The nobility of Holland

This book is the first full-scale analysis of the social and political transformation of the nobility of Holland during the revolt against Spain. In the late medieval county of Holland the nobility played a significant role, but in the seventeenth century it appears to have been obliterated by bourgeois merchants and urban regents. The author argues that this 'decline' needs re-examination, and bases his study on three key aspects: the demographic evidence for the decline of the nobility; the economic vicissitudes of the sixteenth century which gave rise to the myth of its impoverishment; and, finally, the political and administrative powers of the nobility in the reigns of Charles V and Philip II during the Dutch Revolt and in the Republic.

The conclusions are surprising. The nobility of Holland was extremely successful in maintaining its position in a bourgeois republic. In conjunction with the urban regents, the nobles formed the country's administrative, political and economic elite, and, from a social point of view, they maintained a strict apartheid by marrying exclusively within their group.

Widely acclaimed in the Dutch edition of 1984, this is an important contribution to the history of the Netherlands as well as to the more general study of European elites.

CAMBRIDGE STUDIES IN EARLY MODERN HISTORY

Edited by Professor J. H. Elliott, University of Oxford,
Professor Olwen Hufton, Harvard University, and
Professor H. G. Koenigsberger

The idea of an 'early modern' period of European history from the fifteenth to the late eighteenth century is now widely accepted among historians. The purpose of Cambridge Studies in Early Modern History is to publish monographs and studies which illuminate the character of the period as a whole, and in particular focus attention on a dominant theme within it, the interplay of continuity and change as they are presented by the continuity of medieval ideas, political and social organization, and by the impact of new ideas, new methods and new demands on the traditional structures.

For a list of titles published in the series, please see end of book

The nobility of Holland

From knights to regents, 1500–1650

H. F. K. VAN NIEROP

Senior Lecturer in History, University of Amsterdam

Translated by

Maarten Ultee

Professor of History, University of Alabama

CAMBRIDGE
UNIVERSITY PRESS

Published by the Press Syndicate of the University of Cambridge
The Pitt Building, Trumpington Street, Cambridge CB2 1RP
40 West 20th Street, New York, NY 10011–4211, USA
10 Stamford Road, Oakleigh, Victoria 3166, Australia

Originally published in Dutch as *Van ridders tot regenten*
by Hollandse Historische Reeks 1984
and © 1984 H. F. K. van Nierop / Stickting Hollandse Historische Reeks
First published in English by Cambridge University Press 1993 as
The nobility of Holland: from knights to regents, 1500–1650
English translation © Cambridge University Press 1993

Printed in Great Britain at the University Press, Cambridge

A catalogue record for this book is available from the British Library

Library of Congress cataloguing in publication data
Nierop, Henk F. K. van.
[Van ridders tot regenten. English]
The nobility of Holland: from knights to regents, 1500–1650 /
H. F. K. van Nierop: translated by Maarten Ultee.
p.   cm. – (Cambridge studies in early modern history)
Translation of: Van ridders tot regenten.
Includes bibliographical references and index.
ISBN 0 521 39260 8 (hc)
1. Nobility – Netherlands – History – 16th century. 2. Nobility –
Netherlands – History – 17th century. 3. Upper classes – Netherlands –
History – 16th century. 4. Upper classes – Netherlands –
History – 17th century. 5. Netherlands – Social conditions.
I. Title.   II. Series.
DJ152.N5413   1992
949.2'02'08621 – dc20   91–47862   CIP

ISBN 0 521 39260 8 hardback

WV

Contents

List of illustrations		*page* vi
List of tables		vii
Preface to the English edition		ix
List of abbreviations		xiii
Note on currencies		xiv
Map of Holland in 1555		xvi
1	Introduction	1
2	Virtue and descent	19
3	The weight of numbers: demographic trends and forces	46
4	Endogamy and misalliances	67
5	Incomes and expenditures	93
6	Manors and honours	140
7	Beggars and loyalists	177
8	Integration and apartheid	199
9	Conclusion: knights and regents	220
Bibliography		230
Index		245

Illustrations

1 Jan Steen, 'De hoenderhof'. Lokhorst House at Warmond, with *page* 2
Jacoba Maria van Wassenaer, daughter of Johan van
Wassenaer-Duvenvoirde.
2 Anon., 'Jan van Wassenaer'. 3
3 E. van der Maes, 'Johan van Duvenvoirde'. 18
4 Abraham de Bruyn, 'A prince in the Netherlands'. William of
Orange. 40
5 Anon., 'Huis ter Does'. Ter Does House, Leiderdorp. 47
6 Roelof Willemsz. van Culemborg, 'Jan van der Does and his
family'. 48
7 Cornelis Galle jr, after Anselmus van Hulle, 'Johan van
Mathenesse, lord of Mathenesse, Riviere, Opmeer and
Zouteveen, polder-councillor of Schieland'. 68
8 W. Crabeth, 'Elburg van den Boetzelaer (?)', abbess of the
aristocratic convent at Rijnsburg. 123
9 P. Linse after E. van der Maes, 'Maria van Voerst', wife of
Johan van Wassenaer van Duvenvoirde. 136
10 Cornelis Anthonisz., 'Reinoud van Brederode'. 143
11 Jan Mostaert, 'Joost van Bronckhorst'. 151
12 Jan Mostaert, 'Abel van der Coulster'. 172
13 Anon. print in Paulus Merula, *Placaten ende ordonnanciën opt stuck
van de wildernissen* (1605), Warmond House. 178
14 F. Hogenberg, 'Presentation of the nobles' petition to the
Regent Margaret of Parma, 5 April 1566'. 180
15 G. van Honthorst, 'Jacob van Wassenaer-Obdam'. 224
16 Cornelis Anthonisz., 'Genealogical series of the lords of
Brederode'. 226

Tables

3.1 The extinction of twenty-nine Holland noble families, *page* 51
1555–1800

3.2 Average age (mean and median) at first marriage: members of
the Ridderschap of Holland and their children   56

3.3 Average age at first marriage for various elites   56

3.4 Numbers of first and subsequent marriages among members of
the Ridderschap and their children   57

3.5 Childless marriages and marriages without sons, members of
the Ridderschap: individual marriages and successive marriages   59

3.6 Average number of births per mother and gross reproductive
rate   59

3.7 Birth intervals among twenty-one selected families of Holland
nobles   61

3.8 Life-expectancy of members of the Ridderschap and their
children at ages twenty, forty and sixty   63

3.9 Comparative life-expectancy at age twenty of British peers,
Genevan patricians, Danish nobility, Zierikzee patricians and
Holland nobility   63

3.10 Child mortality among twenty-one selected families of Holland
nobles   64

4.1 Marriages of members of the Berckenroede family, *ca.*
1515–1635   72

5.1 Landownership of the lords of Warmond, in several Rijnland
villages, in *morgen, ca.* 1500–1648   99

6.1 The Leiden council, 1481–1574   159

8.1 Manors in Rijnland, 1667   200

8.2 Sales of manors by Egmond, Aremberg and Ligne   202

Preface to the English edition

This book is based on the first Dutch edition of 1984. That edition included eleven appendices, mostly lists of names, as well as additional illustrations, which have been omitted here. The text, notes and bibliography of the English version have been revised by the author and translator.

Since the first edition, historical interest in the nobility and other elites in the Netherlands has increased greatly. We now have studies of the nobility in Groningen, Drente, Utrecht, the Veluwe and Brabant. The general contours of the Netherlands nobility during the *ancien régime* are becoming clear. The particularism of the Netherlands did produce important constitutional differences among the provincial aristocracies. But my view that the nobles adapted creatively and successfully to changing circumstances and remained a significant force in the Dutch Republic appears confirmed in all the provinces. Naturally, on some points there are differences of insight, interpretation and emphasis. Several works might have led to further research and revision, but only minor corrections could be made for this edition. In my opinion, the most important conclusions of this book still stand.

Among recent studies, Sherrin Marshall has written a book about the noble families of Utrecht and their relations in surrounding provinces for the same period.[1] She devoted more attention than I did to the family life and religious life of the nobility: consequently, our two books complement each other. To my mind, it would not be useful to note every point where we differ in facts or interpretation. The reader can be the judge. Nevertheless, the differences in our demographic statistics suggest we should underscore the limited value of these deceptively exact data in a pre-statistical age. H. Feenstra published his revised dissertation on the *jonkers* of Groningen as a book covering the period from the middle ages to the seventeenth century; he has also written about the nobility of Drente during the Republic.[2] S. W. Verstegen studied the *jonkers* in

[1] Sherrin Marshall, *The Dutch Gentry, 1500–1650: Family, Faith, and Fortune* (New York, Westport and London, 1987).
[2] H. Feenstra, *Adel in de Ommelanden. Hoofdelingen, jonkers en eigengeërfden van de late middeleeuwen tot de negentiende eeuw* (Groningen, 1988); *Drentse edelen tijdens de republiek: een onderzoek naar hun economische positie* (n.p., 1985).

the Veluwe region over the 'long' eighteenth century.[3] The great power of the Veluwe group was not a relic of the middle ages, but first arose in the sixteenth and seventeenth centuries. J. Aalbers wrote a fine review article about the nobility of Holland, Utrecht and Guelderland in the early eighteenth century, which was published in a volume with other useful contributions on elites in the northern Netherlands from the middle ages to the present.[4] Various authors have treated the history of the nobility of Brabant in medieval and early modern times.[5] I have also written a short article on noble bastards in the sixteenth century, which may serve as a supplement to chapter 4 of this book.[6]

Several recent studies of the history of Holland shed new light on questions treated here. *Holland under Habsburg Rule, 1506–1566* by James Tracy covers the subject in an impressive manner.[7] Not until this period did Holland develop into a 'body politic' that could bear the burden of the revolt against Philip II and take over sovereignty. This was the result of external circumstances such as the wars with Guelders, the growth of provincial institutions and responsibilities, particularly in the fiscal sphere, and the growth of a communal political consciousness that provincial privileges had to be defended. Tracy's book deals at length with the role of the States, the Ridderschap, the Court of Holland and many noble and non-noble office-holders. Earlier, Tracy had written an important study of the tax system in sixteenth-century Holland.[8] He attaches more significance to the tax exemption of the nobility than I have done.[9] The nobility was exempt from contributions to the *ordinaris-bede* (regular subsidy granted by the States), but did have to pay the *accijnsen* (excise taxes) that were used to finance provincial loans. Furthermore, nobles were exempt from taxes on land that lay 'buiten de schildtalen' (outside the property assessments, last revised in 1514/15). The government had little success in its attempts to make the nobles pay more taxes. Another interesting point is that the Holland nobility disappeared from the group of purchasers of life-annuities and perpetual loans (lenders to the state) at about the same time that nobles ceased to hold administrative offices.

---

[3] S. W. Verstegen, *Gegoede ingezetenen. Jonkers en geërfden op de Veluwe tijdens Ancien Régime, revolutie en restauratie (1650–1830)* (Amsterdam, 1989).

[4] J. Aalbers, 'Geboorte en geld. Adel in Gelderland, Utrecht en Holland tijdens de eerste helft van de achttiende eeuw', in *De Bloem der natie. Adel en patriciaat in de Noordelijke Nederlanden*, ed. J. Aalbers and M. Prak (Meppel and Amsterdam, 1987), pp. 56–78.

[5] J. Verbesselt et al., *De adel in het hertogdom Brabant* (Brussels, 1985).

[6] H. F. K. van Nierop, 'Adellijke bastaarden in de zestiende eeuw', in *Bestuurders en geleerden. Opstellen ... aangeboden aan Prof. Dr J. J. Woltjer ...*, ed. S. Groenveld, M. E. H. N. Mout, and I. Schöffer (Amsterdam and Dieren, 1985), pp. 111–22.

[7] *Holland under Habsburg Rule, 1506–1566: The Formation of a Body Politic* (Berkeley, Los Angeles and Oxford, 1990).

[8] *A Financial Revolution in the Habsburg Netherlands: 'Renten' and 'renteniers' in the County of Holland, 1515–1565* (Berkeley, Los Angeles and London, 1985).

[9] Cf. Tracy's review of my book in *The Sixteenth Century Journal* 17 (1986): 111–12.

Preface to the English edition

On the States of Holland and the position of the Ridderschap in the sixteenth century, we now have a dissertation by J. W. Koopmans.[10] An article by R. H. Vermij on the nobility in meetings of the States examines why the nobles were less inclined to hold offices after 1530.[11] My own answer, that the nobles withdrew of their own volition, no longer appears entirely satisfactory. Vermij suggests that the initiative was taken by the government: in its striving for an obedient officer corps, it no longer wanted nobles in the apparatus. He points out that nobles did continue to hold functions in the service of the States. The disappearance of the nobility from administrative offices must thus be seen in the light of the emancipation of the States from central authority. This explanation is not implausible for the 1550s and 1560s, but it is difficult to see how it could already have been true in the two preceding decades. The disappearance of nobles from offices appears to me inarguable, yet the causes of this process are still very unclear. For an explanation I should be more inclined to consider changes in patronage, also the subject of recent studies.[12] Further research in the correspondence of the regent and the stadholders with the Court of Holland and the bureaucracy will be required to resolve the issue.

The section on the aristocratization of the regents in the Republic in chapter 8 was based on the historical literature available at the time. Since then our knowledge has increased considerably.[13] The view of contemporaries and historians that the regent-patriciate competed with the nobility through the purchase of manors and the pursuit of titles now appears simplistic, to put it mildly. Among the urban patriciate, the possession of manors was exceptional and remained so even in the eighteenth century. This was already apparent from my data on the continuing predominance of nobles as owners of manors. Evidently the regents were able to distinguish themselves from the bourgeois in general without coming into collision with the nobility. For the present, we have no answer to the question of who were the new non-noble owners of manors.

[10] J. W. Koopmans, *De Staten van Holland en de Opstand. De ontwikkeling van hun functies en organisatie in de periode 1544–1588* (The Hague, 1990).

[11] R. H. Vermij, 'De Staten van Holland en de adel in de periode van de opstand', *Holland. Regionaal-historisch tijdschrift* 18 (1986): 215–25.

[12] H. F. K. van Nierop, 'Willem van Oranje als hoog edelman: patronage in de Habsburgse Nederlanden?', *BMGN* 99 (1984): 651–76. Wim Blockmans, 'Corruptie, patronage, makelaardij en venaliteit als symptomen van een ontluikende staatsvorming in de Bourgondisch-Habsburgse Nederlanden', *Tijdschrift voor sociale geschiedenis* 11 (1985): 231–47. *Klientelsysteme im Europa der frühen Neuzeit*, ed. Antoni Mączak (Munich, 1988).

[13] L. Kooijmans, *Onder regenten. De elite in een Hollandse stad. Hoorn 1700–1780* (Amsterdam and Dieren, 1985). M. Prak, *Gezeten burgers. De elite in een Hollandse stad. Leiden 1700–1780* (Amsterdam and Dieren, 1985). J. J. de Jong, *Met goed fatsoen. De elite in een Hollandse stad. Gouda 1700–1780* (Amsterdam and Dieren, 1985). C. Schmidt, *Om de eer van de familie. Het geslacht Teding van Berkhout 1500–1950. Een sociologische benadering* (Amsterdam, 1986). L. Kooijmans, 'Patriciaat en aristocratisering in Holland tijdens de zeventiende en achttiende eeuw', in *De Bloem der natie*, pp. 93–103. Joop de Jong, *Een deftig bestaan. Het dagelijks leven van regenten in de 17de en 18de eeuw* (Utrecht and Antwerp, 1987).

Preface to the English edition

After completing this book I still had a number of questions in my mind. One of the most intriguing was, how was it possible for the members of the Compromise of the Nobility, who were obviously so prosperous, to call themselves 'Geuzen' or beggars? I hope to have solved this problem by interpreting the symbolism of the beggars' movement as a case of carnivalesque inversion.[14]

I am indebted to more people for help and support than I can mention here. Without the encouragement, assistance and tolerance of my parents, I would not have become a historian. It is sad that my father did not live to see the original publication in 1984. Juliaan Woltjer was more than my adviser. He generously shared his unsurpassed knowledge of the sixteenth century, as well as his stack of photocopies. He also taught me the value of common sense for the study of history. The members of his informal sixteenth-century seminar commented on the various chapters as they took shape. My colleagues at the Historisch Seminarium of the University of Amsterdam were generous in allowing me time for research and writing. The employees of various archives and libraries I visited during my research were friendly and helpful without exception: I should like to mention in particular the collaborators of the Amsterdam University Library. Eco Haitsma Mulier was (and is) indispensable both as a stimulator and a critic. I profited immensely from lengthy discussions with Alastair Duke, Jonathan Israel and James Tracy. The late Huub Jansen read the finished manuscript and shared his knowledge of late medieval Holland. L. J. van der Klooster taught me that the Holland nobles I thought I knew so well actually had faces, and assisted me in collecting the illustrations. Walter Wybrand Marcusse was an enthusiastic and patient publisher in 1984, and again for the revised paperback Dutch edition of 1990. Maarten Ultee produced a translation which is both accurate and tasteful. He did not lose his temper when I repeatedly changed the original text in Dutch after he finished translating it. Nothing shows the shortcomings of a text so relentlessly as translation. Tine, Leonie, Samuel and Gulian as they successively entered my life took it for granted that I was busy with a book for most of the time. I am immensely grateful to them all.

The translation of this book was made possible by a grant from the Netherlands Foundation for Scholarly Research (NWO).

[14] H. F. K. van Nierop, 'A Beggars' Banquet. The compromise of the nobility and the politics of inversion', *European History Quarterly* 21 (1991): 419–43.

Abbreviations

AAGB	*Afdeling Agrarische Geschiedenis Bijdragen*
AGN	*Algemene Geschiedenis der Nederlanden*, 12 vols., Utrecht and Antwerp, 1949–58
AH	Archief van het Hoogheemraadschap
ARA	Algemeen Rijksarchief
BGBH	*Bijdragen voor de Geschiedenis van het Bisdom Haarlem*
BMGN	*Bijdragen en Mededelingen betreffende de Geschiedenis der Nederlanden*
BMHG	*Bijdragen en Mededelingen van het Historisch Genootschap*
BVGO	*Bijdragen voor Geschiedenis en Oudheidkunde*
FA	Familiearchief
GA	Gemeentearchief
HA	Huisarchief
HRA	Archief van de Hoge Raad van Adel
JbCBG	*Jaarboek van het Centraal Bureau voor Genealogie*
Kn	W. P. C. Knuttel, *Catalogus van de pamflettenverzameling berustende in de Koninklijke Bibliotheek*, 9 vols., The Hague, 1889–1920
Kron HG	*Kronijk van het Historische Genootschap te Utrecht*
LJ	*Leids Jaarboekje (Jaarboekje voor Geschiedenis en Oudheidkunde van Leiden en Omstreken)*
NAGN	(Nieuwe) *Algemene Geschiedenis der Nederlanden*, 15 vols., Haarlem, 1977–1983
Nav	*De Navorscher*
NL	*Maandblad van het Genealogisch-heraldisch Genootschap: 'De Nederlandsche Leeuw'*
NNBW	*Nieuw Nederlandsch Biografisch Woordenboek*, ed. P. C. Molhuysen and P. J. Blok, 10 vols. (Leiden, 1911–37)
PP	*Past and Present*
RHMC	*Revue d'Histoire Moderne et Contemporaine*
Res. Holland	*Resolutiën van de Heeren Staaten van Holland en Westvriesland*, 276 vols. (The Hague, ca. 1750–98)
TvG	*Tijdschrift voor Geschiedenis*

Abbreviations

TvR	*Tijdschrift voor Rechtsgeschiedenis*
VG	*Verspreide Geschriften*
VW	*Verzamelde Werken*
Wap	*De Wapenheraut. Maandblad gewijd aan geschiedenis, geslacht-, wapen-, oudheidkunde, enz.*

Note on currencies

Two kinds of currency are mentioned in this book. The Holland pound (*Pond Hollands*, abbreviated as £), a money of account, was divided into 20 *schellingen* or shillings (s.), or 240 *penningen* or pence (d.). Thus 1 *schelling* was worth 12 *penningen*. Another system was based on the *gulden* (guilder or florin, abbreviated as *f*). It was divided into 20 *stuivers* or stivers (st.), or 240 *penningen*. A *gulden* (sometimes referred to as *karolusgulden*) had the same value as a pound, a *stuiver* was equivalent to a *schelling*. Because *schellingen* and *stuivers* had the same value, prices were sometimes illogically expressed in pounds and *stuivers*. In some cases, however, the Flemish pound was used; its value was six Holland pounds or guilders. Throughout the text I have followed the language of the sources, rather than convert everything into one particular currency.

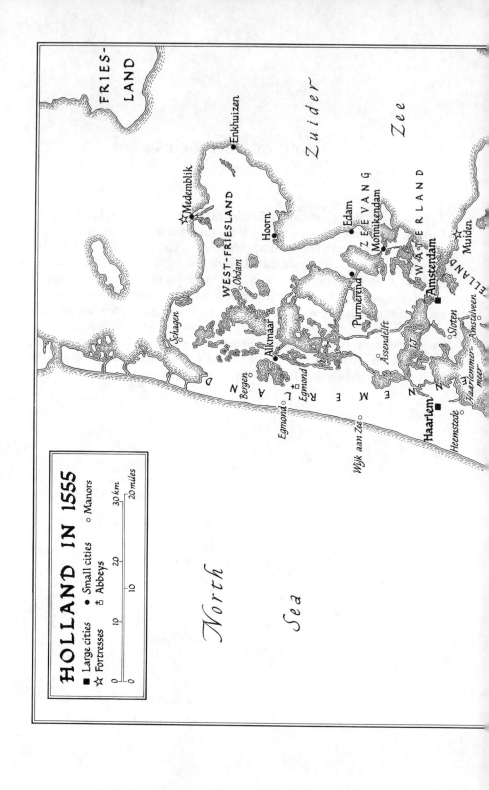

HOLLAND IN 1555

■ Large cities   ● Small cities   ○ Manors
☆ Fortresses   ☩ Abbeys

0   10   20   30 km
0   10   20 miles

North

Sea

FRIES-
LAND

Enkhuizen

Zuider

Zee

Medemblik

WEST-FRIESLAND

Hoorn

Obdam

Edam

Z E E V A N G

Monnikendam

W A T E R L A N D

Schagen

Purmerend

Amsterdam

Muiden

Alkmaar

Assendelft

Sloten

Bergen

Egmond

Amstelveen

Egmond

Haarlemmer-
meer

Wijk aan Zee

Haarlem

Heemstede

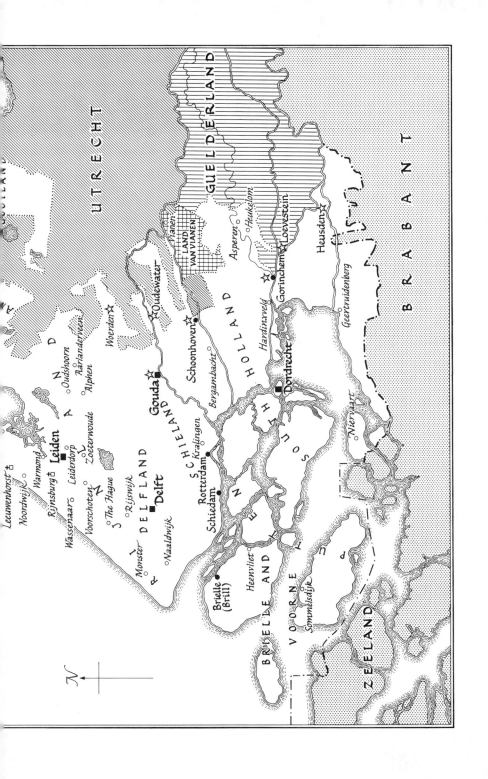

Introduction

On a January afternoon in the year 1524, the people of The Hague turned out in large numbers to gape at the dazzlingly arrayed funeral procession to pay the last respects to Lord Jan van Wassenaer. An anonymous eyewitness described the ceremony in detail.[1] At the head of the procession walked sixty men dressed in black and wearing black hoods. Each of them carried a torch emblazoned with the Wassenaer coat of arms: the silver 'waxing moons' or *wassenaren* on the red field of the house of Wassenaer and the gold crossbeam on the blue field of the burggraviate of Leiden.[2] Behind them paced the clergy: priests, chaplains and other religious from The Hague and the manors of the lord of Wassenaer. Then came the nobles attached to his household, the bailiffs of his manors and a great number of young noblemen who were not in his service, but who were none the less attired in his colours; then the collectors, councillors, steward of the household, chastelain and shield-bearers of his house. They were followed by the grieving friends and kinsmen, each with a page as pall-bearer. These were the son of the lord of Piennes – a cousin of the lord of Wassenaer – and the Holland nobles Raephorst, Oem van Wyngaerden and Spanghen.[3] They were followed by representatives of the central government of the Netherlands: the head of the Privy Council Jean Carondelet, archbishop of Palermo, and Jeroen van Dorp, a nobleman of Holland origin and member of the Great Council of Mechelen. After them came the Holland nobles Duvenvoirde and Schagen, and then followed nearly the entire government of the county of Holland: the president and judges of the Court, the members of the Hague Chamber of Accounts, the collectors of the Domains and the bailiffs, clerks and secretaries of the Court. Only then followed the third estate, representatives of the cities in the States of Holland. At the end of the procession came the ordinary people of The Hague.

[1] Published in *De Navorscher* (*Nav*) 45 (1895): 488–95, and in H. G. A. Obreen, *Geschiedenis van het geslacht van Wassenaer* (Leiden, 1903), pp. 41–5.

[2] One of three gules with three silver 'wassenaars'; two of four azure with a *faas* of gold.

[3] The text reads 'Phls d'Espaigne' but, instead of Philips, his son Cornelis van Spangen must have participated in the procession. Philips had already died in 1509. Cornelis (1487–1546) was a renowned statesman and military leader. A. J. van der Aa, K. J. K. van Harderwijk and G. D. J. Schotel, *Biographisch woordenboek der Nederlanden . . .*, 21 vols. (Haarlem 1852–78), s. v. van Spangen.

1 Jan Steen, 'De hoenderhof' (Mauritshuis, The Hague). Lokhorst House at Warmond, with Jacoba Maria van Wassenaer, daughter of Johan van Wassenaer-Duvenvoirde, lord of Warmond (1672–87), the last male heir of the Warmond branch of the family.

2   Anon., 'Jan van Wassenaer' (Duivenvoorde castle). Jan II, banneret of Wassenaer, burgrave of Leiden (1483–1523).

The destination of the procession was the church of the Dominican monastery, where the lords of Wassenaer had their chapel. It seemed as if the building itself was shrouded in mourning. The decorations that had been placed in the church had to express not only the sorrow of the occasion, but also the power,

3

the prestige and the wealth of the deceased lord and his family. The walls of the nave and the crucifix above the altar were hung with costly woollen cloth. On this cloth, spaced about eight feet apart, were more shields with the Wassenaer coat of arms. Black candelabra hung all around, with so many candles burning that the interior of the church was radiant.

The main altar was draped with a black velvet cloth, which had been decorated with ingenious figures in gold brocade. The altar curtains were of black taffeta silk, and the communion rails were hung with black cloth. Twenty feet in front of the altar a high black canopy had been erected. On it were more than a hundred glowing candles, and on a drapery, the lambrequin, the arms of Lord Wassenaer again appeared. In this small chapel stood the catafalque, the focal point of the funeral rites. A black velvet cloak with a richly decorated gold-brocade cross hung down from it to the ground. Signs of the dignities of the deceased were displayed at the head of the bier: the pointed banner, helmet, and standard, the square flag of battle that only bannerets were allowed to carry.

The obsequies lasted for two days. On the first day, after the funeral procession had settled in the black-draped pews, strictly according to rank and station, the wake was held. The clerical vestments were of black velvet and black damask, with crosses of red satin and green fringe. On the following day the signs of dignity of the deceased were carried in procession. The lord of Schoten carried the banner, Lord Adriaan van Dorp the coat of arms, the lord of Wyngaerden the helmet, and the steward Steenbeke the standard. A herald, arrayed in the livery of Wassenaer, but bare-headed, carried a black velvet cushion with the emblems of the order of the Golden Fleece. The armour and battle-sword of the deceased were displayed on the catafalque. During the offering these attributes were carried solemnly to the altar and held there by two nobles, the brothers Bartholomeus and Adriaan van Egmond. Later these tokens were exhibited in the chapel of the lords of Wassenaer.

These imposing ceremonies were dedicated to Jan II van Wassenaer, burgrave of Leiden, knight of the order of the Golden Fleece, the last male descendant of the main branch of his illustrious clan.[4] He had lived a true knightly life: honourable, luxurious, adventurous – and at times extremely troubled. In 1500, at the age of seventeen, he had formed part of the train of Philip the Fair, when the latter passed through France on his way to collect his inheritance in Spain. But Jan's mother, worried about the dangers attached to the trip, had had her son recalled. In 1507 he accompanied his uncle Lodewijk of Halewyn, the lord of Piennes, stadholder of the king of France in Picardy, who went as French envoy to Venice. He took part in Emperor Maximilian's campaign in Italy, and during the storming of the walls of Padua in 1509 he

---

[4] Obreen, *Wassenaer*, pp. 38–41. Later the Duvenvoirdes, a collateral branch of the Wassenaers, would again bear the family name.

received a bullet in his jaw, by which he lost seven teeth; on that occasion the emperor himself appeared at his camp-bed. The following year he fought on the side of the Danes against Lübeck, and the year thereafter the troops under his command at Jutphaas defeated the Gueldrians. Yet the latter were able to take him prisoner in 1512. They locked him up in an iron cage that was hung from the attic of a strong tower by a rope and pulley. This uncomfortable abode was not lowered except to provide the lord of Wassenaer with food and drink through a small shutter. He was released only after two years, when a ransom of no less than 20,000 gulden had been raised. In 1516 he was received into the order of the Golden Fleece, and his appointment as supreme commander of the Habsburg armies in Friesland followed in that same year. In this role the lord of Wassenaer was mortally wounded at the age of forty, in December 1523, in battle against the Gueldrians.

Jan II van Wassenaer had been one of the emperor's major vassals in Holland.[5] He held as fiefs the high and low justice in Wassenaar, Zuidwijk, Het Zand, Katwijk, Voorschoten, Oegstgeest and Wimmenum, and the justice of Oostbarendrecht, Voorburg, Valkenburg, Sassenheim, Heerjansdam, De Linde and Burggravenveen. In all these villages he also possessed land, tithes, houses, farmsteads and seigneurial rights such as *botting*, tribute-money, tolls, milling rights, the right to keep swans, bridge-crossing, fishing, fowling, market and ferry rights. He also owned feudal rights in several villages where he did not hold the manor: in Ketel, Zoeterwoude, Haagambacht, Vlaardingen, Eikenduinen, Leiderdorp, Zwammerdam and Hillegommerhout, and in the towns of Delft and Leiden. The income from all these rights and possessions made it possible for the lord of Wassenaer to live – and to die – as a nobleman.

Seventy years after the funeral of the lord of Wassenaer, a young Englishman travelled through the Netherlands. He was amazed that in these regions no nobles were to be found. 'The Nobility or Gentry hath long been rooted out by the people', he declared, '. . . after the example of the Sweitzers, especially in *Holland* and *Zealand*.' In these provinces he could find only three noble families, and these 'lived after the Plebeian maner of the other inhabitants, so as it were in vain to seeke for any Order of Knighthood among them. Neither are there Gentlemen – as those of Germany – curious to mary amongst themselves; for those who come to greatest honour in this Commonwealth, are either Advocates of the Law or Sonnes of Merchants', he noted in his travel diary.[6]

The contrast between these two witnesses, the anonymous report of the funeral of the lord of Wassenaer and the travel diary of Fynes Moryson, could hardly be more striking. The spectacle of 1524 was Burgundian. The principal actors were nobles, the symbolism was knightly. Granted, everything that would

---

[5] Ibid., pp. 48–51.
[6] Fynes Moryson, 'Moryson's reis door en zijn karakteristiek van de Nederlanden', ed. J. N. Jacobsen Jensen, *BMHG* 39 (1918): 214–305, at 273–4.

give Holland its exceptional character a century later was already present.[7] Already in 1514 half the population lived in the cities, which made Holland, along with some parts of northern Italy, the most urbanized region of the world. The cities produced an even greater share of the prosperity of the land; accordingly the nobles had only one vote in the provincial states, while the towns had six. But from a social point of view the nobles in the first half of the sixteenth century were still the dominant class.[8] Nobles occupied all the highest administrative posts and a large proportion of the lower ones as well. Of the judges in the Court of Holland who accompanied Jan van Wassenaer to his last resting place in 1524, for example, the majority belonged to families regarded as noble.[9] As lords of the manor, the nobles held practically the entire administrative and judicial power in the countryside. As members of the city councils and the magistracy, they could exert influence in many cities. The highest ranks in the army were occupied by nobles. It may have been 'the waning of the middle ages'; yet society was still unmistakably medieval.

The picture that Moryson sketched seventy years later was already what would become the traditional image of the Golden Age of Holland, where bourgeois patricians and merchants constituted the leading actors, and there seemed no more role for the nobility. By then nearly 60 per cent of the population lived in the cities[10] and, as opposed to the one vote for the nobles in the provincial states, there were not just six, but eighteen voting cities. An Englishman accompanying the earl of Leicester's party in 1586 called his queen's allies, 'Sovereign Lords Millers and Cheesemen'.[11]

Yet on this occasion Moryson did not look closely enough. At the end of the sixteenth century there were more than three noble families in Holland, and his remark that they preferred to marry merchants or patricians is also incorrect. But it does not really matter how well informed Moryson was. It says much that

---

[7] H. P. H. Jansen, *Hollands voorsprong* (Leiden, 1976), pp. 7–8.

[8] H. A. Enno van Gelder, '1548: De eenheid voltooid', in *Van beeldenstorm tot pacificatie. Acht opstellen over de Nederlandse revolutie der zestiende eeuw* (Amsterdam and Brussels, 1964), pp. 9–39, at 28–9.

[9] *Memorialen van het Hof (den Raad) van Holland, Zeeland en West-Friesland van den secretaris Jan Rosa*, ed. A. S. de Blécourt and E. M. Meijers, 3 vols. (Haarlem, 1929), I, pp. xvi–xvii: Floris van Wyngaerden, Jan van Duvenvoirde, Abel van (den) Coulster, Hugo van Assendelft and Gerrit van Assendelft belonged to Holland noble families that appeared in the Ridderschap. Albrecht van Loo and Joost Sasbout belonged to families of high office-holders, although the latter bore the title *ridder* and was lord of Spaland. (Van der Aa, *Biographisch woordenboek*). The two members from Zeeland, Nicolaas Everaerts (president) and Jasper Lievensz. van Hogelande did not belong to the nobility; for the former, cf. A. J. M. Kerckhoffs-de Heij, *De Grote Raad van Mechelen en zijn functionarissen 1477–1531*, 2 vols. (Amsterdam, 1980), II, pp. 69–70. On the definition of the Holland nobility, see chapter 2, below.

[10] Jan de Vries, *The Dutch Rural Economy in the Golden Age* (New Haven and London, 1974), pp. 84–96.

[11] Charles Wilson, *Queen Elizabeth and the Revolt of the Netherlands* (London and Basingstoke, 1970), p. 23.

during his stay he had the impression of a society that had become thoroughly bourgeois.

Only seventy years separated the burial of the lord of Wassenaer and the travels of Fynes Moryson, a space of two generations. An individual might span that period in a lifetime. But these were turbulent years. The list of events is long and dramatic: the continuing campaigns of the emperor in Italy, Germany and France, fought with the help and partly at the expense of his subjects in the Netherlands; the concentration of administrative responsibility in Brussels, the reduction of provincial privileges and the resistance of the States; the Reformation and the religious and social unrest that it produced, the Anabaptist revolts in Münster, Amsterdam and elsewhere; the draconian persecution of heretics, the burning stakes and protests against them, not only by Protestants, but also by moderate Catholic elements who thought that the heretics were perhaps misled, but that they did not therefore deserve the punishment of death; the explosive growth of population, the rise of prices and wages, the growth of cities, of trade and industry, developments that brought wealth to some, but seemed to produce poverty elsewhere; and, finally, the Dutch Revolt against the king of Spain, a civil war that shook the state to its foundations, a guerrilla war that laid waste towns and countryside; a revolt, indeed, that the nobles themselves had helped to unleash by their 'Compromise' of 1565, by which they, in a sort of dialectical somersault, became the founders of a bourgeois merchants' republic, where money seemed to be more important than social origin. Step by step, these developments could not leave undisturbed the position of the nobility of Holland.

Was the transition from the middle ages to the modern period marked by a change of elites, in which the regent-patricians and merchants replaced the old feudal nobility? And if that occurred, what happened to the nobles? Did they simply die out, as did the main branch of the house of Wassenaer in 1523, or were they, much more dramatically, 'rooted out by the people', as our English traveller maintained? Were the nobles impoverished because their incomes remained constant while prices rose? Or did they disappear as a result of the Revolt and the abolition of monarchy? 'Point de monarque, point de noblesse; point de noblesse, point de monarque', as Montesquieu later remarked.[12]

The appearance in 1965 of Lawrence Stone's book on the crisis of the English aristocracy in the period between the accession of Elizabeth I and the outbreak of the English civil war[13] has inspired historians to do research on crises of the nobility in many countries and regions between 1550 and 1650.[14] Admittedly the concept of 'crisis' is hardly applicable to a period lasting a

---

[12] Montesquieu, *De l'esprit des lois*, ed. Gonzague Truc, 2 vols. (Paris, 1956), I, p. 20.
[13] Lawrence Stone, *The Crisis of the Aristocracy, 1558–1641* (Oxford, 1965).
[14] A survey of the literature appears in F. Billacoix, 'La crise de la noblesse Européenne (1550–1650). Une mise au point', *RHMC* 23 (1976): 258–77.

hundred years. But, apart from that, it cannot be denied that nobles everywhere in the sixteenth and the first half of the seventeenth centuries encountered specific problems, to which they formulated different solutions. In some countries the nobles were better able to maintain themselves than in others, but in all countries by the middle of the seventeenth century the concept 'noble' meant something different from what it had a hundred or a hundred and fifty years earlier. The nobles did not disappear from the stage, but the role that they played had changed. In the Netherlands this process of change has not previously been the subject of historical research.

This study covers a century and a half. Its beginning is marked by the birth of Emperor Charles V in 1500, and its end by the death of Stadholder William II in 1650. These dynastic milestones, however, are not very relevant to our subject. It is better to begin around the year 1492, when the factional struggles in Holland between the *Hoeken* (Hooks) and *Kabeljouwen* (Cods) came to an end. This civil war supposedly decimated the nobility, which formed the backbone of the struggling parties, and caused them to lose their influence. Afterwards, it has been argued, markedly different relations prevailed in the county of Holland.[15] As for the end of our study, it is appropriate to choose 1648, when the bourgeois republic received international recognition in the Peace of Westphalia.

This century and a half is important for the study of the nobility of Holland for two reasons. In the first place it coincides with a period of demographic and economic expansion, which has been called 'the long sixteenth century', a rising phase in the secular trend of prices and wages.[16] The period is also significant for political history, for the beginning of the Revolt against the king of Spain falls right in the middle. A distinction can be made between changes in the position of the nobility that were caused by the Revolt, and changes that took place over a longer term. We can divide the age into three parts: the time of Habsburg rule (ca. 1500–72); the beginning of the Revolt in 1565 with the formation of the Compromise or League of the Low Nobility; and finally the time of the Republic between circa 1585 and 1648 (Peace of Westphalia).

The spatial boundaries of this study will be the frontiers of the sixteenth-century county of Holland, partly in order to keep the research within manageable proportions, and partly because the province of Holland may be considered exemplary for the 'bourgeois' Dutch Republic. By studying the changed place of the nobility of Holland we can, in an inverse way, examine the meaning of that shopworn term 'the rise of the bourgeoisie'.

Holland in that period roughly corresponded to the territory of the present-day provinces of North and South Holland. The western boundary was formed

[15] H. P. H. Jansen, *Hoekse en Kabeljauwse twisten* (Bussum, 1966), p. 110.
[16] J. A. Faber, 'De Noordelijke Nederlanden van 1480 tot 1780. Structuren in beweging', *NAGN*, v, pp. 196–250, at 207.

behind the line of dunes by the North Sea; in the northeast it was the Texel channel and the Zuider Zee, the shipping route between Amsterdam and the open sea. South of the diluvial moors of Het Gooi, the ground was low and marshy. The boundary with the bishopric of Utrecht was freakish, the result of countless wars. In the south the islands of Goeree and Overflakkee formed the border with the county of Zeeland. A strip of land south of the Oude Maas and Biesbos, extending as far as Engelen, approximately one hour's walk northwest of 's-Hertogenbosch, formed the boundary with the duchy of Brabant. The arable surface of Holland in the middle of the sixteenth century covered about 309,000 *morgen* or roughly 689,000 acres.[17] A large part of the area of the county, however, consisted of water. In the north the principal lakes (*meren*) were the Schermer, Wormer, Beemster and Purmer. The IJ ran west from Amsterdam through to Beverwijk; it was connected by locks with the Haarlem-mermeer. In the south the estuaries of the Maas and Rhine rivers had many more branches than they do today, so that the country actually consisted of many small islands. During the late middle ages and the sixteenth century, large pieces of Holland disappeared under water. Three lakes that had a surface area of 22,500 acres in 1250 joined together in 1472 to form the Haarlemmermeer, a real inland sea of 28,900 acres. In 1544 the Haarlemmermeer covered 32,650 acres, and with each storm more land was lost.[18] Thus the arable surface of the manor of Aalsmeer was reduced by more than two-thirds between 1544 and 1596.[19] The simultaneous rise of the sea level, the imprudent digging of peat bogs for turf, and the subsidence of land as a result of drainage and cultivation all contributed to the increased water-nuisance.[20] But around 1600 the tide began to turn. In the sixteenth century a start had been made on pumping dry several smaller lakes north of the IJ; between 1600 and 1650, thanks to improved pumping techniques, nearly all of the lakes in this area were made into polders. By constructing dikes, the Hollanders were also able to win much land from the sea.[21]

The uneasy symbiosis with water was partly the reason that an unprecedently large number of people, more than half of the population, lived in the towns. Elsewhere in Europe at that time it was customary to find 70 to 90 per cent of the population working in the agricultural sector. Most foreign travellers devoted few words to the nobility, but without exception they praised the number, extent, power and prosperity of the towns. Around 1525 there were six cities in Holland with more than 10,000 inhabitants. By comparison, in the

[17] J. C. Naber, *Een terugblik. Statistische verwerking van de resultaten van de informacie van 1514* (1885–90; reprint Haarlem, 1970), p. 18.
[18] De Vries, *Dutch Rural Economy*, p. 31.
[19] Morgenboeken Aalsmeer 1544 and 1596, AH Rijnland, Inv. no. 2891 and 2892.
[20] De Vries, *Dutch Rural Economy*, pp. 30–2.
[21] J. D. H. Harten, 'Het sociaal-economische leven, geografie en demografie 1500–1800', *NAGN*, v, pp. 37–77, at 57–60.

entire British Isles there were only three or four cities as large. Around 1675 Holland counted four cities with more than 25,000 inhabitants. Amsterdam with around 200,000 inhabitants towered above the others, followed by Leiden (65,000), Rotterdam (45,000) and Haarlem (37,000). Six Dutch cities in 1675 had populations of 15,000 to 25,000.[22]

The prominent place of the cities in Holland was the reason that neither contemporaries nor later historians gave much thought to the question of what happened to the nobility. The nobles of Holland lived, literally and figuratively, under the smoke of the cities. Seventeenth-century scholars such as Wouter van Gouthoeven, Marcus Zuerius Boxhorn and Simon van Leeuwen indeed confirmed that the nobility of the region had previously been as numerous as in other lands, but they never studied the causes of its obvious decline.[23] In general, later historians overlooked the nobility entirely: when they did mention it, it was only to stress its small numbers as well as its politically and socially unimportant position. In his well-known essay on Dutch civilization in the seventeenth century, Johan Huizinga noted that the importance of the nobility in the Republic was relatively limited, precisely because the nobility in the core-province of Holland was so insignificant. 'As the power of the nobility waned and that of the old church collapsed, so the economic predominance of the merchant class was necessarily transformed into political and social predominance as well.'[24] Consequently the entire Dutch culture was less courtly or aristocratic in nature. It was bourgeois (*burgerlijk*), notably also where it was expressed by the landed nobility.[25] Jan and Annie Romein made the rise of the bourgeoisie virtually the central theme of all Netherlands history from the high middle ages to the present, by which the nobles, 'impoverished squires', disappeared from history: 'First supported by the monarch, later supporting him, still later, in Revolt against him and finally without the monarch, the Cods party, i.e., the urban aristocracy, developed into the ruling class of Holland, and would remain so, although in changed form, to the present day.'[26] All over Europe, according to the British historian Charles Wilson, the nobles preserved their privileges intact, except in the Dutch Republic, where 'the nobility faded

---

[22] A. M. van der Woude, 'Demografische ontwikkeling van de Noordelijke Nederlanden 1500–1800', *NAGN*, v, pp. 102–68, at 135–7; cf. Geoffrey Parker, *The Dutch Revolt* (London, 1977), 23.

[23] Wouter van Gouthoeven, *D'oude chronyke ende historiën van Holland, Zeeland ende Utrecht* (2nd edn, The Hague, 1636), p. 119. Marcus Zuerius Boxhorn, *Toneel ofte beschryvinge der steden van Hollandt* (Amsterdam, 1634), p. 45. Simon van Leeuwen, *Redeningh over den oorspronck, reght, ende onderscheyt der edelen, ende wel-borenen in Hollandt; mitsgaders der selver voor-rechten, soo die nu zijn, ofte van aloude tijden zijn geweest* (Leiden, 1659), p. 23.

[24] J. Huizinga, 'Nederlands beschaving in de zeventiende eeuw', *VW*, 9 vols. (Haarlem, 1948–53), II, pp. 412–507, at 421–3.

[25] J. Huizinga, 'Engelschen en Nederlanders in Shakespeares tijd', *VW*, II, pp. 350–81, at 380.

[26] Jan and Annie Romein, *De lage landen bij de zee. Geïllustreerde geschiedenis van het Nederlandse volk* (3rd edn, Utrecht, 1949), p. 117.

and disappeared from the scene, to be replaced by what Renier picturesquely called "the dictatorship of the middle class"'.[27] Jacques Presser eloquently summed this up when he called the nobles of Holland 'a small fringe on a stately tablecloth. The triumph of the bourgeoisie once and for all pushed them into the background.'[28]

The sparse writings that mention the nobility of Holland do suggest the causes of its decline. First, there is general agreement about what we should now call demographic causes. Most contemporaries confirmed that many noble families failed to produce a male heir.[29] To what degree or how quickly these Holland families died out, however, they did not say. Nowadays historians are inclined to place emphasis on purely demographic factors, such as age at marriage, fertility and mortality. Yet the demography of the nobility of Holland has never been studied.

Contemporaries attributed the decline of the nobility of Holland more to political than to demographic causes. According to Boxhorn, the nobles died out in the 'continual wars'. Van Leeuwen thought specifically of the struggles between the Hooks and Cods, while the English ambassador William Temple emphasized the war against Spain. Fynes Moryson, as we have seen, asserted that the nobles were 'rooted out by the people'.[30]

Later authors regarded the Revolt against Spain and in particular the disappearance of the monarchy as an important cause. According to G. 't Hart, the bourgeoisie took the place of the nobility because the latter 'could not do without the splendour of kingship'. J. L. Price suggested that most Holland nobles had more possessions in the Southern Netherlands than in Holland, and that this was one of the reasons why they chose the king's side in the struggle.[31] The centralizing policy of the government prior to the Revolt has been regarded as the major cause of the decline of the nobles, although this policy naturally attacked the power of the towns just as much as that of the nobles.[32]

The decline of the Holland nobles has also been attributed to economic causes. The story of the sixteenth-century nobles who were reduced to beggary

---

[27] Charles Wilson, *The Transformation of Europe 1558–1648* (London, 1976), pp. 81, 84; cf. G. J. Renier, *The Dutch Nation, an Historical Study* (London, 1944), p. 16.

[28] J. Presser, *De Tachtigjarige Oorlog* (5th edn, Amsterdam, 1975), pp. 179–80.

[29] E.g., Van Leeuwen, *Redeningh*, p. 23.

[30] Boxhorn, *Toneel*, p. 45; Van Leeuwen, *Redeningh*, p. 23; William Temple, *Observations upon the United Provinces of the Netherlands*, ed. George Clark (Oxford, 1972), p. 85; Moryson, *Reis*, p. 273. Cf. Hadrianus Iunius, *Batavia, in qua praeter gentis et insulae antiquitatem, originem, decora, mores, aliaque ad eam historiam pertinentia, declaratur quae fuerit vetus Batavia* ... (Leiden, 1588), p. 325; and Van Gouthoeven, *Chronyke*, p. 119.

[31] G. 't. Hart, *Historische beschrijving der vrije en hoge heerlijkheid van Heenvliet* (n.p., 1949), p. 204. J. L. Price, *Culture and Society in the Dutch Republic during the 17th Century* (London, 1974), p. 59.

[32] H. A. Enno van Gelder, 'De Hollandse adel in de tijd van de Opstand', *TvG* 45 (1930): 113–50, at 132–41; 'Bailleul, Bronkhorst, Brederode', *Van beeldenstorm tot pacificatie* (Amsterdam and Brussels, 1964), pp. 40–79, at 51; 't Hart, *Heenvliet*, pp. 202–4.

by an extravagant lifestyle and inflation on the one hand, and landed incomes that remained constant on the other hand, is too well known to require recounting here.[33] Among others, Cardinal Granvelle and Pontus Payen suggested that the grievances of many nobles in 1566 had more financial than religious causes, an opinion shared by P. C. Hooft and Grotius.[34]

The image of the impoverished nobles also had a social-psychological or moralistic side. As the military significance of the nobles declined, they forgot their 'duty as warriors' and fell into 'idleness, carelessness, drunkenness, immorality, gambling, and blasphemy'. Owing to this 'evil regimen' they had to give up their feudal estates, which were subsequently purchased by patricians ('the ancient bourgeoisie'), thanks to their 'sober and moderate life', or by merchants 'by means of their profits and wealth'.[35]

This negative presentation was corrected to some extent by H. A. Enno van Gelder, the only historian who did serious research on the Holland nobility as a whole.[36] Van Gelder pointed to the great political, social and cultural significance that the nobility still had in the sixteenth century and to its leading role in the Revolt. He emphasized the considerable incomes still enjoyed by many nobles. His work has been of great importance for the historiography of the Revolt, but he did not study the long-term changes in the social position of the nobility.

Contemporaries and historians have thus attributed the decline of the Holland nobility to diverse causes, although it is not clear what weight should be placed on each. Their work suggests a rough hypothesis: the nobility of Holland in the course of the sixteenth century declined in numbers and in social significance as a result of demographic, political, economic or social-psychological causes, or a combination of them. Before studying these factors individually, we shall conduct a provisional test of the hypothesis on two noble families, Cruyningen and Duvenvoirde.

The sad fate of the lords of Cruyningen appears to confirm our hypothesis in all respects.[37] At the beginning of the sixteenth century everything still looked

---

[33] See chapter 5.

[34] *Archives ou correspondance inédite de la Maison d'Orange-Nassau*, ed. G. Groen van Prinsterer, 1st series, 8 vols. and supp. (Leiden, 1835–47), I, pp. 37–9. Wilson, *Queen Elizabeth*, p. 47. Pontus Payen, *Mémoires*, ed. A. Henne, 2 vols. (Brussels and The Hague, 1861), I, pp. 29–30. P. C. Hooft, *Nederlandtsche historiën*, 2 vols. (4th edn, Amsterdam, 1703), I, p. 125. Hugo de Groot, *Nederlandtsche jaerboeken en historiën* (Amsterdam, 1681), p. 8.

[35] Matthijs van der Houve, *Hantvest of Charte Chronyk vande landen van Oud-Batavien, Oud-Vriesland, Oud-Francenland enz.* (2nd edn, Leiden, 1646), p. 60. Van Leeuwen, *Redeningh*, pp. 15–16. Van Gouthoeven, *Chronyke*, p. 119.

[36] Van Gelder, 'Hollandse adel'.

[37] For what follows, see 't Hart, *Heenvliet*, pp. 43–206. The lords of Cruyningen belonged to the nobility of Zeeland, but as lords of Heenvliet they were counted among the Holland nobility. Cf. Boxhorn, *Toneel*, p. 43. In March 1553 the lord of Cruyningen appeared among the nobles at the States of Holland (Simon van Leeuwen, *Batavia illustrata ofte oud-Batavien, vervattende de*

rosy. In 1514 Joost van Cruyningen, aged twenty-five, succeeded his father as banneret of Kruiningen, lord of Heenvliet, Hazerswoude, Montfoort and several other possessions. He also received the title of burgrave of Zeeland. The following year Charles V named him councillor and chamberlain in his household.

The lord was actively involved in village life at Heenvliet, where he had his residence. He promoted economic prosperity, and thanks to his concerns about water-defence, Heenvliet was one of the few polders on Voorne and Putten to be saved from the disastrous floods of 1530. He gave financial aid to villagers in distress. Without himself joining the Protestant Reformation, he supported Angelus Merula, the heretical priest of Heenvliet, and he protected the Anabaptists in his manor of Hazerswoude.

Joost van Cruyningen made two excellent marriages, first to Charlotte of Burgundy, daughter of Philip, lord of Beveren, and Anna van Borsselen, lady of Vlissingen and Veere; then, after her death, to Catharina, a daughter of Lord Jan van Wassenaer. Both the Burgundy family, which had descended from a bastard branch of the ducal house, and the Wassenaer family belonged to the highest nobility of the Netherlands. Joost's first wife bore him a daughter, who died young; his second wife gave him two sons and a daughter.

In 1543 Lord Joost died, and his oldest son, also called Joost, succeeded him. The latter, however, perished four years later, while on campaign as a general in the imperial army in Germany. Since he left no children, his brother Johan succeeded him. He also received the title of burgrave of Zeeland.

Lord Johan occupied various high offices in the service of the emperor, just as his older brother and father had done. Mostly he stayed at the court in Brussels, where he lived in grand style. He too made a brilliant marriage: his wife Jacqueline was a sister of the stadholder of Holland, Zeeland and Utrecht, Maximilian of Burgundy. Since the latter was unmarried, and his sister was his heir, Johan had prospects of gaining the marquisate of Vlissingen and Veere and the status of Maximilian, who was entitled to call himself 'First Noble of Zeeland'.

Now the first dark clouds began to gather above this initially favoured family. Because of Lord Johan's grand life in Brussels, he was obliged in 1549 to mortgage his manor of Heenvliet. Furthermore, when he died in 1559, the succession was endangered. He had left behind three daughters and a four-year-old son, but in view of the high child mortality in that time it was not unthinkable that the boy would die young, threatening the extinction of the male line.

Fortunately Maximilian, as the boy was called, remained alive. Already at age

verhandelinge van den adel en regeringe van Hollandt enz. (The Hague, 1685), p. 766). In 1540 and 1549, however, Joost and Jan van Cruyningen were counted among the Zeeland nobility (Van Gouthoeven, *Chronyke*, p. 620).

eight he was installed as marquis of Vlissingen and Veere; he then had a chance of getting the title of First Noble of Zeeland and by these dignities to gain the stadholdership of Holland, Zeeland and Utrecht, as well as an important career at court in Brussels.

Fate decreed otherwise, however. A struggle soon broke out between the trustees of the property of his deceased uncle, Maximilian of Burgundy, the former stadholder and First Noble of Zeeland, and the current stadholder, Prince William of Orange. At stake was the marquisate. The child was pushed aside, and when Orange temporarily disappeared from the stage in 1567, Philip II assumed the title himself, without paying any regard to young Maximilian.[38]

Meanwhile the Dutch Revolt had begun. Maximilian at first took the king's side. That was not surprising, because his uncle Count Bossu, the royalist stadholder of Holland, Zeeland, and Utrecht, became Maximilian's guardian after the death of his mother. Young Maximilian fought alongside his uncle at the battle of the Zuider Zee (1573) and shared his imprisonment after the defeat. After he was released in 1576 as a result of the Pacification of Ghent, he chose, again just as Bossu had done, to fight for the States-General.

A career in the king's service seemed no longer possible. But how much choice did Maximilian have? If he had remained on the king's side, the States would have confiscated his property. Cut off from the sources of his income, he would never have been able to live in the Southern Netherlands in the manner required by an important position. His chances for a career in the king's service were lost in any case as soon as the separation between North and South became a fact of life, no matter which side he chose.

In the service of the States, Maximilian took part in a number of diplomatic missions, held several high military posts for a short time, and became a member of the Council of State. But these were not the high positions to which he aspired on the grounds of his birth. Endless litigation to recover old manors, offices and rights proved fruitless.

His financial prospects were sombre. The debts incurred by his father – Heenvliet was still heavily mortgaged – the grand style in which he lived and indeed was obliged to live in connection with his diplomatic missions, and his lengthy and costly court cases quickly led to his downfall. Heenvliet brought in less and less income, in part because of the disastrous floods of 1570. While Maximilian's grandfather Joost had given financial aid to the inhabitants of Heenvliet, in 1579 the inhabitants had to take up a collection to support their

---

[38] On developments concerning the marquisate, cf. P. Scherft, *Het sterfhuis van Willem van Oranje* (Leiden, 1966), pp. 105–6; M. Schoockius, *Belgium Federatum, sive distincta descriptio Reip. Federati Belgii etc.* (Amsterdam, 1652), pp. 123–4; A. Meerkamp van Embden, 'De Prins en de staat van eersten edele in Zeeland', *Prins Willem van Oranje 1533–1933* (Haarlem, 1933), pp. 101–24.

lord. A financial settlement with the States in 1591 did not prevent him from having to sell his manor of Hazerswoude several years later.[39]

When Maximilian died in 1612, he left behind five underage daughters. Their guardians then decided to auction the unprofitable manor of Heenvliet, but the estate was so heavily charged with debt that no one bid for it. The manor was only sold fifteen years later, and for a fraction of the original price.

The buyer was Johan van den Kerckhoven Polyander, descendant of a respectable but non-noble family of Ghent. His father had emigrated to the North, where he became professor of theology at Leiden and a delegate to the synod of Dordt. As a favourite of stadholder Frederick Henry, the new lord of Heenvliet advanced to the posts of master of the hunt and chief forester of Holland, offices that previously were reserved for nobles. He travelled regularly on embassies to England, and married into the high English nobility. His son received an English noble title. Under the control of the new lord the income from Heenvliet increased from 2,630 gulden per year to 4,268 gulden, an increase of 63 per cent, which can be attributed as much to his sound management as to the favourable agricultural conjuncture.

All the forces mentioned as causes of the decline of the Holland nobility seemed to work together to ruin the Cruyningen family. Political: because of the intrigues concerning the marquisate of Vlissingen and Veere, but even more as a result of the Revolt, a high function at court was no longer possible. Financial: the lords of Cruyningen lived in such grand style that they had to sell their manors. Demographic: Joost van Cruyningen the elder had two sons; his eldest son died childless, and his brother Johan left behind only one boy aged four; and Maximilian, the last male heir, died leaving five young daughters.

Finally, it can hardly be a coincidence that Heenvliet was bought by a scion of the new regent-aristocracy. Johan van den Kerckhoven Polyander, or 'Heenvliet', as he proudly allowed himself to be called, truly personified the rising bourgeoisie. Thus it is hardly surprising that the author of the monograph on Heenvliet regarded these experiences as typical for the whole nobility of the Republic.[40] Before accepting this conclusion, however, we should place under the magnifying glass another noble lineage: the Duvenvoirde family.

The Duvenvoirdes formed a branch of the Wassenaer family, but they did not belong to the high nobility.[41] When Arend van Duvenvoirde died in 1483, he left behind three sons and four daughters. Two of the daughters were entrusted to convents: Antonia at Nonnenpoel near Leiden, Willemina at

---

[39] Repertoria of the leenregisters, ARA, Archief van de Leen- en Registerkamers van Holland (Leenkamer), inv. no. 229, fo. 893 v.

[40] 't Hart, *Heenvliet*, pp. 202–4.

[41] For what follows, see Obreen, *Wassenaer*, pp. 77–97, 125–35, 151–66.

Hoogstraten in Brabant. Two other daughters were married to Holland nobles: Maria to Jacob Oem, lord of Wyngaerden, and Arnoldina to Floris Oem. The oldest son Jan (d. 1544) continued the main branch of the family as lord of Duvenvoirde, Noordwijkerhout and Starrenburg. In 1503, on his second marriage, the second son Gijsbrecht, lord of Den Bossche, took as his wife the heiress Anna van Noordwijk, lady of Obdam, Hensbroek, Spanbroek and Opmeer in West-Friesland. The youngest son, called Jan, just like the first, studied law and advanced to become a councillor in the Court of Holland. He too was so fortunate as to take an heiress to the altar, Maria van Mathenesse. In 1525, after the death of her aunt Jacoba van Woude, Maria came into possession of the manors of Warmond, Esselikerwoude (or Woude, as it was frequently abbreviated) and Alkemade. Her husband Jan became the founding father of the lords of Duvenvoirde van Warmond. Descendants of all three branches – the lords of Duvenvoirde, the lords of Obdam and the lords of Warmond – sat next to each other in the Ridderschap, or Knighthood, the delegation of nobles in the States of Holland. At the beginning of the troubles we find Arend, lord of Duvenvoirde, and Gijsbrecht van Duvenvoirde, lord of Obdam, among the Union of the Nobility and shortly afterward among the refugees from the duke of Alba's Council of Troubles; Jacob van Duvenvoirde, lord of Warmond, stayed in the country.[42] During the Republic, however, the star of all three branches rose, although the lords of Warmond remained Catholic. Duvenvoirdes held seats in the Ridderschap of the States of Holland and West-Friesland, and in the board of *Gecommitteerde Raden* or Deputy Councils, a permanent body charged with the daily administration of the province. They also sat in the Generality Chamber of Accounts and in the Court of Holland. Duvenvoirdes were keepers of the great seal, lieutenant-foresters of Holland, stadholders of fiefs, curators of the University of Leiden; they held the office of *dijkgraaf* or dike-reeve of Rijnland, received commissions in the States' army, and went on diplomatic missions. The family produced no less than three admirals: Johan van Warmond in 1578; on Johan's recommendation, his second cousin Jacob van Obdam, appointed in 1603; and in 1653, the latter's son Jacob. In 1657 the last of these received the title of 'baron of Wassenaer' after he had bought the manor of that name. Since the end of the sixteenth century, however, all three families had borne the name Wassenaer.

The finances of the Duvenvoirdes went swimmingly. Revenues flowed in from their high offices as well as from their lands. This can be seen by the fact that they were in a position to add new manors to their patrimony. Among others these included former possessions of the lords of Wassenaer, which had passed by marriage and inheritance into the hands of the Southern Netherlands counts of Ligne and were offered for sale during the Twelve Years' Truce (1609–21).

[42] See chapter 7, n. 43.

Finally, let us note the biological survival of the family: although the last male descendant of the Warmond branch died in 1687, the Duvenvoirdes managed as lords and later as barons of Wassenaer to survive into the twentieth century.

The fates of the three branches of the Duvenvoirde family thus do not confirm our hypothesis. They did not die out, they were not impoverished, and they retained important administrative functions; they even saw their importance increase. This example of successful nobles could be supplemented by others such as the Van der Does family, whose members before the Revolt were relatively unimportant landowners who seldom appeared in the Ridderschap. But after Jan van der Does (the renowned humanist Janus Dousa) had actively supported the Revolt, his family rose to wealth and prominence in the government.[43] Similar good fortune came to the Alckemades, one branch of which coalesced with the Catholic patriciate of Amsterdam and rose to prosperity. By 1614 Sybrand van Alckemade was able to buy back the knightly manor of Oud-Alckemade, long out of the family's possession; there he resumed the noble style of life.[44] On the other hand, in the camp of the losers, the lords of Cruyningen could take consolation in the company of the bankrupt lords of Heemstede or Poelgeest.[45]

The problem of the decline of the Holland nobility cannot be solved simply by presenting a number of examples. A thematic study is necessary, one which treats independently the demographic, economic and political factors that influenced the position of nobles in society. This is the goal of this work.

[43] J. Kloos, *Noordwijk in de loop der eeuwen* (Noordwijk, 1928), pp. 37–8, 118–22.
[44] A. van Lommel, SJ, 'Fragment eener genealogie der van Alckemades', *Nav* 23 (1873): 312–14; H. J. Allard, 'Nadere aantekeningen over de Alkemaden', *BGBH* 1 (1873): 374–80; 'Een jachtruzie van voor 200 jaar', *LJ* 13 (1916): 124–31, published anonymously.
[45] Van Gouthoeven, *Chronyke*, p. 179; W. M. C. Regt, 'De burcht Groot-Poelgeest', *LJ* 4 (1907): 93–112.

3 E. van der Maes, 'Johan van Duvenvoirde', 1608 (Duivenvoorde castle). Johan van
Duvenvoirde, later van Wassenaer, lord of Voorschoten (1578–1647).

2

Virtue and descent

CLASSES AND ORDERS

Social equality was not a generally accepted ideal in the sixteenth and seventeenth centuries. Most contemporaries thought that God had placed different social groups into hierarchical order. Not only was it undesirable to change this system, it was impossible, because change in the cosmic order was simply beyond the power of humanity. Contemporaries accepted social inequality: the question is only along which lines the various social groups were divided.

Historians have distinguished between a society of orders and a society of classes.[1] An order is a juridically defined group, to which one belongs by birth or by formal acceptance. Family and lineage, tradition and group character are important. A society of orders is by definition static and traditional. Each order is subject to its own rules of law; each order has certain privileges and obligations. Medieval society is usually divided into three orders: clergy, nobility and third estate. Yet social mobility was more common than this classification suggests.[2]

A class is a socio-economic group. An individual belongs to a class because of his economic activities or his income. In a society of classes, personal achievement is more important than birth. Society can be divided into classes in many ways: for example, into two classes, capitalists and workers, on the grounds of ownership of the means of production; but it is also possible to distinguish a middle class of independent artisans. Some would regard the landowners as a separate class; others prefer to make more class distinctions based on a hierarchy of incomes and the accompanying prestige attached to occupations.[3]

[1] Roland Mousnier, 'Problèmes de méthode dans l'étude des structures sociales des XVIIe et XVIIIe siècles', *La plume, la faucille et le marteau* (Paris, 1970), pp. 12–26; *Les hiérarchies sociales de 1450 à nos jours* (Paris, 1969). Pierre Goubert, *l'Ancien Régime. I: La société* (Paris, 1969). For the Dutch Republic: I. Schöffer, 'La stratification sociale de la République des Provinces-Unies au XVIIe siècle', in *Problèmes de stratification sociale: Actes du colloque international (1966)*, ed. Roland Mousnier (Paris, 1968), pp. 121–32, and G. Groenhuis, *De predikanten. De sociale positie van de gereformeerde predikanten in de Republiek der Verenigde Nederlanden voor ± 1700* (Groningen, 1977).

[2] E.g. J. M. van Winter, *Ministerialiteit en ridderschap in Gelre en Zutphen* (Groningen, 1962).

[3] I. Schöffer, 'De Republiek der Verenigde Nederlanden, 1609–1702', in *De Lage Landen van 1500 tot 1780*, ed. I. Schöffer, H. van der Wee and J. A. Bornewasser (Amsterdam and Brussels, 1978), pp. 167–267, at 178–9. J. M. Winter, *Ridderschap. Ideaal en werkelijkheid* (Bussum, 1965), pp. 81–2; cf. his 'De middeleeuwse ridderschap als "classe sociale"', *TvG* 84 (1971): 262–75. B. H. Slicher van Bath, *Geschiedenis: theorie en praktijk* (Utrecht and Antwerp, 1978), pp. 295–6.

Social change is more pronounced in a society of classes than in a society of orders: social mobility is greater in a society of classes. Joseph Schumpeter has compared a class to a hotel: the rooms are always occupied, but by different people.[4] In an analogous comparison, an order is more like a castle that is inhabited for centuries by successive generations of the same family.

In actuality neither pure societies of orders nor pure societies of classes have ever existed. Every society contains characteristics of both types in varying degrees. A pure society of orders cannot exist, because the different functional elites will die out and require replenishment from below.[5] By contrast, a society of classes will have a tendency to become rigid, because each group that reaches the top will be inclined to reserve privileges for its descendants, and to block the ascent of newcomers. The rate of social mobility will be determined primarily through economic developments and demographic factors. A rapid economic expansion can promote social mobility and give more class-character to the society. It has been suggested that the Dutch Republic between 1580 and 1650 should be described as a society of classes.[6] However, it is hard to establish whether the period from the sixteenth century through the eighteenth century was a society of orders or of classes. On the one hand, this period was marked by tempestuous economic and social developments and the accompanying social mobility; on the other hand, in most countries the juridical inequality of orders was abolished only with the coming of the French Revolution.

Contemporaries were aware of the idea that society consisted of different orders or classes. The threefold medieval division had not entirely disappeared in bourgeois seventeenth-century Holland. In 1620 Wouter van Gouthoeven wrote that inhabitants of all Christian nations were divided into three 'states or sorts', clergy, nobility and third estate, each with its own functions. The nobles were obliged to defend the other two orders with their arms. Van Gouthoeven did recognize a certain social mobility within this scheme. Members of the second and third estates were free to join the first, the clergy. The third estate could join the nobility 'through inborn bravery of mind and exercise of arms and virtues, having acquired great wealth'. But Van Gouthoeven regarded the derogation of nobles and clergy to the third estate as dishonourable.[7]

None the less the concept of the society of three orders had only slight significance in sixteenth- and seventeenth-century Holland. The clergy identified with the group from which they had originated – nobility, grand or petty bourgeoisie. The nuns at the aristocratic convent of Rijnsburg, for example,

---

[4] Cited by Alfred Cobban, *The Social Interpretation of the French Revolution* (Cambridge, 1964), p. 22; cf. Stone, *Crisis*, pp. 38–9.

[5] E. Perroy, 'Social mobility among the French *noblesse* in the later Middle Ages', *PP* 21 (1962): 25–38, at 31–2.

[6] Schöffer, *De Republiek*, p. 179.

[7] Van Gouthoeven, *Chronyke*, p. 119.

regarded themselves more as noblewomen than as nuns.[8] Furthermore, the clergy had never been represented as an independent order in the States of Holland. After the Reformation it ceased to exist. The third estate in heavily urbanized Holland had become much too differentiated to be placed in one category: merchants, small shopkeepers, farmers and day-labourers thought of themselves and each other as clearly distinguished groups. During the Burgundian period, a class of officials began to regard themselves as a separate group, wedged in between the nobility and the patriciate. More important than the threefold scheme of orders was the distinction between those who worked with their hands, which was regarded as not honourable, and those who drew their income from property or offices.[9]

Another view of the social order can be found in the introduction to Martinus Schoockius' *Belgium Federatum* (1652).[10] Schoockius divided the population of the Republic into nine different 'classes': nobles, patricians, merchants, artisans, fishermen, sailors, farmers, workers, and finally, somewhat surprisingly, carters. Schoockius separated this last group from the others because he 'could place them neither among the seamen, nor among the farmers'.[11] After defining these 'classes', he noted that some tradesmen were organized into guilds, while others were not. Small merchants or market-sellers, artisans, seamen, fishermen and carters were guild members. Others remained outside the guild system. These included the farmers, because they could not easily be placed into the system; the nobles, patricians, and great merchants, because of their dignity (*dignitas*); and the 'foul manual labourers' (*sordidi operarii*), precisely because of their limited worth (*vilitas*).[12] By involving the guilds, Schoockius introduced, without explicitly saying so, a division into three classes. These lay immediately below the surface of his nine-class scheme: an upper class, consisting of nobles, patriciate and great merchants; a middle class of independent shopkeepers organized in guilds; and, at the very bottom, an unpropertied class of wage-labourers. In the final analysis, this class division is based on the criterion of ownership of the means of production. The highest class consisted of landowners, *rentiers* and capitalists, living on the income from their property: the middle-class artisans, joined into guilds, worked with their own means of production; the wage-labourers owned no means of production and could only sell their labour. Farmers remained outside this class system. In this manner Schoockius' scheme reflected the extensively developed socio-economic relationships of the Dutch Republic in the Golden Age.

---

[8] See below, pp. 120–5.
[9] R. van Uytven, 'Sociaal-economische evoluties in de Nederlanden vóór de Revoluties (veertiende-zestiende eeuw)', *BMGN* 87 (1972): 60–93, at 84.
[10] Schoockius, *Belgium*, p. 121.
[11] Ibid., p. 158.
[12] Ibid., p. 121.

A DEFINITION OF THE NOBILITY OF HOLLAND

How should the nobility be defined in the context of this partly traditional, partly modern society? It is difficult to give a generally valid definition, because the idea changed over time and also varied from region to region.[13] It may be simplest to state first what the nobility in Holland was *not*.[14]

The nobility cannot be regarded as a class of large landowners. Although it is true that the nobles of Holland received the largest part of their incomes from leases and tithes, they were by no means the only or even the most important landowners in the province. Farmers and town-dwellers collectively owned more land than the nobility. Altogether the nobles in Holland had less than 10 per cent of the arable land.[15]

It is also incorrect to equate the nobility with the fief-holders. By the beginning of the sixteenth century, the names of many vassals who were not regarded as part of the nobility appear in feudal registers. Nor can the nobility be equated with the vassals who held a manor in fief, because some commoners also owned manors, although around 1500 this was still exceptional.[16] The feudal relationship had long ago lost its original significance as a personal bond between lord and vassal. Fiefs could be bought and sold almost without restriction. The purchase of a manorial property did not automatically ennoble the new owner.[17]

The nobility was not a military class either. Although the profession of arms was regarded as the aristocratic task *par excellence*, only a few Holland nobles held military offices. On the other hand, many commoners were employed in the army, even as commissioned officers.[18]

It would also be incorrect to equate the Holland nobility with the Holland Ridderschap. The members of this college did indeed belong to the old nobility, but over the course of time access was limited to a small group of noble families. Furthermore, at meetings of the States it was always possible to find representatives of the cities who were of noble origin.[19]

[13] Cf. P. de Win, 'De adel in het hertogdom Brabant van de vijftiende eeuw. Een terreinverkenning', *TvG* 93 (1980): 391–409, at 392. P. Janssens, 'De Zuidnederlandse adel tijdens het Ancien Régime (17e–18e eeuw)', *TvG* 93 (1980): 445–65, at 449–50. For a seventeenth-century definition of the nobility, see also Wilhelmus Cuminius, *Disputatio politica de nobilitate* (Groningen, 1641), and A. Matthaeus, *De nobilitate, de principibus, de ducibus etc. libri IV* (Amsterdam, 1686).

[14] Cf. Goubert, *Ancien Régime*, pp. 145–54. James B. Wood, *The Nobility of the Election of Bayeux* (Princeton, 1980), pp. 10–14. Janssens, 'De Zuidnederlandse adel', p. 450.

[15] See below, p. 98.

[16] See below, p. 147.

[17] In 1490 six holders of seigneuries were identified only by patronymics: Hendrick Willemsz., Adriaen Ockersz., Adriaen Cornelis Gillisz., Adriaen Cornelisz. (possibly the same person), Aernt Vrancken (schout van Delft) and Catharina Roelofsdr. We may assume that they were not counted among the nobility.

[18] Van Gelder, 'Hollandse adel', p. 150.

[19] See below, pp. 166–75 and 208–12.

Finally, it would be misleading to limit the nobility only to persons who bore noble titles. The titled high nobility in Holland was far exceeded in numbers by the untitled lower nobles, who would at most distinguish themselves with the title *jonkheer*. A nobleman was also not the same as a knight. A man could be of noble origin, but knights were made, not born. Nobles who had received knighthood called themselves *heer* (lord); other nobles were called *knape* or *schildknaap* (squire, or shield-bearer).

The nobility thus cannot be reduced to a specific form of ownership (land, fiefs, manors), nor to a specific social function or profession (soldiers, knights, or lords of the manor). What then was the Holland nobility? The problem can be restated as two separate questions: what did people in Holland understand by the concept of nobility and, second, who belonged to it?

The *concept* 'nobility' can only be defined legally. From a constitutional point of view, the nobility was a group differentiated from the rest of the population by its access to specific constitutional and social privileges, such as the right to hunt, the right to bear coats of arms and titles, the right to be tried by a special court, and the right to be represented as a separate group at meetings of the States.[20] These group privileges, which will be discussed in more detail, remained in existence until 1795. This definition does not state that other groups in the population could not have privileges; some of them enjoyed the same privileges as the nobility. But nobles and non-nobles were not regarded as equal before the law. The nobility distinguished itself from the rest of the population by a special juridical status that was both personal and hereditary in the male line, and gave access to political and social privileges.[21]

Who benefited from these exceptional privileges? To answer this question, we must introduce a social distinction alongside the strict legal criterion. The nobility were those who regarded themselves as noble, and were accepted as such by the rest of the community.[22] In the first place they included those who descended from ancient noble lineages. Someone was noble if his ancestors had been regarded as nobles for several generations. To prove his noble descent, he could use old documents showing that his ancestors in the direct male line had been summoned in the Ridderschap to attend meetings of the States, or had borne the title *ridder* (knight) (or at least *knape*). Thus nobility was defined by birth, yet by itself this genetic definition was not sufficient. On the one hand, by

---

[20] H. A. van Foreest, *Het oude geslacht van Foreest 1250–1570* (Assen, 1950), pp. 170–4. S. J. Fockema Andreae, *De Nederlandse staat onder de Republiek* (7th edn, Amsterdam, 1975), pp. 163–4.

[21] Wood, *Nobility*, p. 12; Goubert, *Ancien Régime*, p. 52, for France. For Holland, see Hugo de Groot, *Inleidinge tot de Hollandsche rechtsgeleerdheid*, ed. F. Dovring, H. F. W. D. Fischer and E. M. Meyers (2nd edn, Leiden, 1965), p. 39.

[22] Cf. H. de Ridder-Symoens, 'Adel en Universiteiten in de zestiende eeuw. Humanistisch ideaal of bittere noodzaak?' *TvG* 93 (1980): 410–32, at 410.

living 'non-nobly' it was possible to lose noble status, and on the other hand commoners could receive letters of nobility.[23]

French historiography has placed great emphasis on the social distinction between nobility of birth (*noblesse de race, noblesse d'épée*) and nobility of office (*noblesse de robe*).[24] It would be misleading, however, to speak of a 'nobility of office' in the sixteenth-century county of Holland. This term suggests that high officials in the provincial administration belonged to the nobility by virtue of their office. Yet they were not regarded as nobles, either by the ancient feudal nobility, or by the rest of the population. They also had no access to aristocratic privileges such as the right to hunt or to sit in the Ridderschap. Some of them nevertheless acquired manors and were even made knights, which sometimes made it difficult in practice to determine whether someone belonged to the nobility or not.[25] The term 'nobility of office' also suggests a sharp distinction between the holders of administrative offices and the nobility of birth. Yet in Holland some descendants of old noble families held administrative offices, such as the councillors Assendelft or Duvenvoirde. Therefore when we speak of 'the nobility' in this work, we mean first of all the old feudal nobility, the descendants of noble families; moreover those who still lived as nobles – a second criterion, which will be discussed. Along with them, we must regard as noble those who had been raised to the noble group by an official letter of nobility, and who thereby shared the exceptional constitutional status of the nobles. In Holland there were few such individuals.

During the Republic there were a fair number of regents of bourgeois origin who received knightly orders from foreign monarchs. They then called themselves *ridder*; most had a family coat of arms and also adopted an aristocratic lifestyle in general.[26] Should they be counted as part of the nobility? In his overview of the various population groups in the Republic around the middle of the seventeenth century, Martinus Schoockius regarded them as *nobiles*, but placed them in a separate category. He discussed this 'nobility of the third rank' or 'recent nobles' after the nobility of birth, whom he divided into high or titled nobility ('who enjoy the prerogatives of nobility') and low nobility (nobility of the

---

[23] H. de Schepper and P. Janssens, 'De Raad van State in de landsheerlijke Nederlanden en zijn voortgang op gescheiden wegen, 1531–1588/1948', *450 jaar Raad van State* (The Hague, 1981), pp. 1–35, at 7; Kerckhoffs-de Heij, *De Grote Raad*, I, p. 86.

[24] Primarily in the work of R. Mousnier; criticisms have been made by Wood, *Nobility*. Cf. for the Netherlands, H. de Ridder-Symoens, 'Adel en Universiteiten', pp. 425–6.

[25] Cf. Kerckhoffs-de Heij, *De Grote Raad*, I, pp. 86–7. Examples in Holland are Arend Sasbout, councillor in the Court of Holland, knight and lord of Spaland (Van der Aa, *Biographisch woordenboek*); Gerrit van Renoy, *eerste rekenmeester*, who was ennobled by Charles V, according to Van Gouthoeven, *Chronyke*, p. 111.

[26] Netherlanders who received foreign orders of knighthood are listed in *Nav* 14 (1864): 259. The most common orders were those of St Michel (France) and St George (England). Foreign titles of nobility had already been granted earlier, e.g. the Amsterdam burgomaster Pompejus Occo received a family coat of arms from Emperor Maximilian in 1504. GA, Familiearchief Bicker, inv. no. 718, fos. 30, 32. Yet this honour did not lead to his acceptance in the Holland nobility.

second rank).[27] In Holland, however, the bearers of foreign titles of knighthood were legally barred from the privileges enjoyed by the old nobility.[28] Furthermore the old nobility was certainly not inclined to accept the knighted regents as their social equals.[29] While grants of nobility were rare under the Habsburg sovereigns, after the abolition of the monarchy no one was raised to noble status in Holland. Because foreign titles of knighthood were not recognized, we can equate the nobility as a whole with the nobility of birth.[30]

People in the sixteenth and seventeenth centuries regarded birth as the criterion for noble status, as is apparent from the means by which an individual could prove that he was noble if anyone had doubts. Arend van Duvenvoirde (1528–ca. 1600) had been a member of the Compromise of the Nobility in 1566 and had favoured the Protestant Reformation. Banished by Alba's Council of Troubles, he had joined the Sea-Beggars. In 1572 he appeared before a notary in England, accompanied by several witnesses who swore that Arend van Duvenvoirde, 'son and heir of the deceased Lord Johan van Duvenvoirde, was a born nobleman from a noble house and family, on his father's as well as on his mother's side, and that this Aernoult's father was the son of the second brother of Lord Willem van Wassenaer, and of the imperial order of the Golden Fleece and his mother of the house of Renesse, barons and children of barons'.[31] Of course this form of proof was tautological. If Arend van Duvenvoirde was noble because his parents had been noble, why then had his parents been noble? Because their parents had belonged to the nobility as well? No one lost any sleep over this problem. It sufficed that the nobility of a family was known 'of old', and the major point is that such proof was accepted. It is not coincidental that Arend van Duvenvoirde pleaded his cause abroad. In Holland no one would have doubted his noble origins. That applied to most noble lineages: they were generally known.

This did not change in the seventeenth century. Adam van der Duyn, lord of Rijswijk and 's-Gravenmoer, who remained Catholic after the Revolt and was to some extent shunted aside, complained in 1620 to the Ridderschap that 'some ignorant persons show little respect for the name and family Van der Duyn'. At his request he received a written declaration from the college, according to which the Van der Duyns, Adam's ancestors, had been nobles since time immemorial; that on this account they had been summoned to the Ridderschap and had actually attended; and that the Van der Duyns were

---

[27] Schoockius, *Belgium*, pp. 121–30.
[28] Eduard van Zurck, *Codex Batavus, waer in het algemeen kerck en burgelijck recht van Hollant, Zeelant, en het ressort der admiraliteit kortelijck is begrepen, enz.* (Delft, 1711), p. 340; cf. De Groot, *Inleidinge*, p. 39.
[29] This point is developed further in chapter 4 and chapter 8.
[30] Fockema Andreae, *Nederlandse staat*, pp. 163–4.
[31] Declaration made by several persons in England, that Arnold van Duivenvoorde is noble, ARA, Huisarchief Duivenvoorde, inv. no. 36.

eligible to attend in the future.[32] That settled the matter. It had already been customary in Holland in the fourteenth and fifteenth centuries, in case of doubt, to prove noble birth by having a number of relatives whose noble status was beyond doubt swear an oath before the court, the so-called *edeltuig* (noble testimony).[33]

None the less, there was still uncertainty about the origins of a number of families. Families that had formerly lived as nobles but suffered financial reverses were unable to maintain their status; they lived as peasants.[34] Other families had settled in the towns and were more or less assimilated to the urban patriciate.[35] Still others had never belonged to the feudal nobility, but had risen in the service of the sovereign, acquired manors and were barely distinguishable from the old nobility in lifestyle. In practice it was difficult to draw a sharp dividing line at the lower edge of the nobility. This is apparent, for example, from the heading written on a list compiled around 1530, with the names of 'Nobles in Holland and also others who behave as nobles, although they are not accepted as such . . . imperial officers [administrative officeholders] not included'.[36] In 1590, Walraven van Brederode and his secretary Arend van Buchell argued about the fate of the noble houses Borsselen and Teylingen. Brederode asserted that there were no more living descendants in the male line of these families; his secretary maintained that there certainly were still living descendants of Teylingen, 'although through unjust fortune they have fallen into the common people' (*plebs*).[37] Indeed, in this period members of the Teylingen family can be found among the town councillors of Alkmaar and Amsterdam.[38]

It was primarily the status of high officers in the provincial administration that gave rise to confusion. Thus, for example, one can find the names of the treasurer-general of the domains, 'Lord' Vincent Corneliszoon van Mierop, lord of Cabau, and his two sons, Jacob, lord of Cabau and Cornelis, dean of Utrecht, on the list of Holland nobles in 1540 and 1549, reported by Van Gouthoeven.[39] Yet they did not belong to an 'ancient' noble family. In 1555 Heijman Vincentszoon and Jacob Vincentszoon were regarded as fief-holders

---

[32] Declaration of the Holland Ridderschap, that Adam van der Duyn is noble, HRA, Collectie Snouckaert, inv. no. 1288.

[33] I. H. Gosses, *Welgeborenen en huislieden. Onderzoekingen over standen en staat in het graafschap Holland* (Groningen, 1926), pp. 2–3.

[34] On the Holland 'welgeborenen', see below, pp. 44–5.

[35] E.g. the Foreest family in Alkmaar, Van Foreest, *Foreest*.

[36] Declaration of several names of nobles in Holland, ARA Brussels, Audiëntie [Aud.], inv. no. 1475/5.

[37] Arend van Buchell, *Diarium*, ed. G. Brom and L. A. van Langeraad (Amsterdam, 1907), p. 253.

[38] C. W. Bruinvis, *De Alkmaarse Vroedschap tot 1795* (n.p., 1904); Johan E. Elias, *De Vroedschap van Amsterdam*, 2 vols. (Haarlem, 1903–5), I, pp. 163–7.

[39] Van Gouthoeven, *Chronyke*, p. 140. Yet Van Gouthoeven and Boxhorn did not regard the family as noble: ibid., pp. 119–20; Boxhorn, *Toneel*, pp. 42–5.

who were not qualified to be summoned to the Ridderschap.[40] The use of the patronymic is in many cases an indication of non-noble origin.[41]

That these prominent officers who possessed manors were no longer gradually raised to the nobility was a comparatively new phenomenon in the sixteenth-century Netherlands. In the middle ages commoners quite often were created knights, and their descendants were regarded as noble.[42] It did not matter to which of the three pre-feudal groups they had belonged – nobles, free, or unfree.[43] Thus in 1315 Bartoud van Assendelft was enfeoffed with the low jurisdiction of Assendelft, a fief formerly held by his father. Not until two years later did the count give him 'the right that free persons have'.[44] By the sixteenth century, however, memories of the servile origin of the Assendelft family had disappeared. Through prudent marriages and the acquisition of property, they then belonged to the most distinguished families of Holland. This suggests that the nobility of the middle ages had been a social class that was open to advancement from below and was continually replenished with new blood. In the course of the fifteenth century, however, fewer and fewer persons of non-noble origin were knighted and raised to the nobility. This privilege was now reserved to persons who already belonged to a noble family (one that was *riddermatig*, worthy of knighthood). Thus the nobility shut itself off and became a closed group defined by birth. Persons either belonged to it or not; if an individual did not belong, it was practically impossible for him to be raised to that status.[45]

Which families were considered to have noble origin? Among contemporaries there was consensus about the status of most families, but confusion and uncertainty prevailed about the status of some. For historians, this is first a question of sources. The most important list was made in 1555 by the president of the Court of Holland, giving the names of the nobles resident in Holland and other vassals of the county, with an indication as to whether they should or should not be included when the Ridderschap was summoned to the States of Holland.[46] That these nobles were summoned, does not say that they

---

[40] See appendix 1 of the Dutch edition.

[41] On the other hand, the use of a family name does not prove noble origin.

[42] Van Foreest, *Foreest*, p. 101, n. 3. An example in Holland is the Ruychrock van de Werve family: cf. Kerckhoffs-de Heij, *De Grote Raad*, I, p. 87, and II, pp. 129–31.

[43] Gosses, *Welgeborenen*, pp. 1–3.   [44] Ibid., p. 8.

[45] Van Winter, 'Middeleeuwse ridderschap', pp. 268–73. She shows that the medieval ridderschap in Gelre and Zutphen (elsewhere as well) fulfilled the criteria set by G. Gurvitch for a social class. One important characteristic of a social class is its openness. In the sixteenth century, however, membership in the ridderschap was made dependent upon ability to participate in meetings of the States, which was established if ancestors had also taken part in such meetings. Newcomers were no longer admitted: as a result the Gueldrian ridderschap became rigid and stopped being a social class. The same point was stated by Van Foreest, *Foreest*, p. 96: 'the ridderschap was a class of fief-holders of the count before it became a condition of birth'.

[46] 'Declaratie van de principale heren edelen en vazallen, gegoed in Holland en aldaar woonachtig, die men vanouds gewoon is tot alle dagvaarten te beschrijven', ARA, Archief van de landsadvo-

actually presented themselves; they were only entitled to do so. The number of nobles that appeared at the meetings was much smaller than the Holland nobility as a whole. First were listed the names of the Holland nobles who were usually summoned. Among them were also several high nobles from other provinces, such as the prince of Orange and the counts of Aremberg, Horne and Ligne: as the heirs of Holland families that had become extinct, they possessed many manors in Holland. In practice, however, these magnates did not appear. We may regard the others, descended from Holland noble families, in possession of manors and entitled to take part in the consultations of the Ridderschap, as the core of the nobility of Holland. Then followed the other vassals who were not usually summoned. These included two abbots and one abbess who held manors. The clergy, however, had never been represented in the States of Holland. Along with them were the burgemeesters of several Holland towns that had come into possession of adjoining manors. In such cases the burgemeesters held the manors ex-officio, but they were not reckoned among the nobility. The third category was the most complicated, 'other vassals whom one is not accustomed to summon to the meetings of the States, as being held not qualified thereunto'. This category included several nobles from other provinces, who had come into possession of Holland manors through marriage or inheritance. Thus they did belong to the nobility, but not to the nobility of Holland. Secondly, we find high officials in the provincial administration who were of non-noble origin, such as the lawyers Jacob de Jonge, Gerrit van Renoy, Arend Sasbout, and Heyman and Jacob Vincentsz. Thirdly, among the ranks of those considered unqualified were manorial lords of urban bourgeois origin, such as Pieter Aertsz, Arend Cornelisz (van der Myle) and Jacob Jansz of Utrecht, later father-in-law of Oldenbarnevelt. The lack of a family name and the use of the simple patronymic reveal their non-noble origin. Fourthly, the list excluded by name several persons who were nevertheless reckoned part of the Holland nobility, such as Dirk van Berckenrode, for example.[47] Why he was not entitled to appear is uncertain. In any event it is clear why the Holland nobleman Klaas van Assendelft was unwelcome: a marginal note reports, 'This one is regarded as a fool.'[48] Within this third category of the unqualified it is often difficult to distinguish Holland nobles, 'foreign' nobles, high officials of the provincial administration, and urban bourgeois or patricians. The Court president's list closes with a fourth category of nobles in Holland, who held no manors and therefore were not summoned. Yet their noble quality was not in doubt. The entire list probably gives a good snapshot of who was reckoned

caat Johan van Oldenbarnevelt, prov. inv. no. 1015; pub. in Van der Houve, *Hantvest*, pp. 62–6, and Van Leeuwen, *Batavia*, pp. 685–6.

[47] M. Thierry de Bye Dólleman, 'Het geslacht Berckenrode', *JbCBG* 12 (1958): 81–132.

[48] This Klaas van Assendelft was not the similarly named son of the president of the Court, who will be discussed in chapter 4.

among the nobility of the county, although it is not complete.[49] This information can be supplemented with two more lists of 'knights and nobles' who lived between 1477 and 1500, and between 1540 and 1549, respectively.[50] From 1620 and 1632 we have the lists of noble family names of Holland compiled by Van Gouthoeven and Boxhorn. Van Gouthoeven's names are those that 'are listed among the Ridderschap and nobles in old or new printed chronicles, in registers, accounts and other written documents, as bearing or having borne various coats of arms'.[51] Boxhorn collected his noble family names 'from the histories as well as public and private documents'.[52] There are few differences between the two lists. They are probably not entirely reliable for the sixteenth century, but at least they allow us to see which family names were regarded as noble in the seventeenth century. Moreover both lists contain many names of noble families that had already died out in the sixteenth century. Furthermore, both lists contain names that had been considered noble in the middle ages, although their descendants in the sixteenth and seventeenth centuries no longer lived as nobles and had consequently lost their noble status. These lists must therefore be used with care in the identification of Holland nobles.

NOBLE VIRTUES

The definition of the nobility was ambiguous. Nobility was first and foremost a status acquired by birth, but there was agreement that nobility was, or ought to be, based on virtue (*virtus*). The concept of virtue was also ambiguous. Depending on the context, it was used to cover all kinds of positive qualities. In a Christian context, virtue meant piety; it could also apply to skill in the arts or to learning. But when the concept was used in connection with the nobility, it pointed to courage in war, leadership, or faithful service to the prince: in short, to the personal qualities that people regarded as characteristic of a nobleman, or at any rate desirable. Virtue was thus a personal quality: that was why Schoockius in his description of the nobility included recent nobles, those who had been rewarded for their virtue with a noble title. Wouter van Gouthoeven agreed that burgers could achieve the status of noblemen 'through inborn bravery of mind, and the exercise of arms and virtues', as well as after acquiring great wealth, provided that the government and the other nobles recognized them as such.[53] 'War makes common men noble through brave deeds', wrote a pamphleteer in

---

[49] In the margin, in another sixteenth-century hand, are the names of several nobles who attended sessions of the States between 1526 and 1572, but are not listed in the text itself. The noble family of Foreest, for example, does not appear, not even under the nobles who did not attend because they had no manors.

[50] Van Gouthoeven, *Chronyke*, pp. 618–20.

[51] Ibid., pp. 119–20.

[52] Boxhorn, *Toneel*, pp. 42–5.

[53] Van Gouthoeven, *Chronyke*, p. 119.

1608.[54] Yet it would be difficult to base nobility simultaneously on personal accomplishments and on descent. On the one hand, there were always persons who had descended from noble houses but did not in the least display the necessary virtue. On the other hand, it was clear that there were many statesmen and soldiers in the service of the sovereign and later of the Republic who could not be reckoned as part of the nobility despite their excellent qualities. The dilemma between *virtus* and *ortus*, virtue and descent, was not new in the sixteenth century. For centuries people had repeated *ad nauseam* that a noble nature was worth more than noble descent.

For the Holland humanist Hadrianus Junius (1511–73), virtue and glory were the foundations of all nobility. He found it much better to make oneself worthy through useful works, than to boast of noble lineage.[55] Consequently he distinguished three kinds of nobility: first, a nobility received from Nature; then one based on Virtue; and finally one based on Art.[56] Those whose nobility was based on Virtue had served the state. Most of these men were of common origin, but they bequeathed a 'generous' name and title to their posterity. Those whose nobility was based on Art were, according to Junius, scholars and artists who served the general interest. Those whose nobility was based on Nature, the first category, however, formed the true nobility of birth. But after he had first praised at length those whose nobility was based on their achievements, at the expense of those who could only appeal to their lineage, Junius subsequently declared that people should not think that he had no respect for the ancient nobility. On the contrary, he was very favourably inclined toward the nobility, not only because it was beneficial to the country that nobles could take the rudder of the ship of state, but also because they kept alive the memory of famous men who had served the country in the past.[57] The nobility of birth deserved to be honoured and beloved 'because God himself has placed the helm of the community in their hands'.[58] Thus Junius did not manage to resolve the latent antithesis of virtue and descent.

The same inconsistency can be found in the legal scholar Simon van Leeuwen.[59] In his 1659 tract on the nobles and well-born of Holland he likewise emphasized achievements as the foundation of nobility. According to him these did not have to be personal, because the accomplishments of the ancestors extended nobility to the descendants. All nobility thus had its origin in services, or in birth. When the nobility of a house was known anciently, it was not necessary to offer further proof. It sufficed for a man to have issued from the lawful marriage of a nobleman and his wife (who did not have to be noble

---

[54] (Anon.), *Den triumph vanden oorloch ende de mis-prijsinghe vanden peys seer genoechlijck ende corts-wijlich om te lesen enz.* ([Leiden], 1608; Kn 1978), fo. B 2 v.
[55] Iunius, *Batavia*, pp. 318–19.
[56] Ibid., p. 320.   [57] Ibid., p. 321.   [58] Ibid., p. 320.
[59] Van Leeuwen, *Redeningh*, pp. 17–20, 31–2.

herself). Yet according to van Leeuwen the nobles of Holland had arisen less from high birth than from their worthy deeds, in particular brave conduct during the war.[60] Van Leeuwen tried to resolve the contradiction between achievement and birth by projecting achievement back into the past. The unspoken assumption was that this characteristic was hereditary: the virtues of the ancestors would live on in the descendants.[61]

Consequently theory was not necessarily in accord with practice. Nobility ought to be based on virtue; in actuality those who were regarded as nobles first and foremost were the lawful descendants in direct male line from a family that had been known anciently as noble.

ENNOBLEMENTS

In Holland during the reigns of Charles V and Philip II, grants of nobility had become exceptional. The ennoblement of Arend Cornelisz van der Myle was a case in point. This burgemeester of Dordrecht received a title of nobility as a reward for his conduct in the 'wonder year' 1566, when he had tried to oppose Protestant open-air sermons and prevent iconoclasm.[62] Van der Myle's nobility was thus based on his achievements, but the notion that nobility ought to be based on birth was so deeply rooted that his deed of ennoblement did everything to project his new status back into the past. In official documents Van der Myle was always cited by his simple patronymic as Arend Cornelisz, and he used to sign his name that way: a clear indication that he did not belong to the nobility. He had only acquired the manor of Myl through his marriage with Cornelia Jan Willem Jan Reyersdr van Alblas.[63] Nevertheless his deed of nobility recalled

how he and his aforesaid wife, outranking others, have lived and conducted themselves as good, honest and excellent persons, bearing the arms continuously descending from

---

[60] Ibid., pp. 31–2.
[61] Abel Eppens tho Equart of Groningen also thought that nobility was defined more by service to the country than by ancestry, *Kroniek*, ed. J. A. Feith and H. Brugmans, 2 vols. (Amsterdam, 1911), I, p. 110. Cf. the outstanding treatment of the same question among the French nobility by Davis Bitton, *The French Nobility in Crisis 1560–1640* (Stanford, 1969), pp. 77–91.
[62] Leenregisters, ARA, Leenkamer, inv. no. 67, fo. 108. The grant of nobility to Van der Myle was published in *Handvesten, privilegiën, vrijheden . . . der stadt Dordrecht*, ed. Pieter Hendrik van de Wall (Dordrecht, 1790), pp. 1321–7. Cf. Van der Aa, *Biographisch woordenboek*, s.v. Van der Myle, and Van Gelder, 'Hollandse adel', p. 115. Van der Myle's title may have involved the confirmation of an earlier grant: see *Nav* 72 (1923): 189. Van Gelder was mistaken in assuming that, because they received fiefs in payment, Willem van Nuyssenberg and Andries the bastard of Wassenaer were also nobles.
[63] In 1555 'Arent Cornelisz. lord of Myle outside of Dordrecht' was among the 'other vassals that would not ordinarily be summoned to the Ridderschap, as not qualified'. Van der Myle's manor had been granted in 1541 to Cornelia Jan Willem Jan Reijersdr on the death of her father; in 1564 she transferred it to 'lord Arent Cornelisz', her husband. ARA, Reportoria op de leenregisters, Leenkamer, inv. no. 231, fo. 645.

their predecessors as is usual among good armigerous men; and as ordinarily happens, the said names became obscured, lost and unknown, both because of the floods occurring around our aforesaid city of Dordrecht; and because the people in Holland over the course of time and by accepted custom acquired the habit of giving children their father's Christian names as family names [i.e. as patronymics], by which their coat of arms has fallen into oblivion.[64]

The document thus tried to create the impression that Van der Myle was not being made into a nobleman, but that his noble status was merely being confirmed.

Later this formula would still have significance. Arend Cornelisz's grandson, Cornelis van der Myle, son-in-law of the provincial advocate Johan van Oldenbarnevelt, was struck from the ranks of the Ridderschap in 1618. Although this was a purely political matter, in one of the numerous pamphlets written at the time he was charged with being 'of lowly origin, being only the third [generation] of nobility appearing at the meetings of the Ridderschap, on which others of older and higher nobility look down'.[65] Van der Myle defended himself by pointing out that his grandfather's title of nobility only reconfirmed the ancient status of his lineage, which had disappeared over time; and he added a lengthy demonstration celebrating both the noble status and the excellent deeds of his ancestors.[66]

It is difficult to determine why the Habsburg sovereigns raised so few persons to the nobility in Holland. The right to grant noble titles was a visible sign of sovereignty, which the Burgundian dukes had used frequently.[67] It is improbable that Charles V and Philip II would have preferred to employ bourgeois rather than nobles as administrative officials. As long as officials competently and loyally carried out the policy of their sovereign, their personal juridical status was irrelevant. All Charles' and Philip's provincial governors, for example, belonged to the high nobility. Furthermore, there was no objection when the monarchs rewarded officials with noble titles, thus binding them even more strongly to themselves. Fiscal concerns were perhaps more important. When Philip the Fair accepted the government in 1494, he found the finances in a deplorable state. He decided to ban ennoblements. Over the following half-century, however, the nobles ceased to be exempt from taxation, so that this consideration was no longer significant.[68] It may also have been thought desir-

---

[64] *Handvesten Dordrecht*, II, p. 1323.

[65] (Anon.), *Practijcke van den Spaenschen Raedt enz.* (n.p., 1618; Kn 2618), p. 47. Cf. H. A. W. van der Vecht, *Cornelis van der Myle, 1579–1642* (Sappemeer, 1907), p. 104.

[66] [Cornelis van der Myle], *Ontdeckinge van de valsche Spaensche Jesuijtische Practijcke enz.* (The Hague, 1618; Kn 2632), pp. 25–9.

[67] C. A. J. Armstrong, 'Had the Burgundian government a policy for the nobility?', in *Britain and the Netherlands*, II, ed. J. S. Bromley and E. H. Kossmann (Groningen, 1964), pp. 9–32, at 17.

[68] P. J. Blok, 'De financiën van het graafschap Holland', *BVGO*, 3rd series, 3 (1886): 36–130, at 45–6.

able to limit the number of nobles who were summoned to the States.[69] Whatever the cause, the nobility was scarcely replenished with new elements.

After the deposition of Philip II in 1581, there was no monarch to grant noble status. It is true that Simon van Leeuwen thought that this prerogative, along with all other sovereign rights, had passed over to the States, but in practice they never made use of it.[70] This is hardly surprising. The monarch not only granted nobility as the sovereign, but also in his quality of first nobleman, first among his peers. A letter of nobility granted by the bourgeois States would have received little recognition from the old or new nobility, in Holland or abroad.

LIVING NOBLY

A man was noble if he descended from a noble lineage. But while this was a necessary condition, it was not sufficient. A man had to prove his noble descent by living as a nobleman. Charles V declared in 1518 that nobles were exempt from taxation on their fiefs, but he expressly limited this privilege to 'the nobles of the country, living and behaving as noble men'.[71] What did this lifestyle consist of? According to Wouter van Gouthoeven, the nobles had to live 'from their own income from lands, tithes and manors, and [refrain] from mercantile activities, and in particular shopkeeping; but practising war and serving in the Prince's court, or in some honourable office, and owing the country and the other two [orders] protection with their weapons against the violence or attack of enemies, provided that they have commission from high authority'.[72]

What people understood by living as a nobleman came to light in a lawsuit that the inhabitants of Wijk aan Zee brought against Koen van Foreest in 1465. They demanded that Koen pay the scot, a land-tax from which nobles were exempt.[73] The defendant claimed exemption on the grounds that he was of noble descent. The arguments of both parties are revealing. The villagers did not deny Koen's noble descent, but they found that his lifestyle did not differ from their own. They charged that he worked the land with his own hands, gathering and raking his own hay. Furthermore he worked land that he had leased, and he lived amidst the peasants of Wijk aan Zee. Koen defended himself by pointing to his noble relatives who owned fiefs. He declared that he did not drive the plough himself, but that he had his servants do it. He did indeed lease land, but only from his brothers, who were regarded as nobles. Countering the argument that he lived among the villagers, he testified that he

---

[69] *Hedendaagsche historie of tegenwoordige staat der Verenigde Nederlanden*, 23 vols. (Amsterdam, 1739–1803), IV, p. 91.

[70] Van Leeuwen, *Redeningh*, pp. 39–40.

[71] *Informacie op den staet, faculteit ende gelegentheyt van de steden ende dorpen van Hollant ende Vrieslant enz.*, ed. R. Fruin (Leiden, 1866), p. 625.

[72] Van Gouthoeven, *Chronyke*, p. 119.

[73] Gosses, *Welgeborenen*, pp. 40–7.

lived in a homestead that belonged to his brother Willem van Foreest, 'a good moated knightly lodging, with moats, fields, and goods thereunto appertaining . . . with bridges and gates and everything that belongs to a [knightly] seat'. He lived a knightly life, 'to wit riding horses, keeping dogs and birds'.[74] This last point showed that he went hunting, an exclusive aristocratic privilege. Moreover, during the trial he offered to serve the count as a knight. This was not a strong argument, however, because it became clear that he had not done so before. Yet Koen van Foreest won the case, although the wording of the sentence does indicate some doubts. In subsequent years we do indeed find him attending meetings of the Ridderschap in the States of Holland.[75]

To refrain from manual labour, trade and industry; to take part in the hunt; to live in a castle or a knightly homestead; and to serve the sovereign – these were the characteristics of a true nobleman. If an individual violated any of these precepts, then derogation, the loss of noble status, could result.

According to the law of Holland, manual labour and trade, at least retail trade, were derogatory occupations for nobles. In the seventeenth century wholesale trade was permitted, 'because commerce is not only the nerve of our state, but also the envy of neighbouring peoples, and the terror of distant lands'.[76] Yet the nobles' own consciousness of status was stronger than the law. Schoockius wrote that among the Netherlands nobles he had met practically no one who was engaged in wholesale trade.[77] The Holland nobles tried to prevent derogation as long as possible. They could maintain their status only if they were wealthy enough to live on the income from their property. If this was no longer the case, they preferred to take up an administrative career rather than trade: government service did not imperil their noble status. Still, there were several derogated noble families in Holland. The Van Toll family gave up their property and lived on as well-to-do farmers.[78] Cornelis van Lockhorst, who boasted that he could trace his family tree back to an Utrecht noble family, became a burgher of Amsterdam in 1600 and settled as a stationer.[79] In 1591 Arend van Buchell met a man who claimed that he was descended from a race of 'Frisian kings', and also a woman from an unnamed noble family who came to Lord Brederode's house and 'did all the most pitiful work'.[80] Yet these derogated families were no longer counted among the nobility. In practice this

---

[74] P. W. A. Immink, 'De Hollandsche "welgeborenen"', *Verslagen en mededeelingen van de Vereeniging tot uitgave der bronnen van het oude vaderlandsche recht* 10 (1948): 253–89, at 281–9.

[75] Van Foreest, *Foreest*, p. 106.

[76] Pieter Loens, *Kort begrip van den staet, en 't onderscheyd der persoonen mitsgaders 't recht daar uyt voortkomende enz.* (Leiden, 1726), p. 30.

[77] Schoockius, *Belgium*, p. 134.

[78] Van Foreest, *Foreest*, p. 101. Van Gouthoeven, *Chronyke*, p. 208, reports that descendants of Maurijn van Tol (living in 1473) had fallen into poverty, but in the first half of the sixteenth century there were burgemeesters of Dordrecht of that name.

[79] Elias, *Vroedschap*, I, p. 201.

[80] Van Buchell, *Diarium*, p. 307.

meant that they had no access to the social and political privileges of the Holland nobility.

NOBLE PRIVILEGES

The nobles were distinguished from others because they had exclusive access to a number of privileges. This exceptional legal position marked the nobility as a separate estate in constitutional terms until 1795. The privileges that the nobility did enjoy, however, were rather limited. Moreover, the nobles always had to share them with several categories of non-noble persons; and finally many of their privileges became hollow over the course of time.[81]

The most important noble privilege was their right to represent the rural areas in meetings of the States of Holland, as a separate order, the Ridderschap. Originally all the Holland nobles who were enfeoffed with a manor with high or low jurisdiction were entitled to appear personally in the Ridderschap. But around the middle of the sixteenth century this privilege was limited to a smaller group of nobles. In 1666 this limitation was formally established. The relative importance of the Ridderschap in meetings of the States declined, however. Before the Revolt, the nobles found themselves facing six voting cities, but during the Republic there were eighteen. Moreover these cities disputed with the nobles over the right to represent the countryside in meetings of the States.[82]

A second major noble privilege was exemption from taxes, but this prerogative was soon lost. In the fifteenth century the nobles had contributed to the state subsidy (*bede*) on several occasions, although with the proviso that their contribution would not be a precedent for the future.[83] In 1515 and 1518 Charles V limited the tax exemption of nobles to the fiefs that they held for their own use. For their fiefs, the reasoning went, they were already required to perform feudal services; but for their allodial possessions they would henceforth have to contribute to the subsidy. Fiefs that the nobles leased to others were no longer exempt either, although here naturally the nobles could shift the burden to the lessees.[84] During the first half of the sixteenth century, the noble exemption from taxes was gradually abolished, as much because of the pressure of the greater financial demands of the government, as because of increasing resistance by the towns represented in the States. Owing to the noble exemption, these towns had to pay a larger portion of the subsidy. In 1544 the towns

[81] On noble privileges, see Van Leeuwen, *Redeningh*, pp. 46–50, and Fockema Andreae, *Nederlandse staat*, pp. 103–4.

[82] See below, pp. 203–5.

[83] Blok, 'Financiën Holland', pp. 106–9; H. Terdenge, 'Zur Geschichte der holländischen Steuern im 15. und 16. Jahrhundert', *Vierteljahrschrift für Sozial- und Wirtschaftsgeschichte* 18 (1925): 95–167, at 147–52. Cf. F. H. M. Grapperhuis, *Alva en de tiende penning* (Zutphen, 1982), pp. 44–6.

[84] *Informacie*, pp. 623, 625.

proposed that nobles and monasteries that did not contribute to the subsidy should henceforth pay excise taxes, but this proposal had no immediate effect. Yet in the same year the government declared that everyone, including the nobles, would in the future have to contribute to the subsidy. Various nobles were now forced to pay by the Great Council of Mechelen. In 1553, the definitive decision was issued. An imperial ordinance decreed that all orders had to contribute to the subsidy. All privileges that were in conflict with this decree were suspended. The greatest resistance now came from Orange, Egmond and Horne, who collectively were liable for some 5 per cent of the provincial subsidy. It is true that Philip II granted an appeal by these three great lords in 1556, but this was a special favour that did not apply to other nobles. Henceforth no more tax exemptions would be given.

This situation applied to the so-called ordinary subsidy. The nobles were not exempt from the tenth penny, a tax on real property collected on several occasions in the first half of the sixteenth century. Nor were they exempt from excise taxes on beer and wine. But the nobles were and remained exempt from payment of the scot. As a result of inflation this tax declined in importance, however, and during the Republic it was no longer levied.[85]

During the Republic the cities took strict care that the nobles should not escape their fiscal duties. In 1627, for example, the Ridderschap resisted the proposal to assess knightly homesteads for the *verponding*, a tax on land and houses, without however achieving their goal.[86] Thus in Holland the very noble prerogative that was most striking and most envied in other countries lost its significance. Holland was exceptional in this regard. As late as 1704 a French traveller was amazed that the *gens de qualité* were not exempt.[87]

In criminal and civil cases nobles had the right to bypass the lower courts and proceed directly before the Court of Holland. Yet the nobles shared this privilege with officials of the provincial administration and the numerous employees of the Court itself.[88]

In 1593 the States of Holland granted nobles the privilege, that in case they were convicted of crimes, confiscation of their property would be limited to the value of £80.[89] Yet a similar privilege had already been granted by most towns to their burghers. Besides, it was in agreement with progressive legal opinion that an individual, not his heirs, should be held responsible for his deeds.

---

[85] Gosses, *Welgeborenen*, p. 191; De Groot, *Inleidinge*, p. 39.

[86] *Resolutiën van de Heeren Staaten van Holland en Westvriesland*, 276 vols. (The Hague, n.d., ca. 1750–98), 13 Jan. 1627 and 2 Aug. 1627.

[87] R. Murris, *La Hollande et les Hollandais aux XVIIe et XVIIIe siècles vus par les Français* (Paris, 1925), p. 232.

[88] Fockema Andreae, *Nederlandse staat*, p. 137. The nobles could also take their cases directly to the Great Council at Mechelen or to the Privy Council.

[89] *Res. Holland*, 9 Jan. 1653. Cf. Van der Houve, *Hantvest*, pp. 189–90, and a copy of the resolution in ARA, Archief van de Ridderschap, 1572–1795, prov. inv. no. 73. On the 'privilege van niet te confisqueren', see M. van de Vrugt, *De criminele ordonnantiën van 1570* (Zutphen, 1978), p. 153.

The nobles also had the right to assume the title of *jonkheer* (squire), but this privilege was not well protected. Schoockius remarked that the title had formerly been reserved for the sons of high nobles, but in his time had come into general use.[90] Simon van Leeuwen wrote sarcastically about the nouveaux-riches bourgeois who bought the lands of the impoverished nobility and now called themselves 'Ionckers ende Me-vrouwen' (squires and ladies); and in 1657 the States of Holland resolved that supplicants would no longer be allowed to use noble titles.[91]

The right of hunting was, according to Hugo Grotius, the only remaining exclusive noble privilege, along with access to the Ridderschap.[92] Members of the Holland nobility enjoyed the right to hunt small game in the 'Wilderness', the dunes along the North Sea that belonged to the provincial domain. But they had to share this privilege with high officials of the provincial administration. In 1586 it was specified who would fall in this category: practically the entire personnel (above the level of clerks and messengers) of the High Council, Court, Chamber of Accounts, Forestry Office and Court of Fiefs, as well as the stewards of North and South Holland, of Voorne and of Kennemerland, and the dike-reeves of Rijnland, Delfland, and Schieland.[93]

Nevertheless, the hunt was regarded as the sole external sign of nobility. Not without good reason had Koen van Foreest testified that he went riding with dogs and birds. It is indicative of the noble character of the hunt and the fear of everything that had to do with derogatory manual labour and retail trade that an ordinance of 1583 reasserted that the right of hunting did not apply to high officials and nobles who 'practise mechanical trades, or sell the hares and rabbits, exchange them, or deliver them for any profit, living thereupon'.[94] A nobleman hunted for his pleasure.

It is understandable that the urban regents looked with envious eyes upon this last noble privilege. In 1660 the representatives of several cities suggested in the meeting of the States that members of city councils, as joint holders of sovereignty, ought to possess hunting rights.[95] Regents and patricians who had been raised to foreign orders of knighthood also tried to add lustre to their new titles with the ancient prerogative of the hunt. In 1666, however, the States expressly excluded this group of newly made nobles from the right of hunting.[96]

---

[90] Schoockius, *Belgium*, p. 122.
[91] Van Leeuwen, *Redeningh*, p. 33; *Res. Holland*, 20 March 1657. The same regulation applied in the Court of Holland, *Groot placaet-boek . . . van de Staten Generaal . . .*, ed. C. Cau, 9 vols. (The Hague, 1658–1796), II, pp. 2926–7; and in Utrecht, *Groot placaatboek . . . der Staten 'slands van Utrecht*, ed. J. van de Water, 3 vols. (Utrecht, 1729), II, p. 1119.
[92] De Groot, *Inleidinge*, p. 39.
[93] Paulus Merula, *Placaten ende ordonnanciën op 't stuck van de Wildernissen* (Dordrecht, 1605), pp. 38–9.   [94] Ibid., p. 76.
[95] Hans Bontemantel, *De regeeringe van Amsterdam, soo in 't civiele als crimineel en militaire (1653–1672)*, ed. G. W. Kernkamp, 2 vols. (The Hague, 1897), II, pp. 49–50.
[96] *Groot placaet-boeck*, III, pp. 608–9.

Only in 1716 was the conflict over hunting rights between the Ridderschap and the towns definitively settled in favour of the latter. Henceforth the burgemeesters and councillors of the voting cities could also enjoy the hunt.[97]

All in all, noble privileges were limited in number and significance, not exclusive, and subject to continual erosion. A nobleman hardly deserved to be envied for his exceptional constitutional position.

STRATIFICATION: THE HIGH NOBILITY

Noble ancestry, noble life and noble privileges – those were the characteristics that all nobles had in common, and, conversely, which differentiated them from the rest of the population. And while it was in practice difficult to specify the lower boundary of the nobility, with the help of these three criteria it was possible to separate the population into two groups: nobles and non-nobles.

Yet great differences existed among the nobles themselves. The most striking was the distinction between 'high' and 'low' nobility. The titled nobles – barons, marquises, counts, dukes, princes – for the most part had been drawn from the untitled nobility only a short time previously by the Burgundian or Habsburg sovereigns. From a constitutional point of view there was no difference between low nobles and the 'Grands Seigneurs'; but in power, wealth and social standing the differences were immense.[98]

Compared to the Walloon provinces – Hainault and Luxembourg in particular – there were few high nobles in Holland. Before the Revolt their number had already been limited, but during the Republic nearly all the high noble titles came into the hands of the house of Orange.[99] Through the extinction of several Holland noble families, a great number of manors in Holland had been inherited by a small number of high nobles. In 1555 the prince of Orange held eighteen manors in fief; the count of Egmond had twelve; the counts of Horne, Aremberg and Ligne had eleven each. Thus these 'Grands Seigneurs' together held sixty-three manors in Holland, more than a third of the total.[100] With the exception of Egmond, however, they did not belong to old Holland families, and none of them had his usual place of residence in the province. Yet the high nobility consisted of more than just titled nobles. The lords of Brederode and the lords of Wassenaer (until 1523) were also reckoned among their number. Formerly these high nobles were called 'bannerets' (*baanderheeren* or *baanrotsen*), because they could carry their own banners in wartime, but in the sixteenth

---

[97] Ibid., v, p. 789; J. Kosters, *Eenige mededeelingen over Oud-Nederlandsch jachtrecht* (Arnhem, 1910), p. 83; Joachim Rendorp, *Verhandeling over het recht van de jagt* (Amsterdam, 1777), p. 145.

[98] On the high nobility of the Netherlands, see Paul Rosenfeld, 'The provincial governors from the minority of Charles V to the Revolt', *Standen en Landen* 17 (1959): 1–63, in particular 5–15.

[99] Schoockius, *Belgium*, 123–7.

[100] See below, p. 146.

century this title fell into disuse.[101] The high nobles usually occupied a high office in the service of the sovereign, as stadholder of a province or as commander in the army. The monarch had bound most of them strongly to himself by honouring them with membership in the prestigious order of the Golden Fleece. By their marriages, the high nobles were closely allied to each other, and some of them were also closely tied to important families in the Empire or in France. The high nobles were also distinguished from the lower ones by their greater wealth. The gross income of the prince of Orange, by far the richest man in the Netherlands, amounted to 157,785 gulden in 1569. The gross income of the count of Egmond came to 62,944 gulden; that of the marquis of Bergen, 50,872 gulden. Much poorer were Montigny with 11,250 gulden and Horne with 8,437 gulden; but that was still much more than the nobles of Holland. The lord of Noordwijk, Jan van der Does (Janus Dousa), for example, had possessions with an annual revenue of 1,491 gulden in 1562. Josua van Alveringen, lord of Hofwegen, had only 666 gulden in 1568.[102]

The most prominent Holland families were Egmond, Wassenaer and Brederode. Jan van Egmond (1438–1516) had received the title of count from Emperor Maximilian I in 1486. Through the marriage of his son Jan II to Françoise van Luxemburg in 1516, an important part of the family's possessions lay in Flanders. In 1553, Lamoraal van Egmond (1522–68) was raised to prince of Gavere, by which the Holland character of the family became even less pronounced.[103] Jan van Wassenaer, who died in 1523, had left behind only one daughter, who married the count of Ligne in Hainault. As a result, the hereditary possessions of the Wassenaers came into 'foreign' hands. Later a younger branch of the Wassenaers, the Duvenvoirde family, reassumed the old family name.[104] Thus in the sixteenth century the Brederodes could be regarded as the leading family among the Holland nobles. Reinoud III van Brederode (1492–1556), was a knight of the Golden Fleece, forester of Holland, and military commander; in 1556 he became a member of the Council of State.[105] His son Hendrik had a military command, but did not rise as high in the sovereign's service. During the Republic the Brederodes held the title of 'First Noble' in the Ridderschap. They claimed that their residence of Vianen

---

[101] H. M. Brokken, 'De creatie van baanderheren door de graven Willem IV en Willem V', *Holland. Regionaal-historisch tijdschrift* 11 (1979): 60–4. Cf. F. Rachfahl, *Wilhelm von Oranien und der niederländische Aufstand*, 3 vols. (The Hague, 1906–24), I, pp. 262–3.

[102] *Correspondance de Philippe II sur les affaires des Pays-Bas*, ed. L. P. Gachard, 6 vols. (Brussels, 1848–1936), II, pp. 115–16; Rachfahl, *Wilhelm von Oranien*, I, pp. 267–8. Cf. *Gegevens betreffende roerend en onroerend bezit in de Nederlanden in de 16e eeuw*, ed. H. A. Enno van Gelder, 2 vols. (The Hague, 1972), I, pp. 15–16 and 228–31; 'Het huwelijkscontract en het testament van Janus Dousa (van der Does)', ed. J. A. Feith, *Algemeen Nederlandsch Familieblad* 5 (1888): 157–63.

[103] A. W. E. Dek, *Genealogie der heren en graven van Egmond* (The Hague, 1958), pp. 50–3.

[104] Obreen, *Wassenaer*, p. 52.

[105] *NNBW*, x, p. 132.

Ein Edler Furst inn Niderlant.

Princeps siue Dominus Belga.

4   Abraham de Bruyn, 'A prince in the Netherlands', ca. 1576–80 (Rijsprentenkabinet, Amsterdam). The nobleman depicted is William of Orange.

was a free manor, not subject to the lordship of the count of Holland. This added to their prestige. Vianen was supposedly a free (allodial) place: it had its own mint, and the Court of Holland had no jurisdiction there. Reinoud van Brederode proudly refused the title of count offered him by Charles V because he realized that he would be acknowledging his subjection to the sovereign if he allowed Charles to make Vianen into a county.[106] The ancestry of the Brederodes added to their prestige. Reinoud van Brederode maintained (incorrectly, as it later appeared) that his family descended from the counts of Holland. When he began to bear the full coat of arms of Holland without indications of descent from a cadet branch, a law-case was brought against him. He was condemned to death for *lèse-majesté*, but the emperor granted him clemency.[107]

However far above the low nobles in wealth, reputation and power, the high nobles were none the less bound to them by ties of patronage and kinship.[108] They could take lower nobles into the *gentilshommes domestiques*. They could let them manage one of their estates, or grant them a military rank in their *bande d'ordinance*. In exchange for these favours, the lower nobles were required to give political support to their patron. This relationship of mutual dependency can no longer be termed feudal because the patron did not grant a fief in exchange for the allegiance of his client.[109] High and low nobles were also bound by blood ties, since younger sons from high noble families would marry into the lower nobility and found new branches. Thus the Egmond van Meresteyn and Egmond van Kenenburg families were cadet branches of the house of the counts of Egmond, and the Duvenvoirdes, as we have seen, descended from the Wassenaer family. These family relations themselves could

---

[106] H. de la Fontaine Verwey, 'Le rôle de Henri de Brederode et la situation juridique de Vianen pendant l'insurrection des Pays-Bas', *Revue du Nord* 40 (1958): 297–302, at 297.

[107] Van Leeuwen, *Batavia*, p. 722; J. Smit, *Den Haag in geuzentijd* (The Hague, 1922), p. 78; *NNBW*, x, p. 132; 'Ie Memoriaal van de griffier Mr Johan de Jonge', ARA, Hof, inv. no. 29, fos. 111, 112, 113, 243 v., 244.

[108] K. B. Macfarlane, 'Bastard feudalism', *Bulletin of the Institute for Historical Research* 20 (1943–5): 161–80. R. Mousnier, 'The Fronde', in *Preconditions of Revolution in Early Modern Europe*, ed. R. Forster and J. P. Greene (Baltimore and London, 1970), pp. 131–59, at 141. Cf. *Hommage à Roland Mousnier. Clientèles et fidélités en Europe à l'époque moderne*, ed. Y. Durand (Paris, 1981). Cf. on patronage and 'good lordship' in England, Mervyn James, *Family, Lineage and Civil Society in the Durham Region 1500–1640* (Oxford, 1974), pp. 32–3. There has not yet been any systematic research into patronage relationships in the Netherlands. See Heinz Schilling, 'Der Aufstand der Niederlande: bürgerliche Revolution oder Elitenkonflikt?', in *Zweihundert Jahre amerikanische Revolution und Moderne Revolutionsforschung*, ed. Hans Ulrich Wehler (Göttingen, 1976), pp. 177–231, at 208; Armstrong, 'Burgundian government', p. 22; and H. G. Koenigsberger, 'Patronage and bribery during the reign of Charles V', in his *Estates and Revolution. Essays in Early Modern European History* (Ithaca and London, 1971), pp. 166–75. Van Gelder stated ('Bailleul, Bronkhorst, Brederode', p. 55) that every 'homme d'armes' in a *bande d'ordinance* was regarded almost as a client of his captain, but he incorrectly saw this as 'an element of feudalism'.

[109] C. van de Kieft, 'De feodale maatschappij der middeleeuwen', *BMGN* 89 (1974): 193–211.

form another part of the patronage system. For example, Viglius, president of the Privy Council, stood at the head of a patronage network; as much as possible he arranged to have his nieces marry high officials of the provincial administrations.[110]

STRATIFICATION: THE LOW NOBILITY

The great majority of the Holland nobles belonged to the low, untitled nobility, which Schoockius called 'nobility of the second rank'. Actually the terms 'high' and 'low' nobility were not used in that period. The low nobility was also far from homogeneous: there were great differences of wealth, power and prestige.

Within the low nobility we can first distinguish a core of those whose noble ancestry and noble lifestyle were indisputable, and who held in fief one or more manors with high or low jurisdiction. On the grounds of their noble ancestry, their lifestyle and the possession of manors, they were in principle entitled to be summoned to the Ridderschap of Holland. In the first decades of the sixteenth century, most of the low nobles who held manors did indeed appear more or less frequently. But when the Ridderschap began to close itself off around the middle of the century, a portion of the lower nobility remained outside the college.[111] In 1555 this core of Holland nobles consisted of those described by the president of the Court as the 'principal lords nobles and vassals, having lands in Holland and living there, whom one has been accustomed since ancient times to summon to all meetings of the States'. The small group of high nobles, who were also included on this list, should be set apart. Examples of noble families that could be listed among the core of the Holland nobility are Assendelft (although their nobility was admittedly not very ancient), the three branches of the Duvenvoirdes, Poelgeest, Mathenesse, Beijeren van Schagen (a bastard branch of the ducal house of Bavaria), Oem van Wyngaerden and Van der Does. Such families had unquestionable noble ancestry. They issued from 'knightly' (*riddermatig*) lineage. Their ancestors had been vassals of the count and had served him as knights or squires. They abstained from commerce and manual labour; they lived only on income from land, tithes, rents and seigneurial rights. Some of them occupied posts in government service or were officers in the army, but in most cases this was not their principal occupation. Above all, they were lords of the manor. They lived in castles, or at least in manor houses in the countryside. The low nobles were much less wealthy than the high nobles, and probably poorer than the richest merchants in the time of the Republic.[112] But most of these nobles still enjoyed a decent income and

---

[110] *Vigliana. Bronnen, brieven en rekeningen betreffende Viglius van Aytta*, ed. E. H. Waterbolk and T. S. H. Bos (Groningen, 1975), p. 7.   [111] See below, pp. 167–74.
[112] Several great fortunes of merchants and industrialists of the seventeenth and eighteenth centuries are reported in Faber, 'De Noordelijke Nederlanden', p. 224.

should certainly be reckoned among the economic elite of society. This core of the Holland nobility forms the subject proper of this study, although higher and lower nobles will also be mentioned often in passing.

There was thus no misunderstanding about the noble status of these families. But next to the core of noble families who were entitled to take part in the Ridderschap stood a fairly numerous group of families who, for various reasons, were regarded as unqualified to appear in the college. This group of families on the periphery of the nobility, who seemed in many respects to occupy a sort of intermediate position between nobility and patriciate, high functionaries and well-to-do farmers, makes the definition of the nobility of Holland so complicated.

In the first place there were in Holland a number of families who belonged to the nobility of some other province. In principle these nobles, most of whom originated in Utrecht, Guelderland and Brabant, even if they possessed manorial properties in Holland, did not have the right to appear in the Ridderschap. In practice, some of them were regarded as the heirs of extinct Holland families, and thus were entitled to sit in the college. The 1555 list of qualified lords mentioned, for example, the lords of Waelwijck and Brecht from Brabant; the lords of Lockhorst, Zuijlen, Zuijlen van Nyevelt and Zoudenbalch from Utrecht; and the count of Culemburg from Guelderland. The previously mentioned lords of Cruijningen were also counted among the Holland nobility as lords of Heenvliet, although they came from a family from Zeeland. But other 'foreign' nobles remained outside the Ridderschap, even if they held manors in Holland. Apart from that, nobles from other provinces stood on the same social level as the nobles of Holland.

It is not a simple matter to establish which families belonged on the periphery of the Holland nobility. Over the course of the sixteenth and seventeenth centuries, some marginal families rose in wealth and reputation, and the Ridderschap was opened to them. Other families who had belonged to the core of the Holland nobility at the beginning of the sixteenth century later fell into obscurity. Furthermore there were noble families in which one branch belonged to the core, while another must be considered peripheral. The cadet branches of a family sometimes held no seigneurial properties, or only insignificant ones; consequently they were not summoned to the Ridderschap. They did however bear the same family name as their relatives who had remained in possession of the patrimony. When the oldest branch of their family died out, they could regain possession of their family properties, and the Ridderschap was opened to them. But they might also acquire prosperity and manors by a favourable marriage, and by this means, independent of their namesakes, they might gain a seat in the Ridderschap. This was the case with the younger sons of the Van Duvenvoirdes, who appeared in the Ridderschap as lords of Obdam and of Warmond, alongside the elder branch, the lords of Duvenvoirde. For these reasons it is difficult to draw a dividing line between core and periphery, and between low and lower nobility. Neither group consisted of a definite number of identifiable families: through demographic, economic, or political factors, noble families (or branches of noble families) could temporarily belong to either group. The lower nobles did, however, refrain from manual labour and trade. Some occupied offices in the urban magistracy, such as the families Spaernwoude, Berckenrode, Bekesteyn and Ruyven in Haarlem; Boshuysen, Van der Laen and Tetroede in Leiden; Van der Dussen in Delft; Foreest and Teylingen in Alkmaar.[113] Others chose an administrative career in the service of the provincial government, such as members of the Van Dorp, Adrichem, Van der Coulster and Van Loo families. Still others served in the household of a high nobleman. Since these peripheral nobles often sought a marriage partner in the official circles they frequented, from a genealogical point of view they formed a bridge between nobility and urban patriciate, or between nobility and high provincial office-holders.

Although they did not belong to the nobility, for the sake of completeness we must also mention the group of 'well-born' (*welgeborenen*). In the countryside of Holland there lived a fairly large number of peasant families who used this title, but actually differed in no other way from the rest of the farmers. Originally the difference between the 'well-born' and common villagers was that the former were exempt from the scot, justiciable before the bailiff's court, and individually liable to military service, i.e. not as members of the village community. Through this exceptional constitutional position, which was based on their ancestry, the 'well-born' formed a true 'estate' or 'order'. These differences had fallen into disuse in the sixteenth century, however. At first the title 'well-born' had been synonymous with 'noble' (*edel*) in ordinary usage. But this changed in the course of the fifteenth century, when 'noble' was reserved for the fief-holding knightly families, and the word 'well-born' was used for those who did indeed have noble origins, but did not belong to the feudal nobility. I. H. Gosses has sought the origin of this order of well-born in the pre-feudal nobility, the Carolingian *nobiles*.[114] The well-born supposedly remained in existence as a separate order by birth alongside the newly developing knighthood. Yet they practised agriculture and cattle-breeding, and thus did not live as nobles. D. T. Enklaar has suggested that not all well-born fell to the level of farmers, but that some of them were taken up into the feudal knighthood.[115] The feudal nobility thus consisted partly of descendants of the old pre-feudal nobility (the well-born), and partly of those of unfree *ministeriale* origin.[116] According to this reasoning,

---

[113] W. P. Blockmans et al., 'Tussen crisis en welvaart: sociale veranderingen 1300–1500', *NAGN*, IV, pp. 42–86, at 62.

[114] Gosses, *Welgeborenen*.

[115] D. T. Enklaar, *De ministerialiteit in het graafschap Holland* (Assen, 1943), p. 17.

[116] Ibid., p. 19.

in the middle ages there were two groups, both called 'well-born': first, the free farmers who could trace their descent from the pre-feudal nobility; and second, the knightly feudal nobility, which consisted partly of descendants of the same pre-feudal nobility, and partly of men of unfree servile origin. P. W. A. Immink has gone a step further and suggested that the entire pre-feudal origin of the well-born order is fictitious. In his view the well-born were descended from the feudal nobility. The well-born, however, were supposedly derogated nobles. They came from knightly families, but for economic reasons they could no longer observe the prohibition against manual labour and trade, and lived as farmers.[117] The problem has been definitively solved by L. Genicot, who discovered similar people in other provinces: these persons indeed had noble origin, but no longer lived as nobles. In Namur, the idea that noble status could be lost by manual labour dates from the sixteenth century, and was applied in practice only in the seventeenth century.[118] The problem of the origin of the well-born need not occupy our attention further. It is sufficient to confirm that a sort of in-between order of well-born existed in sixteenth- and seventeenth-century Holland, a group which should certainly not be counted among the nobility. They did not live as nobles, and they had lost the majority of their original privileges. The only point in which they differed from the other peasants was that as 'well-born men' they were liable to serve in the bailiff's court.[119] It is questionable, however, whether service in the bailiff's courts was always restricted to persons of 'well-born' ancestry in later periods. If that was not the case, then in the seventeenth century the title of 'well-born' became a purely honorific one. In order to distinguish themselves from the well-born, the nobles then called themselves 'high-well-born' (*hoogwelgeboren*).[120] The status of the well-born demonstrates again that having noble descent was not sufficient to be ranked among the nobility. The second condition, living as a nobleman, was equally necessary.

---

[117] Immink, 'Hollandse welgeborenen'.

[118] L. Genicot, *L'économie rurale Namuroise au bas moyen âge*, 2 vols. (Louvain, 1960), II, pp. 251–91. Here the '*welgeborenen*' are called 'hommes de loi' or 'hommes de lignage'. On those of Holland, p. 251, n. 1.

[119] Names of *welgeboren* men of Rijnland appear in Simon van Leeuwen, *Costumen, keuren ende ordonnantiën van het baljuwschap ende lande van Rijnland* (Leiden, 1667), pp. 74–101. Most *welgeborenen* had only a patronymic, but some had surnames such as Van Tol, Van Leeuwen, Van der Laen, etc., which were regarded as noble by Van Gouthoeven and Boxhorn. Yet, in the sixteenth century, bearers of these names did not belong to the Ridderschap. Until 1536 'real' nobles as well as *welgeborenen* served in the bailiff's court, e.g. Duvenvoirde, Alckemade, Wyngaerden, Poelgeest, Swieten, et al.; after 1550 this was very rare. In 1564 the number of *welgeborenen* in Rijnland was reduced. Beginning in the 1580s, many *schouten* (sheriffs) were appointed in the Rijnland bailiff's court. Presumably it was thought that their greater legal knowledge would make them suitable to discuss the law with the bailiff.

[120] A. S. de Blécourt, *Ambacht en gemeente. De regeering van een Hollandsch dorp gedurende de 17e, 18e en 19e eeuw* (Zutphen, 1912), pp. 40–1.

3

The weight of numbers: demographic trends and forces

THE PROBLEM: THE EXTINCTION OF THE HOLLAND NOBILITY

'The nobility was formerly found here in large numbers (considering that it is a small country): but with the passage of time has been much reduced', declared Wouter van Gouthoeven in his 1620 edition of the 'Division Chronicle'. Van Gouthoeven blamed the decline of the nobility in Holland primarily on economic causes. In his view the nobles 'came into a bad state by inundation of lands, or by not observing a good regimen'.[1] The humanist scholar Hadrianus Iunius wrote around 1570 that the great noble houses had disappeared as a result of the continual wars.[2] The English traveller Fynes Moryson wrote a few years later that the nobles had been 'rooted out by the people'.[3] Moryson's countryman William Temple attributed the extinction of the Holland nobility to the war against Spain.[4] But, despite these different explanations, most observers generally agreed on one issue. They pointed out that many a noble family simply ceased to exist through the lack of a male heir.

The extinction of families in the male line is a natural process. However fertile a population, sooner or later some couples will be childless, or have no sons. Other couples will produce only sons who die before they reach the age of marriage, or who never marry. Where the family name is passed on through the male line, one branch of the family will die out. If a family consists of many different branches, the family name will not disappear. But, if only a few families bear the same name, the chance is great that the entire lineage will die out. This process is inevitable and occurs even in periods of population growth. The result is that in every population the number of different family names continually decreases, unless there is immigration.

Thus noble families have a tendency to disappear. The typical noble family in

---

[1] Van Gouthoeven, *Chronyke*, p. 119. Cf. Boxhorn, *Toneel*, p. 45.
[2] Iunius, *Batavia*. On the dating of Iunius' work, see B. A. Vermaseren, 'Het onstaan van Hadrianus Iunius' "Batavia"', *Huldeboek Pater Dr Bonaventura Kruitwagen* (The Hague, 1949), pp. 407–26.
[3] Moryson, 'Reis', pp. 273–4.
[4] Temple, *Observations*, p. 85.

5   Anon., 'Huis ter Does', 1671 (Private collection). Ter Does House, Leiderdorp.

late medieval France seldom lasted longer than three or four generations in the direct male line.[5] Of the 63 aristocratic families living in England in 1559, only 37 remained a century later. Lawrence Stone regards this rate of extinction of 40 per cent in one century as not unusual and even relatively low in comparison with previous centuries.[6] We do have some figures showing the extinction of noble families in the Northern Netherlands. The Frisian nobility declined from 65 families in 1500 to 16 in 1800: a reduction of 11 per cent in the sixteenth century, 41 per cent in the seventeenth century and 53 per cent in the eighteenth century.[7] Of the 45 Groningen noble families that existed in 1600, only 5 remained in 1800. These families declined by 60 per cent in the seventeenth century, and 72 per cent in the eighteenth century.[8]

Ennoblement was the only way to combat the unavoidable numerical decline of the nobility. However much the nobles of old lineage despised their newly minted counterparts, their existence as a group was dependent on the continual

---

[5] Perroy, 'Social mobility', pp. 31–2.

[6] Stone, *Crisis*, pp. 169–70.

[7] J. A. Faber, 'Drie eeuwen Friesland. Economische en sociale ontwikkelingen van 1500 tot 1800', *AAGB* 17 (1972): 346–7, and 512.

[8] Hidde Feenstra, *De bloeitijd en het verval van de Ommelander adel (1600–1800)* (Groningen, 1981), pp. 112, 408–9. Feenstra arrives at somewhat different percentages of extinction, because he repeatedly notes new noble families, in part foreign, in the years under study. My calculations are based on the *jonker* families that existed in the Ommelanden in 1600.

6 Roelof Willemsz. van Culemborg, 'Jan van der Does and his family', ca. 1590–2 (Museum De Lakenhal, Leiden). Jan van der Does (Janus Dousa, 1545–1604) and his wife Elizabeth van Zuylen van der Haer (1545–after 1623) with their nine children. Besides the children shown, the parents had two others who died very young: one child was stillborn during the siege of Leiden. Only three children married: the oldest daughter Anna, the third son Steven and the sixth son Dirk. The others died at young ages.

addition of new men. European monarchs in the early modern period therefore strove to maintain their national nobilities by providing aspiring commoners with patents of nobility. Alongside political objectives such as the creation of a clientele dependent on the monarch, they naturally also had financial motives. Seldom did anyone receive a letter of ennoblement free of charge. Yet in the Netherlands during the sixteenth century the Habsburg sovereigns had already broken with their Burgundian predecessors' custom of raising new members to the noble estate, at least in the county of Holland.[9] After the Revolt, the Dutch Republic lacked a monarch who could bestow nobility; consequently the position of the Holland nobility became even more critical. The number of noble families that existed at the end of the sixteenth century would henceforth not be increased. While a considerable number of Holland patricians did receive letters of nobility from foreign monarchs, this did not lead to their membership in the Holland nobility.[10]

That the number of noble families in Holland was declining did not escape

[9] See above, pp. 32–3. Simon van Leeuwen wrote in 1667 that in the preceding two centuries no non-noble had been made a knight, *Costumen Rijnland*, p. 8.
[10] See above, p. 25.

contemporaries. Scholars such as Junius, Boxhorn, Van Gouthoeven and Van Leeuwen, and foreign observers such as Moryson, Temple and De Parival were convinced that the number of noble families 'formerly' had been much greater than in their own time.[11] In 1786 a pamphleteer found only 3 original Holland noble families entitled to sit in the Ridderschap, and one of them was virtually extinct.[12] The commission charged with preparing a new constitution in 1814 counted 6 noble families.[13] Consequently the new king William I energetically took up the task of creating a new Dutch nobility. In 1913, when a register of the nobility of the Netherlands was published, only 4 families could trace their ancestry in direct male line from the old Holland nobility. Today, 3 of them are left.[14]

Although many authors in the time of the Republic remarked somewhat defensively that the size and reputation of the nobility in Holland were no less than those of other lands, at the beginning of the sixteenth century the nobility was still rather small.[15] Its exact size is hard to determine. As was noted in chapter 2, it is impossible to specify the boundary between the lower echelons of the nobility and the non-noble patricians and high office-holders, who lived in an aristocratic manner. Contemporaries recognized noble status if one truly lived 'as a nobleman'; but in retrospect it is not easy to establish if someone satisfied this criterion. Furthermore, quite a few nobles who had come from other provinces lived in Holland and owned land and manors there. Some of them were recorded among the Holland Ridderschap, so that they could be reckoned among the Holland nobility, although they bore a family name originating in Utrecht or Brabant. Thus all lists of nobles contain names of persons who were not regarded as Holland nobles, as well as the names of 'foreign' nobles living in Holland.

The most complete lists of nobles residing in Holland were compiled by Wouter Van Gouthoeven.[16] His first list has 227 names of the 'knights and nobles' who lived in Holland between 1477 and 1500. They bore 88 different

---

[11] Iunius, *Batavia*, p. 325; Boxhorn, *Toneel*, pp. 45–50; Van Goethoeven, *Chronyke*, p. 119; Van Leeuwen, *Redeningh*, p. 23; Moryson, 'Reis', pp. 273–4; Temple, *Observations*, p. 85; Jean de Parival, *Les délices de la Hollande. Oeuvre panégirique . . .* (Leiden, 1661), p. 121.

[12] Namely the Ridderschap members Wassenaer, Van der Duyn and Van der Does. Anonymus Belga [P. de Wacker van Zon], *De adel* (Alkmaar, 1786, Kn 21299).

[13] *Ontstaan der grondwet. Bronnenverzameling. Eerste deel 1814*, ed. H. T. Colenbrander (The Hague, 1908), pp. 544–5.

[14] Van den Boetzelaer, Van der Duyn, Foreest and Wassenaer. Van der Duyn died out in 1947. E. B. F. F. Wittert van Hoogland, *De Nederlandsche adel, omvattende alle Nederlandsche adellijke geslachten in de Noordelijke en Zuidelijke Nederlanden* (The Hague, 1913), p. lxxiii.

[15] Cf. e.g. De Parival, *Les délices*, p. 121: 'pour fermer la bouche, à quelques étrangers, lesquels par une impudente sottize, ont osé dire qu'il n'y avait presque point de gentils-hommes icy & que c'estoient tous marchans et hollande'. Several noble families had become extinct in the 'civil wars', but there still remained families that were as famous, virtuous and ancient as the nobles in other countries.

[16] Van Goethoeven, *Chronyke*, pp. 618–20. Also pub. in Van Leeuwen, *Batavia*, pp. 757–9.

family names, 78 of which were considered of Holland origin.[17] His second list refers to 'ridderschap and nobles' who lived in Holland in 1540, when Charles V visited the county, and in 1549 when his son Philip was invested at Dordrecht. This list specifies 174 persons bearing 65 different family names, 53 of which were considered of Holland origin. All other enumerations are smaller. A list compiled around 1530 of nobles in Holland 'and also of others, who conduct themselves as nobles, although they are not regarded as such', shows that it was not always simple for contemporaries to determine someone's status either. This enumeration comes to only 94 names.[18] The statement of the president of the Court in 1555, which contains the names of nobles and vassals who were and were not summoned for the meetings of the States, lists 112 persons.[19] After excluding non-noble lords of manors, nearly 75 nobles remain. Of these 55 belonged to ancient Holland families. The list of persons who were required to take the new oath of loyalty to Philip II in 1567 contains 149 names. Among them, however, are many high office-holders and vassals who clearly did not belong to the nobility; on the other hand, some nobles who were living in that year do not appear on this list.[20] From 1572 there is an enumeration of the Holland nobles who signed the 1566 petition to the regent Margaret of Parma, and those who did not.[21] Altogether this list produces 93 names, of which 3 did not belong to the nobility. Of the remaining 90 nobles, 76 were members of old Holland families.

It is difficult to reconcile these different lists. If we begin with the two lists of Van Gouthoeven, it does not seem unreasonable to suppose that about 200 adult noblemen lived in Holland in the first half of the sixteenth century. More than 150 of these belonged to families of Holland origin.[22] If we assume that each adult couple had two or three children, we arrive at an estimate of 800 to 1,000 noble persons.

This was a very small part of the population. At the beginning of the sixteenth century a group of 1,000 persons would have amounted to only 3.6 per 1,000 of population. Owing to strong population growth, by the middle of the century that share had fallen to 2.9 per 1,000.[23] Compared to other European countries, this proportion of nobility is extremely low. A century later in England, Italy and the Scandinavian countries less than 3 per cent of the population belonged to

[17] Van Gouthoeven, *Chronyke*, pp. 119–20.

[18] ARA Brussels, Aud., inv. no. 1475/5.

[19] Appendix 1 of the Dutch edition.

[20] M. L. d'Yvoy van Mijdrecht, *Verbond en smeekschriften der Nederlandsche edelen*, ed. G. J. Beeldsnijder (n.p., n.d. [Utrecht, 1833]), pp. 51–84.

[21] *Nav* 84 (1935): 158–61.

[22] Van Gelder ('Hollandse adel', p. 113) reports that 'from all kinds of reliable sources' he collected the names of 193 nobles from Holland or living in Holland, about whom more is known than simply the name. In his view there must have been 'many more than two hundred'.

[23] The population of Holland in 1514 came to 274,810; in 1550, by a very rough estimate, it was about 350,000. De Vries, *Dutch Rural Economy*, pp. 86, 95.

Table 3.1 *The extinction of twenty-nine Holland noble families, 1555–1800*

	1555	1600	1650	1700	1750	1800
Families	29	25	21	12	6	5
Absolute decline		4	4	9	6	1
Per cent decline		13.8	16.0	42.9	50.0	16.7

the nobility, but in France and the German Empire 5 per cent were noble, while in Hungary, Spain and Poland the figure was as high as 8 per cent.[24]

The list prepared in 1555 by the president of the Court is a good point of departure for establishing the quantitative decline of the Holland nobility. This list does not contain the names of all Holland nobles, but it does have those we regard as the core of the nobility. We will exclude from consideration a few Utrecht and Brabant nobles. These 55 nobles belonged to 29 different families. It was possible to establish the dates of extinction of the male line of this group (see table 3.1).[25]

In the century between 1555 and 1650 the number of noble families declined at a normal rate by the standards of the time (27.6 per cent). Compared with the decline of the English peers and the *jonkers* of Friesland and Groningen, the rate of extinction in Holland was even modest. But between 1650 and 1730 the Holland nobility shrank rapidly. In this eighty-year period it fell from 21 to 6 families, or by 71.4 per cent. The numerical decline of the nobility thus assumed a serious character only in the year with which this study ends. The foundations for this decline, however, must have been laid earlier.

The size of every population is determined by the number of births and deaths, excluding the effects of migration. The number of legitimate births is primarily determined by two factors: the rate of marriage of the population (nuptiality), and fertility. In research on nuptiality two variables are of paramount importance: the percentage of permanent celibates in a community and the age of marriage. It is clear that a population can decline when a large proportion remains unmarried. Furthermore, the rate at which people are inclined to remarry after the death of a spouse is significant. A population containing many widows and widowers is less fertile than a population with many second marriages. Fertility is significantly influenced by the age at which women marry. A woman's age of marriage and age of menopause determine the length of time she can produce children. Several other factors that influence

[24] Geoffrey Parker, *Europe in Crisis 1598–1648* (Glasgow, 1979), p. 63.
[25] Nobles with the same surname have been counted in the same family. An exception has been made, however, for the Duvenvoirde and Egmond families, because representatives of different branches of these families had independent access to the Ridderschap. From the Duvenvoirde family came the lords of Duvenvoirde, Obdam and Warmond; from the Egmond family came the counts of Egmond, the lords of Kenenburg and the lords of Meresteyn.

fertility are the use of contraception, breast-feeding, diet and general health of the parents (in particular of the mother), and variations in the onset of menopause. Moreover, the death rate or mortality can influence fertility. If, for example, a great number of mothers die in childbirth, few marriages will be 'completed' from a demographic point of view, i.e. they will not last until menopause ends the fertile period of the marriage. The death rate also affects the size of a population independently of fertility. Mortality is primarily determined by external factors, such as dietary customs and hygiene, contagious illnesses and epidemics, wars and other violence.

The shifting patterns of births, marriages and deaths thus determine the size of a population. Together these factors were responsible first for the decline and ultimately for the downfall of the Holland nobility.

Not all nobles could be included in this demographic study. For most of them, little or no genealogical information is available. Therefore our study is limited to members of the Ridderschap, their wives and children. Relatively speaking, we know a fair amount about them.[26] The members of the Ridderschap cannot, however, be considered a random sample of the Holland nobility. After the middle of the sixteenth century relatively few nobles appeared at the meetings of the States. They were the wealthy and powerful holders of the most important manors. Most of them were eldest sons, especially in the seventeenth century, when the rules for succession in the college became stricter. Yet, because the children of the members of the Ridderschap are included in our

---

[26] The genealogical material has chiefly been drawn from D. G. van Epen, 'De Ridderschap van Holland en West-Friesland. Namen, stamdelen en kinderen der beschreven edelen', undated manuscript available at the Centraal Bureau voor Genealogie in The Hague. Comparisons with more recent genealogical research show that Van Epen's data are sufficiently complete and reliable for our purposes. When possible, these data have been checked and corrected. Of course, Van Epen did not have any more information than the sources he used: an unknown number of children who died young do not appear in his genealogies. Van Epen's material applies only to those who were enrolled in the Ridderschap since 1568. In order to go back further, I have added data on the nobles enrolled between 1522 and 1568, whose names can be found in Van Leeuwen, *Batavia*, II, pp. 761–7, and Aert and Adriaen van der Goes, *Register van alle die dagvaerden bij deselve Staten gehouden, mitsgaders die resolutiën, propositiën ende andere gebesongneerde in de voirsz dagvaerden gedaen*, 6 vols. (The Hague, n.d., [ca. 1750]). Of the nobles enrolled between 1522 and 1568, I have included in this study only those for whom the published genealogical studies give sufficient data. The research is thus based on *a portion* of the nobles enrolled before 1568, and on *all* nobles enrolled between 1568 and 1650. I have excluded high nobles such as William I of Orange, Maurice and Frederick Henry, and the counts of Hohenlohe and Leicester, who were formally enrolled in the Ridderschap and are thus included in Van Epen's work: they constituted an entirely different social group. On the other hand, I have added nobles enrolled after 1568, such as Van der Duyn, De Jode, Van Hargen and Van der Does, omitted by Van Epen. The data can be found in HRA, Coll. Snouckaert. See also the MS 'Naam en wapenen der Hoog Edele Heeren welke in de Ridderschap van de Provincie van Holland en West Vriesland zijn beschreven geweest', Koninklijke Bibliotheek 's-Gravenhage, MS 135 A 27. Identical manuscripts are available at the HRA and the Centraal Bureau voor Genealogie. A list of nobles whose families constitute the base for my demographic research is found in appendix 2 of the Dutch edition.

study, we do know something about lower strata within the Holland nobility. These children include younger sons, who were not summoned to the Ridderschap, and daughters, not all of whom married members of the college. In addition, data for 18 nobles who were cited to attend an extraordinary meeting of the Ridderschap on 26 September 1584 have been included. These nobles were normally not regarded as qualified to appear in the college.

The 89 nobles who were recorded among the Ridderschap of Holland between 1522 and 1650 contracted 110 marriages, with 109 different women. From these marriages 428 known children were born. The total number of members of the Ridderschap and their married and unmarried children is 487: 256 men and 230 women (the sex of one child who died young is unknown).[27] In order to study changes over time, these persons were divided into cohorts, groups of all those born in the same period. The division of Holland nobles studied was as follows:

Cohort born

	1451–1500	1501–50	1551–1600	1601–50	1651–1700
Men	10	74	88	73	11
Women	no data	46	89	83	12

Even for this rather small sample not all genealogical data were known. The date of birth in particular was often missing, more often for women than for men, and for the earlier cohorts more frequently than in the later ones. Furthermore, we suspect that an unknown number of children who died in infancy were not recorded in the sources and thus remain beyond the scope of research.

THE MARRIAGE PATTERN

The fertility of a population is primarily determined by the number of its members that marry, and the age at which they marry. Our study excludes from consideration children born outside lawful wedlock. The bastards of the Holland nobles were not reckoned among the nobility, and thus did not contribute to the continued existence of the order.

Among members of the Ridderschap the inclination to marry was fairly great.[28] As opposed to the 82 married members of the college there were only 7

---

[27] The total is not the result of simple addition; 89 members of the Ridderschap + 428 children = 517 persons, because some sons of members were themselves enrolled.

[28] Cf. the marriage pattern, number of children and choice of spouses in Ronnie Kaper, 'De Hollandse adel, 1500–1650: huwelijk en gezin', *Skript. Tijdschrift voor geschiedenisstudenten* 2:3 (1980): 48–61.

unmarried members (7.8 per cent). A higher proportion of their children remained unmarried, however. It is difficult to discover exactly how many were in this category. There is no point in researching how many children of members of the Ridderschap died unmarried, because this number was strongly influenced by the prevalence of infant and child mortality. If the infant mortality is high, the number of children who died unmarried will also be high. The percentage of celibates among those who died after their fiftieth birthday is an indication of nuptiality in a population.[29] Yet this figure can be calculated only for those persons whose dates of birth and death are known. Of the 52 sons of members of the Ridderschap for whom these data are known, 6 (11.5 per cent) died after their fiftieth year without ever being married. Of the 36 daughters, 13 (36.1 per cent) died after their fiftieth year without having tasted the fruits of marriage. The sample is small, but these figures suggest that many more women than men remained single. One out of three noble daughters who reached the marriageable age never married.

That more women than men remained single is not surprising, because early modern populations had a fairly sizeable surplus of women. This was probably also the case with the Holland nobility. The nobles in our sample produced 230 daughters and 198 sons, which would represent a sex ratio at birth of 116. Not much faith should be placed in this figure, however, because not all births are known. Generally, somewhat more boys than girls are born, but fewer boys survive. The surplus of women rises in the higher age groups. A portion of the surplus women among the Holland nobility found their way to aristocratic convents, at least during the first three-quarters of the sixteenth century. Of the 46 noble daughters born between 1500 and 1550, 11 (23.9 per cent) took religious vows. As a result of the Reformation, however, the number of religious women in later cohorts became insignificant. Since nearly one-quarter of the noble daughters born in the first half of the sixteenth century went into the cloister, the percentage of nuns among women who reached marriageable age must have been even greater.

On the other hand the custom of the Holland nobles to entrust their daughters to convents was not so universal as these figures may suggest. The 11 nuns born between 1500 and 1550 came from only 5 families. Jan van Duvenvoirde, lord of Warmond (d. 1544) and his son Jacob van Duvenvoirde (d. 1577) together gave 10 daughters to the cloister (2 of the daughters of the latter who became nuns were born after 1550). Both lords of Warmond were indeed blessed with large families. Jan van Duvenvoirde and his wife had 9 daughters and 6 sons. One daughter died at a young age, but of the 8 remaining only 2 married: 6 went to convents at Bedbur (near Cleves), Rijnsburg (near Leiden), Nivelles, Mons and Maubeuge. Jan's son Jacob had 4 sons and 6

[29] L. Henry, *Anciennes familles Génévoises. Etude démographique XVIe-XXe siècle* (Paris, 1956), p. 51.

daughters: once again only 2 daughters married, and 4 became nuns at Nivelles, Rijnsburg and Mons. One of these daughters, Maria, never professed vows and exchanged the cloistered life for the blessings of the married state in 1576, i.e. after the destruction of the Rijnsburg convent.[30] The number of noble nuns was already declining before the Reformation. The abbey of Rijnsburg was designed for 40 noble sisters, but in 1494 it had 29 women, and in 1553 only 20 remained. In 1509 Loosduinen still counted 29 noble nuns; in 1563 there were 21.[31]

At what age did the nobles of Holland marry? The fertility of a population is primarily determined by the age of women at their first marriage. For women marrying young, the period in which they can bring children into the world is longer. Moreover their fecundity, the biological capacity to reproduce, is somewhat greater.[32] Little is known about the age at marriage of noble women in Holland, because their dates of birth are so often shrouded in mist. The number of women in the first cohort (born between 1501 and 1550) whose age at first marriage is known is too small to draw firm conclusions. Yet the individual ages at marriage of these four women (twenty, thirty, thirty-three and forty-six) suggest relatively late marriages for this cohort. Table 3.2 shows the average age at first marriage of the Holland nobles. Although the statistical base remains small, it appears that women born between 1551 and 1600 married fairly late. After 1600, however, the age at marriage of women declined substantially. The husbands' age at marriage was generally somewhat higher than that of their brides. Here too a decline can be observed over time.

In table 3.3 the ages at marriage of Holland nobles are compared with those of several other elites.[33] It appears that the average age at marriage of noblemen born between 1550 and 1600 (28.4) was relatively high. The age at marriage of the noblewomen of Holland in this cohort was much higher than the figures usually found among other groups. This high female age at marriage must have had an unfavourable influence on the fertility of the Holland nobility. In the cohort born 1600–50, however, the age at marriage of both male and female Holland nobles fell and may even be described as low compared to other groups. It is remarkable that the age at marrriage of Holland nobles fell in the seventeenth century, while that of other groups rose. In particular, the female

---

[30] A. G. van der Steur, 'Johan van Duvenvoirde en Woude (1547–1610), heer van Warmond, admiraal van Holland', *Hollandse Studiën* 8 (1975): 179–273, at 245–50.

[31] R. R. Post, *De roeping tot het kloosterleven in de 16e eeuw* (Amsterdam, 1950), pp. 36–7. On the aristocratic convents, see pp. 43–8.

[32] Fertility increases from menarche to the age of twenty to twenty-five years; it then decreases gradually until menopause. Cf. H. van Dijk and D. J. Roorda, 'Het patriciaat van Zierikzee tijdens de Republiek', *Archief. Mededelingen van het koninklijk Zeeuwsch genootschap der wetenschappen* (1979): 1–126, at 36.

[33] Ibid.; Henry, *Anciennes familles*, p. 55; L. Henry, 'Démographie de la noblesse Brittanique', *Population* 20 (1965): 692–704, at 693.

Table 3.2 *Average age (mean and median) at first marriage: members of the Ridderschap of Holland and their children*

	Cohort born		
	1501–50	1551–1600	1601–50
Men:			
mean	31.0	28.4	27.0
median	31.0	27.9	27.0
sample size (N)	17	26	22
Women:			
mean	*	28.0	24.0
median	*	28.1	23.6
sample size (N)	4	12	19

*Not shown; sample too small.

Table 3.3 *Average age at first marriage for various elites*

	Cohort born		
	1501–50	1551–1600	1601–50
Men:			
Holland nobles	31.0	28.4	27.0
Zierikzee patricians	30.6	28.9	31.4
Geneva patricians	—	27.2	29.1
British peers*	—	25.3 / 25.7	26.0 / 27.4
Women:			
Holland nobles	—	28.0	24.0
Zierikzee patricians	25.3	24.2	26.0
Geneva patricians	—	21.4	24.6
British peers*	—	20.3 / 19.7	20.7 / 22.0

*Figures for the British peerage are shown in 25-year cohorts.
— no data.

Holland nobles married at a considerably younger age. Other things being equal, this should have had the result of increasing the fertility of the Holland nobility in the seventeenth century.

The fertility of a marriage is also determined by its duration. If the marriage is ended by the death of either spouse while the woman is still in her fertile period, then from a demographic point of view the marriage is 'incomplete'. Fewer children are born than would have been possible if the marriage had

Table 3.4 *Numbers of first and subsequent marriages among members of the Ridderschap and their children*

	Cohort born		
	1501–50	1551–1600	1601–50
Men:			
First marriages	28 (70.0%)	35 (67.3%)	27 (77.1%)
Subsequent marriages	12 (30.0%)	17 (32.7%)	8 (22.9%)
Women:			
First marriages	12 (80.0%)	35 (64.8%)	38 (88.4%)
Subsequent marriages	3 (20.0%)	14 (35.2%)	5 (11.6%)

lasted until the woman reached menopause. The duration of the first marriages of 32 members of the Ridderschap could be calculated: on the average, these marriages lasted 22.7 years.[34] By comparison, in 1966–70 in the Netherlands the average duration of marriages not interrupted by divorce was about twice as long, namely 46 years.[35] But the chances that an early-modern marriage would be ended by the death of husband or wife were very unevenly divided. The 14 noble marriages ended by death of the husband lasted on average 33.8 years; the 18 marriages ended by death of the wife lasted on average only 13.9 years. When a marriage ended in less than 30 years, by far the most common cause was the death of the female partner. If a marriage lasted longer than 40 years, then the husband had a greater chance of dying first. If we assume that the fertile period of a marriage lasted an average of 20 years, since the average age at marriage of brides of members of the Ridderschap was 28.0 years, then it appears that more than half (56 per cent) of the marriages of this group were incomplete from a demographic point of view. Nearly all incomplete marriages were attributable to the death of the wife: no doubt this was due to the high rate of death in childbirth.

Many first marriages thus remained incomplete. This had a negative influence on the reproductive capacity of the Holland nobility. For this reason alone – although there were naturally also other reasons – it was important for the surviving partner to contract another marriage. Table 3.4 shows to what extent the Holland nobles were inclined to remarry after the end of their first marriages.

For men, nearly 30 per cent of all the marriages were second or later marriages. In general women contracted second or later marriages somewhat

[34] The number (32) is too small to divide into three cohorts.
[35] M. Niphuis-Nell, 'Veranderingen in de duur van de gezinsfasen', in *Gezin en samenleving*, ed. C. J. M. Corver et al. (Assen, 1977), pp. 82–90.

less often (nearly 25 per cent). This is understandable, because on the death of their marital partners they would have been on average older than the men. But it is striking that women born between 1551 and 1600 contracted many second and later marriages, even somewhat more than their male counterparts of the same cohort. Furthermore, it is remarkable that the inclination to remarry was much more limited in the cohort born between 1601 and 1650, for men as well as for women.

NUMBER OF CHILDREN AND FERTILITY

The number of permanent celibates, the age at marriage, the length of their marriages and the number of second and subsequent marriages influenced the reproductive capacity of the Holland nobles. Yet a marriage by itself is no guarantee of the production of children. Some marriages remained childless because at least one of the spouses was sterile; others because they were broken after a short time by the death of one of the two marital partners. The marriages in which the mother as well as the first child died in childbirth would in many cases also have been recorded as childless.

Of the 110 marriages of members of the Ridderschap, 17 (15.5 per cent) remained childless. But since quite a few nobles contracted a second or even a third or fourth marriage, the number of nobles who produced no child at all in any of their successive marriages was lower. Of the 82 married members of the Ridderschap, only 7 (8.5 per cent) died without legitimate issue.

For the continued existence of a family in the male line, only the presence of sons is significant. From a dynastic point of view, a marriage that produces only daughters is just as unfruitful as one that is childless. Of all marriages of members of the Ridderschap, 34 (30.9 per cent) produced no sons. If we study all successive marriages of the nobles, it appears that 15 members of the Ridderschap (18.3 per cent) in all their marriages were unable to produce a male heir. Table 3.5 displays how the childless marriages and the marriages without sons were apportioned over the various cohorts.

The nobles who were born between 1501 and 1550 had the greatest chance of dying without having produced a son, whether in all individual marriages or in their successive marriages. About a quarter of all branches of noble lineages (which is not the same as a quarter of all noble lineages) must have died out shortly afterwards. Furthermore, these figures underscore the importance of contracting a second or even subsequent marriage. Of all marriages of nobles born between 1551 and 1600, 27.3 per cent per cent did not produce sons; but in all successive marriages only 9.5 per cent of the nobles of this generation remained deprived of a male heir. If the possibility of remarriage had not existed, in this generation three times as many branches of nobles would have died out in the male line than was actually the case.

Table 3.5 *Childless marriages and marriages without sons, members of the Ridderschap: individual marriages and successive marriages*

	Cohort born			
	1451–1500	1501–50	1551–1600	1601–50
Individual marriages				
Childless	2 (15.4%)	7 (13.7%)	5 (15.2%)	3 (23.1%)
No sons	3 (23.1%)	18 (35.3%)	9 (27.3%)	4 (30.8%)
N (number of marr.)	13	51	33	13
Successive marriages				
Childless	1 (10.0%)	4 (9.5%)	1 (4.8%)	1 (11.1%)
No sons	1 (10.0%)	11 (26.2%)	2 (9.5%)	1 (11.1%)
N (number of marr.)	10	42	21	9

Table 3.6 *Average number of births per mother and gross reproductive rate*

	(male) Cohort born			
	1451–1500	1501–50	1551–1600	1601–50
Number of births	4.5	3.8	4.0	3.8
Gross rep. rate	2.4	2.0	2.3	1.8
N (number of mothers)	13	51	33	13

The most generally accepted method of stating the fertility of a population is the number of births per thousand mothers. They must be divided into five-year age groups. Unfortunately we possess too little information about the date of birth of these women to apply this procedure in a useful way. It is however possible to calculate how many children were born to each woman (table 3.6). The gross reproductive rate, i.e. the number of daughters that were born to a cohort in relation to the number of mothers, can also be calculated.

The number of live births naturally says little about the average family size that resulted, and even less about the chances of survival for the lineage, because mortality has not been taken into consideration here. With a high mortality, the level of births must likewise be higher if a population is to reproduce itself. However, it is not possible to calculate the net reproductive rate (the number of daughters in a cohort that remain alive until the end of their fertile period, in relation to the number of their mothers), because not enough is known about the age at death of the daughters.

These rather crude statistics suggest that the fertility of the Holland nobility increased during the sixteenth century and the first decades of the seventeenth century; it then fell again around the middle of the seventeenth century.[36] The number of nobles in the first and last cohorts, 13, is too low to draw many conclusions. Remarkably, the cohort with the highest birth rate (the cohort born between 1551 and 1600) was also the cohort most inclined to contract second and later marriages (cf. table 3.4). As a result, the percentage of men who had no children or no sons in all successive marriages was the lowest (cf. table 3.5). The relatively low fertility in the cohort born between 1501 and 1550 can perhaps be attributed to a higher age at marriage, but not enough data are available to establish this point with certainty.

Did the Holland nobles practise any form of birth control? When a population practises contraception, the average intervals between births after the birth of the third or fourth child will be noticeably longer than the intervals between births of the preceding children. In this manner it has been possible to establish that conscious birth control already existed at an early date: among the patricians of Geneva since the middle of the seventeenth century, in the English village of Colyton at the end of the seventeenth and beginning of the eighteenth centuries, and among the patricians of Zierikzee in the eighteenth century.[37] The dates of birth of children of members of the Holland Ridderschap, however, are frequently not known, or insufficiently exact, to apply this procedure. To gain some insight into this question, we have studied twenty-one families for whom sufficient information is available.[38] This number is too small to divide into cohorts. Table 3.7 shows the intervals in months between the date of marriage and the birth of the first child, and between the births of subsequent children.

It is striking that in these twenty-one families the birth intervals were extremely short, on average 20 months. If no contraception is practised in a population, in theory we should expect to find an average birth interval of between 16.5 (minimum) and 31.5 (maximum) months. The lowest average values ever observed among women in their early twenties, thus at the period of their greatest fecundity, ranged between 20 and 23 months.[39] Only if average

[36] Some of those born between 1551 and 1600 did not have children until the first decades of the seventeenth century.

[37] Henry, *Anciennes familles*, pp. 75–81. E. A. Wrigley, *Population in History* (New York, 1969), pp. 120–4. Van Dijk and Roorda, 'Zierikzee', pp. 47–50.

[38] These are the families of the following nobles: Jan van Duvenvoirde (married 1504); Adriaan van Mathenesse (married 1531); Jacob van Duvenvoirde (1542); Jan van Mathenesse (1562); Jan van der Does (1566); Johan van Duvenvoirde (1590); Diederik van Schagen (not a member of the Ridderschap; first marriage 1607, second marriage 1633); Steven van der Does (1601); Cornelis van Aerssen (1630); Reinoud van Brederode (1630); Philip Jacob van den Boetzelaer (1631); Jacob van Duvenvoirde-Obdam (1633); Johan Wolfert van Brederode (1638); Wigbold van der Does (1640); Frederik van Dorp (first marriage 1645, second marriage 1649); Arend van Duvenvoirde-Wassenaer (1646); Adriaan van der Myle (1646); Pieter van Duvenvoirde-Starrenburgh (not a member of the Ridderschap, first marriage 1647, second marriage 1661).

[39] Wrigley, *Population*, pp. 92–3. These are average intervals. Individual intervals could be much shorter or longer.

Table 3.7 *Birth intervals among twenty-one selected families of Holland nobles*

Birth order of children	Average birth interval in months	N (number of families)
1st	18.0	21
2nd	16.6	20
3rd	20.6	18
4th	17.6	18
5th	21.1	16
6th	24.3	14
7th	22.0	12
8th	24.1	7
9th	17.5	4

intervals are longer than 30 months should we consider the effects of conscious birth control. We can therefore conclude that the number of births in these families was not deliberately limited.[40]

These very short birth intervals also suggest that Holland noblewomen did not themselves nurse their babies, or did so only for a short time. It is known that breast-feeding temporarily reduces the fecundity of the mother (so-called lactation-amenorrhea).[41] Among a population whose women are accustomed to breast-feeding their infants for a long period, the average interval between births will therefore be longer than in a population that practises breast-feeding for a short time. The custom of using the services of a wet-nurse leads to shorter birth intervals and greater fertility of the population.

Little is known about the use of wet-nurses in the Netherlands. Most authors who have treated the subject are of the opinion that most mothers nursed their babies themselves, even in higher social circles. Only toward the end of the seventeenth century, under French influence, would the custom have come into vogue to confide babies to a wet-nurse.[42] On the other hand, the Middelburg schoolmaster Johannes de Swaef pointed out in 1621 that 'some women (*primarily among the rich*) . . . neglected the same [i.e. breast-feeding]'.[43] Jean Taffin, court preacher of William of Orange, had earlier noted 'that the Lord God has given her [the woman] two breasts, not in order to show off and be beautiful, but to use the same in the service of God'.[44] It is unlikely that he

[40] The twenty-one families cannot be considered representative of the Holland nobility as a whole. In these families there were 149 births, an average of 7.1 per family. This high birth rate makes it *prima facie* unlikely that these families practised birth control.

[41] Cf. C. Vandenbroeke, F. van Poppel and A. M. van der Woude, 'De zuigelingen- en kindersterfte in België en Nederland in seculair perspectief', *TvG* 94 (1981): 461–91, at 475–80.

[42] L. F. Groenendijk, 'Piëtisten en borstvoeding', *Pedagogisch tijdschrift/Forum voor opvoedkunde* 1 (1976): 583–90, at 583.

[43] Cited ibid.   [44] Cited ibid.

would have directed this propaganda for breast-feeding against an entirely imaginary opposition. A clearer indication is found in 1623, when 'Barber the wet-nurse' apparently lived in the household of the lord of Warmond. He had been married for only a few years and had one daughter.[45] Around 1560, a noblewoman from Artois advised her sister-in-law not to feed her child herself, but to take it to a wet-nurse.[46] This advice suggests that the use of a wet-nurse was not self-evident. People were aware of the hygienic disadvantages: thus the medical doctor Pieter van Foreest (1521–97) warned against the dangers of an infected nurse.[47] In conclusion, we should not assume that the fertility of the Holland nobility was limited by lengthy breast feeding, nor by the practice of contraception.

MORTALITY

Mortality can influence the size of a population in two ways: directly, or via fertility. The fertility of a population declines when many marriages are ended by the death of a spouse. When the mortality rate is greater than the birth rate, however, a population declines without the intervention of reduced fertility.

A generally accepted way of stating mortality is to calculate life-expectancy at given ages. Yet life-expectancy for the nobles can be calculated only for those whose year of birth and year of death are known. These data are more often known for nobles who died at a relatively advanced age, and thus had a greater chance to leave traces in administrative records. Table 3.8 gives the life-expectancy of members of the Ridderschap and their children, at the ages of twenty, forty and sixty.

It appears that mortality in the cohort born between 1501 and 1550 was greater among women than among men. One might be inclined to attribute this higher mortality among women to the dangers of childbirth, if the relationship did not change in later generations. In the cohorts born after 1550, mortality was considerably higher among the men. After the middle of the sixteenth century the mortality among men increased, while among women it decreased. However, the numerical basis for the calculation of female mortality is rather limited. It is difficult to discover why the life-expectancy among adult men declined. One might think of the influence of the war against Spain, but it does not appear that many Holland nobles were killed in action. If we compare the mortality of the Holland nobility with that of the British peerage, the patricians

[45] Calculation of *hoofdgeld* of villages of Rijnland (1623), GA Leiden, Secretarie-archief 1575–1851, inv. no. 7542, fo. 487. For the size of Duvenvoirde's household in that year, see Obreen, *Wassenaer*, p. 161.
[46] R. Muchembled, 'Famille, amour et mariage: mentalités et comportements des nobles artésiens à l'époque de Philippe II', *RHMC* 22 (1975): 233–61, at 239.
[47] L. Burema, *De voeding in Nederland van de middeleeuwen tot de twintigste eeuw* (Assen, 1959), p. 118.

Table 3.8 *Life-expectancy of members of the Ridderschap
and their children at ages twenty, forty and sixty*
(N = size of sample)

	Cohort born					
	1501–50		1551–1600		1601–50	
Ages		N		N		N
Men:						
20	38.0	36	28.0	45	29.4	31
40	24.0	30	19.6	30	17.9	23
60	8.8	21	7.5	14	8.1	8
Women:						
20	31.4	21	33.0	14	36.4	19
40	18.9	15	24.1	10	21.6	16
60	11.0	7	9.1	8	9.9	9

Table 3.9 *Comparative life-expectancy at age twenty of British peers, Genevan
patricians, Danish nobility, Zierikzee patricians and Holland nobility*
(British peers in 25-year cohorts)

	British peers		Geneva		Cohort born Denmark		Zierikzee		Holland	
	m	f	m	f	m	f	m	f	m	f
1551–75	30.1	30.8								
			28.6	29.2			25.8	22.0	28.0	33.0
1576–1600	29.5	30.8								
1601–25	27.2	29.4								
			30.9	34.5	33.3	35.9	25.7	22.4	29.4	36.4
1626–50	28.8	27.8								

of Geneva, the Danish nobility (only for the cohort 1601–50) and the patricians
of Zierikzee (table 3.9), it appears that mortality among the male nobles of
Holland was on approximately the same level as male mortality in Britain and
Geneva. The mortality of the Danish nobility was lower, but the mortality
figures for the Holland nobility compare favourably with those of Zierikzee.
The most remarkable point, however, is that mortality among Holland
noblewomen was lower than that of all other comparable groups.[48]

[48] Van Dijk and Roorda, 'Zierikzee', p. 33.

Table 3.10 *Child mortality among twenty-one selected families of Holland nobles*

	Children born 1500–1600		Children born 1601–1700	
Deaths 0–5 years	9	(15.5%)	37	(39.4%)
Deaths 5–15 years	1	(1.7%)	1	(1.1%)
Total child mortality	10	(17.2%)	38	(40.4%)
Total number of births	58	(100%)	94	(100%)

If we wish to study deaths at an early age, we can most easily refer to the twenty-one selected families for whom all births are known.[49] But even in these families information about the deaths of very young children is scarce, because their age at death is often noted only as 'young'. In these cases it is assumed that they died before the age of five. For these reasons it is not possible to distinguish infant mortality (mortality during the first year of life) from child mortality (mortality to age five). The number of families on which table 3.10 is based is limited; therefore it is dangerous to generalize. But the figures do create the impression that child mortality was significantly higher in the seventeenth century than in the sixteenth century. In particular, between 1600 and 1650 young children aged up to five had a great chance of dying.

Two examples demonstrate how mortality in the seventeenth century could endanger the survival of the Holland nobility. On 30 June 1626, Johan van Mathenesse (ca. 1595–1653) married Judith Wilhelmina Pieck, who bore him fourteen children in a marriage that lasted nineteen years. For the greater part of her married life, she was pregnant.[50] Two children died as infants, one after five days of life, the other after eleven months. In February 1645, seven children died of plague.[51] One month later Johan van Mathenesse had to lay his wife in her grave, too: she had died eleven days after the birth of a son. Whether she died as a result of childbirth or plague is not known. Of the five surviving children, three sons and two daughters, four more died unmarried between age twenty and age thirty. They too died in quick succession, suggesting that the cause was again a contagious disease (24 June 1653, 30 January 1655, between March 1655 and January 1656, 2 February 1656). In the meantime the father Johan van Mathenesse had also died on 30 June 1653, six days after the death of his son Willem. The only survivor of the once-numerous family still alive in 1656 was Gijsbrecht, the youngest son, who was born during the plague epidemic of 1645. The task of continuing his father's lineage now rested on his

---

[49] See above, n. 38.
[50] Van Epen, 'Ridderschap', p. 39.
[51] C. A. van der Zee, *Matenesse en het Huis te Riviere* (Schiedam, 1939), p. 78.

shoulders. He was already married at age twenty-one, in 1666. But a son and a daughter died in infancy, and during the third year of marriage Gijsbrecht's wife died, apparently in childbirth. One year later Gijsbrecht van Mathenesse himself, aged twenty-four, followed her to the grave. When Gijsbrecht's distant relation Willem van Mathenesse died at the age of four only a year later, the noble lineage of Mathenesse ceased to exist. The fourteen children borne by Judith Wilhelmina Pieck were not enough to prevent extinction.

Johan van Mathenesse's contemporary, Johan Wolfert van Brederode (1599–1655), fathered twenty-one children in two marriages. Yet, despite this respectable achievement, he was not able to maintain the existence of his house in the male line.[52] His first wife, Anna Johanna, countess of Nassau-Siegen, bore him twelve children: nine daughters and three sons. Of these, however, seven infants died before baptism. The five surviving children were girls. When Anna Johanna died in December 1636, after about seventeen years of marriage, Johan Wolfert van Brederode hastened to find a new consort. After fourteen months he got married again, to Louise Christina, countess of Solms-Braunfels. Johan Wolfert was then only thirty-eight years old, his bride thirty-one. The couple had nine children, likewise in seventeen years. Only two of these children died very young, but of the seven others four died around age twenty. Of the three children still remaining, only one was a son, Wolfert. He died, aged twenty-nine and childless, on 15 June 1679, as the last male heir of his family. The arms of the Brederodes were broken over his grave.

CONCLUSION

With the extinction of the noble houses of Brederode and Mathenesse we have returned to our starting point. Is it possible to establish a connection between the demographic behaviour of the Holland nobility and the decline in the number of noble families?

From the very summary data available, we can conclude that the generations born in the sixteenth century performed quite well from a demographic point of view. The average age at first marriage was high, but fell among men and perhaps also among women. The number of second and following marriages increased among those born between 1551 and 1600. Probably as a consequence, the percentage of members of the Ridderschap who died without having produced a male heir declined, from 26 per cent in the cohort born between 1501 and 1550, to 9.5 per cent in the cohort born between 1551 and 1600. The average number of children born to each marriage increased slightly, from 3.8 to 4.0. Yet mortality among adult men increased at the same time. This may explain why such a remarkably large number of women in this cohort

[52] Van Epen, 'Ridderschap', p. 61. A. W. E. Dek, 'Genealogie der heren van Brederode', *JbCBG* 13 (1959): 105–46, at 135.

took a second or subsequent husband. Mortality among adult women decreased, and other things being equal this must have led to a greater number of widows. The rate of child mortality among the nobles was at a relatively low level.

The cohort born between 1601 and 1650 had less demographic success. Granted, the average age at first marriage continued to decline. The noblewomen's age at marriage fell so sharply that it came to be lower than that of comparable elites. On the other hand, the number of second and subsequent marriages decreased. It is difficult to establish to what extent these trends were reflected in the fertility of the Holland nobility. The number of nobles who died childless or without a male heir increased somewhat; the number of births per marriage may have declined also. These trends are not very significant, however, because they are based on only thirteen marriages of members of the Ridderschap.

More significant is that mortality, and in particular infant mortality, increased. It is not clear why this happened. A parallel can be found among the patriciate of Zierikzee, where infant mortality in the cohort born between 1600 and 1650 also rose significantly.[53] The examples of the Mathenesse and Brederode families suggest that the extinction of the Holland nobility was not so much a result of low fertility as of high mortality. It is remarkable that the most successful cohort, born between 1551 and 1600, globally experienced its fertile period between 1575 and 1640, roughly the period of the Revolt against Spain. The Revolt certainly did not cause a demographic 'crisis' of the Holland nobility.

[53] Van Dijk and Roorda, 'Zierikzee', p. 26.

4

Endogamy and misalliances

THE CHOICE OF A MARRIAGE PARTNER

The choice of a marriage partner confronted the nobility with a dilemma. On the one hand they were inclined toward endogamy, or marriage within their own group, with the goal of preserving the purity of the noble 'race'.[1] On the other hand, this exclusive marriage policy had disadvantages because it could decrease the number of potential marriage candidates, resulting in a high percentage of celibates and a high average age of marriage. This in turn produced a lower number of children born in each generation and could even lead to extinction of the group in the long run.[2] No doubt the Holland nobles were unaware of the finer points of demography and did not consider the matter so clinically. Yet a tight noble marriage market may have produced a certain pressure in the direction of exogamous marriages, marriages outside their own group. Furthermore, financial considerations may have led nobles to search for a partner with greater wealth, obliging them to accept a lower status as part of the bargain – as contemporaries never tired of repeating and regretting.

Hence, there are two historical interpretations of noble marriage policies. According to the first theory, endogamy was a fundamental characteristic of social life in Europe during the *ancien régime*.[3] People married within their own village, town or region; within their own occupational group, religion, class or order. Social mobility exclusively by means of marriage was practically unknown. Only after a man had enhanced his social position was he able to seal his new status with a marriage to a partner from his new milieu. Usually,

---

[1] On 'racist' ideas among the nobility, see André Devyver, *Le sang épuré. Les préjugés de race chez les gentilshommes français de l'Ancien Régime (1650–1720)* (Brussels, 1973), p. 156; Goubert, *Ancien Régime*, I, pp. 151–2.

[2] This could have been the case in Friesland: Faber, 'Drie eeuwen', pp. 346–8.

[3] Mousnier, 'Problèmes de méthode', p. 20; 'Introduction', in *Problèmes de la stratification sociale. Deux cahiers de la noblesse, 1649–1651*, ed. R. Mousnier (Paris, 1965), pp. 11–24. Lawrence Stone, *The Family, Sex and Marriage in England 1500–1800* (London, 1977), pp. 60–2. Donald Haks, *Huwelijk en gezin in Holland in de 17de en de 18de eeuw* (Assen, 1982), pp. 15–17. The Frisian and Ommelander nobles sought marital partners almost exclusively within their own group (Faber, 'Drie eeuwen', pp. 346–8; Feenstra, *Bloeitijd*, pp. 117–362). In the early seventeenth century 90 per cent of the marriages of the Lancashire gentry were endogamous (Stone, *Family*, p. 61). Between 1430 and 1669, 89 per cent of the marriages of the Norman nobility in the *élection* of Bayeux were endogamous (Wood, *Nobility*, pp. 99–119).

IOHANNES A MATENESSE
D^s in Matenesse, Riuiere, Opmeer, Souteveen, etc.
Deputatus in Concilio DD: Ordinum Generalium Assessor,
ex parte Ordinis Equestris et Nobilium Hollandiæ
et Wessfrisiæ, Magnus Curator Aggerum Schie,
landiæ, dictarumq; Provinciarum nomine ad
Tractatus Pacis Legatus Plenipotentiarius iti

7   Cornelis Galle jr, after Anselmus van Hulle, 'Johan van Mathenesse, lord of Mathenesse, Riviere, Opmeer and Zouteveen, polder-councillor of Schieland', 1648. Johan van Mathenesse (1595–1653) was a member of the Ridderschap of the States of Holland and a delegate at the States-General, and he took part in the negotiations leading to the Peace of Westphalia. His wife Judith Wilhelmina Pieck bore eleven children, yet the family line became extinct soon after his death.

68

however, only his children could acquire a spouse on this level and establish a new tradition of endogamy.

Historians can define a social group as they please: by wealth, profession, relationship to the means of production, or by reputation and prestige. The ideas that historical individuals *themselves* held about their social position came to light in their marital choices. The choice of a spouse may be seen as an external sign of their *mentalité*. The French historian Roland Mousnier regards intermarriage itself as the fundamental characteristic of a social group during the *ancien régime*: 'one could almost say, a social group is those people who marry among themselves'.[4] If the Holland nobles regularly married outside their own order, for example with members of the urban patriciate, one might ask whether they deserve to be considered an independent social group. If, however, they married primarily among themselves, they formed a group according to their own ideas. An increasing number of marriages outside their own circle could be interpreted as an external sign of increasing integration.

However, we have yet to see whether endogamy was characteristic of the marital choices of nobles in bourgeois Holland. Its economic and social structure differed so much from the European pattern that we cannot simply assume that the European model of marital choices applied here. Thus there is a second theory, constructed more specifically for the nobility of Holland, which stresses the relatively insignificant position of the nobility compared to the regent class. Accordingly, the original 'apartheid' of the nobles became blurred by intermarriage with regents of bourgeois origin. There is, however, no empirical research to provide a foundation for this theory.[5]

The lamentations of contemporaries suggest the worst. Fynes Moryson maintained in the 1590s that the Holland nobles, unlike their counterparts in Germany, were not inclined to marry among themselves, 'for those who come to greatest honour in this Commonwealth, are either Advocates of the Law, or Sonnes of Merchants'.[6] Schoockius in 1652 was of the opinion that many nobles no longer gave any thought to the ancestry of their bride, 'since a rich dowry can lighten the obscure ancestry of a family'.[7] In his 1659 discussion of the origin of the Holland nobles Simon van Leeuwen pointed to the phenomenon of persons of bourgeois origin buying manors and adopting an aristocratic style of life: 'Which ingrained corruption moves and necessitates many nobles, in order to maintain their condition next to the same [i.e. the bourgeoisie], that they marry their children to Rich Men, although these are not of noble ancestry ... By this means a great deviation and degeneration of old Noble families has come to pass.'[8] But contemporary testimonies are not

---

[4] Mousnier, 'Problèmes de méthode', p. 14.
[5] Renier, *Dutch Nation*, p. 230; Schöffer, 'De Republiek', p. 180.
[6] Moryson, 'Reis', pp. 273–4.   [7] Schoockius, *Belgium*, p. 128.
[8] Van Leeuwen, *Redeningh*, pp. 33–4. Cf. the remark by *griffier* Fagel in 1732: '... depuis l'érection

unanimous. Sir William Temple remarked that it was precisely the nobles in bourgeois Holland who had a much stronger group identity than those in other countries where nobility was more numerous. The Holland nobles 'would think themselves utterly dishonoured by the marriage of one that were not of their Rank, though it were to make up the Fortune of a Noble Family, by the wealth of a Plebean'.[9]

In order to establish the rate of endogamy among the Holland nobles, we have studied all marriages contracted by members of the Holland Ridderschap and their children between 1500 and 1650.[10] To avoid a distorted picture of the marital choices of the Holland nobility, we shall subsequently devote some attention to marriages of several families whose members were never recorded among that college.

Between 1500 and 1650 the members of the Holland Ridderschap and their children (the descendants of 29 different lineages) contracted 279 marriages in all. Of these, to begin with the most important conclusion, 253 or 90.7 per cent were with other nobles, and 26 or 9.3 per cent were outside their own group. Exogamous marriages appear to have increased over time. Of the 31 marriages contracted in the first half of the sixteenth century, only one (3.2 per cent) was exogamous, the sensational misalliance of Gerrit van Assendelft, of which more later. Of the 123 marriages contracted between 1550 and 1600, 6 (4.9 per cent) were with non-nobles. Of the 125 marriages contracted between 1600 and 1650, however, 19 (15.2 per cent) were exogamous. Yet that figure stands in contrast to the 36 marriages contracted after 1650 by children of members of the Ridderschap (who were first recorded among the college before 1650): as far as can be determined, only 2 (5.6 per cent) of them were exogamous. Thus there was no question of a continuing process of integration between the nobility and the bourgeoisie.[11]

With the exception of the lowly born wife of Gerrit van Assendelft, all non-noble marital partners were children of regents or patricians. Many of them held seigneurial manors and led lives that differed little from those of the nobles. Some had acquired foreign orders of knighthood or patents of nobility, and, although they were not thereby recognized as nobles in Holland, we can regard them as a sort of new aristocracy. Thus Theophilus Damman, the non-

---

de la République plusieurs de ces familles [nobles] sont éteintes, et celles qui restent en partie n'ont pas conservé la pureté de leur noblesse, par des alliances qu'elles ont fait avec des familles, dont la naissance n'est pas également hors de critique, à quoi présentement dans une République marchande on ne regarde pas si près'. Quoted by J. Aalbers, 'Factieuze tegenstellingen binnen het college van de ridderschap van Holland na de Vrede van Utrecht', *BMGN* 93 (1978): 412–45, at 416.

[9] Temple, *Observations*, p. 85.

[10] Van Epen, 'Ridderschap'. This material has been supplemented with various genealogical publications. See above, pp. 52–3, esp. n. 26.

[11] In the eighteenth century endogamous marriage was still the norm for the Holland Ridderschap. Cf. Aalbers, 'Factieuze tegenstellingen', pp. 416–17; Haks, *Huwelijk*, pp. 116, 118.

noble husband of Maria van Swieten, came from a prominent family of Ghent; his father was lord of Bijsterveld and was known as 'knight of Fairhill'.[12] Philips Rataller, the husband of Maria's sister Geertruid, was secretary of the Court of Utrecht and came from a family of high office-holders in the service of the emperor; his mother, Margaretha van Loo, belonged to the lower Holland nobility.[13] The wife of Wigbold van der Does was a daughter of Johan van den Kerckhoven Polyander, a diplomat from a prominent family of Ghent; he had bought the manors of Sassenheim and Heenvliet, and advanced to lieutenant-forester of Holland.[14]

Three members of the Van Dorp family accounted for four of the twenty-six exogamous marriages, while the four Van Swieten sisters added eight more. Nearly half of all exogamous marriages were thus contracted by members of only two families, which further underscores the exceptional nature of exogamy. Both families were impoverished: earlier they had already been forced to divest themselves of their manorial property.[15] It was primarily owing to contingent political factors that they still appeared in the Ridderschap in the sixteenth century. On the one hand, by marriages to aristocratic regents who held manors they were able to restore their ruined fortunes and 'live nobly'; on the other hand, noble daughters, even though poor, could increase the prestige of their spouses.

Sometimes mixed marriages had political motives. Reinoud van Brederode and Cornelis van der Myle, who married two daughters of Johan van Oldenbarnevelt in 1597 and 1603, may have found the ancestry of their brides less important than the protection and patronage they expected from the provincial advocate. Indeed, in the political controversies during the truce with Spain (1609–21), they were faithful supporters of the party of their father-in-law.[16] Van der Myle came from a family that had been raised to the nobility only in 1570,[17] while Reinoud van Brederode was descended from a bastard branch of the Brederode family.

We must now consider the social origins of marriage partners of the lower nobility, who were not represented in the Ridderschap. Were their marriages equally endogamous, or did they form a bridge between the nobility and the patricians? Since these lower nobles occupied a less prominent position, relatively little is known about them. The marriages of a few families must serve as a sample.

---

[12] *NNBW*, III, pp. 273–4.   [13] *NNBW*, II, p. 1164.

[14] 't Hart, *Heenvliet*, pp. 207–19.

[15] Arend van Dorp, *Brieven en onuitgegeven stukken*, ed. J. B. J. N. de van der Schueren, 2 vols. (Utrecht, 1887–8), I, p. xvi; E. C. G. Brünner, *De order op de buitennering van 1531* (Utrecht, 1918), p. 167; Repertoria op de leenregisters, ARA, Leenkamer, inv. no. 229, fo. 849; Van Epen, 'Ridderschap', p. 55.

[16] Jan den Tex, *Oldenbarnevelt*, 5 vols. (Haarlem and Groningen, 1960–72), III, p. 645.

[17] See above, pp. 31–2.

Table 4.1 *Marriages of members of the Berckenroede family, ca. 1515–1635*

	1515–50	1551–1600	1601–35
Men:			
To nobles	3	2	1
To patricians	2	5	0
Women:			
To nobles	2	1	1
To patricians	4	9	0

The Berckenroedes were lords of the homestead of Berckenroede and the manor of Schoter Vlieland in Kennemerland, but these possessions were apparently not important enough for them to be received in the Ridderschap.[18] Members of this family occupied many political and administrative posts in Haarlem until the last male heir died in 1642. Of the thirty marriages contracted by members of this family between circa 1515 and 1635, ten were with other nobles and twenty with members of the patriciate. The male Berckenroedes were more likely to marry nobles than were the female members of the family (table 4.1). By occupying regent-offices the Berckenroedes were apparently so well integrated into the Haarlem patriciate that they sought many of their marital partners among this group. Their marriage strategy suggests that lower nobles, and in particular noblewomen, were more inclined to marry patricians than those who belonged to the core of the Holland nobility.

The noble families Ruyven and Spaernwoude belonged to the same circle of Haarlem regents as the Berckenroedes.[19] Members of both families filled offices in the city and in the surrounding area; Ruyvens served as stewards and bailiffs of Kennemerland, Spaernwoudes were stewards and bailiffs in the manor of Brederode. Between 1500 and 1550, all members of the Ruyven family (three men and four women) married other nobles. Between 1514 and 1615, the Spaernwoude family (also three men and four women) contracted seven marriages, of which only one was to a patrician.

Why the Ruyvens and the Spaernwoudes were more keen to marry within the nobility than the Berckenroedes remains a mystery. Perhaps differences of wealth played a role, or the social and psychological distinctions were so subtle as to render them invisible after four centuries.

[18] M. Thierry de Bye Dólleman, 'Het geslacht Berkenrode'. Cf. on Haarlem families who were or were not enrolled in the Ridderschap, Van Foreest, *Foreest*, p. 95.

[19] M. Thierry de Bye Dólleman, 'Genealogie Van Ruyven', *JbCBG* 20 (1966): 140–73; J. F. Jacobs and M. Thierry de Bye Dólleman, 'Het familiekroniekje van Ysbrant van Spaernwoude', *JbCBG* 18 (1964): 81–116.

The Van der Does family was more prominent than the three Haarlem families.[20] As lords of Noordwijk, they sat in the Ridderschap after the Revolt; another branch, who lived at the house of Ter Does near Leiden, held somewhat lower status. Hendrik van der Does was a knight, member of the Leiden Council, and sheriff of Leiden 1515–23; his son Jacob was a councillor of William of Orange and commander during the siege of Leiden. In turn his son Pieter was lord of Rijnsaterwoude, Leimuiden and Vriesekoop, bailiff and dike-reeve of Rijnland, sheriff of Leiden, admiral of Holland and general of the artillery. This branch thus improved its social standing during the sixteenth century. Between 1500 and 1610, ten members of this family married nobles, while two (one man and one woman) married patricians.

A remarkable example of the marital choices of the lower nobles of Holland is furnished by the Foreest family. Several branches of this family existed in the fifteenth century. The heirs of the eldest branch, the lords of Middelburg (near Gouda) and Schoterbosch, appeared in the Ridderschap and generally lived as nobles. They married primarily among the nobility: in 1477 Herpert van Foreest, alderman, burgemeester, member of the city council of Delft, keeper of the castle of Woerden, a man recorded as appearing at the Ridderschap, married the substantial Zeeland dowager Maria van Cats. Their three daughters married a Borsselen, a Raephorst and an Egmond van Meresteyn.[21] A junior branch of the Foreest family had settled in Haarlem, where various members occupied important functions in the magistracy. For several years Jan van Foreest (d. 1501) appeared in the States of Holland among the urban delegation as burgemeester of Haarlem, but in other years he was present among the nobles in his quality of fief-holder of the county.[22] Most marital partners of this Harlem branch of the Foreests also had their social origins in the Haarlem nobility. Cornelis van Foreest, alderman, married Aechte Potter van der Loo in 1497; their son Jan (1498–1557), who held no office, married the non-noble Maria van Heuckesloot from Delft. Their daughter Magdalena was married first to Jan van Ruyven, the last male heir of that noble family, and second to Jan van Duvenvoirde, a younger brother of the lord of Warmond. Jan van Duvenvoirde built a career in municipal government as alderman and burgemeester of Haarlem.[23] A third branch of the Foreest family had settled in Alkmaar, where they occupied many offices in the magistracy and acquired reputation and great wealth.[24] The members of this Alkmaar branch never gave up their claims to noble status, as may be seen by their use of noble titles (e.g. *vir nobilis*), their bearing of the unbroken arms of the Foreest family, and – what

[20] C. J. Polvliet, *Genealogie van het oud adellijk geslacht van der Does* (The Hague, 1893), pp. 65–8.
[21] Van Foreest, *Foreest*, pp. 120–4, 142–5.
[22] Ibid., pp. 94–6.
[23] Ibid., pp. 124, 147–50.
[24] Ibid., pp. 157–77.

was much more convincing in a century of increasing noble pretensions – their unquestioned exercise of hunting rights.[25] But because they held no manor or homestead in fief from the county of Holland, they remained outside the Ridderschap. Without having suffered derogation in a formal sense, the Foreests of Alkmaar in the sixteenth century belonged on the periphery of the Holland nobility. This is also apparent from their marital choices. In the sixteenth and seventeenth centuries they chose practically all their marital partners from the circles of the respectable, but non-noble, patriciate of Alkmaar.

The number of marriages in this sample is too small to draw far-reaching conclusions. But we can establish that the lower nobles were more likely to marry outside their own group than members of the Ridderschap and their families. None the less the general rule of marriages within one's own group applied in large measure here also.[26]

Up to this point we have understood the concept of endogamy as relating to a marriage between one noble and another. In principle all nobles were equal, from the king down to the poorest squire.[27] But in practice there were vast differences in standing, wealth and power. Strictly speaking, a misalliance is a marriage in which one party is regarded as inferior. This may be so on grounds of birth, but also on grounds of fortune, power, prestige, education, or occupation. Most Holland nobles not only married other nobles, but their spouses were also descended from families who held a more or less equivalent position *within* the nobility. Thus the Berckenroedes married nobles who, like themselves, neither held important manors nor gained admittance to the Ridderschap (Naeltwijck, Bekesteyn, Van Sijl, Adrichem van Dorp, Persijn, Alckemade). Among the high nobility, Lamoraal, count of Egmond, married the daughter of the imperial count of Sponheim; the spouses of his children bore the names of Horne, Lalaing, Mansfeld and Aubigny.[28] The high nobles drew their marital partners from a wider geographical area than the lower nobles: the Walloon provinces, France and Germany. And the middle-range nobles of Holland who held manors chose marital partners of similar prestige and wealth.

According to the laws of Holland, nobility could be passed on only through the male line.[29] Children of a noble father were noble, while those with only a

---

[25] See above, p. 37.

[26] This may be compared to the situation in Deventer, where H. Kronenberg established that, while nobility and patriciate each supplied about half of the Council until ca. 1550, marriages between the two groups were practically non-existent. Yet the so-called 'half-nobility' of *hoveluden* or *haveluden* intermarried with both groups and formed a bridge between them. 'Verhouding tussen adel en patriciaat in Deventer', *Bijdragen en Mededelingen van de Vereeniging tot Beoefening van Overijselsch Regt en Geschiedenis* 65 (1950): 88.

[27] Devyver, *Sang épuré*, p. 155.

[28] Dek, *Genealogie Egmond*, p. 53.

[29] De Groot, *Inleidinge*, p. 39; Van Leeuwen, *Redeningh*, p. 18.

noble mother were not. We might therefore expect that more noblemen than noblewomen would marry outside their order, thus preserving the nobility of the family. If we examine the marriages of members of the Ridderschap and their children, however, at first glance this does not appear to be the case. Fourteen exogamous marriages were contracted by men, and thirteen by women. But among the twenty-one nobles who contracted these marriages, there were thirteen men and only eight women; and of the latter, the four Van Swieten sisters and their eight exogamous marriages accounted for a disproportionately great share of the female exogamy. Furthermore, one noblewoman, Philipotte van der Duyn, had already been married previously to a nobleman, before she married a patrician husband. Finally, among the eight Holland nobles who married outside their order between 1600 and 1650, there was only one woman. We can thus confirm that male nobles were more likely to contract a misalliance than female nobles. None the less in the Berckenroede family more women than men married outside their order. We do not know if this is representative of the lower nobility.

We might also expect that younger sons would more readily seek a bride from the patriciate than their older brothers. Even though primogeniture did not apply in Holland, the eldest sons were more richly endowed with manorial properties and generally followed in the footsteps of their fathers in the Ridderschap and in offices. Yet this is incorrect. Among the thirteen men in our group who married beneath their station, we find eight eldest sons and also three younger sons who became heirs after the death of their older brothers. Nine of them were themselves members of the Ridderschap. Exogamy was thus somewhat more frequent among noble heirs than among younger sons.

The age at marriage of these exogamous nobles does not differ significantly from that of the Holland nobility in general. The age at marriage is known for eight men who married beneath their station: on the average, 28.9 years. Josina van der Does married at age fifteen in 1618 and was therefore considerably younger than the norm.[30] Yet it is possible that in some cases age mitigated feelings of group identity. Sophia, the dowager of Johan van den Boetzelaer, remarried at age seventy to Johannes Hey, a lawyer from Zevender. The ceremony was held privately, 'without clamour or solemnity'.[31] And the Catholic nobleman Willem van der Duyn (1537–1607), who had previously had an illegitimate daughter by Cornelia Adriaansdr. van Stakenbroeck, married his paramour at the age of fifty-three, as he said 'for the sake of the times and religion'.[32]

The Holland nobles sought marital partners in their immediate surroundings. Of the 110 brides of members of the Ridderschap, 40 (36.4 per cent)

---

[30] For the age at marriage, see above, pp. 55–7.
[31] Van Buchell, *Diarium*, p. 383.
[32] HRA, Coll. Snouckaert, inv. no. 1288.

came from Holland, and 49 (44.5 per cent) from the adjoining provinces of Guelderland (15), Brabant (12), Utrecht (11), and Zeeland (11). The more distant provinces supplied only a few brides: Friesland 2, Groningen 1, Overijssel 2, Flanders 1, Hainault 2. Eight brides came from the German Empire, and one from France; one bride came from distant Cyprus. The origin of three brides could not be determined. The marriages of the children of the Holland Ridderschap show approximately the same pattern of concentric circles. With the passage of time, however, the large share of marital partners from Holland did decline. This can be related to the increasing integration of the provinces that formed the Dutch Republic. During the war against Spain, foreign military officers were suitable marital partners for daughters of members of the Ridderschap.

IDEAS ABOUT MARITAL CHOICES: THE MEANING OF THE NOBLE 'LINEAGE'

The high rate of endogamy among the nobles of Holland was in accordance with prevailing tendencies elsewhere in Europe. Yet, in the context of bourgeois Holland, it requires further explanation. The cause of the great number of marriages within the group must first be sought in the nobles' own ideas about the value and meaning of lineage, i.e. the succession of generations in the male line from one forefather.

The nobles believed that they belonged to a special 'race'. They were convinced that their superior qualities were based on their ancestry, on their 'blood'. Scholars might dispute whether nobility rested on ancestry or on virtue;[33] for the nobles themselves this was not a problem. Precisely the antiquity of their lineage and the great deeds of their forefathers guaranteed that the nobles of the sixteenth and seventeenth centuries would also distinguish themselves by their virtue, bravery and leadership, qualities which constituted their honour or reputation. Thus a pamphlet of 1583 speaks about true nobility: 'which is ennobled and exalted on the one hand by the pious deeds of their ancestors, and on the other by their bold advancement of Fatherland and justice'.[34] The writer saw no conflict between nobility through ancestry and nobility by service; he simply placed the two alongside each other. In the sixteenth century people were convinced of the overwhelmingly hereditary nature of mental capacities.[35] The nobles thus had a very practical interest in maintaining the purity of their lineage. Their quasi-natural right to occupy leading functions in the government, the courts, and the army, the respect they

---

[33] See above, pp. 29–31.
[34] Cited by P. A. M. Geurts, *De Nederlandse Opstand in pamfletten* (Nijmegen, 1956; reprint Utrecht, 1978), p. 195.
[35] Devyver, *Sang épuré*, pp. 164–75.

enjoyed, in short their entire privileged place in society depended on qualities that they themselves regarded as hereditary. They believed that the welfare of the entire community was enhanced by preserving the individual character of the various classes as much as possible.[36]

The intense interest of the Holland nobles in family history, genealogy and heraldry reveals their preoccupation with their ancestry. The rapidly increasing number of writings on these subjects in the fifteenth and sixteenth centuries reflects more than increasing literacy. It also testifies to the desire to demarcate their own noble race sharply from other groups.[37] This was a general European phenomenon.[38] Holland nobles such as Johan van Duvenvoirde van Woude (1547–1610) and Johan van Mathenesse (1538–1602) themselves wrote about the origins of their own and other noble families.[39] Others, such as Johan Wolfert van Brederode (1599–1655), commissioned renowned scholars to write their family histories.[40] These works did not always adhere strictly to the truth. The farther back in time one could trace one's lineage, the greater its prestige. The Brederodes pretended – without foundation – to be descended from the counts of Holland.[41] The Wassenaers traced their ancestry, via the burgraves of Leiden, back to 'Veromerus, prince of the Hollanders' in the time of Caesar Augustus; the champion of Batavian freedom, Claudius Civilis, supposedly belonged to this family.[42] The lords of Batenburg, from the Bronckhorst family of Guelderland, carried their family tree back to a certain prince Batto, who was alleged to have been given his name to the Batavians.[43] This sort of pseudo-etymological derivation was extraordinarily popular. By means of etymological conjuring, the Van de Merwede family could be traced back to the Merovingian kings; the Cralingen family, 'or rather Carolingen', to Charlemagne.[44] In the humanistic climate of the age, classical antiquity was particularly popular. The Van Arckel family (*Herculana familiar*) was related to the Trojans. In a fine mixture of Germanic and classical mythology it was suggested that in the time of the Frankish king Pepin the Short a member of this family 'had followed a swan to Holland', where he settled at a place that he named for his ancestor Hercules

---

[36] For France, ibid., pp. 156–9. For the Netherlands, see e.g. Iunius, *Batavia*, p. 318, and (Anon.), *Een onderscheyt boeckje ofte tractaetje vande fouten en dwalingen der politie in ons vaderlant* (Amsterdam, 1662; Kn 8670).

[37] J. Romein, *Geschiedenis van de Noord-Nederlandsche geschiedschrijving in de middeleeuwen* (Haarlem, 1932), pp. 212–15.

[38] Jean-Pierre Labatut, *Les noblesses Européennes de la fin du XVe siècle à la fin du XVIIIe siècle* (Paris, 1978), pp. 73–8.

[39] Van der Steur, 'Johan van Duvenvoirde', p. 238; W. A. Beelaerts van Blokland, 'Het geslacht van Mathenesse', *NL* 39 (1921): 34–9 and 375–6, at 36–7.

[40] De la Fontaine Verwey, 'Le rôle', p. 301.

[41] Ibid., p. 297; A. W. E. Dek, 'Genealogie der heren van Brederode', p. 1.

[42] Obreen, *Wassenaer*, p. 2.

[43] Iunius, *Batavia*, p. 326; Jean-François Le Petit, *Nederlantsche Republycke* (Arnhem, 1615), p. 161.

[44] Ibid., p. 162.

Alemanicus, Castra Herculana or Arkel.[45] The Teylingens began their family tree with 'Priam, king of Troy'.[46] The Alckemades traced their ancestry back to Alcmena, the mother of Hercules, 'who used to have her ordinary residence here' (i.e. in the village of Warmond, near Leiden).[47]

Yet the Holland nobles were not living only in a dream world. They tried to maintain the purity of their families by practical means, for example by testamentary arrangements. In July 1607 Johan van Schagen and his wife Anna van Assendelft drew up a testament in which they specified that their children, if they wished to receive their share of the inheritance, had to marry 'to noble families, with prior approval and consent of both of us'.[48] These were not idle threats, as Willem van Praet van Moerkercken had discovered: after he had 'mismarried' at Schoonhoven, according to the testament of his father (d. 1537), Willem was not allowed to take possession of the latter's fiefs.[49]

The developments around the striking misalliance of Gerrit van Assendelft (ca. 1487–1558) clearly illustrate the importance that the Holland nobles attached to the purity of their blood. Often we learn most about the rule by observing the exceptions. Every year countless nobles married quietly within their order, without revealing anything about their attitudes toward marital choice. But this single misalliance led to so much agitation that nearly a century and a half after the marriage was contracted it was still in litigation.[50]

The lords of Assendelft did not belong to one of the oldest noble families, but by the sixteenth century they were among the richest, most powerful and most prestigious nobles of Holland.[51] They owned extensive feudal and allodial properties, and occupied high offices in the service of the sovereign. Gerrit's father Klaas (d. 1501) had been a judge in the Court of Holland, treasurer of West-Friesland and military governor of Schoonhoven. Gerrit himself was a knight, enfeoffed with the high justice in the manors of Assendelft and Heemskerk, and low justice in the manors of Castricum, Kralingen, Overschie, de Hoogeban and Schiebroek. As president of the Court of Holland in The Hague, he was the highest imperial office-holder in the province after the stadholder.[52]

In the first years of the sixteenth century, Gerrit studied law at the University of Orléans.[53] There he entered into a love affair with an innkeeper's daughter,

---

[45] Iunius, *Batavia*, pp. 331–3. On the Trojan ancestry of Brederode and Arckel, cf. J. Romein, 'De functie van een historische fictie. De vermeende afstamming der Germanen uit Troje in verband met het begrip der translatio imperii', *Historische lijnen en patronen* (Amsterdam, 1971), p. 20.

[46] 'Een jachtruzie van voor 200 jaar', *LJ* 13 (1916): 124–31, at 129.   [47] Ibid.

[48] F. A. Holleman, *Dirk van Assendelft, schout van Breda en de zijnen* (Zutphen, 1953), p. 336.

[49] Van Gouthoeven, *Chronyke*, p. 190.

[50] The following material is primarily based on J. Craandijk, 'De geschiedenis van Nicolaas van Assendelft', *BVGO*, 4th series, 10 (1912): 1–38, and Holleman, *Dirk van Assendelft*, pp. 240–60.

[51] See above, p. 27.

[52] ARA, Landsadvocaat Oldenbarnevelt, prov. inv. no. 1015, and Holleman, *Dirk van Assendelft*.

[53] Gerrit van Assendelft was born about 1487. At the time of his marriage he was 'not yet twenty

Catharina le Chasseur. So far there was nothing exceptional: many nobles had pre-marital and extra-marital affairs with girls of plebeian backgrounds. It was certainly exceptional, however, that Gerrit married his girlfriend. Why he took this unusual step is unclear. According to his own testimony it had been 'thoughtless', and he pointed out that he had been still 'below his twenty years of age'.[54] It may be assumed that the marriage came about under duress: Catharina's father 'when he found them together, forced him to marry her in the presence of a notary and witnesses'. Gerrit supposedly also took Catharina 'for the sake of [her] beauty'.[55] Be that as it may, the bridegroom quickly regretted his misalliance. After his return to Holland he refused to live together with his wife, which caused her to go to court. The Court of Holland sentenced Gerrit, who admitted having contracted a lawful marriage with Catharina, 'to receive his wife to live with him in one house, [to share] his table and his bed, and to treat her, to supply her with food and drink and clothes according to his station and the capacity of his means, such as a noble man is obliged to treat his lawful wife as long as they both shall live'.[56] The young lord of Assendelft seems to have accepted this judgment outwardly, but not in his heart. Not until 1517, eight years later, did the couple have a son, who was named Klaas, after Gerrit's father. Klaas remained an only child; his parents continued their litigation. Finally, on 11 April 1532, an agreement was reached by which Gerrit would pay his wife an annual sum and she would live separately in a house in The Hague. It appears that Assendelft was under strong pressure from his family. Gerrit's mother, Alijd van Kyffhoeck, who 'did not like at all' her daughter-in-law and grandson, specified in her testament (8 June 1530) that Gerrit would not be allowed to alienate the goods he would inherit from her, and 'that also the aforesaid Catharina de Chasseur, housewife of the same, must absolutely not enjoy and profit [therefrom] in any manner whatsoever'.[57] Also, Gerrit's sister, Catharina of Helmond, had 'never ceased inducing, exacerbating, tormenting, inciting and instigating her brother, the aforesaid lord Gerrit van Assendelft, president, against the aforesaid Catharina de Chasseur as well as against the aforesaid Nicolaes, son of the same'.[58]

The legal separation of 1532 did not settle the matter: the difficulties were only just beginning. The household of Catharina van Assendelft, *née* le Chasseur, included a chaplain, two chambermaids and a page. The chaplain, a Frenchman named Mathurin Alys, had invited two young compatriots 'earning

---

years old'; the marriage must therefore have taken place before 1507, and not in or shortly before 1514, as Craandijk thought. Craandijk, 'Nicolaas van Assendelft', p. 9; Holleman, *Dirk van Assendelft*, pp. 241–2.

[54] Craandijk, 'Nicolaas van Assendelft', p. 8.
[55] Ibid., p. 38; Holleman, *Dirk van Assendelft*, p. 241.
[56] Ibid.
[57] Ibid., p. 250.
[58] Ibid., pp. 250–1.

their living by striking coins'. Soon a flourishing counterfeiting operation was begun in the house of the wife of the Court president, under the inspired leadership of a priest. Gold and silver imperial coins were clipped, and counterfeit coins were struck and placed into circulation with the help of Lombards in Delft and Haarlem.

In February 1541 the crime was discovered. Catharina, her chambermaid Huguette and chaplain Mathurin Alys were imprisoned. On 9 April the Court, in the absence of president Assendelft, condemned Catharina to be burnt at the stake. The execution was carried out two days later, but 'with water' instead: by pouring water through a funnel into the mouth of the victim until death resulted. The chaplain was beheaded, and as accomplices both chambermaids and the page were banished. Thus ended the marriage of Gerrit van Assendelft.[59]

The son Klaas was about twenty-four years old when this drama occurred. To Gerrit's dynastic way of thinking, the 'very vile and slight origin' of Catharina lived on in her son, and this made him unfit to succeed his father as lord of Assendelft. Shortly after the death of his mother, Klaas entered the religious life – he became dean of the chapter at Arnhem – under strong pressure from his father and against his own wishes. Gerrit had reportedly wanted his son to enter the church 'in order to please his sister Catharina van Helmond and to be relieved of her insufferable torments', since she 'did not cease repeatedly, day and night, to impress upon him the misalliance and the lowly origin of the aforesaid Claes his son from his mother's side'.[60] Now the way was open for Gerrit to find another heir. In 1544 he received a patent to testate, the necessary consent of the sovereign to dispose of his fiefs by testament, on the grounds that his son 'being [a] religious, will not be allowed to beget in lawful marriage or to leave behind any children, who would be qualified to succeed [to the fiefs]'.[61] In his request that the patent be granted, Gerrit had again pointed to his misalliance and to the fact that he was 'very desirous to uphold the honour and reputation of his lineage, name and ancestry, which is both one of the oldest and most principal of Holland', in order that his family should be better able to serve the Emperor and his successors.[62] He thus made a direct connection between ancestry and virtue: the first would guarantee the second. After he had received the patent to testate, Gerrit made his will on 24 April 1547. 'In view of the inexpressible affection and desire that I have always had and still have today, to uphold my lineage and ancestry in worth and reputation and greatness', again for the benefit of the Emperor 'such as my forefathers had always faithfully served the same Emperor's predecessors', he

[59] Craandijk, 'Nicolaas van Assendelft', p. 9.
[60] Holleman, *Dirk van Assendelft*, p. 251.
[61] Craandijk, 'Nicolaas van Assendelft', p. 8.
[62] Holleman, *Dirk van Assendelft*, p. 243.

bestowed on Klaas only the son's minimum legal portion (one-third of all allodial possessions) and made his nephew Otto van Assendelft, the son of his brother Floris, his principal feudal successor and heir.[63]

Matters would turn out otherwise. Barely had the president breathed his last in December 1558, when his son Klaas, the dean of Arnhem, rode to Holland. Klaas took possession of the family estate of Assumburg at Assendelft, contested his father's will, and had himself invested with his feudal possessions in expectation of the legal judgment. Naturally his cousin Otto was not satisfied with this turn of events, but after a multitude of lawsuits Gerrit's testament was finally declared invalid and judgment rendered in favour of Klaas. Furthermore Klaas requested and received a dispensation from the pope, on the grounds that he had not consented voluntarily to his religious vows and wanted to marry and have children. As lord of Assendelft, he lived the normal life of a Holland nobleman. He married, became a member of the Ridderschap and continued to appear at the States of Holland, even under Alba's regime, until his death in 1570.

What does this extraordinary history tell us about prevailing attitudes toward marriage, marital choice and the value of the family among the nobles of Holland? In the first place, it shows how seriously they regarded misalliances. Naturally this was an extreme case, because the president's wife was condemned for counterfeiting by the very same Court. But his mother's crime was probably not grounds for excluding Klaas from the succession. Everything suggests that Gerrit was already contemplating steps in that direction before 1541, when Catharina's counterfeiting became known.[64] Moreover, in the countless documents on this case that have been preserved, Catharina's crime is never mentioned, but only her lowly origin. Perhaps Gerrit regarded his wife's criminal career as a natural consequence of her low birth, just as he thought high birth guaranteed faithful service to the sovereign. We should be more inclined to explain Catharina's fall at least partly by her disappointment with life in Holland, as a result of the attitude of her husband and in-laws.

From a judicial point of view, the case presented no problem at all. According to the law of Holland, nobility was patrilineal. Anyone born of a lawful marriage, in direct male line from a noble family, was noble. The origins of the mother had no effects on the status of the children. Indeed, after Klaas had set himself up as successor to his father, no one contested his nobility. The Assendelft case does not tell us anything about the judicial determination of nobility, but it speaks volumes about the mentality of the Holland nobles, their ideas about the value of the noble lineage, about marriage and family, about themselves and their place in society. The problem was not that Catharina was not noble, but that she was 'of very vile and slight origin': in other words, that

---

[63] Ibid.; Craandijk, 'Nicolaas van Assendelft', p. 17.
[64] Ibid., p. 25.

she came from the working class. Little fuss was made about the few nobles who married daughters of patricians.

Other Holland nobles shared Gerrit van Assendelft's ideas about racial purity. His misalliance was exceptional, the only case of exogamy among members of the Ridderschap and their children in this period. At the lower levels of the nobility there was some mixing with the patriciate, but reports of flagrant misalliances, marriages with persons from the working class, are scarce. Around the same time there was only a certain Maria van Teylingen, the second daughter of Dirk, a nobleman in the service of the lord of Wassenaer, 'misallied with a journeyman'.[65]

MARRIAGE: ARRANGEMENTS AND ABDUCTIONS

Group identity was not the only concern in the search for a marital partner. Vast material and political interests were at stake in any marriage between two nobles. Marriage served to bind families closer to each other: property, protection and patronage were exchanged along with spouses. In the sixteenth and seventeenth centuries people regarded marriage as a matter that was too important to allow the future partners to decide for themselves.

The marriages of the Holland nobles were minutely prepared by the parents and relatives of the bride and bridegroom. Marriage was not in the first place a tie between two individuals, but an alliance between two families. Each marriage meant a transfer of property from one family to another, and simultaneously a call on future political support, favours, offices, revenues and patronage. In these circumstances it is not surprising that the nobles, when they sought marital partners for their children, looked around primarily in their own social milieu. They involved their entire network of relatives and friends, and, since this group by definition consisted of persons of more or less equal status, it tended to reinforce the already existing tendency toward endogamy.[66] The means by which marriages were arranged had as a result that the noble marriage market remained a closed circuit.

Countless marriage contracts from this period indicate that marriage was seen as a family matter. The parties to a marriage contract were generally not the bride and bridegroom themselves, nor their parents, but rather extended groups of relatives of the future couple. The property they brought to their marriage was regarded as family capital that was being alienated. The entire family had to be consulted about the conditions under which this transfer would take place.

The terms for the marriage between Gerrit van Assendelft's father Klaas and

[65] D. J. M. Wüstenhoff, 'De geslachten van Teylingen', *Wap* 8 (1904): 265–80, 289–304, 401–16, 433–48, at 442.
[66] Muchembled, 'Famille', pp. 247–51.

Alijd van Kyffhoeck (1480) were arranged on one side by the father and an uncle of the bridegroom, along with the bridegroom himself; on the other side, by an uncle and two godparents of the bride (then still a minor), her mother's second husband, and three of her 'nearest kinsmen'.[67] The conditions for the marriage of Dirk van Assendelft and Adriana van Nassau (1527) were arranged by the two brothers and a brother-in-law of the bridegroom, 'in his name, the said *joncker* Dirck also being present', with a group of five 'friends and relations' of Adriana, an orphan. These two parties had decided, in the telling language of the contract, 'to conclude a marriage between Dirck and Adriana'.[68] At the wedding of Jan van der Does and Elizabeth van Zuylen (1566) there were three uncles of the bridegroom – his father had died – and five relations of the bride who declared themselves present as 'proxies or witnesses [*hijlicxluden*] and parties' in the company of the bride and groom, along with the father and mother of the bride.[69]

Marriage contracts specified precisely the properties that bride and groom brought to the union, often with an account of the annual income, and furthermore how these properties should be disposed in the event either of the spouses died. Generally they held that, if either spouse died childless, properties would return to the family from which they came. If there were children or grandchildren, however, they would inherit the property. Finally, the parties negotiated the dower, the goods which the wife would receive from the possessions of her husband in case he died first.

Sometimes the future spouses were still very young when these agreements were made. In 1476, Jan van Assendelft was destined for the heiress Alijd van Kyffhoeck, who was six years old. When Jan unexpectedly died four years later, the families made a new contract in which Alijd was to marry Jan's younger brother Klaas. The religious ceremony took place when Alijd was about fifteen.[70] Klaas van Assendelft was fifteen to twenty years older than his bride, but sometimes men were also betrothed at an early age: the marriage of Joost van Cruyningen was arranged for him in 1498, when he was eight.[71] Sometimes the agreement specified that a bride who was still a minor would be raised in the household of her future in-laws. In 1480 the ten-year-old Alijd van Kyffhoeck had to be brought to the house of her future father-in-law 'in order to be raised there nobly (*heerlicken*) by the aforesaid Lady his wife and instructed and taught good and decent morals and manners, as is and will be reasonable and proper, according to her station'. Her father-in-law also had to take on the burden of

---

[67] Holleman, *Dirk van Assendelft*, p. 545.

[68] Ibid., p. 553.

[69] 'Huwelijkscontract Janus Dousa', p. 158.

[70] They were already described as husband and wife on 31 January, presumably because the engagement was binding. Holleman, *Dirk van Assendelft*, pp. 5–7.

[71] 't Hart, *Heenvliet*, p. 44.

her present and future litigation.[72] The reasons for this arrangement are not clear. Perhaps the parents of the bride found it easy to be rid of their daughter quickly; or perhaps her in-laws thought they could thereby better enforce observance of the contract. In any event, the arrangement ensured that the future spouses had a chance to become acquainted. Walraven van Brederode and Margaretha van Borsselen had grown up together in childhood. On hearing the news that Margaretha's father wanted to marry her off to another, Walraven abducted her and married her in Vianen (1492).[73] But we do not know if he wanted above all to win her love, or to make a good match.

It is clear that in these marriages, so carefully arranged by the families, love between man and woman cannot have been the motive.[74] This applies *a fortiori* when the future spouses were still children. From the letters of several Artois nobles of the second half of the sixteenth century, however, it appears that, while their marriages were organized just as carefully as those of their Holland counterparts, they did not regard the idea of love as contrary to marriage. At the least, they maintained the fiction of marriage for love. Nor were the word and the concept absent from marital relationships, though it is difficult to establish its meaning.[75]

Among the Holland nobles there are also signs that mutual inclination, love, and even passion played a role. Even when a marriage was arranged by the family over the heads of the partners, we may suppose that affection later developed. But the language in which the Holland nobles expressed themselves seldom allows us to judge the proper worth of these feelings. Thus on 2 May 1514 Gerrit van Spaernwoude married Josina Bol. He was twenty-four, she only fourteen.[76] In the nearly fourteen years that the marriage lasted, Josina bore twelve children, of whom six died very young. She herself died barely short of her twenty-ninth year, presumably again in labour. 'On the VIIIth day of January anno XV^{C}XXVII died my beloved worthy wife Lady Josina Florys Bollen's daughter in the morning around eight o'clock and was XXIX years old less seven days', Gerrit noted in his chronicle, '. . . thus we had lived together with great friendship for more than XIIII years, but then God did not allow more and took her away from me in the flower of her life.'[77] Perhaps these words speak of affection and even marital love; then again, we may read in them nothing more than a conventional formula and religious resignation. The 1507 testament of Andries van Foreest and his wife Wilhelmina Adriaansdr van

[72] Holleman, *Dirk van Assendelft*, p. 546.
[73] P. Horden Jz., *Een kleine geschiedenis van het land van Vianen* (n.p., 1953), p. 41.
[74] Cf. for France, Jean-Louis Flandrin, *Familles, parenté, maison, sexualité dans l'ancienne société* (Paris, 1976), p. 161; for England, Stone, *Family*, pp. 5, 86, 180–1; for the Republic, Haks, *Huwelijk*, pp. 138–40.
[75] Muchembled, 'Famille', pp. 244–5.
[76] Jacobs and Thierry de Bye Dólleman, 'Familiekroniekje Spaernwoude', pp. 100–1.
[77] Ibid., p. 101.

Adrichem states that they drew up their last will 'out of right love and affection, that they have for each other'.[78] Yet here too it is unclear whether the language describes feelings of love. None the less, Holland nobles were interested in the quality of relations between husband and wife. Magdalena van Dorp separated from Daniël van Cralingen in 1509 'because of his reckless life, and because he treated her badly'.[79] In 1592 the countess van Culemborg lived apart from her husband because he was jealous and hit her.[80] One year later a daughter of the lord of Brederode returned to her mother because her husband had mistreated her.[81] In the last two cases, however, Holland nobles negotiated successfully to reconcile the spouses.

Infatuation did occur, but the Holland nobles did not regard this illness as sufficient grounds for marriage. Walraven van den Boetzelaer, son of the lord of Asperen, fell in love with Josina van Dorp, a girl 'not so famed for the nobility of her parents, as for their wealth'.[82] None the less she put him off by quoting a verse expressing her preference for her freedom over the constraints of love; at which the unhappy lover stabbed himself with a dagger in her presence. Maurice of Nassau told him that such an action did not befit an heir of a noble family, and Walraven's friends henceforth called him 'Hartaff' (Heart-off).

This was an innocent happening. It was more serious when nobles abducted their loves and endangered the entire system of marital politics by which noble origin, capital and family alliances had to be kept in precarious equilibrium. Here we should distinguish between abductions, by which the perpetrator carried off his victim against her will, and elopements, when the woman co-operated with the man. Elopement was a well-tried means of putting pressure on parents who opposed a marriage. Abduction and elopement occurred quite regularly among the Holland nobles. They were the only way for noble children to escape from a parentally arranged marriage that was not to their liking. Once a marriage had been contracted, it could not be undone. But not all abductions should be regarded as rebellions against parental marriage-politics. In 1654 the aristocratic regent George Rataller Doubleth, a councillor in the Chambre-Mipartie of Mechelen who lived there with his two carefully guarded daughters, thought that rich girls were in more danger than beautiful girls.[83]

Money seems to have been the mainspring of action of one destitute adventurer: in 1664, after he had frittered away his inheritance, he ran off with a rich and prominent heiress of The Hague.[84] Yet the kidnapped bride had willingly

---

[78] Van Foreest, *Foreest*, p. 127.
[79] Van Gouthoeven, *Chronyke*, pp. 161, 171.
[80] Van Buchell, *Diarium*, pp. 329–30.
[81] Ibid., p. 349.   [82] Ibid., p. 224.
[83] R. Fruin, 'Uit het dagboek van een oud-Hollander', *VG*, IV, pp. 195–244, at 206. On abductions in the Republic, see Haks, *Huwelijk*, pp. 125–8.
[84] Lieuwe van Aitzema, *Saken van Staet en oorlogh in, ende omtrent de Vereenigde Nederlanden*, 6 vols. (2nd edn, The Hague, 1669–72), V, pp. 144–66.

collaborated in the abduction because her relations had wanted to marry her off against her will, and she then prevented that. She was an especially attractive match because her parents were dead, and she had collected her inheritance. Money also seems to have played a role in 1531 when the Holland nobleman Frederik van Rhoon abducted the thirteen- or fourteen-year-old *jonkvrouw* Van der Haer.[85] The girl had come to Rijnsburg with her mother to visit an aunt who lived as a nun in the convent. Frederick sought an opportunity to kidnap her and make her his wife, 'noting that the same young daughter was very wealthy'.[86] His aunt Martina, the wife of the bailiff of Rijnsburg, Joost van Wijngaerden, where he 'was maintained', was helpful to him. Frederik managed to lure his victim 'with guile' from the convent to the garden of his aunt, and began to walk with her behind the orchard. At the back gate Frederik grabbed the girl and threw her on a waiting wagon containing several accomplices armed 'with arquebuses and other weapons'. The evildoers sped away and left the county of Holland. The victim had 'screamed terribly', but her abductor placed her on his lap, folded his cloak around her and pressed his hand over her mouth. He married her at Helmond in the duchy of Brabant and subsequently held her prisoner, against her will, at IJsselstein. Finally, however, she managed to escape to the house of her mother. Although in this case the motive was apparently the girl's fortune, it is doubtful whether the kidnapping produced any material gain for Frederik: the Court condemned him to banishment and confiscated his property. In most cases an abduction produced little profit. Sometimes the parents had already stipulated beforehand in their testaments that their children had to contract an approved marriage if they wished to receive their share of the inheritance. In this fashion Floris van Assendelft and his wife Henrika van Arckel van Heukelom declared in 1549 that their son Otto would be their universal heir, provided that he contracted a desired marriage.[87] Sometimes it was still possible afterwards for parents to cut off their children from the inheritance.[88] Therefore most abductors were probably less motivated by material gain than by love.

In 1509 Gerrit van Raephorst abducted the thirteen-year-old Catharina de Grebber, but certainly not for her money.[89] The truth about his motives and the feelings of his bride is difficult to determine, because in the court case that ensued from this incident he put forward a version completely different from

---

[85] Register van criminele sententiën 1529–1538, ARA, Hof, inv. no. 5653, fos. 18 v., 24; Rekeningen van de rentmeesters van de exploiten, ARA, Grafelijkheidsrekenkamer, rekeningen, inv. no. 4454, ff. 75–9, 92–5, and inv. no. 4455, fos. 37 v., 38, 46.

[86] ARA, Hof, inv. no. 5653, fo. 24.

[87] Holleman, *Dirk van Assendelft*, p. 366.

[88] On financial penalties applied to children who married without the consent of their parents, see Haks, *Huwelijk*, pp. 127–8.

[89] *Sententie, gegeven op het interinement van Brieven van pardon, noopende d'ontschakinge van seecker Jonge-Dochter, gedaan by Gerrit van Raephorst (ged. 15 juli 1515)* (n.p., n.d., Kn 9; reprint 1664, Kn 8960). Also in Aitzema, *Saken*, v, pp. 158–60.

that of the girl's parents. Both parties were in agreement, however, about the facts of the abduction itself, carried out with force and against the wishes of the victim.

Jonker Gerrit and four accomplices had lain in wait for the carriage taking Catharina and her parents to high mass in the church of Wassenaar. They sprang on the carriage with drawn bows and took Catharina 'forcefully and violently from her father's lap'. They carried her in a wagon to Leimuiden, where, according to the kidnapper's story, Catharina of her own free will 'had a talk' with him in the presence of many people. A short time later they were married. Catharina's parents however denied that their daughter had 'been content' at Leimuiden. On the contrary, 'while she was there, the aforesaid Raephorst acted in such a manner, that he threw her on the ground, and *de facto* indeed raped, violated, and assaulted her, so that she was crying out with force and violence, and in order that people would not hear it, [Raephorst's accomplices] also cried out, screamed, and sang . . .'.[90] Her parents and their son-in-law also had conflicting interpretations of the period after the wedding. According to Raephorst the couple had lived together 'well and properly' for some months; yet his parents-in-law declared that he 'had lived so harshly with their daughter and kept her in such a way that she had neither consolation nor pleasure with him, but he used her with so much rigour and force, that she had to go with him to the Buurkerk [a church] in Utrecht, where she had to say everything that he wanted said, and he lived with her before and after in such a manner that she had not a kerchief on her head, nor a daily gown on her body'. As soon as she saw her chance, she fled back to her parents, 'who received her in friendly manner'.[91]

It is significant that both parties, the kidnapper and the parents of the victim, brought up arguments based on the mutual feelings of Gerrit and Catharina, and the quality of their marriage. One party did that positively, the other negatively. Both must have thought that these considerations would influence the Court, because they were in agreement about the fact of the kidnapping, which was of course by itself a criminal deed. Raephorst excused his action on the grounds that he had acted 'out of great love and affection that he had for . . . *juffrouw* Catharina'. Her parents argued to the contrary, not entirely illogically, 'that it could be presumed that the aforesaid Raephorst had and has neither affection nor love for their daughter, since he had never in all his days spoken to her [i.e. before the abduction]'.[92] According to the kidnapper the marriage had been happy; according to his parents-in-law Catharina had left her husband 'because he was doing her great impetuosity and injury' – she herself had asked her parents to prosecute him.[93] It is true that during the trial she was again living with her husband, but her parents said that 'because she was young'

90 Aitzema, *Saken*, v, p. 159.   91 Ibid.
92 Ibid., p. 158.   93 Ibid., p. 159.

Raephorst had induced her to come back to him with 'a pair of slippers'.

Catharina de Grebber's tender age at the time of her abduction was not exceptional. The *jonkvrouw* van der Haer kidnapped from Rijnsburg was the same age; and in 1589 Gerrit van Bevervoirde, a nobleman from Gelderland, ran off with the eleven- or twelve-year-old Anna Magdalena van Reede, when she and her parents were guests in his house.[94] The daughter of the Utrecht nobleman Jan van Isselt must have been about the same age when she was kidnapped. Arend van Buchell, a great fancier of such tales, reported the incident:

Around the 27th [of October 1593] a common lout [*juvenis villicus*], a former servant of lord Jan van Isselt, who used to say that he was engaged to the lord's daughter, kidnapped her from the midst of her little friends, after he had built a raft at night. Her mother, and subsequently also her father, went after him; and the latter found his daughter the next day at Bodegraven and brought her back. Thus he experienced what he earlier had done to another. Because this knight himself had by force of arms abducted his own wife.[95]

The difference of station between kidnapper and victim made this case extraordinarily serious. But generally both parties were on the same social level. In 1589 Sir Thomas Morgan, the English military governor of Bergen op Zoom, and Thomas Knollys (another English officer, and younger son of the statesman Sir Francis Knollys) kidnapped the two daughters of Jan van Merode, the marquis of Bergen.[96] Their parents sent a warship after them, but they did not succeed in getting their daughters back. The mother subsequently complained to the States-General, who took the case seriously. The English argued that the abduction was allowed 'by all godly and natural rights' because the girls themselves had asked for it. Anna, the elder, supposedly asked Morgan to save her, because her mother wanted to marry her to a Catholic cousin and thus bring her 'to the enemy's side'. Her sister reportedly threw herself into the arms of Knollys because the mother also wanted to marry her to the enemy's side, 'against her wish, will, and conscience'. One may have doubts about the religious or political motives of the two girls, but it is clear that they co-operated fully with the plans of the two English officers. Van Buchell's commentary was, 'So many of our girls and women [are] given over to foreigners; the Spaniards have tried the virginity of a good number, and our proud and haughty English have deceived many of them.'[97]

---

[94] L. A. J. W. Sloet, 'Gerrit van Bevervoorde schaakt iure militari juffer Anna Magdalena van Rheden in het jaar 1589', *BVGO*, 2nd series, 10 (1880): 259–92. J. I. D. Nepveu, 'Gerrit van Bevervoorde, wegens schaking van Anna Magdalena van Reede te Brussel ter dood gebracht', *BMHG* 8 (1885): 29–44; R. Fruin, 'Het proces van Gerrit van Bevervoorde', *VG*, IX, pp. 70–2.

[95] Van Buchell, *Diarium*, pp. 353–4.

[96] Pieter Bor, *Oorsprongk, begin ende vervolgh der Nederlantscher oorlogen*, 4 vols. (Amsterdam, 1679–84), III, p. 381; Van Buchell, *Diarium*, p. 195.   [97] Van Buchell, *Diarium*, p. 195.

Pieter van Myerop clearly went too far on St Joris day, 1556, when he tried to abduct *jonkvrouw* Van Cralingen, a 'professed and religious nun' in the convent of Koningsveld, who none the less gave her co-operation to the plan. He had talked her into leaving the cloister and going with him to 'Oostland' [the Baltic]. On the appointed day she summoned him to the cloister in order that they might elope. But the plot came to light, and the case ended for the abductor with banishment and confiscation of his property – and he could think himself fortunate, for abduction of nuns carried the death penalty.[98]

The sisters Margaretha and Adriana van Assendelft also co-operated heartily in their abductions.[99] Margaretha allowed herself to be abducted around 1640 by Simon du Faget, a noble ensign in the States army. The kidnapper took the underage Margaret from the house of her parents in Delft 'by night and at an unseasonable hour', and brought her to Delfshaven, whence they travelled by night-barge to Heusden. Only after they had had children together were they married, 'in a very confused fashion and without making a marriage contract', against the will of her parents.

Perhaps encouraged by the example of her older sister, Adriana van Assendelft eloped late in the evening of 19 October 1644, with cornet Frederik Conincx. He had come in contact with her at an inn in The Hague where Adriana was staying with her mother. On the evening in question the kidnapper had arranged for a coach, and at his call the girl threw some luggage out of the window and secretly left the house. They rode in the carriage as far as Delft, where they took the barge for Delfshaven and then departed by ship to an unknown destination. Some years later they appeared to be legally married. The Court of Holland, not having the power to condemn the fugitive abductor to death, sentenced him in absentia to perpetual banishment and confiscation of his property.

These are only a few examples of abductions, possibly only the tip of the iceberg. Councillor Rataller Doubleth declared in 1654, on the occasion of the elopement of the young *juffrouw* d'Ivrea and Mr Van der Nath, that abductions of young daughters were not rare occurrences.[100] The authorities tried to prosecute the crime vigorously, as seen by the heavy penalties that were demanded and carried out. In 1664 a poor wretch who was hired to assist a kidnapper died on the scaffold. Another one was banished for life; a third accomplice, Frederik Hendrik van den Boetzelaer, a Holland nobleman, was stripped of his captaincy in the cavalry and banished for five years.[101] Generally the kidnapper himself was not put to death, although in principle this punishment was possible. Gerrit van Raephorst was condemned in 1515 to go bareheaded in a linen

[98] Register van criminele sententiën 1538–1572, ARA, Hof, inv. no. 5654, fos. 322 v.–324.
[99] Holleman, *Dirk van Assendelft*, pp. 430, 444–5.
[100] R. Fruin, 'Dagboek van een oud-Hollander', p. 206.
[101] Aitzema, *Saken*, v, pp. 144–60; Holleman, *Dirk van Assendelft*, p. 430.

robe, carrying a burning candle, to beg forgiveness from the court as well as his offended parents-in-law. In addition he had to have a glass window made for the church at Wassenaar, bearing the arms of the sovereign and the following ignominious text: 'This glass was placed here by order of the Court of Holland, by Gerrit van Raephorst, as reparation for the abduction perpetrated by him.'[102] Yet the same sentence did lift an earlier order of banishment. The church window, which should have recalled Raephorst's shameful deed for all eternity, decorated the church for only half a century. In 1566 the glass was broken into fragments – and the iconoclastic movement at Wassenaar was led by none other than Herbert van Raephorst, a descendant of the kidnapper.[103] In the case of Frederik Conincx, the kidnapper of Adriana van Assendelft, the prosecutor-general of the Court had wanted to demand the death penalty. But, since Conincx was a fugitive, the sentence was left at banishment, which however did not prevent him from repeatedly showing himself in Holland, apparently with impunity.[104] The concerned father, Rataller Doubleth, thought that the system of justice was too lenient in these cases.[105] Only Gerrit van Bevervoirde appears to have been beheaded at Brussels, some years after the kidnapping of Anna Magdalena van Reede.[106]

The abductions can be divided into two types according to the motives of the kidnappers – abductions for greed and abductions for passion. The first variant was rare. In order to conquer an inheritance along with an heiress it was imperative that she already be in possession of her share. If the parents were still living, there was a chance they would disinherit their daughter. Abductions for passion can be subdivided into cases where the girl was carried off by force and against her will, and those in which she lent her co-operation. The second category appears to have been the most common. The daughters of the lord of Merode and the girl from The Hague in 1664 allowed themselves to be abducted in order to avoid a forced marriage. Elopements were thus the undesired consequences of the careful marriage policies of the Holland nobles.

The youthful age of many abducted girls is striking. The *jonkvrouw* Van der Haer and Catharina de Grebber were thirteen, Anna Magdalena van Reede eleven or twelve. Rataller Doubleth mentioned the case of *jonkvrouw* Van Adrichem, who ran away from her grandfather's house at age thirteen in order to marry.[107] The daughter of Jan van Isselt and the Assendelft sisters were also minors. These ages are far below the usual age of marriage for Holland noblewomen.[108] It is however possible that mostly abductions of very young

---

[102] Aitzema, *Saken*, v, p. 160.
[103] Smit, *Den Haag in geuzentijd*, pp. 59–60; W. A. Beelaerts van Blokland, 'Wassenaar in den geuzentijd', *LJ* 23 (1930–1): 67–97.
[104] Holleman, *Dirk van Assendelft*, p. 445.
[105] Fruin, 'Dagboek van een oud-Hollander', p. 208.   [106] See above, n. 94.
[107] Fruin, 'Dagboek van een oud-Hollander', p. 208.   [108] See above, pp. 55–6.

girls have been recorded in the archives, because in such cases the parents were more inclined to press court cases. Perhaps incidents of abduction or elopement at an older age were more often followed by reconciliation between the parents and the kidnapper. Yet it is also probable that the noble girls of Holland gained more mature understanding with advancing years, and that when they were older they were more attracted by a carefully arranged marriage of status and money than by a romantic adventure.

Most kidnappers of noble daughters were themselves nobles. Endogamy was also the rule in abductions, which were none the less the negation of status-marriages arranged by the parents. Endogamy was not a duty imposed on the nobles from without, but rather an internalized pattern of behaviour.

When the parents did take action against the kidnappers of their daughter, the mother was especially active. After the abduction of *jonkvrouw* van Isselt, her mother and 'subsequently' her father went after the perpetrators.[109] After Morgan and Knollys abducted the Merode girls, their mother contacted the States General. Likewise the mother of Anna Magdalena van Reede pressed all the lawsuits against Gerrit van Bevervoirde. The best story is the unconfirmed report that the mother, bent on vengeance, sat with her daughter on a balcony and witnessed the execution of Bevervoirde: later she forced her daughter to wear a dress made of the black velvet material on which the execution had taken place.[110]

The harshness with which many parents pursued the abductors of their daughters leads us to suppose that more was at stake here than simply tarnished family honour and damaged family interests. When Bevervoirde wanted to drag Anna Magdalena van Reede from her bedroom, her mother sprang out of bed, attacked the abductor and tore 'the ruffles of his neck'. When she could not prevent him from entering her daughter's room, she fell powerless to the ground. Her husband had also 'fallen out of bed', as much to stop Bevervoirde as to 'assist' his wife. These facts are not in accord with the opinion of Van Buchell, who as secretary of Brederode was in a good position to observe first-hand the lives of the nobles. He was amazed that the feelings of the magnates toward their children were so cool. Reinoud van Brederode had cast off his children 'as strangers'; therefore Van Buchell had often heard Reinoud's son Walraven say that God had rightly cursed his lineage. The parents treated their children badly, threatening the near-total annihilation of the Brederode family and their possessions. Van Buchell's later patron, the baron of Boxtel, had sent his children to friends after the death of his wife. Not only had he not seen his children in fifteen years, wrote Van Buchell indignantly, but he did not even answer their letters and had sent them nothing as keepsakes.[111] Elsewhere Van

[109] Van Buchell, *Diarium*, pp. 353–4: 'Insequitur mater, hinc pater'.
[110] Sloet, 'Gerrit van Bevervoorde', p. 291.
[111] Van Buchell, *Diarium*, p. 309.

Buchell reports that Anthonis van Aemstel en Mynden went insane, because his father preferred the children of Anthonis' stepmother.[112] May we draw conclusions about the entire Holland nobility from these cases of bad fathers? Van Buchell's indignation suggests that parental love was not an unknown phenomenon in the sixteenth century.

[112] Ibid., p. 311.

5

Incomes and expenditures

THE ECONOMIC DECLINE OF THE NOBILITY – A MYTH?

The economic decline of the nobility is as proverbial as the rise of the bourgeoisie. 'The trouble with the middle class is that it is always rising', one historian has remarked.[1] The trouble with the nobility is that it is always declining.

The scenario of this tragedy has been produced in many versions with several common elements. Rising prices in a time of constant incomes; a luxurious, wasteful style of life; debts; the loss of official functions at princely courts and the ascendancy of mercenary infantry over heavily armoured cavalry – these are supposedly the foremost causes of the decline of the nobility and simultaneously those of the rise of its perpetual adversary, the bourgeoisie. Nobles and bourgeois formed mirror images of each other. Merchants could take advantage of rising prices. The wastefulness of nobles was the complement of sober saving, the 'Protestant ethic' of the bourgeoisie. The nobles ran up debts, the bourgeois were their creditors. In their attempts to tame the nobility the 'new monarchies' depended for their support on money and salaried employees from urban backgrounds.[2]

Recent research on the nobility in early-modern Europe, however, has stressed its economic vitality. In an age of population growth, the nobles as land-owners could profit from rising food prices. Moreover sixteenth- and seventeenth-century rulers drew upon noble services for support, more than was previously thought.[3]

Perhaps even more than in other countries, the myth of the declining nobility in the Netherlands has affected the writing of history. After all, its purpose is to

---

[1] M. Karpovich, cited by I. Schöffer, 'Did Holland's golden age coincide with a period of crisis?', in *The General Crisis of the Seventeenth Century*, ed. Geoffrey Parker and Lesley M. Smith (London, Henley and Boston, 1978), pp. 83–109, at 100.

[2] This interpretation was formulated in a classical manner by J. D. M. Cornelissen, *Waarom zij geuzen werden genoemd* (Tilburg, 1936), pp. 21–2.

[3] The neo-marxist scheme of rising bourgeoisie and declining nobility was criticized by J. H. Hexter, 'The myth of the middle class in Tudor England', *Reappraisals in History* (London, 1961), pp. 71–116. The decline of the French nobility in the sixteenth century is disputed by Wood, *Nobility*. For Europe in general, see G. R. Elton, *Reformation Europe, 1517–1559* (New York, 1963), pp. 305–18.

explain retrospectively the rise of the merchant republic of the seventeenth century. At first glance there is no place for a prosperous nobility in such a schematic history.

'The poor nobility longed for all that money could buy', wrote Robert Fruin.[4] 'As empty as their heads were of any higher civilization, so poor were the purses of the high nobility', declared R. C. Bakhuizen van den Brink. He compared the nobility, 'exhausted, powerless, corrupt in their nature, [who] had to perish at the first blow that the Revolt struck against them', with 'the antagonists of the nobility, the bourgeoisie, in all their power and activity'.[5] According to Pieter Geyl, the rising prices presented insurmountable financial difficulties for the nobles, which led them to cast a covetous eye on the possessions of the church.[6] L. J. Rogier saw the increasing tax burden as the primary cause of the financial decline of the nobles and the origin of the Compromise of the Nobility.[7] 'Penniless squires', Jan and Annie Romein called the members of the Compromise of 1565.[8] Finally, the most recent standard work on Dutch history reports that the position of the nobles was damaged by the continual inflation, particularly where noble incomes consisted of fixed sums such as long leases and ground rents. Although admitting that sixteenth-century nobles could enter the service of the sovereign, this work questions whether they could do so without private wealth, in view of the costs of maintaining noble status and consumption patterns.[9]

This image finds support in the opinions of contemporaries. Cardinal Granvelle saw the impoverishment of the nobility as the primary cause of the Revolt – after God's will.[10] Pontus Payen also thought that the desire of destitute nobles to seize church property was one of the causes of the outbreak of the Revolt.[11] Pieter Cornelisz Hooft wrote that some nobles, because they were 'up to their teeth' in debts, tried to make use of the Troubles 'in order to keep their heads [above water] in a choppy sea';[12] and Grotius chimed in that many nobles 'sought the general troubles, as [a means of] rescue or disguise for their own'.[13] The poverty of nobles served not only as an explanation for war, but also as an explanation for peace. The author of a pamphlet declared that it

---

[4] R. Fruin, 'Het voorspel van den tachtigjarigen oorlog', *VG*, I, pp. 266–449, at 288.

[5] R. C. Bakhuizen van den Brink, 'De adel', *Cartons voor de geschiedenis van den Nederlandschen vrijheidsoorlog* (3rd edn, The Hague, 1891), pp. 1–78, at 49, 77.

[6] P. Geyl, *Geschiedenis van de Nederlandse stam*, 6 vols. (paperback edn, Amsterdam and Antwerp, 1961–2), I, p. 211.

[7] L. J. Rogier, *Eenheid en scheiding. Geschiedenis der Nederlanden 1477–1813* (3rd edn, Utrecht and Antwerp, 1973), p. 34.

[8] Romein, *Lage Landen*, p. 254.

[9] Faber, 'Noordelijke Nederlanden', p. 208.

[10] *The Low Countries in Early Modern Times*, ed. H. H. Rowen (New York, 1972), pp. 27–9. Cf. Wilson, *Queen Elizabeth*, p. 47.

[11] Payen, *Mémoires*, I, p. 31.

[12] Hooft, *Nederlandsche historien*, I, p. 125.

[13] De Groot, *Nederlandsche jaerboeken*, p. 8.

was precisely the nobles who favoured a truce with Spain, 'because among the ancient nobility there are many who cannot suffer that the merchants are prospering so much, [and] they are falling behind, since they are not being paid well by their land-leases, rents, and tithes'.[14] As for the nobility of the province of Holland in particular, Wouter van Gouthoeven, Matthijs van der Houve and Simon van Leeuwen unanimously bemoaned their bad financial management, by which the merchants were able to make themselves masters of their fiefs.[15]

There is one dissenting voice among the historians. H. A. Enno van Gelder concluded that the Holland nobility was prosperous and wealthy on the eve of the Revolt.[16] The nobles who started the Revolt in 1566 were a significant economic force. Perhaps they were deep in debt at times, but on the other hand both the urban and rural population had many monetary obligations to them. 'And the conclusion cannot be otherwise: the possessions of a nobleman and the revenues tied to a manor truly represented a considerable capital for that time.'[17] Van Gelder called Granvelle's economic explanation of the Revolt 'slanderous in every respect'.[18] Van Gelder is the only historian who based his judgment on a thorough knowledge of the sources. The surviving financial documents of the nobles around the middle of the sixteenth century do indeed give the impression of vast wealth.[19] Yet Van Gelder did not succeed in relating the incomes of the nobles to their expenditures.[20] The charge that the nobles spent their money like water is not answered by pointing to the size of their capital. By systematically living beyond his means, anyone can fritter away the greatest fortune. Furthermore, Van Gelder did not take sufficient account of the fact that part of the noble patrimony was permanently burdened with rents and mortgages. The disposable part of income for consumption and investment was smaller than the gross revenue of a noble estate.

Van Gelder did not attempt to set his picture of the Holland nobles in the context of the time. His study is a still photograph, not a film; it shows a situation, not a process. Although the wealth of the nobles on the eve of the Revolt was indeed considerable, if we could place the nobles on a downward slope the economic explanation for their resistance would still be tenable. If, however, the nobles were becoming richer, this explanation would be groundless.

Van Gelder should not be reproached for having made a somewhat impres-

---

[14] (Anon.), *Schuyt-praetgens, op de vaert naer Amsterdam, tusschen een lantman, een hovelinck, een borger, ende schipper* (n.p., n.d., but after Easter 1608; Kn 1450), fo. A3 v.

[15] Van Gouthoeven, *Chronyke*, p. 119; Van der Houve, *Hantvest*, p. 60; Van Leeuwen, *Redeningh*, p. 60.

[16] Van Gelder, 'Hollandse adel'.

[17] Ibid., pp. 118–23.

[18] Ibid., p. 121.

[19] Cf. *Gegevens betreffende roerend en onroerend bezit*, esp. I, pp. 215–38.

[20] J. W. Smit, 'The present position of studies regarding the revolt of the Netherlands', in *Britain and the Netherlands*, I, ed. J. S. Bromley and E. H. Kossmann (London, 1960), p. 20.

sionistic study. The available sources are too fragmented to serve as a basis for modern statistical analysis. With only a few exceptions, manorial accounts running over a long period have not been preserved. Periodic appraisals of the possessions of all nobles, such as those made in France, are lacking in Holland.[21] Accounts of individual nobles, which could give a picture of their incomes and expenditures, have not been preserved either.

Nobles could not practise any trade or commerce, but had to live 'from their own incomes from lands, tithes and manors'.[22] In this chapter we shall present a picture of these sources of income. Owing to a shortage of source material, in some respects our picture will seem as impressionistic as that of Van Gelder. A statistical study, based on a great number of serial data, will probably remain impossible. But in contrast to Van Gelder, we shall attempt to trace developments over one and a half centuries. Where possible, numerical series will be used; where not, examples will take their place.

THE NOBLES AS LANDOWNERS

The largest part of the wealth of most Holland nobles consisted of land: consequently the largest part of their income came from land-leases. Income from tithes and seigneurial rights was secondary. Around 1500 the lord of Warmond, for example, received £194 in rents from land and farms. The lease of the ferry, the mill and some fishing rights brought in £75, so that leases of land (not counting tithes) produced 72 per cent of the income.[23] In 1531 the manors of Amstelveen, Sloten, Sloterdijk and Osdorp, which Reinoud van Brederode had sold to Amsterdam shortly before, produced an income of 52 pounds Flemish: of that sum, £34 or 65 per cent came from land-leases.[24] The manor of Zuid-Polsbroek, which belonged to the count of Aremberg, brought in £945 in 1555; of that, £596 or 63 per cent came from land-leases.[25] In 1567–8 the revenues of the county of Culemborg were £9,313 5s. 4d. The largest portion, £6,682 4s. 3d., or 72 per cent, again came from leased lands. Various

---

[21] J. B. Wood based his study of the incomes of the nobility of the *élection* of Bayeux on periodic assessments of noble wealth, pp. 120–55.

[22] Van Goethoeven, *Chronyke*, p. 119.

[23] Staat van inkomsten van de heer van Warmond (ca. 1500), GA Leiden, Huisarchief van de heren van Warmond, inv. no. 66. In 1510 the revenues from leases in this manor came to 171 gulden 14s., or 46 per cent of the total (57 per cent of the total if tithes are excluded). *Gegevens betreffende roerend en onroerend bezit*, I, pp. 215–18. Unless noted otherwise, all sums are stated in Holland pounds.

[24] Yet land revenues fell to 28 per cent in 1560, 29 per cent in 1590, and 24 per cent in 1619. GA Amsterdam, Archief Burgemeesters, stadsrekeningen 1531, 1560, 1590, 1619. Cf. Van Gelder, 'Hollandse adel', pp. 141–2 (appendix): an account of the same manors in 1521, where the share of leases was much smaller, 13 per cent.

[25] Accounts of the manor of Zuid-Polsbroek, GA Amsterdam, FA De Graeff (particulier archief no. 76), inv. no. 433. Hereditary leases valued at £1 16s. 0d. have not been included in the calculation.

tithe rights amounted to only 5 per cent of the total, while seigneurial rights such as fishing, milling, *gruit* (the exclusive right to supply the herbs used for flavouring beer), ferries, excise taxes and tolls came to 16 per cent.[26] In 1625 the possessions of the lord of Lisse in the manor of the same name had an assessed valuation of £121,353. Land and farms were worth £102,516 or 84 per cent of the total.[27] The preponderance of land-leases in the incomes of Holland nobles was, however, a rule that did have some exceptions: thus the revenues of Dirk van Assendelft in Besoyen in 1527 came to nearly £1,100, about half of which came from tithes. Only one-third came from land-leases, the rest from hereditary leases and various seigneurial rights.[28]

Three factors significantly affected the nobles' incomes from leases: the size of their landed possessions; the measure in which they were in a position to raise their lease prices periodically (in other words, the relationship between term leases, hereditary leases, and other forms of lease); and, finally, the trend of lease prices.

How important were the nobles as landowners? Already at the beginning of the sixteenth century the patterns of landownership in the countryside of Holland were distinctly modern. The peasants owned a great deal of land, and the urban bourgeois as a group owned more land than the nobles or the church. Local conditions varied greatly, however. On the islands of Texel and Wieringen in 1514 the peasants owned all the land, and in the Gooi region they held 85 per cent. Yet around the town of Woerden peasants owned only 10 per cent, and on the islands of South Holland 8 per cent. In the entire county of Holland in 1514, the peasants owned 42 per cent of the land that they worked. The peasants exploited 94.5 per cent of all arable and pasture land; the remaining 5.5 per cent was used by urban bourgeois, clergy, and nobles.[29] In the polder district of Rijnland, the peasants in 1544 owned 39,834 of the 64,302 *morgen*, or 62 per cent of the land. But here too differences between manors were great. In the lands along the foot of the dunes and the fertile clay along the banks of the Old Rhine, the peasants owned less than 40 per cent; while in the peat-bogs of the eastern part of the district they held over 70 per cent. The peasants north of the IJ owned less land than their counterparts in the south.[30]

---

[26] *Gegevens betreffende roerend en onroerend bezit*, I, pp. 78–86. Hereditary leases valued at £248 19s. 2d. have not been included in the calculation.

[27] Valuation of the real property of Johan van Mathenesse, ARA, FA Heereman van Zuijtwijck, prov. inv. no. 34.

[28] Holleman, *Dirk van Assendelft*, pp. 552–9. In Groningen land also formed the bulk of the wealth of the *jonkers*: 40 to 70 per cent of their capital. Feenstra, *Bloeitijd*, pp. 10–21 and 357. Cf., for the sixteenth century, H. A. Enno van Gelder, 'Friesche en Groningsche edelen in den tijd van den Opstand tegen Spanje', *Historische opstellen opgedragen aan prof. dr. H. Brugmans . . .* (Amsterdam, 1929), pp. 78–94, at 78–9. [29] Naber, *Terugblik*, pp. 47, 50–1.

[30] De Vries, *Dutch Rural Economy*, pp. 49–51; E. F. van Dissel, 'Grond in eigendom en huur in de ambachten van Rijnland omstreeks 1545', *Handelingen en mededelingen van de Maatschappij der Nederlandsche Letterkunde* (1896–7): 152–4.

Most land that was not owned by the peasants belonged to the urban bourgeois. Landownership by town-dwellers also varied from place to place. In some villages in the Noorderkwartier and marsh-villages where the proportion of land belonging to the urban bourgeois was more limited, peasant ownership was correspondingly greater: 3.5 per cent in Ter Aar in 1543, 2.5 per cent in Tekkop in 1562, 14.6 per cent in Nieuwkoop in 1562, 18 per cent in Lambertschaag in 1514. In Twisk and Ursum, town-dwellers none the less owned nearly 50 per cent of the land; in Haastrecht 66.5 per cent; in Noord-Schermer as much as 72.5 per cent.[31] The total landownership of the urban bourgeois at the beginning of the sixteenth century is unknown, but may be estimated at 20 to 30 per cent of the total.

Ecclesiastical institutions held third place as landowners in Holland. In most villages less than 10 per cent of the land was owned by the church; only in a few villages was the proportion higher than 20 per cent. Most of the church lands were to be found near the two great abbeys of Egmond and Rijnsburg.[32] Besides the abbeys, other ecclesiastical landowners included local parishes, priests, charitable institutions (the 'Holy Spirit'), urban convents, chapters of canons and other religious foundations.

The nobility were minor landowners in Holland. Jan de Vries estimates the landed possessions of the nobility in the entire county of Holland in the sixteenth century at less than 10 per cent of the total.[33] Yet while the nobility as a class owned less land than the peasants, the town-dwellers and the ecclesiastical institutions, many individual nobles were still important landowners. We have already established that not more than two hundred noble families lived in Holland in the first half of the sixteenth century.[34] In 1514 the total cultivated surface of the province came to 308,000 *morgen*.[35] If the nobles owned some 5 per cent of the land, then each adult nobleman would have held an *average* of 77 *morgen*, circa 160 acres. This is not a vast landed estate, but it still represented considerable wealth. Since the possessions of the nobles varied greatly in size, however, this theoretical estimate is not very significant.

The land registers (*morgenboeken*) of Rijnland enable us to study noble landownership in detail.[36] In a large number of Rijnland manors the nobles held quite a few parcels, but nowhere did they own a large percentage of the land. The differences between manors were great on this point. In Aalsmeer, for example, in 1544 not a single parcel was owned by a nobleman, while in Hillegom in that same year approximately a quarter of all land belonged to

[31] De Vries, *Dutch Rural Economy*, pp. 43–9.
[32] Ibid., p. 42.
[33] Ibid., p. 36.
[34] See above, p. 50.
[35] Naber, *Terugblik*, p. 17.
[36] Beginning in 1544, all parcels in Rijnland were surveyed every four years. The *morgenboeken* have been preserved in the AH Rijnland.

Table 5.1 *Landownership of the lords of Warmond in several Rijnland villages, in morgen, ca. 1500–1648*

Manor	ca. 1500	ca. 1544	1586/90	ca. 1600	ca. 1648
Warmond	13.66	43.70	51.75	48.83	83.1
Aalsmeer	—	—	—	17.5	—
Alkemade	—	5.2	—	—	—
Alphen	—	—	—	10.08	10.08
Esselikerwoude	—	21.13	—	23.50	13.68
Katwijk	—	3.73	—	6.64	0.66
Koudekerk	—	20.82	—	3.99	3

— no data.

nobles. In Aarlanderveen, Alkemade, Alphen and Esselikerwoude in that year between 1 and 5 per cent of the land was owned by nobles; in Warmond, Koudekerk and Lisse between 10 and 15 per cent.[37] S. J. Fockema Andreae estimated that in 1544, of the circa 60,000 *morgen* of land in Rijnland, around 3,700 *morgen* or 6.2 per cent belonged to 'nobles of old Holland lineage' and a further 1,600 *morgen* or 2.6 per cent belonged to 'what could be called nobles of office': thus altogether 8.8 per cent.[38] Yet it is unclear what he meant by these terms, and how he came to this estimate. Noble landownership in the Rijnland in 1544 was concentrated around Leiden, near the old mouth of the Rhine. Since peasant ownership predominated on the less fertile marshlands, it is reasonable to assume that the nobles owned primarily the better riverbank clay and lands at the foot of the dunes.

The Rijnland *morgenboeken* do make it possible to compare noble landownership at different periods. It appears that many nobles were in a position to increase their landholdings. Table 5.1 shows the possessions of the lords of Warmond in a sample of several Rijnland villages. These possessions constituted only part of their entire property.[39]

It is noteworthy that, while their possessions in the other villages fluctuated, those in Warmond progressively expanded. Perhaps the lords of Warmond sold land outside their own manor with the goal of consolidating their landed

[37] AH Rijnland, Morgenboeken. Noble landholding in Hillegom: 252 *morgen* out of a total of 995; Aarlanderveen, 47 of 2,511; Alkemade, 50 of 3,138; Alphen, 76 of 2,239; Esselikerwoude, 56 of 2,526; Warmond, 169 of 1,329; Koudekerk, 179 of 1,168; Lisse, 215 of 1,551.

[38] S. J. Fockema Andreae, 'De Rijnlandse kastelen en landhuizen in hun maatschappelijk verband', in S. J. Fockema Andreae, J. G. N. Renaud and E. Pellinck, *Kastelen, ridderhofsteden en buitenplaatsen in Rijnland* (Arnhem, 1974), pp. 1–20, at 8.

[39] AH Rijnland, Morgenboeken Warmond, Aalsmeer, Alkemade, Alphen, Esselikerwoude, Katwijk, Koudekerk; GA Leiden, HA Warmond, inv. no. 66; Van der Steur, 'Johan van Duvenvoirde', pp. 258–64.

property in Warmond; but these fluctuations were also caused by the accidents of birth and death, and the much less accidental factor of marital choice. As a result of marriages and inheritances, the lords of Warmond regularly gained control of properties spread over the entire country. In their testaments they often bequeathed lands in the patrimonial manor of Warmond to the eldest son, and other lands to the younger children.[40] Each successive lord of Warmond owned a number of widely distributed lands, which differed in their constitution and extent. If we wish to eliminate these genealogical accidents, we should consider only their possessions in Warmond. Between 1590 and 1606 Johan van Duvenvoirde, lord of Warmond, spent no less than 50,000 *gulden* for the purchase of landed property, life annuities and reimbursable rents.[41]

Gerrit VIII, lord of Poelgeest, whose castle stood in Koudekerk, owned 38 *morgen* of land in that manor in 1544. In 1600 his grandson Gerrit X van Poelgeest owned 83 *morgen*. In 1648 in turn his grandson Gerrit XII held only 37 *morgen* in Koudekerk, but genealogical circumstances mask the total ownership of the family here. The family owners in 1648, namely the lord of Poelgeest, his two unmarried aunts and the lord of Valckenes, who was married to a cousin of his father, held altogether 134 *morgen*. Thus the landownership of the van Poelgeests had further increased between 1600 and 1648 by more than 60 per cent.[42] In addition, the lords of Poelgeest acquired land in Esselikerwoude. In 1543 they owned 32 *morgen* there, in 1604 37 *morgen*, and in 1644 48 *morgen*.[43] The last lord of Poelgeest, Gerrit XII (ca. 1625–78), did indeed come into financial difficulties, which meant that after his death his widow had to sell the manors of Koudekerk and Poelgeest in order to pay his debts.[44]

Nicolaas van Mathenesse (post 1508–64), the second son of Johan van Mathenesse, had inherited his non-patrimonial possession in Lisse. In 1544 he and his mother together owned 45 *morgen* in that manor. In 1592 his only son Johan owned 100 *morgen* there; in 1625 this complex of lands had grown to 123 *morgen*.[45] Both Nicolaas and Johan van Mathenesse bought much land in Lisse.[46] But they also bought land in other Rijnland manors: four parcels (6 *morgen*) in Noordwijk in 1604, five parcels (15 *morgen*) in Aalsmeer in 1596, etc.

Various nobles also expanded their landownership in Noordwijk. The most important noble landowners in this manor were members of the Van den Bouchorst family. In 1542 Adriaan van den Bouchorst owned twenty parcels

[40] Van der Steur, 'Johan van Duvenvoirde', pp. 264–7.
[41] Ibid., p. 212. It is possible that the lord of Warmond was investing prize moneys he had received as admiral of Holland.
[42] AH Rijnland, Morgenboeken Koudekerk. Cf. genealogical data in *NNBW*, VII, pp. 995–9.
[43] AH Rijnland, Morgenboeken Esselikerwoude. In 1644 the lady of Poelgeest was the owner.
[44] See below, pp. 131–2.
[45] AH Rijnland, Morgenboeken Lisse. ARA, FA Heereman van Zuijtwijck, prov. inv. no. 34.
[46] Cf. land purchases by the lords of Mathenesse, A. M. Hulkenberg, *Het huis Dever te Lisse* (Zaltbommel, 1966), pp. 76–98, and ARA, HA Lisse, inv. no. 6.

with a combined area of 46 *morgen*, which was only slightly more than 1 per cent of the total area of Noordwijk. Shortly after 1600, Amelis van den Bouchorst (d. 1603) owned thirty-three parcels there, with a total area of 64 *morgen*, while his son Nicolaas also owned several parcels. In 1648 the various heirs of this estate owned together forty-two parcels, nearly 76 *morgen* of land. Here, too, noble landownership had increased, by two-thirds in one century.[47] It is exceptional that the lords of the manor of Noordwijk, members of the Van der Does family, owned practically no land there. In 1542 and 1604 they had only one parcel, smaller than one *morgen*; in 1648 the lord of Noordwijk had expanded his possessions to six parcels, altogether a modest 16 *morgen*.[48] Probably this discrepancy between the possession of seigneurial rights and the ownership of land formed the background for the remarkable transaction of 1620, by which Steven van der Does, the lord of Noordwijk, and Nicolaas van den Bouchorst, the lord of Wimmenum, exchanged their manors with each other. The transaction was annulled seven years later, however, by a sentence of the Hoge Raad of Holland. This court of appeal ruled in favour of Caspar van Eussum, who was married to Anna van der Does, sister of Steven van der Does, who had died in the meantime.[49]

These are only a few examples of nobles who increased their land ownership. Careful research in the archives of Rijnland would bring to light many others. Countless contracts of land purchases can also be found in family and manorial archives. The total area of lands owned by the nobles cannot be calculated. Yet the conclusion is inescapable that many nobles were in a position to increase their landed property.

The nobles reserved a portion of the land for their own use. Mostly this land was located close to their houses. Thus about 6 *morgen* of land went with the house at Warmond, and the lord of Poelgeest used 19 *morgen* in Koudekerk in 1600.[50] The lord of Mathenesse used 5 *morgen* near Dever house in Lisse, 4.6 per cent of the land he possessed in this manor. Besides the house, there was a shed, an orchard and a moat.[51] Most noble houses did have an orchard, a kitchen-garden, and a small meadow with some livestock. The produce of these lands found its way to noble tables. In a time of rapidly rising food prices, the

---

[47] AH Rijnland, Morgenboeken Noordwijk. The owners in 1648 were Amelis van den Bouchorst, lord of Wimmenum, with twenty parcels (42 *morgen*); his mother, the lady of Wimmenum, with eleven parcels (14.5 *morgen*); and the heirs of Nicolaes van den Bouchorst, also with eleven parcels (19.4 *morgen*). Furthermore Daniël van den Bouchorst owned nine more parcels, amounting to 24.2 *morgen*.

[48] Ibid.

[49] Repertoria op de leenregisters, ARA, Leenkamer, inv. no. 229, fo. 1052. Cf. Kloos, *Noordwijk*, pp. 119–20.

[50] Staat van het leengoed, bezeten door Jacoba van den Woude (1521), GA Leiden, HA Warmond, inv. no. 67; AH Rijnland, Morgenboeken Koudekerk.

[51] ARA, FA Heereman van Zuijtwijck, prov. inv. no. 34.

harvest of the nobles' own lands had a significance that should not be underestimated.

A second part of the land was let on hereditary leasehold. Most nobles had at least some income from hereditary tenures, always modest sums. The lord of Zuid-Polsbroek received £1 16s. annually from hereditary tenures. In 1555 that was 1.9 per cent of the income of the manor; in 1614, because total revenues had increased, it was only 0.13 per cent. The lord of 's-Heeraartsbergen received £25 4s. from hereditary tenures: in 1528 that was 1.2 per cent of total revenues, in 1626 0.75 per cent.[52] Although this part of the nobles' incomes consisted of fixed sums, their overall revenues were not seriously undermined.

The greatest part of the nobles' land was let on term leases. These terms were not long, mostly five years.[53] Share-cropping occurred rarely if at all in Holland.[54] Every five or six years the conditions of the lease, in particular the price, could be revised. As a result lease prices followed the general tendencies of agricultural prices and nobles could benefit from the upward trend in this period. While an owner often let a piece of land term by term to the same tenant and his heirs there was no sliding transition to hereditary leasehold.[55] The laws regarding land tenure made such a development almost impossible. An edict of 1515, confirmed in 1580, required the making of a new contract for each new term. Moreover it gave the owners the means to take action against tenants who remained in possession of the land against the owners' wishes after the expiration of the leasehold contract. These regulations were reconfirmed in 1658.[56]

A study of farm lease prices in Holland between 1500 and 1650 indicates that landowners were doing very well indeed.[57] Lease prices rose during the entire period, with the exception of 1570–80, when war raged in the countryside of Holland. Between 1530 and 1540, and again between 1580 and 1600, lease prices rose sharply. Between 1500 and 1570, lease prices rose an average of 28 per cent per decade, with the peak increase at 59 per cent between 1530 and 1540. After 1580 lease prices rose an average of 23 per cent per decade. In 1650 the lease price per *morgen* was between ten and fifteen times as high as in 1500. Yet there were remarkable differences in the price levels of various landlords. It is unclear whether these differences were caused

[52] GA Amsterdam, FA De Graeff, inv. no. 433. Valuation of the revenues of farms and rights belonging to the manor of 's-Heeraartsberg (1528), ARA, Archief van de heerlijkheid 's-Heeraartsberg, Bergambacht en Ammerstol, inv. no. 258; Cash book with all revenues in Ammers, 's-Heeraartsberg and Bergambacht (1626), ARA, HA 's-Heeraartsberg, inv. no. 262-a; Accounts of the manor of Niervaart (1563–1652), ARA, Nassause Domeinraad na 1581, inv. nos. 8171–211.

[53] J. Kuys and J. T. Schoenmakers, *Landpachten in Holland, 1500–1650* (Amsterdam, 1981), p. 22.

[54] Ibid., p. 23. A. M. van der Woude, 'Het Noorderkwartier', *AAGB* 16 (1972): 527; C. Baars, *De geschiedenis van de landbouw in de Beijerlanden* (Wageningen, 1973), p. 123.

[55] Kuys and Schoenmakers, *Landpachten*, p. 24.

[56] Ibid.

[57] Ibid., pp. 66–8 and 35–40.

by qualitative differences in the land, or by different leasehold policies. The various price series, however, always display the same trends.[58]

There is no reason to suppose that noble lease prices followed different trends. Few data on the revenues of noble lands over a long period have been preserved. Moreover it is difficult to compare revenues from different years, because there was no uniform method of bookkeeping. Because the name of the land, its size and natural conditions such as the level of the water table could vary continuously, it is seldom possible to build consistent series of lease prices from different accounts. The few cases for which this is possible show a continual increase of lease prices, except during the war years. The revenues of *jonker* Johan van Mathenesse from leaseholds rose between 1580 and 1597 with the average lease price in Holland, if not faster.[59] The leases of two polders in the manor of Niervaart, in the possession of the prince of Orange, stagnated as long as the military front was nearby.[60] After 1600, when the threat of war disappeared, lease prices moved upward. In Zuid-Polsbroek, leasehold revenues declined during the war, but in 1588 they rose again along with the average lease price.[61] The accounts and registers of the lords of Warmond show that they continually raised the lease prices, although the data are insufficient for the construction of price series.[62]

Since prices of raw materials, industrial products and nominal wages also rose strongly during this period, the increase in leasehold revenues does not demonstrate that the purchasing power of the nobles increased accordingly. In order to know the real incomes of nobles, we should have to express lease prices in relation to the prices for commodities that a typical nobleman would have purchased. Yet not enough is known about the consumption pattern of the Holland nobles to construct a typical 'market basket'. Besides, the great differences in prosperity and living standards among the Holland nobles would make this a useless undertaking. The nobles spent money on food for their families and their servants (in so far as their own land did not produce it), on raw materials such as building products, on horses, clothing, furniture, luxury articles and wages for their own staff and day-labourers; but the proportions cannot be determined.[63]

The nobles were partly protected from a fall in purchasing power because a

---

[58] Ibid., pp. 37–9.

[59] Revenues of Johan van Mathenesse from leases, ARA, FA Wassenaer van Rozande, inv. no. XVI-z.

[60] ARA, Nassause Domeinraad, inv. nos. 8171, 8174, 8175, 8177, 8178, 8187, 8196, 8197, 8211.

[61] GA Amsterdam, FA De Graeff, inv. no. 433.

[62] GA Leiden, HA Warmond, inv. nos. 66 and 67; inv. no. 71 (Register of properties at Warmond, 1685–97) and no. 76 (Accounts of Warmond, 1510, 1511 and 1525); *Gegevens betreffende roerend en onroerend bezit* I, pp. 215–18.

[63] The cash book kept by Johan van Mathenesse for six weeks during 1587 shows the expenditures of a Holland nobleman of the period. ARA, HA Lisse, inv. no. 17; pub. by A. M. Hulkenberg, 'Het kasboek van Jan van Mathenesse, heer van Dever, 1587', *LJ* 54 (1962): 50–66.

portion of their leasehold incomes was often paid in kind. The annual revenues of the manor of Warmond came to £609 8s. 6d. at the end of the 1580s; 77.34 per cent of this sum came from leases. But the lord of Warmond also received 'crooked-tail [*cromstaerte*] capons', 'good hams', lambs and birds from a great number of tenants. In one year he thus received 42 capons, 5 hams (and 13 more hams every five years), six lambs and two birds.[64]

THE NOBLES AS SEIGNEURIAL LORDS

As lords of the manors the nobles left a greater mark on the Holland countryside than they did as landowners. While they owned less than 10 per cent of the land in the sixteenth century, they held more than 80 per cent of all manors. Their share declined to around 60 per cent in 1650, but they still remained the largest group of seigneurs.[65] The discrepancy between their influence as landowners and their importance as manorial lords was possible because in Holland their manors were judicial seigneuries (*seigneuries justicières*) rather than landed seigneuries (*seigneuries foncières*).[66] Strictly speaking, a manor or seigneurie was the right to exercise justice in a specified area.[67] In the sixteenth century the seigneurs no longer exercised the right of justice personally. They leased out the office of sheriff and reserved for themselves a portion, generally one-third, of the revenues from fines. Besides the lesser judicial rights, the right of high justice was sometimes also granted in fief. By 'high justice' we mean that the lord had the right to apply the death penalty in capital crimes. If he could only punish for lesser offences, he held 'low justice'. The right of high justice was then reserved to the bailiff of the district in which the manor lay.

Other seigneurial rights might include rights to catch birds and fish, to claim flotsam on the beaches, to hold markets, to keep swans, to claim inheritances of bastards, to establish ferries and tolls, and wind or milling rights. Often a number of other rights that were not actually seigneurial were granted in fief along with a manor. For example, the lord frequently enjoyed the right of nomination or collation to the parish, not as seigneur, but as legal successor to the founder of the church. Although the tithe was not actually a seigneurial right, it was often granted at the same time as the manor. The lords of the

---

[64] Van der Steur, 'Johan van Duvenvoirde', pp. 258–64.
[65] See below, pp. 147, 199.
[66] Van Gelder, 'Bailleul, Bronkhorst, Brederode', p. 49.
[67] De Blécourt, *Ambacht en gemeente*, pp. 6–7. J. V. Rijpperda Wierdsma, *Politie en justitie. Een studie over Hollandschen staatsbouw tijdens de Republiek* (Zwolle, 1937), pp. 149–249. A. S. de Blécourt, 'Heerlijkheden en Heerlijke rechten', *TvR* 1 (1918–19): 45–107, 175–90, 489–519. Van Gelder, 'Hollandse adel', pp. 125–31; A. A. Beekman, *Het dijk- en waterschapsrecht in Nederland vóór 1795*, 2 vols. (The Hague, 1904–7), 1, pp. 66–80.

manor had no automatic right to collect tithes; rather, it had to be stated expressly in the charter granting the fief.[68]

The rights granted with a manor differed from case to case. The lord of Hardinxveld had the right to annul and intervene in land transactions. He collected levies on orphans and houses where auctions of the effects of deceased persons took place. He enjoyed all the revenues from civil cases in the low justice, and one-third of those in the high justice. He collected an annual tax, the *oirtgelt*, and tithes on cereals, hemp, turnips, rapeseed, pulse, lambs, bees and mire. His seigneurial rights included the *gruit*, the right to claim alluvial accretions, fishing rights, the right to keep swans and to catch birds. Finally, the lord had a monopoly on the fulling mill and the windmill.[69]

The lady of Warmond in 1521 held the high and low justice, the scot, fishing, birding and milling rights. At nearby Esselikerwoude she owned the *botting* (a tax), *tijns* or tribute money, and levies on peat and *gruit* in addition to the scot, fishing and birding rights. In Alkemade she owned birding and fishing rights, and a turf tax.[70]

As a result of all these rights, the lord was an important figure in his jurisdiction. It is not necessary to regard the lord as a relentless exploiter of the peasants to realize that the latter were continually confronted with the former, especially in financial matters. Whether the lord resided in the village or elsewhere, allowing a steward to manage his interests, was immaterial. Once a year the peasants had to pay the scot or other ancient taxes. They also paid tribute money on their houses. At every harvest the eleventh sheaf of grain disappeared to the manor-house. From their other crops, legumes, turnips, rapeseed, slaughtered livestock and honey, one-tenth or one-eleventh went to the lord. From the grain that they were required to grind at his mill, he took his portion. The peasants paid excise duties for their beer. The lord demanded his share of every transfer of land. Anyone who wanted to go fishing had to lease the fishing rights from the lord. Unless they had paid him a fee, peasants were forbidden to hunt the birds that pecked at their seed. Nor were they allowed to hunt the rabbits that devoured their harvest. If the villagers violated any of the countless regulations, they were arrested and fined by an officer appointed by the lord; and one-third of the fines went into the lord's pockets. The lord was not merely a representative of governmental authority in his village: rather, governmental authority was in his possession. This gave him power and esteem; it also gave him income.

How important was this income? And could the seigneurial lords increase their income from rights in such a way that they compensated for inflation? In all theories about the economic decline of the nobility, their stagnating incomes

[68] Beekman, *Dijk- en waterschapsrecht*, II, pp. 1559–64.
[69] List of seigneurial rights in Hardinxveld, AH Alblasserwaard, inv. no. 649.
[70] GA Leiden, HA Warmond, inv. no. 67. The *botting* was an old annual fixed levy.

in a time of rising prices occupy a central place. Precisely these seigneurial rights supposedly contributed to the relative impoverishment of the nobility. Many ancient seigneurial levies, such as *botting, bede*, scot and tribute money were fixed amounts that could not be increased.

The reality was more complex. We can divide seigneurial rights into two types. On the one hand, some rights were expressed in fixed amounts of money, which declined steadily in real value as a result of inflation. Yet other rights actually increased in value so much that they partly or wholly nullified the effects of inflation.

Levies such as scot, *botting*, and *lentebede* were never increased. The revenues typically varied between £5 and £15 per manor. Nor were hereditary leaseholds and tribute money increased, but the revenues could grow when the number of taxable farms increased. This was, however, never enough to compensate for inflation. When a levy was expressed in kind, the money value could sometimes be increased. Thus the inhabitants of Zuid-Polsbroek paid a tribute of one capon for each *morgen* of land in the manor. One capon was originally valued at $2\frac{1}{2}$ *stuivers*, but in 1591 the amount was doubled.[71]

The leases of other seigneurial rights, such as the office of sheriff, were periodically raised. This office did not produce much income, however. The lease for the sheriff of Ammers came to £10 in 1528; in 1626, £15; in 1683, £40.[72] The same office at Amstelveen was more profitable: in 1531, £32 4s.; in 1560, £40; in 1590, £115 12s.; in 1619, £150.[73] The revenues from fines collected were also limited. In Zuid-Polsbroek the fines came to £4 10s. in 1555, in 1562 £1 10s. In later years fines are no longer reported in the accounts.[74] In the accounts of Niervaart the revenue from fines was listed year by year only as a formality.[75] The lady of Warmond was probably correct in 1521 when she declared that justice in her three manors cost her more than it brought in.[76]

But there were also rights whose revenues could be increased substantially. The lease of fishing rights was generally very advantageous. Sometimes the fishermen paid only a nominal fee for fishing, as at Bergambacht, where the 'taking of salmon on the Snackaert' brought in $12\frac{1}{2}$ gulden for centuries.[77] Mostly, however, the lord exploited his fishing rights intensively by leasing them to the highest bidder. The income from fishing then rose in line with the

---

[71] GA Amsterdam, FA De Graeff, inv. no. 433.

[72] ARA, HA 's-Heeraartsberg, inv. nos. 258, 260 (revenues from seigneurial rights in Ammers, 1683), 262 (idem), 262-a (cash book with revenues in Ammers, 's-Heeraartsberg and Bergambacht, 1626) and 264 (valuation of 's-Heeraartsberg, Bergambacht and Ammerstol, 1720).

[73] GA Amsterdam, stadsrekeningen 1531, 1560, 1590, 1619.

[74] GA Amsterdam, FA De Graeff, inv. no. 433.

[75] ARA, Nassause Domeinraad, inv. nos. 8171–211.

[76] GA Leiden, HA Warmond, inv. no. 67.

[77] See above, n. 72.

increasing demand for food, and compensated for inflation. The lord of Hardinxveld leased his fishing rights per parcel to a great number of different lessees.[78] The lease revenues from fishing in the Diemermeer were as follows:

1531	£48 15s.
1560	£102 18s.
1590	£225
1619	£905

Between 1531 and 1590 the revenues more than doubled every thirty years, and in the last thirty-year period the revenues quadrupled.[79]

Another right that produced continually rising revenues was the tithe. As noted, the tithe was not actually a seigneurial right. Yet, because the tithes were often granted simultaneously with the manor, they will be discussed here. Nobles also owned tithe rights independent of their manors. Most tithes were granted in fief, but some were allodial property. Sometimes the lord collected the tithe personally; often he leased the tithe in his manor, in its entirety or in parts. The advantage of doing so was that he could stabilize his revenues to some extent. Tithe revenues could fluctuate greatly from year to year, depending on the harvest and market prices.[80] In any case the owners of tithe rights could take full advantage of rising agricultural prices in Holland. In Zuid-Polsbroek the tithes formed between 16 and 22 per cent of total revenues of the seigneurie (inclusive of land-leases).[81]

It is difficult to draw up a balance sheet. To each seigneurie belonged both rights carrying fixed revenues and rights whose revenues could be increased. The proportions of these two elements varied. As expressed in money, however, rights whose income was stagnant made up a steadily falling share of all estates; this share became relatively less significant as revenues from land and tithes increased. In 1555, for example, the gross income of Zuid-Polsbroek came to 945 gulden. Of this sum 63 per cent had come from land-leases, 17 per cent from tithes and 20 per cent from seigneurial rights. In later years, however, the income from seigneurial rights at Zuid-Polsbroek did not exceed 5 to 10 per cent.[82] In 1521 the revenues from land-leases in Warmond came to £97 17s.; tithes brought in £60, and seigneurial rights £39, or 19.8 per cent of the total revenues of the seigneurie. In 1606 the scot of Warmond still brought in 13 gulden, but the total revenues of the seigneurie had risen to 2,883 gulden.[83] In

---

[78] Revenues from the manor of Hardinxveld (1539–40), ARA, HA Hardinxveld, inv. no. 1.
[79] GA Amsterdam, stadsrekeningen 1531, 1560, 1590, 1619.
[80] This can be seen clearly in the graph in the Dutch edition of revenues from grain tithes at Moerkerken, owned by *jonker* Johan van Raesveld. Tithe records of Moerkerken (1584–1633), ARA, HA Mijnsheerenland van Moerkerken, inv. no. 40.
[81] GA Amsterdam, FA De Graeff, inv. no. 433.
[82] Ibid.
[83] Van der Steur, 'Johan van Duvenvoirde', pp. 253–4.

the manor of Niervaart the imbalance was even more extreme. In 1563 this seigneurie produced the vast sum of 20,535 gulden. Yet justice, rights to bastard-goods, and salvage rights brought in nothing at all; tribute money came to 82 gulden (0.4 per cent of the total revenues); excise duties and *berrygeld* (a market levy) came to 340 gulden (1.6 per cent); fishing and birding 283 gulden (1.4 per cent). Leases on land produced more than 90 per cent of the income of the seigneurie.[84] Since the Holland nobles depended primarily on land for their incomes, and not on seigneurial rights, the stagnation in revenues on a portion of those rights did not threaten their financial position.

THE NOBLES AS OFFICE-HOLDERS

Little is known about the gains nobles derived from offices. Office-holding was the only profession that the nobles regarded as worthy. Not only were offices not derogatory, but they were also consistent with the knightly ideal of service to the sovereign. Feudal ties had lost much of their meaning by the beginning of the sixteenth century, but the growing administrative apparatus of the Habsburgs offered nobles the opportunity to devote their lives to their country and their lord. Yet we cannot determine how significant income from offices was in the context of total income for the entire Holland nobility.[85]

Around 1530 the stadholder received a salary of £2,040, and the next highest office-holder of the province, the president of the Court, received £800. Yet an ordinary judge of the Court earned only £252; an auditor in the Chamber of Accounts, £258. Military offices did not produce much income either: the commander of Gouda, Floris van Assendelft, received £230; Johan van Vliet, the commander of Oudewater, got £150.[86] This was more money, but not overwhelmingly more, than the wages of a master carpenter at Alkmaar, who earned 6 *stuivers* per day; on the basis of 240 workdays per year, that would come to an annual income of 70 gulden.[87] Naturally the salaries of these office-holders do not include their extra emoluments. In the seventeenth century the base salaries of office-holders were still regarded as low.[88]

Many office-holders received no salary at all, but leased their offices. This procedure was customary among officials required to handle accounts. These

[84] ARA, Nassause Domeinraad, inv. no. 8171.

[85] Research on the history of officialdom in the Netherlands is in its infancy. Little is known about conditions of employment, salaries and career prospects. Within the bounds of our study, it is not possible to devote extensive research to this subject. Cf. O. Vries, 'Geschapen tot ieders nut. Een verkennend onderzoek naar de Noord-Nederlandse ambtenaar in de tijd van het Ancien Régime', *TvG* 90 (1977): 328–49.

[86] List of office-holders in Holland and Zeeland (ca. 1530), ARA Brussels, Aud., inv. no. 1184, fos. 54–72 v.

[87] L. Noordegraaf, *Daglonen in Alkmaar 1500–1850* (n.p., 1980), p. 138.

[88] Temple, *Observations*, p. 84.

functionaries paid a fixed sum annually to the Chamber of Accounts. Whatever their office produced in fines, confiscations and other benefits, they kept as their income. It is not known how lucrative these leased offices were in practice.

The emoluments that went with an office were often more important than the actual salary. These emoluments can be divided between fixed sums and variable emoluments, such as a share of the fines levied.[89] Thus the salary of the lieutenant-forester of Holland came to 300 gulden per year. The emoluments consisted of the supply of rabbits from Keukenduin – in 1560 there were 1,200 of them. Each year the villagers of Monster paid a half sack of oats and a sack of peas in recognition of their right to allow dogs to roam freely. Probably for the same reason, the inhabitants of Naaldwijk and Wateringen supplied a sack of wheat; those of De Lier a cask of butter; those of Maasland and Schipluiden two casks of 'red butter'; those of Zandambacht a sack of wheat, and a green and a white sheep's cheese. Half of all fines belonged to the forester; the other half he had on lease. The most significant part of his income was probably formed by several leases of farms located around Teylingen, the forester's official residence.[90] The value of these bits and pieces must have been much more than his salary. When the supply of rabbits from Keukenduin stopped as a result of sand mining, the forester received compensation of 600 gulden per year.[91] Since many emoluments were paid in kind, the office-holder was protected from the effects of monetary inflation.

The functions of dike-reeve (*dijkgraaf*) and polder-councillor (*hoogheemraad*) were also regarded as desirable. Here too the wages were low, but the emoluments were high. Fines were divided equally between the dike-reeve and the polder-councillors. Provincial functionaries had considerable influence in the appointment of lesser officials. In 1642, for example, the steward of Rijnland had to pay 26,000 gulden for his office. The provision of offices in Rijnland was made within the college by rotation, as was the custom among the urban regents.[92] In Delfland, however, the polder-councillors had already been deprived of their share of the fines in 1518, in order to avoid giving the impression that the administration had a vested interest in levying high fines.[93] Henceforth the entire income from fines went to the dike-reeve.[94]

During the Republic, membership in the Ridderschap of the States of Holland and West-Friesland opened the door to many important functions and revenues. In practice only a portion of the noble seigneurs had access to the Ridderschap. In the first half of the seventeenth century membership became

[89] Vries, 'Geschapen tot ieders nut', p. 343.
[90] Van der Steur, 'Johan van Duvenvoirde', pp. 235–6.
[91] Ibid.
[92] S. J. Fockema Andreae, *Het Hoogheemraadschap van Rijnland: zijn recht en zijn bestuur van den vroegsten tijd tot 1857* (Leiden, 1934), pp. 188–9.
[93] T. F. J. A. Dolk, *Geschiedenis van het hoogheemraadschap Delfland* (The Hague, 1939), pp. 101–2.
[94] Ibid., p. 114.

practically hereditary. The intention was to keep the number of eligible nobles small, and thereby to increase the benefits of membership for each.[95]

The Ridderschap appointed the chairman of the Deputized Councils of the Zuiderkwartier; a representative to the States General and to the Council of State; the admiralty colleges; the Chamber of Accounts of the Generality; the College of Curators of the University of Leiden; two judges of the Court of Holland; and two directors of the East India Company.[96] The members of the Ridderschap occupied most of these posts themselves; sometimes they named a noble relative or friend. Furthermore, the nobles were members of countless commissions and embassies.

The combined allowances for members of the Ridderschap amounted to £3,000 per year from 1579 onward. In 1590 this sum was increased to £4,500, 'provided that in all gatherings a sufficient number attend'.[97] That same year the States decided that nobles travelling on official business would receive in addition to travel expenses 4 gulden of *per-diem* remuneration, one guilder more than representatives of the towns.[98] Nobles holding offices in the gift of the Ridderschap also received higher salaries than the urban representatives.[99] The revenues from the former aristocratic convents of Rijnsburg and Leeuwenhorst, which were available to members of the Ridderschap, will be discussed later.[100]

The problem of the income from offices is further complicated because honourable offices sometimes cost the holders more than they were paid in salary. It is difficult to reconstruct to what extent these offices had a positive or a negative balance. For example, military officers advanced the pay of their troops and had to hope their money would be reimbursed. This practice of delayed payment led the officers to borrow funds from *solliciteurs*, and to compensate themselves by maintaining fictitious rolls listing many more troops than their actual strength. At one point during the war against Spain the States army, nominally consisting of 80,000 men, actually had only 60,000.[101] Many servants of the administration were expected to maintain a high standard of living, appropriate to the respect due to their offices. In particular the Dutch ambassadors abroad had to bear heavy costs. Gideon van den Boetzelaer (1569–1634), the ambassador in France, reckoned that the States General owed him

---

[95] R. Fruin, *Geschiedenis der staatsinstellingen in Nederland tot den val der Republiek*, ed. H. T. Colenbrander (2nd edn, The Hague, 1922), p. 234; Aitzema, *Saken*, v, p. 857; Van Zurck, *Codex Batavus*, p. 247.

[96] ARA, Ridderschap, inv. no. 73; *Hedendaagsche historie*, IV, pp. 99–100.

[97] Fruin, *Staatsinstellingen*, p. 233; *Res. Holland*, 20 Jan. 1590.

[98] Van der Houve, *Hantvest*, p. 22.

[99] A. J. C. M. Gabriëls, 'De Edel Mogende Heeren Gecommitteerde Raaden van de Staaten van Holland en Westvriesland, 1747–1795', *TvG* 94 (1981): 527–64.

[100] See below, pp. 120–5.

[101] P. B. de Troeyer, *Lamoraal van Egmont. Een critische studie over zijn rol in de jaren 1559–1564 in verband met het schuldvraagstuk* (Brussels, 1961), p. 16.

£37,489 2s. 8d. for the years 1619 to 1621 inclusive. His salary had just been reduced from 12,000 to 9,000 gulden, and he complained that it was 'impossible to maintain his onerous household in such an expensive and brilliant court on such a small salary of IX m £, without falling into considerable debt and thereby consuming his own patrimony'.[102] He budgeted his annual expenses for rent, household fuel, maintenance of horses and carriage, clothing and livery for himself and his family, food and wages for his servants at 14,720 gulden. To his 'train' belonged himself, his wife and his three sons, two ladies in waiting, a secretary and a clerk, a steward, a nobleman, a chamberlain, a coachman, a groom and six horses (*sic!*), a cook and kitchen boy, a porter, two pages, four lackeys and three maids – in all, 26 persons.[103]

All things considered, it is not possible to establish how much the nobles gained or lost from office-holding. Everhard van Reyd wrote around 1600 that the country 'overflowed with money and goods, and all who were in offices and government, could become rich, if they wished it'.[104] There is no reason to doubt his judgment; some nobles certainly knew how to take advantage of their opportunities.

THE NOBLES AND LAND RECLAMATION

Because the practice of trade or commerce caused a loss of noble status, the nobles of Holland were seldom involved in capitalistic enterprises on a grand scale. The oldest register of stock-holders of the Amsterdam Chamber of the Dutch East India Company does not contain the name of even one Holland nobleman.[105] The only enterprises in which the nobles played a significant role from their inception were the land-drainage projects. Holland nobles probably were among the first to occupy themselves with these projects in the sixteenth century. In 1566 Lamoraal van Egmond began the drainage of the Alk-

---

[102] 'Staat van onkosten van den heer van den Boetzelaer van Langerak gemaakt als afgezant in Frankrijk 1619–1622', ed. F. H. C. Drieling, *Kron HG* 5 (1849): 15–18.

[103] Ibid., p. 18.

[104] Cited by A. T. van Deursen, *Het kopergeld van de gouden eeuw*, 4 vols. (Assen, 1978–9), III, p. 11.

[105] J. G. Van Dillen, *Het oudste aandeelhoudersregister van de Kamer Amsterdam der Oost-Indische Compagnie* (The Hague, 1958). The few noble names listed belong to persons who had long been integrated into the merchant class: Jacob van Alckemade, merchant and soap-boiler of Amsterdam; Dirck Jacobsz. van Foreest, probably the father of an Amsterdam merchant (ibid., pp. 146, 226; Elias, *Vroedschap*, I, p. 105). Adryaen van der Myle, who registered for ƒ 3,600 of shares, must have been a relation of Arend Cornelisz. van der Myle, who was raised to the nobility in 1570. His son Adriaan van der Myle had already died in 1590, however. The lack of Holland nobles is all the more remarkable because nobles were among the participants at Utrecht, although they invested relatively modest sums (Van Dillen, *Aandeelhoudersregister*, p. 48). Participation in the Dutch East India Company was evidently not regarded as derogatory; the structure of this venture was so modern that the participants were not considered merchants, but rather financiers.

maardermeer.[106] Likewise, in the Noorderkwartier, Hendrik van Brederode took on the drainage of the Bergermeer. The investment evidently brought grist to his mill. While he tarried over his polder projects, he wrote to Louis of Nassau in 1566: 'I well understand that the good Lord is one of our Beggars. He has sent me the sum of 300,000 florins which will be, my brother, at your service . . .'[107]

The count of Egmond was actively involved in the diking of new land south of the Oude Maas river. He named these new lands the Beijerlanden, after his wife Sabina van Beijeren.[108] He often attended meetings where the plans for dike building were discussed, and he personally designed the plans for opening up the polder.[109] It is possible that Egmond expedited the polder works in conjunction with his own financial difficulties. As soon as the works had been completed, he borrowed large sums of money, using the new land as collateral.[110] Soon afterwards he was no longer the only landowner in the Beijerlanden. In 1556 he received permission to sell a portion of the land in the diked area, because otherwise he would not be able to pay the costs of dike building. It was customary in the sixteenth century for a landowner to sell his saltings while retaining the seigneurial rights and tithes. The astute steward of the Prince of Orange at Steenbergen, Andries Vierlingh, who wrote a standard work on dike building, remarked that 'it is much more secure and more profitable for the owner of the said salt marshes, in so far as he holds the seigneurial rights and tithes, to let them at a reasonable hereditary lease or annual sum or term of payment after the first harvest, rather than to repair them himself, build dikes and await the perils and adventures aforesaid, in particular for princes and lords . . .'.[111]

Although the involvements of Egmond and other nobles were substantial, they did not act primarily as landowners. Their activities were based on their position as manorial lords. The count of Egmond retained for himself the right to name polder-officials, not as the landowner, but as seigneur. Vierlingh did not agree on this point, because he questioned the expertise of the nobles and the polder-officials they appointed. In this manner, he wrote, persons were employed 'who have never seen water . . . our prosperity and our land depend on a slender silk thread, and what is worse: they believe that their authority would be lessened and thus they do not want to be instructed; before they begin to learn they cost the landholders lots of money'.[112] Egmond, however, did take the advice of the landholders on the appointment of polder-officials.

[106] W. C. Mees, *Lamoraal van Egmond* (Assen, 1963), pp. 17–18. According to De Vries, *Dutch Rural Economy*, p. 193, the first polder works in the Noorderkwartier began in 1561.
[107] Archives, 1st series, II, p. 130. These 300,000 gulden probably refer to the extent of his entire fortune. 'Geu du tout' means completely devoted to the rebels.
[108] Baars, *Beijerlanden*, p. 12.
[109] Ibid., p. 29.   [110] Ibid., p. 31.
[111] Ibid., p. 29.   [112] Ibid., p. 30.

As seigneurial lords the lesser Holland nobles also had an interest in polder administration. Their manorial jurisdiction sometimes included rights to salt-marshes, holms, and mud-flats. If they could exploit these additions to their lands, their theoretical rights were transformed into financial interests. Thus the accounts of the manor of 's-Heeraartsbergen note revenues from osiers, alders, grasses and reeds from various accretions. An account from 1528 mentions 'a new accretion in the River Lek, which could be planted profitably'.[113]

Some nobles also invested in more speculative drainage projects. Johan van Duvenvoirde, lord of Warmond, took part in 1608 in the drainage of the Beemster through the purchase of two parcels of 25 *morgen*. To obtain the ready money, he first had to liquidate a loan in favour of a benefice at Roelof-arendsveen and a prebend on a house at Warmond. The total capital of 123 investors came to 1,492,500 gulden. Almost immediately the investors received an annual income of nearly 17 per cent.[114]

A comparable enterprise involving the lord of Warmond was the mining of sand (*afzanding*) at Keukenduin. As lieutenant-forester of Holland, Warmond had a direct interest in the project because he received a portion of the revenues from the dune. The Holland nobleman Johan van Beijeren van Schagen was among the participants in this project, while others such as Andries van Thienen, the bailiff of Noordwijkerhout, 'jonkheer' Willem van Oudshoorn, Gerard van der Laen and Johan van Sypesteijn also had more or less aristocratic backgrounds.[115]

This sort of activity remained marginal, however. Nobles who had money to invest – and there were many – preferred to invest in land, tithes or seigneurial rights; or they bought financial paper. Consequently the nobles did not contribute to the flourishing of trade and industry in the Golden Age of Holland, except perhaps as consumers.

THE NOBLES AND THE SECULARIZATION OF CHURCH PROPERTIES

Did the Holland nobles profit from the confiscation of church properties after the Reformation? H. A. Enno van Gelder said that it was 'slander' to attribute an economic motive to the Holland nobles who participated in the Compromise of the Nobility,[116] but reports that the nobles enriched themselves at the expense of the church are so persistent that we cannot ignore them here. The problem consists of two independent questions. To what extent was the *prospect* of personal enrichment by means of the possessions of the church a motive for

---

[113] ARA, HA 's-Heeraartsberg, inv. no. 258.

[114] Van der Steur, 'Johan van Duvenvoirde', p. 241; De Vries, *Dutch Rural Economy*, pp. 193–4.

[115] The lord of Warmond was also involved in Willem Barentsz.'s 1594 voyage in search of a northern passage to the Indies, but that was probably in his capacity as admiral and not as speculator. Van der Steur, 'Johan van Duvenvoirde', pp. 240–1.

[116] Van Gelder, 'Hollandse adel', p. 121.

the rebellious nobles in 1566 and 1572? And to what extent did they *really* profit from it after the Reformation?

The first question is difficult to answer. Perhaps some did cast a covetous eye on the possessions of the church. Foreign examples were certainly not unknown in the Low Countries. Attitudes toward the temporal power of the church changed during the sixteenth century, among Catholics as well as Protestants. In 1536 King Henry VIII of England had secularized the monasteries for the benefit of the Crown. He sold their lands below market value, and the gentry were the first to reap the gains.[117] As a result of religious wars in Germany, ecclesiastical properties also came into the hands of the nobility. Why would it be impossible for similar things to happen in the Netherlands? Some contemporaries thought that the prospect of material gain was partly responsible for the grievances of the nobles in 1565 and 1566. Pontus Payen reported that

some persons of good judgment who have carefully considered the views actually held by some seigneurs and gentlemen of the court and their behaviour . . . were of the opinion that the most impoverished [of them] had cast their eye on the great possessions of the Church. Because these wonderful managers who had so wisely governed the affairs of their own houses, had no other proposal to suggest than to reform the rich abbeys.[118]

Christoffel d'Assonleville, a member of the Secret Council, held a more nuanced view. Under the cloak of the Petition of 1566 there were, he thought, three kinds of people. Some really wanted to get rid of the Inquisition and the edicts against heresy; others were indifferent on the question of religion. But there were also some 'who in all likelihood wanted to change the prince, sack the churches and pillage the rich, and to accomplish this used the Spanish Inquisition as a pretext'.[119] According to the Franciscan Brother Cornelis, the 'shabby squires' wanted only to enrich themselves: 'Bah, if only they had the church property, the priests' property, and the monasteries' property of these lands also in their claws!'[120]

It is difficult to make a judgment. In every polarized difference of opinion, parties attribute low motives to their opponents. These frequently cited accusations by the royalist party are not supported by other sources. Consequently there is little reason to emphasize the material motive, as some historians have done.[121] We can join in the judgment of Payen and d'Assonleville: among some noble rebels the hope of acquiring church property may have played a role.

[117] S. T. Bindoff, *Tudor England* (Harmondsworth, 1967), pp. 114–16, 136.

[118] Payen, *Mémoires*, I, p. 31.

[119] *Correspondance du Cardinal Granvelle*, ed. E. Poullet and C. Piot, 12 vols. (Brussels, 1877–96), I, pp. 222–3. Cf. Cornelissen, *Waarom zij geuzen werden genoemd*, p. 81.

[120] Cited by Cornelissen, ibid.

[121] Erich Kuttner, *Het hongerjaar 1566* (3rd edn, Amsterdam, 1974), pp. 65–73, and to a lesser degree Geyl, *Stam*, I, p. 211, and Rogier, *Eenheid en scheiding*, p. 34.

Thereby the Compromise of the Nobles is by no means reduced to a revolt of 'shabby squires'.

More important is the question of whether such enrichment actually occurred after the Reformation. The States of Holland quickly brought all ecclesiastical properties under the management of a foundation, with the intention of paying the salaries of Protestant preachers from its funds. At first glance there are no grounds for assuming that the nobles enriched themselves at the expense of the church. In actuality the situation was more complex, however, and that is why the rumours remained current.

In the first place there was the incidental embezzlement of various church possessions, which had already occurred before 1572.[122] In 1567 the priest of Langerak made a deposition against the lord of the village, Wessel van den Boetzelaer (1529–75), who with his family had forced the Reformation on his unwilling subjects in 1566, and had 'purified' the church of its images.[123] Eight or nine years previously, Wessel as collator of the church had already seized 34 *morgen* of land from two vicarages, and furthermore had sold 7½ *morgen*. This happened against the will of the community, and only with the consent of the churchwardens of Nieuwpoort. Besides the priest, the church then had no other persons in its service. Moreover the lord's steward, who was also churchwarden to boot, had forbidden the peasants to pay the priest.[124] Now it is true that the Van den Boetzelaers were notorious supporters of the Reformation, and it is not surprising that Lord Wessel showed little respect for the possessions of the church, even before 1566. Yet nobles who remained faithful to Rome also profited from ecclesiastical properties both before and after the Reformation. This does not necessarily point to cynical opportunism among these nobles: even among nobles who finally chose to remain within the mother-church, more modern attitudes toward its temporal power were gaining ground at this time. That some of them lined their own pockets does not prove that they were devoid of religious conviction. One of these Catholic nobles was the lord of Warmond, who according to a visitation report had gradually stolen the properties of the chapel of Roelofarendsveen, and those of the chapel of Rijnsaterwoude as well.[125]

After the rebel States of Holland had taken over authority, the chances to profit from ecclesiastical possessions increased. The States complained in 1574

---

[122] The opinion of the Catholic historian L. J. Rogier, that 'a decadent nobility *became bent on* a more or less cautious alienation of funds for the maintenance of priests, vicars, and deacons', is certainly exaggerated: *Eenheid en scheiding*, p. 45 (emphasis mine).

[123] See below, pp. 190–1.

[124] A. van L[ommel], 'De kerkelijke toestand der gemeente Langerak in den Alblasserwaard A° 1567, 27 jan.', *BGBH* 10 (1882): 441. Cf. A. C. Duke, 'An inquiry into the troubles in Asperen, 1566–1567', *BMHG* 82 (1968): 207–27.

[125] L. J. Rogier, *Geschiedenis van het katholicisme in Noord-Nederland in de 16de en 17de eeuw*, 3 vols. (Amsterdam, 1946–8), I, p. 19.

that many collators, primarily nobles, recovered the lands that had been granted by their ancestors for benefices and vicarages. Three years later they again expressed the suspicion that many ecclesiastical properties, despite the order for registration, had been improperly seized.[126] Yet some nobles also profited from the possessions of the old church in legal ways. In 1577 the lord of Warmond, Johan van Duvenvoirde, asked the States if he might use the remnants of the monasteries in Warmond, which had been burnt during the siege of Leiden, in order to restore his house, which had been destroyed at the same time. Simultaneously he asked if he might make the land on which the monasteries had stood suitable for agriculture, and enjoy the fruits. Van Duvenvoirde had been appointed as steward of the ruined Warmond monasteries four years earlier by the States, and thus may have increased the chances that they would look favourably upon his request. In any event, the States responded positively, 'in view of the great damage that Van Duvenvoirde has suffered for the common cause'.[127]

A short time afterwards the mother of the lord of Warmond asked if she might purchase the ground on which the monasteries had stood, and live there. In 1584 the States decided that she would get the land for nothing, because her ancestors had given the land to both monasteries. This was analogous to the fact, declared the States, that land belonging to urban cloisters had been given to the towns. Thus the monastic properties of Warmond came into the possession of the Van Duvenvoirde family. Extraordinary circumstances (the lord's merits as admiral of Holland) and the fact that the ancestors of the petitioner had given the land to the monasteries played a part here. We shall note both factors again in all transfers of ecclesiastical properties to nobles.

Arend van Dorp (ca. 1530–1600), 'because of his great possessions called the rich Dorp' by contemporaries, was one of the nobles who profited on a large scale from the Reformation and the seizure of ecclesiastical properties.[128] As younger son of an impoverished noble family, he had to take on various occupations in order to support himself. He was an accomplished financier and was able to acquire a great fortune by dubious transactions. He had begun his career as steward of the marquis of Vlissingen and Veere, Maximilian of Burgundy. Later, in the service of the count of Aremberg, he became bailiff of Zevenbergen. His fortunes improved when he was appointed curator of the estate of the marquis of Vlissingen and Veere. By creative accounting he was able to extract large sums from the inheritance, with which he purchased manors, farms, and a house in Mechelen – which he had furnished richly at a

---

[126] J. F. van Beeck Calkoen, *Onderzoek naar den rechtstoestand der geestelijke goederen in Holland na de Reformatie* (Amsterdam, 1910), pp. 160 and 53; *Res. Holland*, 12 Nov. 1574 and 17 April 1577.
[127] Van der Steur, 'Johan van Duvenvoirde', p. 225.
[128] The following material is based on Van Dorp, *Brieven*, I, pp. xiii–xlix; cf. Van der Aa, *Biographisch woordenboek*, s.v. Arend van Dorp.

cost of 10,000 gulden. The lord of Cruijningen, one of the creditors of the estate, asserted that Van Dorp had cheated the creditors as a group of more than 387,700 Flemish pounds, an enormous sum. Over time, however, Van Dorp found it increasingly difficult to hold off his creditors. The Revolt thus came to him as a godsend.

In 1565 and 1566 he had remained more or less on the sidelines, and in 1568 he offered help to Orange so cautiously that he escaped the notice of the duke of Alba. In the beginning of 1572 Van Dorp was informed that Orange was again planning an armed invasion of the Netherlands. Yet the lack of money prevented him from raising an army. Shortly before, Van Dorp had sold several farms for 25,000 gulden. At Antwerp he borrowed 10,000 gulden with the bond he had received as security for these properties. With this sum he travelled to meet Orange at Dillenburg. He arrived just in time in order to convince the assembled German generals, who had little faith in Orange's financial soundness. But Van Dorp was not a man to put down his money without some interest and some conditions. In exchange he desired that, once the prince had arrived in Brabant, he would conquer Mechelen first. The accounts Van Dorp had already presented were kept at the Great Council in Mechelen, and in his own house Van Dorp held the papers of the estate of the marquis of Vlissingen and Veere. It was in his interest to make a large part of both archives disappear. Strategic objections by Orange – the city of Mechelen was supposedly too far inland – were brushed aside by Van Dorp. That Arend van Dorp succeeded in his plan is clearly seen in the fact that the publisher of Van Dorp's letters found numerous papers relating to the estate – which he could not have had in his possession if he had not brought them from Mechelen to Holland. The lord of Cruijningen also was able to show in a later trial that Van Dorp had made use of some papers that he had earlier sent to the Great Council – and which should, therefore, have been kept in Mechelen. After the success of the Revolt in Holland, Van Dorp continued his dishonest but profitable practices there. In his capacity as superintendent of provisions, he was repeatedly and probably with good justification accused of having converted to his own use moneys belonging to the intendancy. At the same time he purchased ecclesiastical properties at low prices either from the States, who sold them out of financial necessity, or from the owners, who were glad to get even a low price and thereby escape complete confiscation.[129]

In 1574 the States of Holland compensated Van Dorp for the 10,000 gulden he had earlier lent Orange as well as for a second loan of 6,000 gulden, by granting him ownership of the monastery of Engelendaal and several other religious properties in Leiderdorp, altogether 134 *morgen* of land.[130] Owing to

---

[129] Van Dorp, *Brieven*, I, p. xliii.

[130] J. B. J. N. de van der Schueren, 'Eenige mededeelingen omtrent het regulieren-convent en andere geestelijke goederen onder Leijderdorp', *BGBH* 10 (1882): 210–39.

the siege of Leiden, these properties were then flooded and brought little revenue. Van Dorp had the monastery torn down and sold the building materials. In 1577, however, Van Dorp's ownership rights were contested by two of the former owners of the farms, the commander of the Teutonic Order in Haarlem and the churchwardens of Leiderdorp; and the commander's claim was based on the relevant terms of the Pacification of Ghent. It is noteworthy that the peasants overwhelmingly opposed Van Dorp in this conflict. Many of them refused to pay him rent. When the lease contracts had to be renewed, only one prospective tenant presented himself, and the public auction of the lease could not take place. Eventually the States of Holland passed judgment in favour of the Commandery of Haarlem. After many protests Van Dorp relinquished the religious properties in Leiderdorp, and the States had to repay him the borrowed money with interest, which in the meantime had risen to 19,000 gulden. Van Dorp was allowed to keep the revenues already collected, some £2,100 or £2,200.

For many reasons Arend van Dorp was not representative of the Holland nobility. The circumstance that he came from an impoverished family and had to pursue an occupation, as well as his financial improprieties and their extraordinary success, set him apart. But his case shows that in the early years of the Revolt it was possible to take advantage of the uncertain situation surrounding ecclesiastical property.

He was not the only one. An irreproachable nobleman such as Johan van Wassenaer, lord of Duvenvoirde, bought the manor of Voorschoten from the properties of the prince de Ligne during the Twelve Years' Truce. Because the manor had cost him a great deal of money, he asked the States to allow him to sell a vicarage: the collation right belonged to the manor. The States permitted him to treat the properties of the vicarage as allodial lands.[131] Likewise the States allowed the curator of the estate of the bankrupt lord of Cruijningen 'to sell vicarage properties as allodials in view of the great decline of the house of Cruyningen'.[132]

Many other cases could be cited, but they do not justify the charge that the nobles systematically seized ecclesiastical property. In two situations, however, a systematic transfer of religious properties to the nobility did occur: first, at vicarages where nobles held collation rights; and second, at the aristocratic convents of Rijnsburg and Leeuwenhorst, which came under the administration of the Ridderschap.

Disputes over the vicarage properties continued until the end of the Republic.[133] The States passed a regulation in 1578, but it was largely ineffec-

[131] Van Beeck Calkoen, *Rechtstoestand*, pp. 170–1.
[132] Ibid., p. 171. On Cruijningen, see above, pp. 12–15.
[133] For what follows, Van Beeck Calkoen, *Rechtstoestand*, pp. 156–91.

tive owing to the refusal of church patrons, primarily nobles, to observe it – and to the support they enjoyed in the Ridderschap.

In former times many nobles and other landowners had set aside a portion of their properties for the support of a priest, who was required to perform certain religious services. According to the interpretation held by the Ridderschap, most of them had appointed a member of their families to such offices. If no relatives in the priesthood were available, however, others might be appointed. When the Reformation abolished these religious services, the question arose of what to do with these vicarages. Most collators declared that vicarage properties had never been alienated from family ownership. The family had only taken on the obligation to devote these properties *ad pios usus*, but maintained their rights of ownership. Consequently it was purely for them to decide whether some new pious purposes had to be found after the Reformation, or whether the properties would simply return to the family as allodial patrimony. Others argued to the contrary that vicarage properties definitively left family ownership at the moment of foundation, and that the founding family kept only the right to name the holder of the religious office (the right of collation). In the eyes of this party, vicarage properties essentially did not differ from other ecclesiastical properties: thus after the Reformation they should be used for the support of Protestant clergy.

In the first years of the Revolt – and probably earlier as well – many collators decided on their own authority to recover the vicarage properties.[134] In 1575 the States decreed that the revenues from vicarages still had to be given to vicars who had not thrown in their lot with the enemy. Any remainder would serve for the support of ministers and other servants of the Reformed church. Apparently the States were not in a position to enforce this rule, because in 1578 they came to a compromise. The States resolved that one-third of the revenue from benefices and vicarages in the gift of laymen (*de iure patronatus laicalis*) would be devoted to the support of the Protestant clergy. This one-third share (*de tertiën*) had to be paid to the Religious Bureau (*Geestelijk Kantoor*) in Delft, which administered the other ecclesiastical properties as well. Two-thirds of the revenues would remain at the disposal of the collator, but for pious purposes, 'for relief, support of boys or school-pupils, or otherwise *ad pios usus*'. In practice, the remaining two-thirds of the vicarage revenues thus became scholarships.

The nobles fought vigorously against this regulation. In their eyes the vicarages had been founded in the first place for the benefit of members of their families, who were required to perform religious services to boot. When the distinction between religious and lay persons ceased to exist as a result of the Reformation, and simultaneously Roman Catholic services were forbidden, the

---

[134] *Res. Holland,* 12 Nov. 1574.

only remaining purpose of the vicarage properties was the support of a family member. Therefore most nobles did not obey the resolution of 1578 and disposed of the properties as they thought best. Attempts to solve the question in a 'friendly' manner led to deadlock. To force the issue, the States threatened to haul resisting nobles before the Court of Holland. Apparently matters never went so far, because as late as 1658 it was necessary to summarize the resolution of 1578 in a new proclamation.

In 1622 the parties again attempted to reach agreement. The existing vicarages would be liquidated, with the payment of the one-third share (*tertiën*) in one lump sum for the support of the Protestant ministers. In exchange the requirement that the rest of the revenue had to be spent *ad pios usus* would be abolished. But on this occasion also the issue was not settled.

In 1657 the States once again tried to establish a more satisfactory settlement. The Protestant ministers were demanding increases in their salaries, and the Religious Bureau in Delft was hard pressed. In a resolution the States confirmed the regulation of 1578, but the nobles raised such an outcry that the proclamation was scrapped. A decision was indefinitely postponed.

Thus the old state of affairs continued until the end of the Republic. The regulation of 1578 was not entirely ignored. The *tertiën* were collected, although with difficulty and by no means everywhere. In a number of cases the remaining two-thirds share was used for scholarships or other pious purposes. But on the whole the nobles had recovered a portion of their capital, which their ancestors had previously alienated for benefices or vicarages. In this regard the nobles did profit materially from the Reformation.

Similar reasoning was applied by the nobles to the aristocratic convents. When the States wanted to raise cash in 1581 and sell several parcels of former convent property, the Ridderschap protested because in their opinion these lands were destined 'for the support of children of impoverished nobles'.[135] The nobles thought that the counts and countesses of Holland in former times had specially founded these convents for their benefit ('for the honour of God and support of Noble daughters'), because the nobles had always served the lords of the land with deeds and counsel.[136] The ancestors of the Holland nobles had also richly endowed the convents. The nobles thus regarded these houses in the same way as the vicarages, family possessions which did indeed have a pious purpose yet had to be used for their primary goal, the support of noble daughters. The Reformation had caused the pious purpose to disappear, since the cloistered life was now regarded as contrary to the word of God. The care of unmarried noblewomen was now the sole remaining purpose.

Unlike in the matter of the vicarage properties, here the Ridderschap received full satisfaction. Besides the support of Wiliam of Orange, the cause

---

[135] Van Beeck Calkoen, *Rechtstoestand*, p. 234. [136] Ibid., p. 235.

may have been that the religious aspect of cloistered life at the aristocratic convents had gradually faded into the background. These convents had developed into aristocratic communes, where unmarried noblewomen could live a pleasant life among their social peers, only barely separated from the world. It may be doubted whether the cloisters were specially destined for daughters of *poor* nobles. More likely, poverty was a relative concept here. Nobles who had too many daughters to marry them all with respectable dowries to suitable candidates could deposit their surplus offspring in an aristocratic convent. These girls did not have to remain behind neglected, nor marry below their station; meanwhile their fathers could keep the family capital more or less intact. According to the nobles, the convents served 'for the relief of noblemen who are burdened with many children, and to the conservation of noble families'.[137] The convents functioned as a safety-valve in the subtle mechanism of the noble marriage market.

This secularized concept of the convent life is strikingly illustrated in a letter from the (Protestant) Cornelis van Aerssen van Sommelsdijck (1600–62), in which he voiced his concerns about marrying off his smallpox-scarred daughters:

Until now the smallpox has not passed us by, and treated my three daughters very graciously, already having placed them out of danger of dying and of increase in ugliness, but because I have a great deal of that *bad merchandise*, I very much doubt, notwithstanding the good opinion that people have of my wealth, if it is sufficient to allow me to get rid of them, but because I belong to a religion that promises no relief whatsoever, and in which our daughters mock the vow of virginity, it will be necessary to see what their grandmother has saved up to settle them properly.[138]

The lord of Sommelsdijck had exceptionally bad luck. His wife bore him sixteen children, of whom eleven belonged to the 'wrong' sex.[139]

Parents often decided very early which daughters were destined for the convent. This made it improbable that religious vocation played a great role. Klaas van Assendelft decided in his testament of 1501 that his youngest daughter Catharina would go to the convent. She received several possessions 'in order with them to be brought to an enclosed convent; of which goods she shall have the usufruct her life long and not longer, and [the goods] shall after her death come back to and be inherited by Gerrit van Assendelft [Catharina's eldest brother] and his heirs . . .'.[140] Thus the capital of the family would remain intact. Yet in this case Catharina herself decided otherwise and got married. At Rijnsburg daughters could be entered at ten years of age.[141] The rule that only

[137] Cited by G. D. J. Schotel, *De abdij van Rijnsburg* ('s-Hertogenbosch, 1851), p. 326.
[138] *Archives*, 2nd series, 5 vols. (Utrecht, 1857–61), V, p. 30 (emphasis mine).
[139] Van Epen, 'Ridderschap', p. 71.
[140] Holleman, *Dirk van Assendelft*, p. 550.
[141] R. R. Post, *Kerkelijke verhoudingen in Nederland vóór de Reformatie van ± 1500 tot ± 1580*

girls with four noble grandparents could be accepted guaranteed that they would be raised according to their family station.[142]

The nuns were not in the slightest separated from the world. The abbess and the nuns from Leeuwenhorst went on a visit to the convent of Warmond and dined there festively; the sisters from Warmond made a return visit and were equally grandly received.[143] In 1540 lord Gerrit van Poelgeest and his wife organized a reception for the sisters from Warmond that was so 'friendly, festive, and lordly with great expense, in such a way, that the convent will never forget it'.[144] The sisters had brought along wine, ham, a half suckling pig or lamb, and two bitterns. Several sisters of the admiral of Holland, Johan van Duvenvoirde, lived in convents in the Southern Netherlands. After the reconstruction of Van Duvenvoirde house, which had been destroyed by the Spaniards, they visited several times during the summers, bringing girlfriends with them.[145]

In 1553 an official enquiry at Rijnsburg revealed that 'the said ladies are often visited by persons from outside and even by their parents and friends who occasionally stay there three four five six days more or less'.[146] The nuns appeared to lead a worldly life: nearly all those questioned admitted that they were accustomed to wear secular clothing and sometimes danced all night long. In particular the recently deceased abbess, Maria Schenck van Tautenburgh, had gone too far. The steward of the convent thought that in general the nuns behaved respectably, but 'that it is none the less true, that the deceased lady abbess was somewhat extroverted and dissolute in her manner of acting, as in making good cheer in her room, dancing and springing and also wearing gold bracelets and jewels on her body, as if she had been a true great princess, by which many persons were scandalized'.[147]

It is not surprising that the Rijnsburg nuns wanted to convert the convent into a lay community (*stift*) or 'college of canonesses'. Nuns had to make a vow of chastity; by contrast residents of a *stift* were free to return to the world and marry.[148] In 1536 the nuns petitioned the emperor Charles V to make the convent into a *stift*.[149] Charles seems to have postponed granting his consent, so

---

(Utrecht and Antwerp, 1954), p. 171. Post also maintains that vocation and suitability were important for admission to a convent, p. 167 ff.

[142] M. Hüffer, *De adellijke vrouwenabdij van Rijnsburg, 1133–1574* (Nijmegen and Utrecht, 1923), p. 187; Schotel, *Rijnsburg*, p. 189.

[143] W. J. J. C. Bijleveld and W. Nolet, 'Het klooster van St Ursula of der Elfduizend Maagden in Warmond', *BGBH* 43 (1925): 40–58, and 45 (1927): 54–76, at 59–60.

[144] Ibid., p. 62.

[145] Van der Steur, 'Johan van Duvenvoirde', p. 208.

[146] 'Actestukken betreffende de verkiezing van vrouwe Elburch van Langerak tot abdis van Rijnsburg in 1553 en eene Informatie, tegelijkertijd gehouden', *BGBH* 23 (1898): 321–71, at 326.

[147] Ibid., p. 364.   [148] Hüffer, *Rijnsburg*, p. 213.

[149] The text of the request appears in Schotel, *Rijnsburg*, pp. 185–91.

8 W. Crabeth, 'Elburg van den Boetzelaer (?)' (Rijskprentenkabinet, Amsterdam).
Elburg van den Boetzelaer (ca. 1505–68) became abbess of the aristocratic convent at
Rijnsburg, which she had entered at the age of ten. She was a sister of Wessel van den
Boetzelaer, the lord of Asperen, who together with his sons organized the iconoclasm
there.

that the matter was tabled.[150] In 1539, however, the nuns did make an agreement among themselves, by which the rules of the house were relaxed. Whether the emperor ultimately gave his consent or not is of little import: despite their vows, there were always some nuns who left the cloister in order to marry, and at the convent the sisters of Rijnsburg lived more like lay women than like religious.

From a material point of view little changed when Rijnsburg and Leeuwenhorst were placed under the administration of the Ridderschap. The convents had indeed served primarily for the support of noble daughters, and this purpose was maintained. Yet from a Catholic standpoint, there was indeed a loss of property devoted to spiritual purposes and a transfer of ecclesiastical possessions to lay hands, those of the Ridderschap. For the noblewomen beneficiaries, life changed drastically when Rijnsburg and Leeuwenhorst were levelled to the ground during the war. Thereby the communal life ended, although initially several former nuns continued to live in the house of the abbess in Leiden.

In 1581 the abbess of Rijnsburg and several members of the Ridderschap drew up an agreement for the assignment of prebends.[151] Prospective prebendaries of Rijnsburg were still required to prove four quarters of nobility; those of Leeuwenhorst, two. Prebends would be given only to girls between seven and fourteen years of age. At the time of her marriage the girl lost her prebend, but to cover the cost of her wedding gown the payments would be continued for one additional year, provided that the girl had married 'in accord with her state and quality and with the consent of father and mother or close relatives'.[152] The noble young ladies who held prebends were obliged to obey the abbess. Until they reached fifteen years of age, they lived in her house and received an education. Rijnsburg thus became a boarding school for noble girls. To guarantee that the chosen girl would enjoy the fruits of her living, the regulation specified that payments must not be made to parents if 'they had gone into debt by bad management and decline of their property'.[153]

Thus members of the Ridderschap carefully regulated the future of their daughters. But in so doing they did not forget themselves. The two oldest members of the Ridderschap assumed the grand if somewhat anachronistic titles of abbot of Rijnsburg and abbot of Leeuwenhorst, and received 2,000 gulden annually from the convent properties. The next four members were called superintendents of Rijnsburg and Leeuwenhorst and got 500 gulden each.[154]

---

[150] Hüffer, *Rijnsburg*, p. 218; according to Schotel, *Rijnsburg*, p. 191, the change to a lay community did take place.
[151] Schotel, *Rijnsburg*, pp. 326–8; Hüffer, *Rijnsburg*, pp. 263–4.
[152] Schotel, *Rijnsburg*, p. 327.
[153] Ibid.   [154] Ibid., p. 324.

In 1620, after the death of the last abbess of Rijnsburg, the regulation of 1581 fell into abeyance. The girls were now educated in the homes of their relatives. No regard was given to the minimum age: girls aged three and four received prebends. Members of the Ridderschap took turns allocating the prebends to each other's children. In 1581 these payments came to 250 gulden per year, but the former prioress received 360 gulden. These sums were soon increased to 300 and 450 gulden, respectively. In 1629, besides the abbess, twenty-nine women received support. Most collected 500 gulden, but the daughter of the prince of Orange, Emilia of Nassau, who was married and therefore should not have had a prebend at all, received 1,950 gulden.[155] The value of the prebends remained unchanged until 1672. In that year they were reduced to 250 gulden, perhaps because of unfavourable agricultural conditions.[156] In the eighteenth century it was possible to maintain payments at this level, but there were only eighteen noblewomen prebendaries from Rijnsburg, and of those only the twelve oldest received livings. At Leeuwenhorst there were twelve noblewomen prebendaries, and eight of those received livings.

The question of whether the nobles profited from the secularization of ecclesiastical properties thus requires a nuanced answer. The ecclesiastical property of Holland was destined for the maintenance of ministers of the public church, not as a reward for supporters of the Revolt. Yet financial necessity regularly forced the States to sell pieces of land, and in these troubled times some church properties might escape registration and be sold for less than market value: these facts made it possible for speculators such as Arend van Dorp to seize the properties. Only in regard to vicarage properties did the nobles escape from regulations of the States. By not paying the *tertiën* and keeping the remaining two-thirds of revenues – in their own eyes, recovering their own property – they took control of church property. The administrative takeover of Rijnsburg and Leeuwenhorst did mean a transfer of spiritual property to lay hands. In practice, however, not much changed. The ecclesiastical properties had always served as a source of revenues for noble daughters. In theory the pious purposes had been lost, yet in practice they were not much respected before the Reformation either.

Finally, it should be noted that most accusations of intended or actual theft of ecclesiastical properties are not based on evidence, but only upon the supposed poverty of the nobles. As the commonly held reasoning goes, they were poor, and thus they probably took advantage of ecclesiastical properties. This applies both to contemporaries such as Brother Cornelis and historians such as Geyl and Rogier. The entire theory of the impoverishment of the nobility, however, rests on insufficient evidence. Consequently the most important grounds for accusing nobles of plundering the church fall away.

---

[155] Ibid., p. 328.   [156] Ibid., p. 330.

DEBTS

It is likely that farms, tithes and seigneurial rights gave the nobles enough income to live comfortably. Yet there are too many reports of debts and even bankruptcies of nobles to pass over this subject in silence. Precisely on this point the optimistic interpretation of H. A. Enno van Gelder has been criticized.[157] The incomes of the nobles must be related to their expenditures.

Balanced against the incomes of the nobles stood a great number of fixed expenses. Lodewijk van der Werve, for example, held the manor of De Werve in fief, with 160 *morgen* of land, worth 300 gulden per year. The annual charges against the estate included £25 for his mother, £42 for the wife of Jan van der Werve, 35 *andriesguldens* for the heirs of Engelram de Jonge and 46 gulden for Jacob van Domburch. Furthermore, there was provision for a 'perpetual mass' costing 20 gulden from his estate.[158] In 1544 the manor of 's-Heeraartsberg had the following charges: a perpetual rent of £6 to the emperor, a reimbursable rent of 61 gold gulden in the name of Gielis van Zoutelande; and 20 *schilden* (écus) or 14 gulden to Jacob Gijsbrechtsz, reimbursable for 210 gulden. To each of his two sisters the lord of 's-Heeraartsberg paid 24 *karolusguldens* annually; to *jonkvrouw* Sibilla of Koningsveld 12 *karolusguldens*. Another financial obligation of this manor was the contribution of 13 *morgen* of land in the apportionment of Bergambacht and the maintenance of 44 *roeden* of dike and 18 *roeden* of road.[159] The possessions of the lord of Warmond in 1606 were charged with rents with a total value of £316 13s. The gross income that year was £2,883 13s., so that charges amounted to 11 per cent of income. The four sisters of the lord of Warmond (two of whom were nuns at Nivelles in Brabant) received annual pensions. But there were also charges for the lord's nephew and other persons who were not members of the family. The revenues from three parcels of land were destined for the church of Warmond. The steward of the University of Leiden collected 4 gulden per year.[160] The prince of Orange had set aside a portion of the revenues from his manor of Niervaart for the payment of rents and pensions to all kinds of persons in his circle, among others pensions to the widows of deceased officers. In 1610, 6,266 gulden were devoted to this purpose, 22 per cent of the gross income of the manor.[161]

From these examples it appears that the purpose, nature and extent of the charges pressing on the nobles' possessions were so diverse that it is not

---

[157] J. W. Smit, 'Present position', p. 20.

[158] Waarde van lenen (1504), ARA, Archief van de graven van Holland, inv. no. 885, fo. 24.

[159] Letter from Gerolf van Vliet, lord of 's-Heeraartsberg etc. with a list of revenues from 's-Heeraartsberg, Bergambacht and Ammerstol (1544), ARA, HA 's-Heeraartsberg, inv. no. 259.

[160] Van der Steur, 'Johan van Duvenvoirde', pp. 254–5.

[161] ARA, Nassause Domeinraad, 8187. When Maurice accepted the administration of these rich domains, the steward had already freed them of most of their charges. Scherft, *Sterfhuis*, pp. 226–7.

possible to generalize about the burden of debt. Gross revenues, however, tell us little about disposable income.

The lands of the Holland nobles were chiefly burdened with two kinds of obligations. In the first place, there were obligations to members of the immediate family and relations. Mostly this was in the form of a perpetual rent, which was set at a certain share of the capital. Often a testator had bequeathed a great deal of his property to one heir – generally the eldest son – with the obligation to care for his unmarried sisters. Furthermore, part of the property was always set aside to provide support for the widow after the death of her husband. The extent of the charges thus depended on all kinds of coincidental demographic factors. We have to take these obligations into account in calculating the disposable income of a given nobleman at a particular moment, but they play no role in our judgment of the financial position of the nobles as a whole. As long as their sources of income did not dry up, the distribution of incomes among members of the nobility is not important.

Financial obligations to persons outside the nobility, however, belong to another category. Some nobles had borrowed great sums of money, for which they had pledged land as collateral. If they did not reinvest the money they borrowed, repayment of the interest and principal could present such difficulties that it became necessary to sell off some of their property. Thus they were consuming their own capital. In this way the use of consumer credit offered by bourgeois money-lenders could lead to the relative impoverishment of the nobility.

Contemporaries who criticized the wasteful aristocratic lifestyle probably had in mind the high nobles. Lamoraal, count of Egmond, had vast properties, but he saw a large share of his annual revenues disappear into the pockets of his creditors. In 1569 the revenues from Egmond's (confiscated) possessions came to 62,944 gulden, which probably made him the second richest man in the Netherlands.[162] As military commander under Charles V and Philip II, Egmond had high expenses. Not only was he required to live in great state because of his high position, but he had also sometimes advanced the pay of his troops from his own pocket. In February 1566 he mortgaged his properties at Gaasbeek in order to ransom his possessions at Heeze and Leende, which his creditors had already seized more than a year earlier. At the confiscation of his property it became apparent that the revenues were barely enough to amortize his debts.[163] The drainage projects in Holland had served only as a means of getting credit.[164] Lamoraal's youngest son Karel, who lived in the Southern Nether-

---

[162] De Troeyer, *Lamoraal van Egmont*, pp. 15–17; cf. the somewhat different figures in *Gegevens betreffende roerend en onroerend bezit*, I, pp. 15–16: probably £60,375 for Egmond and £152,886 for Orange.

[163] De Troeyer, *Lamoraal van Egmont*, p. 17.

[164] Baars, *Beijerlanden*, p. 31.

lands, took advantage of the Truce in order to sell the Beijerlanden. Yet this did not leave him any cash in hand, because the entire sale price was needed to pay debts. First he had to pay off a mortgage debt of 210,161 gulden, and the rest served to satisfy the creditors of his deceased brother Lamoraal.[165]

Some high nobles lost great sums in gambling. Reinoud van Brederode supposedly played against a burgemeester of Amsterdam in 1529. The latter had bet 3,000 *karolusguldens*, while Brederode laid down his manors of Amstelveen, Sloten and Osdorp, which bordered on Amsterdam. Brederode lost, and Amsterdam acquired the manors.[166] In 1566 Louis of Nassau owed £399 2s. to the count of Hoogstraten; in various card games he had lost £994 to him, and won £594 18s. from him.[167]

Johan van Cruijningen (d. 1559) lived in very grand style at the court in Brussels. In 1549 he borrowed a sum of 40,000 gulden in cash and pledged against it a rent of 250 *karolusguldens* on his manors of Kruiningen, Heenvliet and Hazerswoude.[168] This was the beginning of a financial decline, which continued under his son Maximiliaan.[169] In the service of the States, Maximiliaan had great expenses on various diplomatic missions. His many court cases also swallowed up money. The creditors of his deceased uncle, Maximilian of Burgundy, hindered his installation as marquis of Vlissingen and Veere. In 1591 the States aided his attempts to pay off his debts by paying him a lump sum, but to no avail: he sold his manor of Hazerswoude to Nicolaas van Mathenesse, who was invested with it in 1600.[170] Moreover, the income from his seigneuries was steadily declining – Heenvliet was hit hard by the economic recession and the flood of 1570.[171] After Maximiliaan's death in 1612, it appeared that revenues from Heenvliet, still 2,480 gulden per year, were insufficient to cover the expenses. The curators of the estate then decided to sell the manor. But the estate was so heavily charged with debt, and the financial reputation of the testator was so bad, that no one made an offer: the seigneurie was withdrawn from sale at 180,000 gulden. Not until 1627 did the curators try again to sell it at auction, impelled by the steadily increasing burden of debt. The bidding was opened at 130,000 gulden, but the property was finally sold for only 87,000 gulden; and the proceeds were reduced by 20,000 gulden that had been borrowed from the States. The purchaser was a favourite of the stadholder, Johan van den Kerckhoven Polyander, forester of Holland.[172]

---

[165] Ibid., p. 24.

[166] On this unusual transaction, see E. Smith, 'Koop of spel. Eenige aanteekeningen uit de geschiedenis van den aankoop door Amsterdam der ambachtsheerlijkheden van Amstelveen, Sloten, Sloterdijk en Osdorp van Reinoud van Brederode in 1529', *Jaarboek Amstelodamum* 36 (1939): 39–86.

[167] *Archives*, 1st series, II, pp. 54–6.   [168] 't Hart, *Heenvliet*, pp. 81, 453.

[169] Ibid., pp. 133–85; Van der Aa, *Biographisch Woodenboek*, s.v. Maximiliaan van Cruijningen.

[170] Repertoria op de leenregisters ARA, Leenkamer, inv. no. 229, fo. 893 v.

[171] 't Hart, *Heenvliet*, p. 154.   [172] Ibid. pp. 205, 206.

Roeland Lefebvre, lord of Heemstede, was another financial disaster maker. First he had traded the barony of Liesveld with his uncle for the lands of Aarlanderveen, Oudshoorn and Vrijhoef. Then he sold these possessions to his aunt Anna van Bernemicourt. In 1545 he was so deeply in debt that the Court of Holland ordered the seizure of his goods. Lord Roeland asked for eight days' respite, 'in order to prevent my further expense, damage and scandal',[173] but when the bailiff came the bird had flown. Furniture, small household goods and five horses were seized. The court-ordered sale of these items by public auction brought in so little money that seizure also had to be enforced on his lands, the house and manor of Heemstede. The manor was not sold until 1552, for 18,000 gulden. Roeland van Heemstede continued his resistance for several more years, but in 1557 he agreed to give up his rights. Van Gouthoeven reports that Roeland's wife 'was almost obliged to separate from him because of his great debts that he had made'.[174]

Bad financial management was not a monopoly of the high nobles. 'If the seigneurs of the court were magnificent in banquets, masquerades and foolish expenditures, you can be sure that the majority of the lesser noblemen followed in their footsteps; for the little ones ordinarily ape the great ones', wrote Pontus Payen.[175] Cornelis van Dorp, the grandfather of Arend van Dorp, was forced to sell the manor of Benthuizen. His son Adriaan also had to sell lands, and after the latter's death his widow did likewise. The count of Egmond was the purchaser in this case. Adriaan's son Arend, however, was able to achieve great prosperity once again.[176]

After the death of Cornelis van Swieten in 1544, the guardians of his son Adriaan decided to sell the manor of Zoeterwoude to cover the debts of the estate.[177] Adriaan remained the lord of Swieten, Kalslagen and Schrevelsrecht, but he sold the latter two manors in 1592. He was still enrolled in the Ridder-schap in 1574, and he held the offices of bailiff of Gouda and commander of Woerden.[178] His son, also named Adriaan, sold the remainder of the rights and possessions of Kalslagen in 1602 and had to earn his living as a soldier. Only in 1618, thanks to the *coup d'état* of Prince Maurice, did he receive his seat in the Ridderschap: he was one of the judges of Oldenbarnevelt. Consequently he also gained access to all kinds of offices in provincial administration: for example, he was a curator of the University of Leiden. It is remarkable that the four sisters of this Adriaan van Swieten married non-noble husbands, although these did indeed come from the genteel regent-patriciate.[179] In 1630 his only

---

[173] J. G. N. Renaud, *Het huis en de heren van Heemstede* (Heemstede, 1952), p. 49.
[174] Van Gouthoeven, *Chronyke*, p. 179.
[175] Payen, *Mémoires*, I, p. 29.
[176] Van Dorp, *Brieven*, I, p. xvi.
[177] Brünner, *Order op de buitennering*, p. 167; ARA, Leenkamer, inv. no. 229, fo. 849.
[178] Van Epen, 'Ridderschap', p. 55.
[179] Ibid., p. 10.

son, again named Adriaan (b. 1593), was reportedly living 'in poor and decrepit state'. He did not become a member of the Ridderschap.[180]

The Assendelft family was also beset by financial problems. Klaas van Assendelft (1517–70) complained that he was harassed daily by creditors of his deceased father. Klaas had been eager to get possession of his father's fiefs, which had been denied to him by testament;[181] but in matters of debt he took the position that he was not his father's heir.[182] Yet these threats did not lead to the sale of his lands. His cousin Otto van Assendelft, lord of Goudriaan, likewise declared in 1563 that he 'found himself buried under many debts, made by my late father of blessed memory, so that I have no idea how to pay the same, except to sell my lands'. Otto sold Nieuw-Lekkerland and Streefkerk for 5,000 *karolusguldens* to his cousin Klaas, whose financial problems were apparently not so disastrous as he had made them appear.[183] Yet this transaction did not provide adequate relief. When Otto died in 1569 he left an insolvent estate, and his son Cornelis renounced the inheritance. Shortly afterwards, however, Cornelis became the heir to his father's cousin Klaas, who died childless in 1570, so that Otto's former manors as well as the hereditary possessions of the Assendelfts came into his hands. Consequently he was enrolled in the Ridderschap. But in 1581 the Court of Holland appointed two curators for the bankrupt estate of the late Otto van Assendelft, which led to the public auction of Oud- and Nieuw-Goudriaan. The Holland nobleman Jan van Beijeren van Schagen became the new owner.[184]

Another scion of the same family, Jan van Assendelft, Otto's cousin, in 1594 used his manor of Albrandswaard as collateral for a loan of 11,200 gulden. Two years later he had to sell the manor to the treasurer-general of the United Provinces, Joris de Bye.[185] Yet all of this did not lead the Assendelft family to financial ruin. Until the last male heir died in 1653, they seem to have lived in prosperity.

The Van den Boetzelaer family also suffered from financial problems, but these did not lead to their ruin either. After Floris van den Boetzelaer died in 1574 or 1575, it appeared that he had debts to the heirs of Hendrik van Brederode. The latter tried to collect them from his widow, and indeed in 1583 they even had her held hostage for a few days in Utrecht.[186] She managed to escape and fled to the free territory of Vianen, but there too she soon had to run from her creditors.[187]

---

[180] Ibid. Cf. *NL* 65 (1948): 167, where Adriaan van Swieten appears to have been the standard-bearer of a regiment.
[181] See above, pp. 80–1.
[182] Holleman, *Dirk van Assendelft*, p. 260.
[183] Ibid., p. 173. [184] Ibid. [185] Ibid., p. 279.
[186] J. W. Destombe, *Het geslacht van den Boetzelaer*, ed. C. W. L. van Boetzelaer (Assen, 1969), p. 181.
[187] Van Buchell, *Diarium*, p. 83. Was this perchance because the free manor of Vianen was in the

The great expenses of the Dutch ambassador in Paris, Gideon van den Boetzelaer, have already been mentioned.[188] The ambassador was forced to take a mortgage on his possessions at Langerak, and after his death in 1634 his estate was heavily burdened with debts. His son and heir Rutger Wessel had to sell the manor of Willige-Langerak in 1639. Because this sale did not bring in enough money to pay off his father's debts, in 1642 he sold the house and manor of Langestein with 24 *morgen* of land.[189] These sales did not, however, ruin the family. Rutger Wessel remained lord of Langerak, Carnisse and half of Nieuwpoort, and he remained a member of the Ridderschap of Utrecht.

After the middle of the seventeenth century, the number of sales and bankruptcies among the Holland nobility increased. On account of his debts, Willem van Beijeren van Schagen sold his patrimonial manor of Schagen to the Zeeland nobleman George van Cats for 263,000 gulden in 1658; but in 1676 Floris Karel van Beijeren van Schagen, count of Warfusé, a first cousin of Willem, bought back the ancestral properties.[190]

The Brederodes also came into financial difficulties. The last male Brederode died in 1679. In 1687 his estate was still charged with debts of 488,356 gulden, for which 18,679 gulden in interest had to be paid annually. In addition there was another 8,782 gulden in fixed annual expenses. Against a total of interest and expenses of 27,461 gulden, there was an income from landed property and seigneurial rights of only 21,873 gulden, resulting in an annual deficit of 5,588 gulden.[191]

The extravagant lifestyle of Gijsbrecht van Mathenesse, who died childless in 1670, caused heavy indebtedness on the family properties. His heiress Florentina van Mathenesse and her husband Johan van Hardenbroeck likewise had financial difficulties. In 1686 they were obliged to pledge Oud- and Nieuw-Mathenesse as collateral for loans. After Florentina's death two years later, the property was sold by public auction at Delft. The city of Schiedam took advantage of the situation by purchasing Riviere House, the ancestral castle of the Mathenesses, and the manors of Oud- and Nieuw-Mathenesse, for a total of 13,400 gulden.[192]

The lords of Poelgeest, perhaps because they had remained Catholic, were not enrolled in the Ridderschap. After the death of his father, Gerrit XII van Poelgeest (ca. 1625–78) was invested with the manors of Hoogmade, Koudekerk and Poelgeest. After his mother's death, he received Onzenoord

---

Brederodes' possession? Van Buchell speaks of *debita*; according to Destombe these were gambling debts.

[188] See above, p. 111.

[189] Destombe, *Van den Boetzelaer*, p. 226.

[190] A. W. E. Dek, *Genealogie van de graven van Holland* (The Hague, 1954), p. 66.

[191] Horden, *Vianen*, pp. 92 ff.

[192] Van der Zee, *Matenesse en het Huis te Riviere*, p. 83. Florentina was a sister of the last male heir, Willem van Mathenesse, who died young.

and Nieuwkuik, hereditary properties of the Malsen family. Yet neither his extensive possessions nor his marriage to the daughter of the count of Merode could protect him from financial ruin. He lived in grand style, beyond his means, and he appears to have been a bad financial manager as well. Thus he had to mortgage his lands. His need was so great that he even seems to have embezzled the money of the diaconate that was on deposit in the castle. Accordingly, after his death his widow had to sell his manorial properties to pay the debts of the estate. In 1692 she sold the seigneurie of Koudekerk, the house at Poelgeest and 18 *morgen* of land. Their son Gerrit tried until his death in 1713 to recover the possessions, but without success. Because he was the last male heir, the seigneurie reverted to the States of Holland.[193]

These are only a few examples of financial mismanagement. Some nobles brought themselves to bankruptcy; for others the danger was only temporary. Yet we can draw several general conclusions.

First, it appears that the core of the Holland nobility, the manorial lords who had seats in the Ridderschap, were fairly immune to financial difficulties. In the sixteenth century most reports of excessive debts come from high nobles such as Egmond, Cruijningen and Lefebvre. Lower nobles such as Assendelft and Van den Boetzelaer could also encounter difficulties, but these did not lead to their ruin. The Van Swietens, who had to sell their manors and really do seem to have fallen into poverty, were an exception. The Van Dorp family, which became impoverished in the first half of the sixteenth century, were able to recover thanks to the manipulations of Arend van Dorp.

Only in the second half of the seventeenth century did a greater number of Holland nobles experience problems. It may be supposed that the cause of these difficulties was the declining agricultural conjuncture. If we are to speak of a 'crisis' in aristocratic finances, it must be situated after 1650 and not in the sixteenth century, a period of economic expansion. Noble incomes were for the most part drawn from landownership, and thus were very sensitive to fluctuations in the rural economy.

Yet a number of nobles in the sixteenth and the first half of the seventeenth centuries did come into difficulties. What was the cause? Two types of explanation have been offered for the financial decline of the nobles. The first explanation stresses the lagging tendency of noble incomes. The most important element of this explanation is the lag in relatively fixed incomes in a period of rising prices. The second explanation emphasizes the excessive expenditures of the nobles. Their wasteful lifestyle, the mirror-image of bourgeois frugality, the need to maintain their status and their acceptance of honourable but costly administrative service explain why their expenses exceeded their incomes.

In most cases it is not possible to discover precise details of the how and why

---

[193] *NNBW*, II, pp. 998–9; Regt, 'Groot-Poelgeest', pp. 93–112.

of noble debts. The examples cited, however, appear to fit the second model. Lamoraal van Egmond and Johan van Cruyningen ran up debts in the service of Charles V; Maximiliaan van Cruyningen ruined himself in the service of the States. More often we hear of an extravagant lifestyle. Reinoud van Brederode and Floris van den Boetzelaer lost great sums in gambling. Lamoraal van Egmond Jr was known as a wastrel;[194] so was Gijsbrecht van Mathenesse.

By contrast, the first explanatory model lacks supporting evidence. Since the greatest portion of the nobles' capital consisted of land, on which the rents could be increased regularly, it is implausible that their incomes declined. Only nobles whose incomes were primarily derived from seigneurial rights, and in particular those types of rights whose revenues could not be sufficiently increased, could become impoverished in this manner.

Consequently it appears that incomes remained in step with rising prices, but the high expenditures of some nobles exceeded their rising incomes. If they were forced to mortgage their possessions, or to sell a portion of their lands to pay their debts, they reduced their annual income. They fell into a downward spiral that inevitably led to bankruptcy, unless they adjusted their exorbitant pattern of spending to match their income – which seldom occurred. It is, however, misleading to speak of a general economic decline of the nobility.

Often it was not the wasteful nobles themselves who had to give up their possessions, but their heirs. Otto van Assendelft blamed his financial troubles on the debts made by his father. Otto sold manors, but he still left behind an insolvent estate, and his son renounced the inheritance. Maximiliaan van Cruyningen was burdened all his life with the debts that his father had contracted in Brussels. Karel van Egmond had no money left over after the sale of the Beijerlanden, because he had to pay his father's debts. Rutger Wessel van den Boetzelaer sold Willige-Langerak for the same reason. The fact that it was always the fathers of the selling nobles who had caused financial chaos, suggests that they tried to hold on to their seigneurial properties as long as possible, often longer than was financially prudent. Apparently nobles were able to live beyond their means for quite a long time before their creditors put their furniture out in the street. Perhaps this was related to their social position, but also to the circumstance that some nobles had such extensive possessions that they could keep going for a long while by borrowing. Arend van Buchell complained that the *grands seigneurs* always paid badly. They promised much, they used beautiful words, but they paid only in 'voix et vent'.[195]

The bad management of some individuals does not imply the economic failure of the nobility as a whole. Many nobles who had to sell their seigneurial possessions found buyers in other nobles, sometimes family members. In con-

[194] J. A. Wijs, *Bijdrage tot de kennis van het leenstelsel in de Republiek Holland* (The Hague, 1939), p. 46.
[195] Van Buchell, *Diarium*, pp. 248–9.

trast to the impoverished nobles, others were so prosperous that they could expand their holdings. Cornelis van Dorp and his son Adriaan sold to the Holland nobleman Cornelis Croesingh and to the count of Egmond.[196] Cornelie van Driebergen, a noblewoman of Utrecht, bought the goods of the bankrupt lord of Heemstede. The holdings of Otto van Assendelft went to his cousin Klaas, who was already Otto's liege-lord for these possessions; by this transaction the sub-feudal relationship was dissolved. Another part of Otto's possessions went to the lord of Schagen. Maximiliaan van Cruijningen sold Hazerswoude to *jonker* Nicolaas van Mathenesse. Willem van Beijeren van Schagen sold Schagen to the Zeeland noble George van Cats; eighteen years later Willem's cousin brought the seigneurie back into the Schagen family. The Holland manors sold by Egmond, Aremberg and Ligne during the Twelve Years' Truce and after 1648 largely came into the hands of other nobles who were able to expand their holdings.[197]

The cases described here thus do not point to a general decline of the nobility. While some nobles became poorer, others became richer. This is hardly surprising. Vertical mobility seldom operates in one direction only. As a seventeenth-century pamphlet put it, 'Thus has always been the way of the world – one rises, the other falls.'[198]

PROSPERITY AROUND 1600

There is much evidence that the Holland nobility was flourishing around the end of the sixteenth and the beginning of the seventeenth centuries. Many nobles had their castles repaired, modernized and embellished. In the Rijnland alone in the first half of the seventeenth century nobles built or rebuilt eight manor houses. Johan van Duvenvoirde restored the house at Warmond that had been destroyed by the Spaniards; he made it 'more beautiful and more comfortable than it had been before, with his great expenditures'. Between 1589 and 1601 – the construction had already begun ten years previously – he spent no less than 25,000 gulden.[199] In Koudekerk, the castle of Groot Poelgeest, which had also been destroyed in the war, was rebuilt 'fine and glorious' on the old foundations by Gerrit van Poelgeest.[200] Pieter van der Does had Huis ter Does in Leiderdorp modernized around 1600.[201] Between 1631 and 1634 Johan van Schagen had Dever house in Lisse rebuilt and redecorated. He had to borrow 'money at interest' not only to finance the 'heavy costs' of the project, but also

---

[196] Repertoria op de leenregisters, ARA, Leenkamer, inv. no. 229, fo. 915.
[197] See below, p. 201.
[198] *Schuyt-praetgens*, fo. A 1 v.
[199] Van der Steur, 'Johan van Duvenvoirde', p. 219.
[200] Regt, 'Groot-Poelgeest', p. 105.
[201] Fockema Andreae et al., *Kastelen*, p. 73: 'Modernised at the beginning of the seventeenth century by *jonker* Pieter van der Does'. But Pieter had already died in 1599.

'in order to live more comfortably than I otherwise should have done'.[202] The lords of Wassenaer restored Huis Duvenvoirde in Voorschoten and founded Huis Meerenburgh in Lisse.[203] Sybrand van Alckemade bought the ruins of the old family home in Alckemade in 1615 and had it rebuilt.[204] The lord Van Mathenesse founded Haaswijk in Oegstgeest.[205] The building of great houses testifies both to the prosperity of the Holland nobles and to their willingness to make large expenditures required by their station.

Many documents give further indications of the wealth of the nobles. The cash-book that Johan van Mathenesse kept for six weeks in 1587 shows that he led a modest existence.[206] Yet in the assessment for the 200th penny-tax in 1602, his capital was estimated at 160,000 gulden.[207] After his death his possessions in Lisse alone were valued at £121,353. In addition he owned farms in Zwammerdam and Bodegraven, Snellerwaard and Linschoten, Aarlanderveen, Voorhout, Noordwijk and Offem, and in the polders of Hille, Robbenoord and De Plompert and Karnemelksland. Furthermore, as the heir of his mother, Geertruid Pieck, he owned the manor of Giessen and many farms there and in Guelderland.[208] In the home of the deceased was found the fabulous sum of 42,684 gulden in cash, along with an unspecified quantity of jewels, valuables, gold and silver vessels.[209]

At the same time that Johan van Duvenvoirde rebuilt his house at Warmond, he bought another house in Rotterdam for 2,790 gulden. Simultaneously he owned a house in the Breestraat in Leiden, one or two houses in The Hague, one in Nijmegen and one in Utrecht.[210] Besides the great house at Warmond, he had country houses in Woubrugge and near Rhenen.[211] Often he acquired his properties not by inheritance or marriage, but by active purchases – the possessions of Woudenburg 'which we bought during our marriage', with 58 *morgen* of land; properties near de Grebbe, also in the province of Utrecht, bought in 1608; and in Holland two parcels of 25 *morgen* each in the newly reclaimed Beemster, bought that same year.[212]

A list of inhabitants of the district of Noord-Holland (that part of the present-day province of South Holland located north of the Maas) who were assessed at 300 gulden or more in the forced loan of 1599 clearly shows that the

---

[202] Hulkenberg, *Huis Dever*, p. 102.
[203] Fockema Andreae et al., *Kastelen*, pp. 73, 80.
[204] Ibid., p. 67; cf. Van Lommel, 'Fragment genealogie Alckemades', pp. 213–13.
[205] Fockema Andreae et al., *Kastelen*, p. 75.
[206] ARA, HA Lisse, inv. no. 17. Cf. above, n. 63.
[207] Hulkenberg, *Huis Dever*, p. 90.
[208] Ibid., p. 95.
[209] Inventory of the property of *jonkheer* Johan van Mathenesse, lord of Lisse etc. (1625), ARA, HA Lisse, inv. no. 4. Cf. Hulkenberg, *Huis Dever*, p. 95.
[210] Van der Steur, 'Johan van Duvenvoirde', p. 210.
[211] Ibid., pp. 264–7.
[212] Ibid., and p. 241.

9   P. Linse after E. van der Maes, 'Maria van Voerst' (Private collection). Maria van Voerst (1575–1610), wife of Johan van Wassenaer van Duvenvoirde (1578–1647, in illust. p. 18). Her costly clothing and jewels do not indicate an economic decline among the Holland nobility. The gold chain alone was valued at £995. See L. J. van der Klooster, 'De juwelen en kleding van Maria van Voerst van Doorwerth', *Nederlands Kunsthistorisch Jaarboek* 31 (1980): 50–64.

nobles were among the richest people of the province, both in the countryside and, remarkably enough, in the towns.[213] In the rural Rijnland, no less than seven of the ten assessed persons bore the title of *jonkheer*: Nicolaas van Mathenesse (*f* 1,000), Johan van Mathenesse (*f* 800), Andries (*f* 900) and Willem (*f* 500) van Bronchorst, Henrik van der Werve (*f* 500), Jan van Persijn 'with mother and sister' (*f* 350) and Hendrik van der Laen (*f* 300). In Zeven-huizen the only person assessed was *jonkheer* Bartoud van Assendelft, at *f* 400; in the Overmaze it was *jonkheer* Pieter van Duveland, lord of Rhoon. While Rotterdam and Schiedam had no noble taxpayers, The Hague had a surpris-ingly large number of them. At the head of the list stood 'the Ridderschap and Nobles appearing at the meeting of the States, with the Lord Advocate van Oldenbarnevelt', together at *f* 9,000.[214] Along with them in The Hague were noted Amelis van den Bouchorst(*f* 800), Pauwels van Assendelft (*f* 600), Johan van der Myle (*f* 600), Philips van der Aa (*f* 900), *joffrou* Cornelia van der Myle (*f* 500), the lord of Tilburg (*f* 500), Johan van der Does, lord of Noordwijk (*f* 400), Arend van Dorp (*f* 400), Reinoud van Brederode, lord of Veenhuizen (*f* 300), Boudewijn and Jan van Rhoon (*f* 300), Johan van Egmond (*f* 300) and Dirk van der Does (*f* 300). Of the thirty-five assessed persons in The Hague who were outside the Ridderschap, thirteen belonged to the nobility. Even in the industrial city of Leiden there were surprisingly many nobles among the persons with the highest assessments, such as Lady Johanna van Lier (*f* 1,000), Cornelis van der Myle (*f* 600), *jonkheer* Jacob van Duvenvoirde, lord of Obdam (*f* 400), *jonkheer* Pieter van Rhoon (*f* 600), Adam van der Duyn (*f* 500), *jonkvrouwe* Van Loo (*f* 400), the Lady van Sint Aldegonde (*f* 300) and *jonkheer* Pieter Suys (*f* 300). A more detailed study of persons assessed in the capital imposition of 1600, one year later, has shown that at Leiden the nobles received by far the highest assessments. The thirty-one taxpayers who bore the title of *jonkheer* or *jonkvrouw* paid on average 456 gulden; half of them had to pay 250 gulden or more, while the average tax on regents came to only 260 gulden, and the average for the city as a whole was 99 gulden.[215]

Although the list of the assessed persons for the loan of 1599 applies to only

[213] List of persons assessed *f* 300 and above in the capital loan (end of sixteenth century), ARA, Archief van de Financie van Holland, inv. no. 440. The document must refer to the loan of 1599. *Jonkheer* Nicolaas van Mathenesse is listed as *hoogheemraad* of Rijnland, an office he first held in 1594, establishing a *terminus a quo*. Gerrit de Bont, who died in 1599, is named as rector of Leiden University, thus setting a *terminus ad quem*. Between 1588 and 1599, however, no capital loans were levied; consequently this document can only date from the last-mentioned year. Cf. R. C. J. van Maanen, 'De vermogensopbouw van de Leidse bevolking in het laatste kwart van de zestiende eeuw', *BMHG* 93 (1978): 1–42, at 26.

[214] In 1599, at most ten nobles attended. That means that each noble (and Oldenbarnevelt) was assessed between 800 and 900 gulden. Cf. Van Leeuwen, *Batavia*, p. 771.

[215] Van Maanen, 'Vermogensopbouw', pp. 30–6. Cf. J. J. Woltjer, 'De "alderrijcste" te Leiden in 1584', in *Leidse facetten*, ed. D. E. H. de Boer (Zwolle, 1982), pp. 23–34. Three of the eighteen richest inhabitants of Leiden in 1584 bore noble titles.

part of the province, nearly all of the family names of nobles who were regarded as qualified for the Ridderschap in 1555 appear on the list. Yet from these data it is apparent that prosperity was shared by a much wider group of noble families. It is noteworthy that the assessments of most nobles were well above the minimum sum of 300 gulden. The conclusion is inescapable that the nobles belonged to the richest inhabitants of the province at the turn of the century.

H. A. Enno van Gelder has already shown that the same point can be made about the Holland nobility just before the outbreak of the Revolt.[216] Thus there is no question of economic decline of the nobility in the sixteenth century. The Holland nobility was prosperous before the Revolt, and it remained so during the Revolt. It is just as unlikely that the alleged impoverishment of the nobility was a cause of the Revolt, as it was a result. Even in the 'bourgeois' province of Holland, the economic decline of the nobility was a myth.

CONCLUSION

The largest part of the capital of the Holland nobles consisted of land. They were largely dependent on land-leases for their income. Only a small part of their land was farmed on hereditary leases; on the rest they could continually raise the rent. The income of the nobles therefore increased in line with agricultural conjuncture. Whether their landed incomes increased sufficiently to maintain their purchasing power, or even to raise it, cannot be stated with certainty: yet it is not unlikely. Since nobles were able to expand their landholdings, they apparently regarded investment in land as lucrative, and they were in a position to set aside enough money for new investments.

The nobles were much less dependent on revenues from seigneurial rights. Some rights brought in limited sums that had been fixed once and for all time; others, such as fishing rights, could be exploited intensively. Overall revenues from seigneurial rights probably increased less than revenues from land leases. Yet because these revenues formed only a limited part of the total income of nobles, their financial situation was not seriously threatened. Revenues from tithes augmented noble incomes substantially. These revenues also increased with the agricultural conjuncture.

Salaries formed an unknown quantity. Younger sons, who were endowed with little or no land and seigneurial possessions, had to seek their living through office-holding. This suggests that administrative offices were not indispensable to the typical landed nobleman. The circumstance that nobles occupied relatively few offices after 1530 leads us to suppose that land and seigneurial rights provided them with adequate income.

A separate category is formed by the offices that were the exclusive domain of

[216] Van Gelder, 'Hollandse adel'.

members of the Ridderschap in the Dutch Republic. These high regents' offices were probably very lucrative, although there is no evidence that members of the Ridderschap had to occupy them to keep their heads above water. To the advantages that flowed to members of the Ridderschap, we must add the revenues of the abbeys of Rijnsburg and Leeuwenhorst.

Nevertheless, some nobles landed in financial difficulties. This led to the sale of their possessions, and sometimes to bankruptcy. It is reasonable to suppose that the cause lay not in the decline of their revenues, but in their excessive expenditures. Wastefulness, conspicuous consumption, the costs of maintaining their status and their expenses in public service placed a heavy burden on their incomes. From the financial ruin of several noble families, however, we cannot infer that the entire Holland nobility was in economic decline. In many cases other Holland nobles acquired the possessions that their heavily indebted friends and relations had to put on the market. Moreover, manors that came up for sale for other reasons, such as the properties of the Southern Netherlandish nobles who wished to unload their holdings in the North, often found noble buyers.

After 1650 more nobles had financial problems. If there was an economic decline of the nobility, it must have taken place in the second half of the seventeenth century. Even at that time other nobles, such as the lords of Duvenvoirde-Wassenaer, managed to maintain their prosperity. This decline suggests anew that the incomes of nobles were closely tied to agricultural conjuncture. When agricultural prices began to fall, and revenues from leases and tithes went down along with them, many nobles were not able to adjust their pattern of expenditures.

It is possible that some nobles reacted to the changed conditions by again seeking refuge in administrative offices. In 1666 the sitting members of the Ridderschap sharpened the admissions criteria of their college. By this means they reserved the lucrative offices for a small circle, to which membership in the Ridderschap gave access. But this falls beyond the scope of our history.

6

Manors and honours

NOBILITY AND ELITE

Despite the growth and increasing importance of the urban bourgeoisie, at the end of the middle ages the nobility still formed the political elite *par excellence*. Many nobles found their life's purpose in the service of the monarch. Nobles held seats in the sovereign's council, and during wartime they served in person as heavily armed knights. As seigneurial lords the nobles represented the sovereign's authority in the countryside. Nobles found honourable employment in the expanding Burgundian bureaucracy, but by no means all of those who held official posts were noble. In the fifteenth century it was not unusual for high non-noble officials to acquire fiefs, adopt a noble style of life and receive knighthood – through which they were gradually assimilated to the nobility. Consequently, in the late middle ages, nobility and political elite were largely identical.

In the course of the sixteenth century the nobles apparently lost their leading role in politics. H. A. Enno van Gelder remarked that during the first years of Philip II's reign the greater part of the nobles of Holland no longer held administrative offices.[1] Jan den Tex stated that in the entire sixteenth century hardly any noble played a significant political role.[2] This situation appears to have continued in the time of the Republic. The 'bourgeois' character of the Republic was exemplified by its rulers. G. J. Renier's description of the Republic as 'the dictatorship of the upper middle class' illustrates the political dominance of the grand bourgeoisie.[3] None the less, many authors have emphasized the continuing political importance of the nobles within the bourgeois-republican framework. The influence of the Ridderschap in the States of Holland was greater than its numerical representation might suggest – one vote for the nobility as opposed to eighteen for the towns. Moreover, some nobles who enjoyed the prestige of being descendants of old families converted this status into political power. Nobles also played an important role at the stadholder's court.[4] Around 1670 Sir William Temple, the well-informed

[1] Van Gelder, 'Hollandse adel', p. 114.
[2] Den Tex, *Oldenbarnevelt*, II, p. 250.
[3] Renier, *Dutch Nation*, pp. 16–24.
[4] Schöffer, 'De Republiek', pp. 179–80; Aalbers, 'Factieuze tegenstellingen'.

English ambassador in The Hague, noted that the Holland nobles 'are in a manner all employ'd in the Military or Civil Charges of the Province or States'.[5] This remark conflicts with the professed 'bourgeois' character of the Republic, as well as with the situation in the sixteenth century. It seems as if Temple was writing about the middle ages.

THE NOBLES AS SEIGNEURS

The sixteenth-century nobles were primarily manorial lords. Most nobles had seigneurial jurisdiction; and most of those who held such jurisdiction belonged to the nobility.[6] The nobles regarded the management of their estates as an important social duty. Nobles who held several manors often tried to ensure that each of their sons would inherit at least one of them, so that they also could live as true nobles. In a will made in 1500 Klaas van Assendelft declared that his oldest son Gerrit would inherit the manor of Assendelft; after the death of Klaas's wife, Gerrit would also receive the adjoining manors of Heemskerk and Castricum. Floris, Klaas's second son, was to receive Goudriaan; Jan, his third son, Kralingen and the castle of Honingen; Dirk, the fourth son, Heinenoord and Bezooien. The oldest daughter Beatrix received Hendrik-Ido-Ambacht and a one-third share of Kijfhoek; two other daughters received farms without jurisdiction in Westland.[7] During his lifetime Jacob van Duvenvoirde divided his three manors of Warmond, Woude and Alkemade among his three sons. His oldest son Johan in turn took care that each of *his* three oldest sons would get a manor, but there was none left for the fourth son.[8]

The greatest prestige was attached to the manor bearing the family name. The lord of Assendelft was actually lord of the manor of Assendelft, the lords of Mathenesse held Mathenesse, the lords of Brederode the manor of Brederode, the counts of Egmond both Egmond-Binnen (inland) and Egmond-aan-Zee (by the sea). Some nobles tried to recover family manors that had come into the hands of others by inheritance or sale. Thus in 1629 Arend van Dorp (1599–1652) was invested with the manor of Dorp (in Delfland), which had belonged to one of his ancestors in the fourteenth century. In 1648 he tried to get a new manor with the appealing name of Arendsdorp from the Wassenaer family possessions.[9] The possessions of the Wassenaers were in the hands of the Ligne family, nobles from Hainault, but in 1657 Jacob van Wassenaer, the lord of Obdam, was again invested with the high jurisdiction of Wassenaar.[10] The

[5] Temple, *Observations*, p. 85.
[6] Van Gelder, 'Hollandse adel', p. 114.
[7] Holleman, *Dirk van Assendelft*, pp. 546–52.
[8] Van der Steur, 'Johan van Duvenvoirde', pp. 214, 264–7.
[9] Van Zurck, *Codex*, p. 511; Wijs, *Leenstelsel*, p. 115. The manor of Dorp belonged to the Wassenaar Chamber of Fiefs.
[10] Repertoria op de leenregisters, ARA, Leenkamer, inv. no. 228, fo. 542.

rich Amsterdam merchant family De Vlaminck traced its family tree back to the noble Oudshoorn lineage; and in 1627 Dirck de Vlaminck 'van Oudshoorn' had himself invested with the seigneurie of Oudshoorn near Alphen.[11]

The seigneurial lords had originally been representatives of the sovereign in the villages of the countryside. They held their offices as fiefs. As feudal ties gradually lost their original significance, the seigneurs became virtual owners of their manors. Sovereign authority was thus alienated; it came into the possession of private persons. Strictly speaking, the seigneurie was not a specific territory, but rather the right to administer justice within a jurisdiction.[12] The low justice consisted of jurisdiction over everyday civil cases. A lord who was invested with high justice was empowered to judge capital cases.[13] But the area within which justice was exercised was also known as the manor (*heerlijkheid*), jurisdiction (*ambacht*), or seigneurie (*ambachtsheerlijkheid*). In practice the right of justice was limited to the authority to appoint the sheriff (*schout*). This functionary was charged with daily operations while the lord enjoyed the revenues of the office, such as a share of the fines. In addition the lord received revenues from other seigneurial rights that were associated wth the manor, the *ambachtsgevolg*.[14]

Although seigneurial lords occupied key positions in the countryside and enjoyed great social prestige, we should not exaggerate their power. Some nobles such as Johan van Duvenvoirde of Warmond administered their manors personally, but their authority was local and counted for little on the provincial level. Low seigneurial jurisdiction was subordinate to that of the bailiffs (*baljuws*); high justice was subordinate to the Court of Holland, which expanded its judicial powers during the reign of Charles V. As a consequence of their possession of manors, however, the nobles had the right to be represented in the Ridderschap at the meetings of the States. Thus the possession of manors was a precondition for the exercise of political power on the provincial level.

The relationship between noble seigneurs and their subjects was influenced by the lords' place of residence.[15] If the lord lived among his villagers, he was as a rule closely involved in village life. Van Gelder speaks of a 'fairly intimate relationship' between lord and subjects, and characterizes the lord as a 'helper in need'.[16] Although a social chasm divided the lord from his peasants, personal contact was frequent and often cordial. Reinoud van Brederode (1492–1556)

[11] Elias, *Vroedschap*, I, p. 279.
[12] See above, p. 104.
[13] De Blécourt, *Ambacht en gemeente*, pp. 6–7; Rijpperda Wierdsma, *Politie en justitie*, pp. 149–249; De Blécourt, 'Heerlijkheden'; Van Gelder, 'Hollandse adel', pp. 125–31; Beekman, *Waterschapsrecht*, I, pp. 66–80, and II, p. 1058.
[14] See above, pp. 104–8.
[15] H. A. Enno van Gelder, *Nederlandse dorpen in de 16e eeuw* (Amsterdam, 1953), pp. 14–39, 67–89.
[16] Ibid., p. 69; 'Hollandse adel', p. 123.

10 Cornelis Anthonisz., 'Reinoud van Brederode' (Rijksmuseum, Amsterdam). Reinoud van Brederode (1492–1556), the eleventh lord of Brederode, was condemned to death by Charles V because he claimed descent from the counts of Holland and bore the unbroken arms of Holland. He was pardoned, however. He deeded his manors of Amstelveen, Sloten, Sloterdijk and Osdorp to the city of Amsterdam, reportedly following the loss of a bet.

had a portrait of his old gardener hanging among other paintings in his castle.[17] One farmer of Johan van Mathenesse, lord of Lisse, used to drive the lord to town on his waggon to do errands for himself and his mother. In 1587 *jonker* Johan noted in his account book the expense for a cake that his mother had given to Klaas, this farmer's little boy.[18] Adriana van Nassau (born from a bastard line of the Breda counts of Nassau), the widow of Dirk van Assendelft, declared in her testament in 1558 'that Rochus, a hired hand and two other poor boys with him shall be taught a trade and given the necessary support to learn the same in order to earn a living in the future'.[19] Rochus was Adriana's page; after her death he was indeed established in the tailor's trade.[20] Owing to 'great and good-hearted services shown and done for many years to [the testator] and her husband of blessed memory', Godert Bosman was granted eighteen *karolusguldens* and 'four quarters of rye' in the same testament; 'on account of various matters, affection, friendship and services shown and done', another servant likewise received four quarters of rye.[21] In 1581 Johan van Duvenvoirde van Woude granted a tenant free occupancy of a small house 'by God's will'; in 1600 he destined it 'for my servants or servant-women who may fall into poverty and have faithfully served the house of Warmond'.[22]

It was only a small step from the care of old servants to poor relief in general, and there the Holland nobles were also active. In her will Adriana van Nassau decreed that 'eight poor widows' should be clothed annually.[23] In 1587 Johan van Mathenesse met with the brothers of the guilds of Our Lady and St Catharine at Lisse to create a foundation to own the lands of these formerly Catholic confraternities. The foundation would be devoted to poor relief, in particular for those not already helped by the reformed diaconate. The annual income came to 300 gulden, but 'out of pure affection, love, and inclination' *jonker* Johan gave another 500 gulden, with the promise that he would grant the future inhabitants of the House at Lisse a further 25 gulden each year.[24] The tithes belonging to the House at Alkemade were dedicated to the poor in 1606 'until further notice'.[25]

The administration of their seigneuries kept the lords busy. Apparently it was owing to the flood-control efforts of Joost van Cruijningen, lord of Heenvliet, that Heenvliet was one of the few polders on Voorne and Putten not flooded during the storm of 1530.[26] The lord and lady of Heenvliet were members of

---

[17] J. J. Salverda de Grave, 'Twee inventarissen van het huis van Brederode', *BMHG* 39 (1918): 1–72, at 54.

[18] Hulkenberg, *Huis Dever*, p. 87.

[19] Holleman, *Dirk van Assendelft*, pp. 569–70.

[20] Ibid., p. 66.   [21] Ibid., p. 570.

[22] Van der Steur, 'Johan van Duvenvoirde', p. 210.

[23] Holleman, *Dirk van Assendelft*, pp. 569–70.

[24] Hulkenberg, *Huis Dever*, p. 87.

[25] Van der Steur, 'Johan van Duvenvoirde', p. 256.   [26] 't Hart, *Heenvliet*, p. 44.

the Our Blessed Lady guild, and they supported the local chamber of rhetoric.[27] In 1541 when the parish treasury was in deficit because of carelessness by the churchwardens, the lord of Heenvliet had them dismissed and sold the household goods of the negligent.[28] In 1576, when Warmond was plundered by unpaid Spanish soldiers, the lord took immediate action: Jacob van Duvenvoirde allowed the damages to be deducted from leases and other obligations, while his son Johan got in touch with the bailiff of Noordwijk, where the troops were quartered. He obtained the names of the commanders and held them responsible for damages suffered.[29] Johan van Duvenvoirde promulgated all kinds of by-laws.[30] He farmed out the offices of sheriff, secretary and messenger, but retained that of bailiff, exercising the high justice in the seigneurie himself.[31] In Heenvliet also the lord sometimes presided over the criminal court.[32]

In return for the lord's favour, the common people had to promise their obedience and loyalty. Furthermore, they had many material obligations, such as on the investiture of a new lord or his marriage. The inhabitants of Wassenaar complained in 1514 that they had to raise loans to pay 'for the investiture of the lord of Wassenaer'; the inhabitants of Leiderdorp had to pay 'for the ransom of their seigneur', the very same lord of Wassenaer, who had been taken captive by the Gueldrians.[33] In 1568 the people of Burghorn and Schagerkogge made a gift to Jan van Schagen on the occasion of his marriage, and in 1595 Barsingerhorn, Haringhuizen and Schagen gave a wedding present to his daughter Adriana.[34] In 1627 Johan Polyander van den Kerckhoven 'on his investiture as Lord of Heenvliet . . . was honoured by the inhabitants . . . with a silver ewer and basin and a festive meal, which cost a considerable sum of money for which each *gemet* [one-half *morgen*] in the said manor was assessed and contributed six *stuivers*, by right according to the letters, papers and records'.[35]

Contact between the lord and the villagers was partly determined by the place where the lord resided. Nobles who held only one manor mostly resided there, and often were actively concerned with village life. If a lord held several manors that formed a more or less contiguous unit, close relations were also possible. When nobles held many manors spread over a large area, however, they played a far less significant role in village life, especially if they held high offices in the

27 Ibid., pp. 44, 48.
28 Ibid., p. 50.
29 Van der Steur, 'Johan van Duvenvoirde', pp. 218–19.
30 Ibid., pp. 222–4.
31 Ibid., p. 263.
32 't Hart, *Heenvliet*, p. 172.
33 Van Gelder, *Nederlandse dorpen*, p. 76; cf. above, p. 5.
34 Holleman, *Dirk van Assendelft*, p. 331.
35 't Hart, *Heenvliet*, p. 207.

sovereign's service. From the survey of all manors and their lords in 1555, it is possible to determine how many manors the seigneurial lords of Holland possessed, and indirectly to consider the rate of absenteeism.[36] The manors were distributed very unevenly among the nobles. A great number of manors had come into the hands of a small group. Twelve nobles (13 per cent of the seigneurs) collectively held 45 per cent of all manors. The greatest seigneur in the province was the prince of Orange. As the heir to the lords of Polanen and De Lek, he held eighteen manors. Furthermore, Orange owned extensive possessions outside Holland. The difference between great and small fief-holders was closely correlated to the difference between high and low nobility. The prince of Orange was followed by the count of Egmond with twelve manors; next came the count of Horne as lord of the Land van Altena, the prince of Ligne (heir to Wassenaer), and the count of Aremberg (heir to Naeltwijck), each with eleven manors. The lord of Brederode had nine manors, the marquis of Bergen seven. Gerrit van Assendelft, president of the Court of Holland, also had seven: among the lower nobles, he held the greatest number. Gerrit's brother Floris and his nephews Otto and Nicolaas van Assendelft together held another nine manors, so that the total holdings of the Assendelft family can be regarded as very sizeable. Several other high nobles, such as the countess of Hoogstraten, the lord of Cruijningen, the burgrave of Montfoort and the lord of Merode each held between two and five manors in Holland.

A great number of manors were thus held by lords who resided elsewhere. This does not mean that absentee lords never concerned themselves with their subjects. In 1533, 1562, 1569 and 1614, for example, the inhabitants of Oosthuizen and Etersheim received privileges from their seigneurs, the counts of Aremberg.[37] Yet the great concentration of manorial possessions and the resulting high rate of absenteeism remind us not to idealize the paternalistic relationship between lords and inhabitants.

Of the ninety-two seigneurs recorded in 1555, forty-five (49 per cent) belonged to the nobility of Holland and twenty-one (23 per cent) to the nobility of other provinces. Nineteen lords (21 per cent) belonged to the bourgeoisie: three lords were urban burgemeesters, *sterfmannen*, who were ex-officio holders of the manors belonging to the cities. Three seigneurs were ecclesiastics. Thus nearly three out of four seigneuries were held by the nobility, and the nobles still enjoyed a great preponderance of seigneurial power in Holland.

The evolution of manorial holdings can be studied through the registers of the Chamber of Fiefs.[38] This source produces different totals for seigneuries

---

[36] See appendix 1 of the Dutch edition.

[37] Rijksarchief Noord-Holland, Archief van de heerlijkheid Oosthuizen, inv. nos. 32, 38, 39, 43, 47.

[38] See appendices 5 and 6 of the Dutch edition. Cf. H. F. K. van Nierop, '"Het quaede regiment". De Hollandse edelen als ambachtsheren, 1490–1650', *TvG* 93 (1980): 433–44. For the possession of manors from 1585 until 1650, see below, pp. 199–203.

and lords because the registers sometimes mention several fief-holders who were invested with various fiefs simultaneously in one investiture. According to these registers, the proportion of noble fief-holders remained fairly constant between 1490 and 1585 at around 80 per cent. The proportion of non-noble fief-holders rose from 11 to 15 per cent, but remained limited. The number of fief-holders of bourgeois origin began to grow significantly only in the seventeenth century. Cities and clergy remained insignificant.

The most important development in this period was the increase in the number of 'foreign' nobles at the expense of the nobles from Holland families. The proportion of noble seigneurs of Holland origin remained constant at 59 per cent between 1490 and 1525, but fell to 50 per cent in 1555 and 46 per cent in 1585. That of the non-Holland nobles rose from 22 per cent in 1525 to 30 per cent in 1555 and 35 per cent in 1585. This process was primarily caused by the extinction of the male line of several Holland lineages (or their branches); nobles from other regions who had married heiresses could then obtain Holland manors. By this means, after the death of Hendrik van Naeltwijck in 1496, the Naeltwijck family possessions passed via the female line to the Van der Marcks, lords (later counts) of Aremberg.[39] The manors of the lord of Wassenaer, who died in 1523, passed by the marriage of his daughter Maria in 1525 into the Ligne family.[40] Lesser nobles, especially those of adjoining Utrecht, Gelderland and Brabant, likewise acquired Holland manors by marriages to heiresses. This was possible because a fairly large proportion of manors, between 14 and 20 per cent, was held by women.[41]

Conversely, Holland nobles acquired possessions in other provinces. We have already mentioned the marriage of Jan van Egmond to the rich heiress Françoise van Luxemburg, by which part of the Egmond family possessions came to be in Flanders.[42] It is not possible to determine to what extent the Holland nobles were able to compensate for their decline as seigneurial lords by acquiring manors elsewhere. It is, however, apparent that the high nobility, whom Charles V favoured above the great mass of lower nobles, also differentiated themselves from the lesser nobility as seigneurs. Not only did the nobility as a whole constitute the largest group of seigneurial lords in Holland, but also their position was not threatened by the 'rise of the bourgeoisie', at least not before 1585.

---

[39] Van Gouthoeven, *Chronyke*, p. 193.
[40] Obreen, *Wassenaer*, p. 52.
[41] On property ownership of noblewomen of the northern Netherlands at this time, see Sherrin Marshall Wyntjes, 'Survivors and status: widowhood and family in the early modern Netherlands', *Journal of Family History* 7 (1982): 396–405.
[42] See above, p. 39; Dek, *Genealogie Egmond*, pp. 50–3.

THE NOBLES AS OFFICE-HOLDERS

If there were practically no quantitative changes in manorial holdings until 1585, the situation with administrative offices was different. At the beginning of the sixteenth century a great number of nobles occupied important official posts in Holland, but by mid-century the overwhelming majority of the offices were held by persons of bourgeois origin. The nobility's withdrawal from administration has not been studied previously. Before explaining the decline of the nobility in this area, we must sketch its outlines. Since it is not possible to survey all provincial offices, we shall examine only the most important posts.

The chief organ of central administration in Holland was the Court. This institution had developed gradually from the count's council.[43] Just as the sovereign himself, his councillors fulfilled judicial, legislative, and administrative functions.[44] These functions were difficult to distinguish from each other: in the sixteenth century there was as yet no question of formal separation of powers.[45] The Court had as its task to substitute for the stadholder in his absence. The Court then functioned as the direct representative of sovereign power in the province.[46] At first the political aspects of the Court had been paramount, but gradually its judicial role became more important. Since the beginning of the sixteenth century, appointments to the Court were given almost exclusively to law graduates.[47] In 1531 the Court received a new instruction placing greater emphasis on its judicial functions.[48]

The nucleus of the Court consisted of nine salaried councillors, including the president.[49] The stadholder was ex-officio chairman, but since 1510 he had allowed the president to take his place. Along with the salaried councillors,

---

[43] T. S. Jansma, *Raad en Rekenkamer in Holland en Zeeland tijdens hertog Philips van Bourgondië* (Utrecht, 1932); T. van Riemsdijk, 'De oorsprong van het Hof van Holland', in *Geschiedkundige opstellen aangeboden aan Robert Fruin* (The Hague, 1894), pp. 183–208; *Memorialen van het Hof (den Raad) van Holland, Zeeland en West-Friesland van den secretaris Jan Rosa*, ed. A. S. de Blécourt and E. M. Meijers, 3 vols. (Haarlem, 1929), I, pp. i–xxi.

[44] Fruin, *Staatsinstellingen*, p. 65.

[45] Hugo de Schepper, *Rechter en administratie in de Nederlanden tijdens de zestiende eeuw*, inaugural lecture (Alphen aan den Rijn, 1981).

[46] Fruin, *Staatsinstellingen*, pp. 63–4. The Court was responsible for summoning the States, renewing the law in the cities (i.e. appointing magistrates), provisional appointment and swearing-in of office-holders, supervision of bailiffs and other officials, and maintenance of fortifications and city walls. In consultation with the stadholder, the Court could issue ordinances that had the force of law within the province.

[47] *Memorialen Rosa*, I, pp. xlv–xlviii. According to A. A. Beekman, *Geschiedkundige atlas van Nederland*, 19 vols. (The Hague, 1912–39), 'Tekst bij kaart XIV, de Republiek in 1795', p. 82, it was decided in 1582 that only lawyers could be appointed councillors. After that year most but not all councillors were identified with the title *mr* (*meester* = master of law). I have not found Beekman's source for this information.

[48] *Groot placaet-boeck*, II, pp. 703–60.

[49] J. Smit, 'De omzetting van het Hof van Holland', *BVGO*, 6th series, 2 (1925): 179–223, at 220–3; and *Memoriaelen Rosa*, I, pp. i and ix.

however, there was a fairly large number of unpaid councillors, and their position is difficult to specify. Other councillors took part in the work of the Court on a very irregular basis.[50] Several councillors were always drawn from Zeeland, because the Court also had authority in that province.

The role of the Holland nobles in the Court declined gradually. At its foundation in 1428, the Court as the extension of the count's council had offered places to the most important nobles of the province.[51] In the last quarter of the fifteenth century the number of lawyers in the Court increased, but that does not mean that the nobility disappeared, since there were also lawyers among the nobles. At the beginning of the sixteenth century, approximately half of the members of the Court belonged to the nobility.[52] In 1500, five of the ten salaried members who held seats that year bore noble names (Almonde, Van Dorp, Spanghen, Oem van Wyngaerden, Oudheusden); in 1520, so did six out of thirteen (Oem van Wyngaerden, Duvenvoirde, Coulster, two Assendelfts, and Cats from Zeeland). In 1528, when the government in Brussels made a list of the office-holders of Holland, four of the six ordinary councillors were Holland nobles. The president, Nicolaas Everaerts of Zeeland, was not noble, but among the three extraordinary councillors named that year there was an ecclesiastic of noble origin, Hugo van Assendelft, canon of the court chapel.[53] Of the seven unpaid councillors that year, two or three others were noble (Frederik van Renesse, Andries van Bronckhorst and Guillam Zegers).[54] Among the ordinary councillors were several of the most important nobles of the province. We have already encountered Gerrit van Assendelft, knight, the greatest holder of manors among the lesser nobles: he was also renowned for his remarkable marriage.[55] In 1528 he succeeded as president of the Court and held that office until his death in 1558. Floris Oem van Wyngaerden was knight and lord of IJsselmonde.[56] As a younger son, Johan van Duvenvoirde had not inherited any seigneurial possessions, and he had therefore chosen to pursue an administrative career. Yet he married an heiress and acquired the manors of Warmond, Woude and Alkemade, thus becoming the founder of the War-mond branch of the Duvenvoirde family.[57] As important fief-holders, councillors Assendelft, Duvenvoirde and Wyngaerden appeared regularly in the

---

[50] *Memoriaelen Rosa*, I, pp. ix–x.

[51] Ibid., I, pp. xxxvi–xxxvii.

[52] Councillors of the Court are listed in ibid., I, pp. xliv–l.

[53] ARA Brussels, Aud., inv. no. 1184, fos. 54–54 v.

[54] *Memoriaelen Rosa*, I, pp. xlv–xlvi. Guillam Zegers came from a Flemish family that had settled in Holland. He was listed among the nobles in 1540 and 1549, but did not appear at the States meetings. J. W. te Water, *Historie van het verbond en de smeekschriften der Nederlandsche edelen*, 4 vols. (Middelburg, 1776–96), III, pp. 412–13. Andries van Bronckhorst was from a Gueldrian noble family that had settled in Holland.

[55] See above, pp. 78–81.

[56] Van der Aa, *Biographisch woordenboek*, s.v. Floris Oem van Wyngaerden.

[57] Van der Steur, 'Johan van Duvenvoirde', p. 57; Obreen, *Wassenaer*, p. 151.

Ridderschap of the States of Holland, serving as a bridge between sovereign and representative bodies.[58] Abel van Coulster was also a knight.[59] Joost Sasbout was probably not regarded as noble, although he did bear the title 'knight' and was lord of the manor of Spaland.[60]

In subsequent years the noble element in the Court declined as a result of resignations or deaths of noble councillors: Wyngaerden in 1532, Duvenvoirde in 1543, Coulster in 1548 and finally president Assendelft in 1558. Nobles were still appointed in these years, but they belonged to the minor nobility who were not enrolled in the Ridderschap. When the Court moved to Utrecht in 1572, at the outbreak of the Revolt in Holland, two or three of the nine ordinary councillors still bore noble names.[61] The president, Cornelis Suys, knight, lord of Rijswijk, was probably not regarded as noble despite holding these titles.[62] Nicolaas van der Laen did have a noble name, but probably should be reckoned among the circles of the Haarlem patriciate.[63] Only Cornelis Oem van Wyngaerden had relatives who appeared in the Ridderschap, but he belonged to a cadet branch and was not himself enrolled in it.[64]

The numerical decline of the nobility in the Court of Holland was not an isolated case. Officials of bourgeois origin also gained ground at the expense of nobles in the judicial councils of other provinces,[65] and even in the distant Palatinate between 1546 and 1550 a great number of bourgeois law graduates were named councillors.[66]

In the Chamber of Accounts, also located at The Hague, the nobility was less strongly represented.[67] Before 1428, accounts had been audited by the count's councillors, who were recruited from the most important nobles of the province, representatives of the cities and clerks of the chancellery.[68] In 1428 the

58 See below, p. 168.
59 Van der Aa, *Biographisch woordenboek*, s.v. Van Coulster; cf. J. Belonje, *Ter Coulster* (Wormerveer, 1946), pp. 26 and 70.
60 Van der Aa, *Biographisch woordenboek*, s.v. Sasbout; *NNBW*, II, p. 1265. He became a member of the Court of Friesland in 1526, and chancellor of Guelderland in 1543. Nevertheless, Van Gouthoeven and Boxhorn regard the name Sasbout as noble.
61 Smit, 'Omzetting', pp. 190–1.
62 Van der Aa, *Biographisch woordenboek*, s.v. Suys. Van Gouthoeven and Boxhorn regard the name as noble.
63 Van der Aa, *Biographisch woordenboek*, s.v. Van der Laen.
64 He was probably the half-brother of the similarly named Cornelis Oem van Wyngaerden who worked with Diederik Sonoy and Lodewijk van den Binckhorst to introduce the new religion in The Hague in 1566. *Sententiën en indagingen van den Hertog van Alba*, ed. J. Marcus (Amsterdam, 1735), pp. 51–3. It is not clear which of the two half-brothers was a member of the Compromise of the Nobles. See D'Yvoy van Mijdrecht, *Verbond*, no. 22 and below, pp. 183–4.
65 H. de Schepper, 'Vorstelijke ambtenarij en bureaukratisering in regering en gewesten van 's Konings Nederlanden, 16e–17e eeuw', *TvG* 90 (1977): 358–77, at 362, and the literature cited there in n. 26.
66 Volker Press, *Calvinismus und Territorialstaat. Regierung und Zentralbehörden der Kurpfalz 1559–1619* (Stuttgart, 1970), p. 194.
67 Members of the Chamber of Accounts are listed in Van Gouthoeven, *Chronyke*, pp. 110–12.
68 Jansma, *Raad en Rekenkamer*, pp. 12–76; Fruin, *Staatsinstellingen*, pp. 56–7.

11   Jan Mostaert, 'Joost van Bronckhorst' (Musée du Petit Palais, Paris). Joost van Bronckhorst, knight, master of accounts in the Chamber of Accounts at The Hague, lord of Bleiswijk. He was descended from a branch of a Gueldrian noble family, which had settled in Holland.

newly created Court was charged with this task, but in 1446 a separate Chamber of Accounts was established to audit accounts and to administer the count's domain. The personnel of the Chamber consisted of two masters of accounts, an auditor and a clerk.

There were no important Holland nobles in the Chamber of Accounts in the sixteenth century. We do find professional bureaucrats, graduates in law, who had assumed an aristocratic style of life and often held manors as well; but they were not counted among the nobility – families such as De Jonge, Van Mierop and Stalpert. The office of master of accounts (*rekenmeester*) was sometimes passed from father to son in these lineages. Cornelis de Jonge, lord of Baard-wijk, was master of accounts in 1504, Jacob de Jonge in 1526. In 1572, Cornelis de Jonge, 'master of accounts in place of his father', went with the Chamber to Utrecht, and in 1573 Joos de Jonge Cornelisz became auditor there.[69] Never-theless, a minority of the Chamber, five of the thirty-two members appointed between 1502 and 1572, did belong to the lower nobility. Joost van Bronckhorst (1525), knight, lord of Bleiswijk, belonged to a family of Gueldrian origin that had settled in Holland. Gerrit (1529) and Albrecht van Loo belonged to the lower strata of Holland nobility. Zeger van Alveringen, knight, lord of Hofwe-gen, belonged to a foreign noble family. *Jonkheer* Jacob Coppier, lord of Kalsla-gen, was presumably not reckoned among the nobility. Only Reinier van der Does, master of accounts in 1555, was probably a relation of the family that was enrolled in the Ridderschap. Finally, Gerrit van Renoij, lord of Spijk, first master of accounts in 1555 and 1568, did not belong to the old Holland nobility, but was ennobled by Charles V.

Why so few nobles chose a career in the Chamber of Accounts is unclear. Perhaps there were not enough nobles with sufficient expertise in this area. It is also striking that few members of the Holland nobility were represented among the stewards of the domain, an office that reported to the Chamber of Accounts.

In the Forestry Office, also found in The Hague, the nobility was better able to preserve its position. The forester and three chief assistants (*meesterknapen*) were charged with judicial functions in hunting cases.[70] Among other duties, they had to prevent unqualified persons from hunting in the 'wildernesses' (sand dunes along the North Sea), a noble privilege in Holland. Thus it is understandable that the Forestry Office was more aristocratic than the other administrative bodies. Since not only nobles, but also the highest administrative officials of Holland were allowed to hunt, not all of the *meesterknapen* belonged to the nobility.[71] 'To this lordly station', wrote Paulus Merula in 1605, 'were admitted (besides bannerets and knights) persons of nobility, together with the most qualified of the land, and men of State.'[72] Of the sixteen persons who were appointed *meesterknapen* between 1515 and 1572, only three did not belong to the nobility.[73] These men, Aart Boot (1531), Vincent van Lebesteijn (1535) and *jonkheer* Guillaume le Grand (1566), combined their office with that of bailiff of The Hague. Possibly this function involved them in the management of the

[69] Van Gouthoeven, *Chronyke*, pp. 110–12.
[70] Merula, *Placaten Wildernissen*, p. 24.
[71] On hunting rights, see above, p. 37.
[72] Merula, *Placaten Wildernissen*, p. 24.
[73] Names of *meesterknapen* in ibid., pp. 24–5, and in the commission books of the Rekenkamer, ARA, Archief van de Graflijkheidsrekenkamer, registers, inv. nos. 492–5.

Wildernesses.[74] The foresters of Holland, who were ex-officio governors of the hunting estate of Teylingen, almost all belonged to the high nobility.[75] One may suppose that the offices of forester and *meesterknaap* were less time-consuming than offices in the Court and Chamber of Accounts.

In the Court of Fiefs (*Leenhof*), which had jurisdiction over disputes involving fiefs, the significance of the nobility declined to some extent in favour of the bureaucrats with legal training. Originally the count had pronounced judgment personally in disputes over fiefs, and was assisted by an unspecified number of vassals, all of whom belonged to the nobility.[76] In 1469 Charles the Bold established a separate Court of Fiefs, in which the stadholder, assisted by a number of vassals appointed by him, would issue judgments.[77] In practice this arrangement proved unsatisfactory, and Charles V issued a new instruction in 1520.[78] Henceforth the Court of Fiefs would consist of twelve vassals, six of whom had to be nobles 'or other good men *coustumiers*' (those acquainted with customary law), and the other six 'learned men' (graduates in law) who would be recruited from the Court of Holland or elsewhere. On the same day that the Chamber of Fiefs received its instruction, nine members took the oath of office.[79] These were the 'knights' Gerrit van Assendelft, Floris Oem van Wyngaerden, Jan van Duvenvoirde, Frank van Borsselen and Willem van Alcke-made; and the lawyers Albrecht van Loo, Joost Sasbout, Anthonis van Bronck-horst and Jacob Stalpert. The distinction between nobles and men learned in the law must not be drawn too sharply. Of the five 'knights', Assendelft, Wyngaerden and Duvenvoirde were also lawyers and councillors in the Court of Holland; whereas councillor Van Loo and solicitor Bronckhorst were members of the lesser nobility. The office of councillor in the Chamber of Fiefs can probably also be seen as a secondary activity.

All the institutions mentioned thus far had their seat in The Hague. Outside The Hague the most important officials of provincial administration in the countryside were the bailiffs. They formed the connection between the provincial administration, in particular the Court, and local administration in the seigneuries. Practically the entire countryside was divided into bailiwicks.[80] They were headed by bailiffs, who were named by the central administration in

---

74 ARA, Grafelijkheidsrekenkamer, registers, inv. no. 493, fos. 178 and 260 v.; inv. no. 495, fo. 21 v.

75 Wolfert van Borsselen (1478); Jan van Egmond (1492); Cornelis Croesingh (1504; had been lieutenant-forester earlier 'under the hand' of the two previous); Jan van Wassenaer (1520); Reinoud van Brederode (1525); Lamoraal van Egmond (1556); William of Orange (1560); Maximiliaan van Bossu (1567). Merula, *Placaten Wildernissen*, pp. 14–15.

76 P. Bort, 'Hollants leenrecht', *Alle de wercken* (3rd edn, Leiden, 1731), pp. 325–7.

77 *Groot placaet-boek*, II, p. 682.   78 New style dating. Ibid., pp. 682–92.

79 Henricus Stephanus van Son, *De nature et indole curiae Hollandiae (vulgo het Hof van Holland) sub comitibus* (Leiden, 1783), appendix D.

80 Rijpperda Wierdsma, *Politie en justitie*, pp. 250–78. West-Friesland had a different administrative organization.

Brussels. The bailiffs received no salaries; instead they paid a set lease-sum to the Chamber of Accounts. Their incomes consisted of the surplus revenue of the bailiwick above and beyond the lease.[81] Although the bailiff leased his office for a specified number of years, he could be removed. The cities and high jurisdictions located within his bailiwick did not come under his authority. The bailiffs were charged with criminal proceedings and the execution of punishments, the promulgation of local by-laws and administration in their districts. They functioned as presiding officers of the college of lay judges, who administered justice in capital cases. Furthermore, the bailiff's court heard appeals for civil cases decided by manorial courts. Some bailiffs were also ex-officio dike reeves in their districts, such as in Rijnland, Delfland and Schieland. Other bailiffs were governors of castles located in their bailiwicks. The powers of the bailiffs were reduced, however, as the cities in their districts increased in importance. In 1388 parties to litigation in Amstelland and Gooiland were already allowed to appeal to the Amsterdam courts. During the sixteenth century the significance of the bailiffs' courts further decreased, because more and more frequently judgments of the manorial courts were appealed directly to the Court of Holland, thus bypassing the bailiffs.[82]

The appointments of bailiffs, sheriffs, treasurers and other financial officials are noted in the commission books of the Chamber of Accounts.[83] The bailiwicks that were attached to governorships of castles were generally rather small. The military aspect of these offices was probably the most important, but governors were also charged with the exercise of justice and administration. These governorships remained the preserve of the nobility. In Gorinchem, Gouda, Heusden, Loevestein and Woerden between 1506 and 1572 only nobles were appointed governors; in Muiden there were six nobles as opposed to two non-nobles. Only in Medemblik did noble governors not form the majority.[84] In contrast to most other offices in Holland, here the government made extensive use of high nobles and nobles from outside Holland. Count Hendrik van Nassau was appointed governor of Loevestein in 1510; Count Jan van Egmond and later his son Lamoraal were governors of Gorinchem (1515

---

[81] ARA Brussels, Aud., inv. no. 1184, fos. 59 v.–60.

[82] Jan Wagenaar, *Amsterdam, in zyne opkomst, aanwas, geschiedenissen*, 3 vols. (Amsterdam, 1760–7), III, p. 67. H. de Schepper, 'De burgerlijke overheden en hun permanente kaders 1480–1579', *NAGN*, v, pp. 312–49, at 344.

[83] ARA, Grafelijkheidsrekenkamer, registers, inv. nos. 492–5. Inv. no. 492 begins in October 1506; the commission book covering November 1493 to September 1506 is missing. Cf. for appointments by Orange from 1565 to 1574, ARA, Staten van Holland 1572–1795, inv. no. 1788. See J. Fox, 'Baljuwen en schouten in Holland. Hoe bij de Derde Afdeling van het Algemeen Rijksarchief naar hun benoeming te zoeken', *Holland. Regionaal-historisch tijdschrift* 12 (1980): 35–7. Names of bailiffs of Rijnland were pub. in Fockema Andreae, *Rijnland*, p. 399; bailiffs of Zuid-Holland are in Matthijs Balen Jansz., *Beschrijvinge der stad Dordrecht* (Dordrecht, 1677), p. 7; those of Delfland in Dolk, *Delfland*, p. 707.

[84] See appendix 8 of the Dutch edition.

and 1541); the count of Horne was keeper of Muiden (1522). The high nobles did not, however, exercise the offices themselves. Lord Gerrit van Renesse was named bailiff and dike-reeve of Woerden in 1541 'under the hand of Count Chaerles van Egmondt', who had been appointed to this office in 1528.[85] Shortly after Lamoraal van Egmond succeeded his brother Karel, Gerrit van Renesse again received the office, 'under the hand of Lamorael'.[86]

Yet in bailiwicks that were not tied to governorships, the number of bailiffs with noble names declined drastically. At the head of the great bailiwicks of Amstelland, Waterland and Zeevang,[87] Kennemerland, Rijnland, Delfland, Schieland, Brielle and Voorne, Putten, Strijen and South Holland there were about equal numbers of noble and non-noble bailiffs, until around 1530.[88] Afterwards the number of noble bailiffs decreased, until around 1570 there was only one noble (Adriaan van der Does in Schieland) alongside eight non-noble colleagues.[89]

Among the bailiffs we find primarily nobles of the second rank: scions of impoverished noble families, younger sons of important noble families, and nobles who had been integrated into urban patriciates. Only a few bailiffs were enrolled in the Ridderschap.[90] Gijsbrecht van Duvenvoirde, lord of Den Bossche, was bailiff of Amstelland, Waterland and Zeevang until 1507; he was the second son of Arend lord of Duvenvoirde.[91] Adriaan van der Does, bailiff of Delfland (1559–63) and of Schieland (after 1563) was the third son of Dirk van der Does, lord of Noordwijk.[92] But proportionately more significant than the younger sons were nobles associated with urban councils.

The cities had many interests in dominating the countryside: economic, judicial, military, hydraulic and even demographic.[93] To make rural areas dependent on them, cities used various means, including buying the surrounding manors and exercising pressure in the States. Thus in 1529 Amsterdam bought the seigneuries of Amstelveen and Nieuweramstel, Sloten, Sloterdijk and Osdorp; Leiden bought the seigneuries of Leiderdorp in 1582 and Oegstgeest in 1616.[94] In 1531 the cities obtained from the States a ban on rural

---

[85] ARA, Grafelijkheidsrekenkamer, registers, inv. no. 494, fos. 35 v., 36.
[86] Ibid., fos. 36 v., 37 v.
[87] Until 1545 under one bailiff; afterwards Amstelland had one, and another was appointed for Waterland and Zeevang.
[88] There were a few other noble bailiffs, who sat for shorter periods.
[89] See appendix 9 of the Dutch edition.
[90] Besides Jasper van Treslong, bailiff of Den Briel and Voorne (1541–58).
[91] Obreen, *Wassenaer*, p. 125. Indeed, in 1503 he had already married an heiress, Anna van Noordwijk, lady of Obdam.
[92] C. J. Polvliet, *Genealogie van het ond adellijk geslacht van der Does* (The Hague, 1893), pp. 69–70.
[93] T. S. Jansma, 'Het economisch overwicht van de laat-middeleeuwse stad t.a.v. haar agrarisch ommeland, in het bijzonder toegelicht met de verhouding tussen Leiden en Rijnland', *Tekst en uitleg. Historische opstellen* . . . (The Hague, 1974), pp. 35–53.
[94] Wagenaar, *Amsterdam*, I, p. 227; Wijs, *Leenstelsel*, pp. 103–5.

industry (*buitennering*), in favour of urban industry and urban excise taxes. Partly as a result of resistance by the Ridderschap, however, this order was not very effective.[95] Naturally the cities had a great interest in getting control of the surrounding bailiwicks as well, especially when these were tied to the office of dike-reeve. The cities were then able to influence the waterworks, by-laws, police, justice and economic life to their advantage.

Already in 1488 Amsterdam had received the revenues from the bailiwicks of Amstelland, Waterland and Zeevang as security for a loan to Maximilian, and in 1495 the burgemeesters received the right to name the bailiff, who none the less received his letter of appointment from the sovereign.[96] In 1484 Delft leased the combined bailiwick and dike-reeveship of Delfland; the office of bailiff and dike-reeve was filled by one of the burgemeesters. In 1500, however, these offices were returned to the sovereign.[97] The bailiffs of South Holland had to be selected by the central government from a list of burghers of Dordrecht, drawn up by the Dordrecht magistrates.[98] In 1576 the city of Rotterdam took advantage of the States' shortage of money to purchase the entire bailiwick of Schieland; henceforth the bailiff and dike-reeve were appointed from the Rotterdam council.[99] Even when a city did not appoint the bailiff, it had influence on his administration. In 1387 Amsterdam had the privilege of requiring the bailiffs of Amstelland and Gooiland to swear an oath to the Amsterdam magistracy that they would respect the rights and privileges of the city. Likewise, the bailiffs of Rijnland and Delfland swore an oath to the burgemeesters of Leiden and Delft.[100]

The dominance of the 'metropolis' located in the bailiwick was expressed in the choice of bailiffs. These officers were nearly always drawn from the councils of the city. This applies not only to bourgeois bailiffs, but also to bailiffs with noble names. In Kennemerland between 1507 and 1572 there were eleven bailiffs, of whom seven or eight belonged to the nobility; most of them, including the nobles, appear on lists of Haarlem magistrates.[101] In Rijnland between 1489 and 1573 seven bailiffs were appointed, four of them nobles; all belonged to the council of Leiden.[102] The dominance of Dordrecht over the South

---

[95] Brünner, *Order op de buitennering*.

[96] Wagenaar, *Amsterdam*, I, pp. 188, 193–4, and III, p. 181. ARA, Grafelijkheidsrekenkamer, registers, inv. no. 492, fo. 123.

[97] Dolk, *Delfland*, p. 58.

[98] Balen, *Dordrecht*, p. 7.

[99] J. L. van der Gouw, 'Schieland als koloniaal gebied van Rotterdam', *Rotterdams Jaarboekje* (1977): 235–55.

[100] Van Leeuwen, *Costumen Rijnland*, p. 52; Rijpperda Wierdsma, *Politie en justitie*, p. 26.

[101] *Naam-register van de Heeren van de Regeering der Stad Haarlem, van de ministers van dien; en van derzelven commissien; alsmeede van eenige ampten en employen binnen dezelve* (Haarlem, 1733). E.g., Gerrit van Schoten, 1505–9 burgemeester, 1510 *baljuw*; Jan van Alckemade, 1511 *schepen*, 1513 *baljuw*; Ysbrant van Schoten, *schout* in 1510, *baljuw* in 1524.

[102] Willem en Gomme van Bosschuyzen, Geryt van Lockhorst (dike-reeve only, not bailiff), Dirck

Holland islands appears in the preponderance of Dordrecht names among the bailiffs of Strijen and South Holland.[103] Amsterdam dominated Amstelland, Waterland and Zeevang; the fact that Amsterdam had no nobles in its council is reflected in the small number of noble bailiffs in these districts.[104]

Even noble preserves such as the military governorships were not safe from the expansive tendencies of the cities. Thus in 1477 Amsterdam took over the occupation of the strategically important castle at Muiden.[105] After the death of governor Jan van Nyenrode, a nobleman of Utrecht, the city declared that the defences of the castle were not strong enough; on its own initiative it named an Amsterdam burgemeester to Nyenrode's post. Some months later he received his official appointment as governor of Muiden and bailiff of Gooiland.[106]

The office of sheriff in the cities was in many respects comparable to that of bailiff in the countryside. The sheriff represented sovereign authority. He received his appointment from the central government, and like the bailiff he leased his office for a specified term. Together with the alderman he was responsible for 'police and justice'. Although the sheriff thus formally represented the sovereign, the cities had also acquired influence over his appointment. Since the sheriff had to lease his office, a city could, with the sovereign's permission, pay the lease sum and appoint the officer itself. Thus Amsterdam leased the office of sheriff in 1469, from 1509 to 1550, and from 1564 to 1581. In 1581 Amsterdam was relieved of its obligation to pay the annual lease of 300 gulden. Henceforth, the sheriff was appointed by the burgemeesters and was responsible only to them. The ties to sovereign authority were almost completely broken; the sheriff was one of the city regents. After 1578 no one was appointed sheriff in Amsterdam unless he had previously been alderman, burgemeester, or a member of the council.[107] Something similar occurred in Leiden. In the fourteenth century the city had already established that only councillors of Leiden could be appointed sheriff, and that the office could not be alienated; compensation was paid to the burgrave of Leiden for the sum that he used to receive from the sheriff's office. In the sixteenth century the

van der Does. J. J. Orlers, *Beschryvinge der stadt Leyden* (2nd edn, Leiden, 1641), pp. 591–6; Fockema Andreae, *Rijnland*, p. 399.

[103] Jacob Oem Jacobsz., burgemeester of Dordrecht and Baudewijn Heerman, bailiff of Styen in 1550 and 1558 respectively. In Zuid-Holland Dirck Oem van Wyngaerden, *knape* (1491), Jacob Oem, *ridder*, heer van Wyngaerden and Florens and Ysbrand van den Coulster.

[104] Coen van Bosschuyzen, who could be reckoned among the lower nobility of Holland, was bailiff of Amstelland, Waterland and Zeevang from 1515 to 1533; at the same time he was a member of the Leiden Council. Orlers, *Leyden*, pp. 591–7.

[105] Wagenaar, *Amsterdam*, I, p. 178.

[106] Lambertus Hortensius, *Over de opkomst en den ondergang van Naarden*, ed. P. H. Peerlkamp and A. Perk (Utrecht, 1866), p. 253. In 1482 nobles who had no connection with Amsterdam were again appointed; in 1510 the post went to another Amsterdammer, Heyman Jacobsz. van Ouderamstel. Cf. Jacobus Koning, *Geschiedenis van het slot te Muiden en Hoofts leven op hetzelve* (Amsterdam, 1827), pp. 117–18.

[107] Wagenaar, *Amsterdam*, III, pp. 280–1.

sheriff was chosen by the stadholder from a proposed list of three persons.[108]

Just as with the bailiffs, the influence of the cities was expressed in the choice of sheriffs. The sheriffs of Haarlem, whether they had noble names or bourgeois origins, were largely drawn from the Haarlem council; the sheriffs of Leiden, both nobles and others, were members of the Leiden council; and the sheriffs of Dordrecht were Dordrecht patricians such as Bueckelaer and Van Drenckwaert.[109]

Among the sheriffs the decline of the noble presence was even more pronounced than among the bailiffs. Until about 1530, there were more sheriffs with noble names than others in the six voting cities of Holland. But after that year the proportion of nobles fell, and in 1570 there was no more a noble sheriff in these cities. There were differences among these cities. All sheriffs of Haarlem belonged to the nobility until mid-century, and in Leiden they were noble until 1540. In Dordrecht, Gouda and Delft noble sheriffs were in the minority, and in Amsterdam in the entire period not a single nobleman was appointed.[110]

All officers discussed so far were appointed by the sovereign, although the cities had in practice acquired much say over them. Burgemeester, alderman, and member of the council were urban offices. The council was a closed college, consisting of twenty-four to forty persons. Here lay the real power. Burgemeesters and aldermen were regularly named from the council. The councillors sat for life and were appointed by co-optation.[111]

The proportion of nobles among the councillors, burgemeesters and aldermen varied in the six voting towns. Amsterdam and Gouda had no noble magistrates.[112] During the early decades of the sixteenth century, Dordrecht had regularly chosen members of the noble families Van Alblas, De Jode and Van Coulster as burgemeesters.[113] In Haarlem one or two of the four ruling burgemeesters were regularly drawn from the noble families Berckenroede, Bekesteyn, Foreest, Schagen, Schoten, Van Loo, Treslong, Van Dorp, Bronckhorst, Duvenvoirde and Van Vliet.[114] In the magistracy of Delft sat the knightly

---

[108] Orlers, *Leyden*, pp. 601–3.

[109] Leiden: Jacob van Bosschuyzen (schout 1490–1503), Jan van Swieten (to 1509), Hendrik van der Does (1515) and Gerrit van Lockhorst (1527) were members of the Council (Orlers, *Leyden*, pp. 607–8, and 591–7; ARA, Grafelijkheidsrekenkamer, registers, inv. no. 492, fo. 96 v.). Haarlem: Dirk van Almonde (1501) Gillis van Valckesteyn (1503), Gerrit van Berckenrode (1504), Dirk van Almonde (1507), Ysbrant van Schooten (1510), Jan van Schagen (1515), Jan van Heemstede (1518), Joost van Bronckhorst (1519), Frans van Hoogstraten (1521), Jan van Alkemade (1524), Jasper van Treslong (1527) (*Naam-register Haarlem*).

[110] See appendix 10 of the Dutch edition.

[111] Fruin, *Staatsinstellingen*, pp. 71–2.

[112] Wagenaar, *Amsterdam*, III, pp. 355–60; J. Walvis, *Beschrijving der stad Gouda* (Gouda and Leiden, 1713), pp. 109–15.

[113] J. Van Beverwijck, 't Begin van Hollant in Dordrecht. Mitsgaders der eerster Stede beschryvinge, regeringe, ende regeerders (Dordrecht, 1640), pp. 175 ff.

[114] *Naam-register Haarlem*.

Table 6.1 *The Leiden council, 1481–1574*

	1481	1481–1510	1510	1519–74
Nobles	17 (42.5%)	21 (40%)	11 (27.5%)	17 (12%)
Burghers	23 (57.5%)	31 (60%)	29 (72.5%)	126 (88%)
Totals	40	52	40	143

families Van der Dussen, Adrichem, Almonde, Van Dorp, Foreest and Rhoon.[115] Among the council of Leiden there were many descendants of the noble families Raephorst, Alckemade, Poelgeest, Swieten, Boechorst, Boschuyzen, Heerman, Lockhorst, Van der Does, Van der Laen, Tetroede, Coulster and Van Loo.[116] But the representation of nobles in urban councils also declined. This can be seen clearly in the composition of the Leiden council (table 6.1).[117]

The Holland nobles served the government not only as administrators, but also as soldiers. Yet it is difficult to determine how many nobles were employed in the army. At the beginning of the sixteenth century the military importance of the nobility was still based on its feudal relationship to the sovereign. In exchange for the possession of fiefs, nobles were required to take part personally in the feudal ban. In practice personal military service by vassals was probably infrequent, and during the reign of Charles V such required service was permanently discontinued.[118] None the less, a great number of sixteenth-century nobles were still called 'knight'. This title was conferred upon being dubbed a knight, but did not necessarily imply skill in the profession of arms. Nobles who had the title 'knight' should not be regarded as professional soldiers. Many of them fulfilled quite peaceable functions at Court, in the Forestry Office, as bailiff or sheriff. Even in the urban councils one can find

[115] Reinier Boitet, *Beschrijving der stadt Delft* (Delft, 1729), pp. 81 ff.

[116] Orlers, *Leyden*, pp. 591–7.

[117] See appendix 11 of the Dutch edition.

[118] Van der Houve, *Hantvest*, I, p. 60, and Van Leeuwen, *Redeningh*, p. 22. Cf. Van Zurck, *Codex*, pp. 344 and 461. On 3 July 1500 Emperor Maximilian summoned all vassals, knights, nobles, fief-holders and sub-fief-holders (*mansmannen*) to appear with their armed followers at a survey of arms in Haarlem (Petrus Rendorp, *De origine ac potestate ordinum sub comitibus Hollandiae* (Leiden, 1782), appendix C). Van Zurck cites a placard of 31 Dec. 1517, 'dat alle edelmannen in Holland zig in wapenen, elks na hun faculteit zullen vinden onder 't regiment van den Stadhouder, ter resistentie van de vyanden' (that all noblemen in Holland should be armed, each in accord with his capacity, under the command of the stadholder, to resist the enemy), *Codex*, p. 345. But on 27 Jan. 1567 the Ridderschap in the States of Holland declared that nobles did not have to perform military service because they were not exempt from taxes (*Res. Holland*, 27 Jan. 1566. In the published resolutions the first months of 1567 have been incorrectly bound with those of 1566.) In Breda, fief-holders still had to perform military service in 1573, according to Bor, *Nederlantscher oorlogen*, I, p. 489.

nobles who had received knighthood.[119] The continuing presence of nobles in the governorships, however, indicates that their military significance was not entirely lost.

The castles where the nobles resided in the countryside had lost their military importance.[120] In fifteenth-century conflicts the castles had played a role, but in most cases that role ended with their destruction. Their stone walls no longer offered adequate protection against the improved artillery. During the siege of Leiden by the Spaniards, the Rijnland castles served only for the quartering of troops – a reason why they were destroyed, first by the Leideners, and later by the Spaniards.[121]

The high nobility was better able to retain its military significance. Jan van Wassenaer was killed as commander of the imperial troops in Friesland; Joost van Cruijningen, the lord of Heenvliet, was killed in action as general of the imperial army during the Schmalkalden War. Lamoraal van Egmond led the army to victory in battles at St Quentin (1557) and Gravelines (1558).[122] Hendrik van Brederode had command of a *bande d'ordonnance*.[123]

These *bandes d'ordonnance* retained little military importance.[124] They stood under the command of a member of the high nobility. A band consisted of thirty, forty, or fifty *hommes d'armes*, heavily armed horsemen, each with three horses; most of these men belonged to the nobility. Alongside them stood twice as many 'archers', light cavalry, a great number of whom also were noble. Apparently, however, few Holland nobles belonged to these units: most of the *bandes* came from Hainault and Artois.

It is difficult to judge the military significance of the Holland nobles in this period. Presumably the military heritage of the nobles lived on in their memory, as many nobles bore the title of knight, lived in castles, and had themselves depicted in full armour.[125] In practice not that many Holland nobles were

---

[119] The knights Gerrit van Assendelft, Floris Oem van Wyngaerden and Jan van Duvenvoirde were councillors in the Court of Holland and the Court of Fiefs; they were also graduates in law. Floris van Assendelft, knight, lord of Kijfhoek, the younger brother of Gerrit, was bailiff of The Hague and bailiff and dike-reeve of Schieland. However, he also fulfilled military duties as governor, bailiff, and sheriff of Gouda and Oudewater. Willem van Alckemade, knight, was councillor in the Court of Fiefs, sheriff of Leiden and steward of the abbey of Leeuwenhorst. Dirk van Duvenvoirde, knight, was bailiff and dike-reeve of Schieland. Gerrit van Lockhorst, knight, was bailiff and dike-reeve of Rijnland and sheriff, burgemeester, and member of the council of Leiden. Jacob van Wyngaerden, knight, was bailiff of Zuid-Holland. Willem van Bosschuyzen, knight, was member of the Leiden Council in 1510.

[120] J. G. N. Renaud, 'De Rijnlandse kastelen in hun krijgsbouwkundige betekenis', in Fockema Andreae, Renaud and Pellinck, *Kastelen*, pp. 21–52, at 44–5.

[121] Ibid., pp. 48–9. The castles lay within the firing range of artillery, and furthermore the Leideners were afraid that the Spaniards would use them as cover for their assaults.

[122] Obreen, *Wassenaer*, pp. 38–41; 't Hart, *Heenvliet*, p. 77; Dek, *Egmond*, p. 53.

[123] De la Fontaine Verwey, 'Le rôle'; H. L. G. Guillaume, *Histoire des Bandes d'Ordonnance des Pays-Bas* (Brussels, 1873), p. 104.

[124] See Guillaume, *Bandes d'Ordonnance*.

[125] E.g., the illustrations on pp. 3, 224, 226–9.

employed as soldiers. Yet during the Revolt nobles suddenly played important military roles: in 1566 and 1567 with Brederode's troops, later among the bands of Sea-Beggars, in the prince of Orange's army, or in the defence of the cities of Holland. Their military heritage was thus not without consequences.

To recapitulate, the proportion of nobles declined in many administrative offices. This decline was not observed in all offices, nor was it equally pronounced. In the Chamber of Accounts, nobles had never been very important. In the governorships and the Forestry Office they retained their leading position. But in the Court, as bailiffs and as sheriffs, the nobles lost ground. In 1528 four of the six ordinary councillors at Court still belonged to the nobility; in 1572 the number had fallen to two out of eight, whereby the personal connection with the Ridderschap was lost. In 1515 nobles held six of the ten great bailiwicks in Holland, but in 1570 only one of them. The six great cities of Holland counted four noble sheriffs in 1515, but in 1570 not a single sheriff was still noble. Noble representation also declined in urban councils and colleges of aldermen and burgemeesters.

The causes of the declining noble presence in administration are unclear. In all likelihood, however, the nobles did not disappear from these offices against their will. First, there is no sign of any protest from them. Second, there are signs that many nobles preferred to live on their manors without official responsibilities. The family of Beijeren van Schagen, descendants of a bastard of Count Albrecht van Beieren, furnish an example. At the turn of the sixteenth century, scions of a lesser branch of this family were employed in the magistracy of Haarlem. Jan, second son of the lord of Schagen (ante 1450 – post 1518), was sheriff of Haarlem; his son Jan was burgemeester six times between 1527 and 1540. But after the latter had inherited the ancestral manor of Schagen from his childless cousin Josina in 1542, just prior to his own death, his heirs settled in the castle of Schagen and ceased to hold offices in the city administration. Jan's grandson, also called Jan (1544–1618), became a member of the Ridderschap after the Revolt.[126]

High nobles likewise did not always have the opportunity or the desire to become engaged in official business. When important decisions had to be made after the death of the regent Margaret of Austria, several nobles excused themselves: the count of Nassau 'for various necessary and urgent affairs at Breda, about which he wrote us'. The lord of Beveren and the count of Buren were preoccupied with their dike works; the lord of Gavere said he was ill.[127]

In 1558 a post that had to be filled by a nobleman became vacant at the Court of Friesland. The Court considered all three candidates who had applied for

---

[126] Dek, *Genealogie graven van Holland*, pp. 63–5.
[127] M. Baelde, 'Edellieden en juristen in het centrale bestuur der zestiende-eeuwse Nederlanden (1531–1578)', *TvG* 80 (1967): 39–51, at 45; *De Collaterale raden onder Karel V en Filips II, 1531–1578* (Brussels, 1965), p. 15.

the position qualified, but found two of them rather young. Thus the Court thought it better to ask the most prominent nobles of Friesland to fill this important post. Yet the search for a leading nobleman to accept the position was unsuccessful. Indeed, 'none of these, *because they are rich and comfortable gentlemen*, wanted to hear about or subject himself to continual residence and attendance at the said council'.[128] Those who refused were Frisian nobles, but there is no reason to think that their counterparts in Holland, who were no less rich and comfortable, thought otherwise. Nor were nobles the only ones who tried to avoid office-holding. In 1563 a certain Frans Teyng wanted to move from Amsterdam to Haarlem and 'spend his money' there, but only on the condition that he would not have to occupy any offices.[129] Adriaan Pauwels of Brill was chosen alderman in 1547, but repeatedly refused to appear at sessions of the Court. His colleagues complained: 'We too have things to do at home. If anyone is allowed to go home and absent himself, we too should like to go home.' The negligent Pauwels received a fine, but was never again chosen as alderman.[130]

The Holland nobleman Anthonie van Woerden van Vliet, who chose the king's side during the time of Troubles and had lived in Mechelen, settled in Haarlem in 1579. But, because he was annoyed that the magistrates of the city required him to accept public office, he moved to his house Ter Coulster in Heiloo.[131] We do not know whether this Catholic nobleman wanted to avoid compromising himself by siding with the rebels, or simply found all offices troublesome. Political and personal motives could also blend imperceptibly for those involved. The Amsterdam poet Hendrik Laurensz. Spieghel would rather pay a stiff fine than sit in the college of Admiralty in 1589. He based his refusal on an oath he had taken at the 'Satisfaction' in 1578, when he had promised to preserve the old magistrates in the government and the Catholic religion in the city. He supposedly resigned from his burghership in order not to hold any offices.[132] Yet it is likely that, along with this principled political position, he felt a more general philosophical aversion to administrative responsibilities. Spieghel was the author of 'Numa, or Refusal of Office', an allegorical play based on Plutarch, describing how the Sabine Numa Pompilius refused the throne of Rome. Spieghel wrote it after his own refusal of office, probably

---

[128] ARA Brussels, Aud., inv. no. 1704/1 (emphasis mine).
[129] J. J. Woltjer, 'De "alderrijcste" te Leiden in 1584', in *Leidse facetten*, ed. D. E. H. de Boer (Zwolle, 1982), p. 31.
[130] W. Troost and J. J. Woltjer, 'Brielle in hervormingstijd', *BMGN* 87 (1972): 307–53, at 309.
[131] ARA Brussels, Aud., inv. no. 1472/1.
[132] C. Kramer, 'De datering van Hendrick Laurensz. Spieghels zinspel Numa ofte Amptsweygheringe', *Jaarboek Amstelodamum*, 66 (1974): 80–95. To avoid being an alderman, Spieghel had lived in Haarlem for several years. According to his own words, he *ontpoorterde* (disenfranchised, or 'uncitizened') himself. [Translator's note: The 'Satisfaction' was a treaty concluded after the Pacification of Ghent (1576), by which the cities in Holland and Zeeland that had remained loyal to the king of Spain accepted the authority of William of Orange.]

between 1600 and 1603, but the same considerations that motivated Numa may have played a part in the author's decision in 1589.[133] Spieghel makes Numa describe the differences between himself and Rome as follows:

> You people have been restlessly fed on arguments and partisanship,
> I am of a tranquil and sedate mind.
> You seek external wars, fights and battles;
> I seek to enjoy inner peace.
> You seek force, power over all your neighbours;
> I try only to guide my own spirit well.
> You strive to the utmost for wealth and power;
> I value nothing more than disdain for all that is transient.
> And because our design and customs thus sharply conflict,
> My government of your people would be improper.
>
> (verses 337–46)

Pieter Adriaansz. van der Werff had no objections in principle to the States' government when he declined membership in the Deputy Councils in 1585. The Leiden regent based his refusal on 'weighty affairs' that he had to settle in Amsterdam, else he would 'find himself suffering great damage'; on the care of the orphaned children of his deceased brother 'who by my absence would be likely to fall into great corruption'; and on his own household, 'which is not small, [filled with] children as well as many other problems'.[134] It is unclear whether Van der Werff was honestly expressing his cares for his business affairs and his family, or simply frightened away by the thorny political problems that would await him if he became a councillor in 1585. The same applies to the lord of Mathenesse, who was also nominated to the Deputy Councils in 1586. The States attached to his nomination the proviso that 'the same [lord] will be very earnestly admonished by the Noble Lords, henceforth to attend more regularly at the college [of the Ridderschap], than he has hitherto done'.[135] In 1576 the lords of Kenenburg (Egmond), Carnisse (Van den Boetzelaer) and Warmond (Duvenvoirde) all wanted to reduce their duties to their country. Apparently it was not easy to find successors, because on 24 October of that year the Ridderschap decided that these lords would provisionally continue in their offices. But this would not bind them in any way: if their presence was required elsewhere or if they had something else to do, then a substitute would be engaged to take their place.[136]

These examples have brought us to the time of the Revolt, when political

---

[133] Hendrick Laurensz Spieghel, 'Zinspel Numa ofte Ambtsweigeringe', in *Noordnederlandse rederijkersspelen*, ed. N. van der Laan (Amsterdam, 1941), pp. 295–320; Kramer, 'Datering', pp. 91–5.

[134] The correspondence between Van der Werff and the States is published in A. Kluit, *Historie der Hollandsche staatsregeering tot aan het jaar 1795*, 5 vols. (Amsterdam, 1802–5), III, pp. 433–4.

[135] Ibid., p. 440.

[136] *Res. Holland*, 24 Oct. 1576.

considerations could have played a role in the decision to decline offices. But it is quite possible that the Holland nobles had already felt reservations about office-holding earlier. If this supposition is correct, we must still explain why nobles continued to hold many offices in the first three decades of the sixteenth century, and why a decline set in afterwards.

Charles V remained in the Netherlands almost the entire year of 1531, bringing about an intensification of state activity.[137] In 1530 both the imperial chancellor Mercurino Gattinara and the regent Margaret of Austria had died. The emperor did not name a successor to the chancellor and retained personal authority over a number of important official matters.[138] The chancellor's duties were assigned to several councillors devoted to the emperor and dependent upon him.[139] Along with the new regent Mary of Hungary he appointed three 'collateral' councils, in which high nobles as well as professional jurists were represented. Owing to their permament presence, the jurists acquired a certain predominance. Although the rise of non-noble jurists at the expense of the nobility is an older phenomenon, this process was accelerated at the level of central administration by the reforms of 1531.[140] One week after the establishment of the collateral councils the emperor ordered the codification and homologation of all existing provincial rights and customs; he himself retained the power to give them the force of law. Provincial particularism was still so strong that not much came of this gigantic project. Simultaneously the emperor reconfirmed a number of strict measures against heretics, which were likewise in conflict with old laws and customs.[141] In Holland these reforms of 1531 did not lead to institutional changes, except for the Court receiving a new instruction that placed greater emphasis upon its powers as a judicial body.[142] As a result of the changes in Brussels, however, the pressure of central authority increased. The declining number of nobles in administrative offices cannot be regarded as principled opposition to the policy of Charles V, although this policy did indeed make office-holding less attractive. The new administration required a new type of official. More specialized knowledge was required in finance and law. The office-holders lost some of their former independence as more decisions

---

[137] M. Baelde, 'De Nederlanden van Spaanse erfopvolging tot beeldenstorm, 1506–1566', in *De Lage Landen*, ed. Schöffer, Van der Wee and Bornewasser, pp. 38–101, at 46.
[138] Baelde, *Collaterale raden*, pp. 17–22.
[139] Ibid., p. 47.
[140] Baelde, 'Edellieden en juristen', p. 51. Cf. De Schepper and Janssens, 'De Raad van State in de landsheerlijke Nederlanden', pp. 3–4.
[141] W. P. Blockmans and J. van Herwaarden, 'De Nederlanden van 1493 tot 1555: binnenlandse en buitenlandse politiek', *NAGN*, v, pp. 443–91, at 465. J. Gillissen, 'Les phases de la codification et l'homologation des coutumes dans les XVII Provinces des Pays-Bas', *TvR* 18 (1950): 36–67 and 239–90.
[142] *Groot placaet-boeck*, II, pp. 703–60. For various social and economic regulations, see A. F. Mellink, *De wederdopers in de Noordelijke Nederlanden 1531–1544* (Groningen, 1953; reprint, Leeuwarden, 1981), pp. 5–7.

required the consent of higher authorities. In many offices, emphasis came to rest on the administrative aspects. As their activities were extended, governing bodies had to meet more often and for longer periods.[143] The nobles who were asked to sit in the Court of Friesland in 1558 complained precisely about the 'continual residence and attendance'.[144] Sitting in the Court and other institutions was transformed from an honorary office to a profession.[145] This applies equally to city administrations. The towns did not lose their traditional independence, but increased government activity called for frequent trips to The Hague, Mechelen and Brussels.[146] Earlier, nobles had no objections to office-holding, as long as it did not take too much time and the matters were not too complicated. This attitude was consistent with the aristocratic ethos that regarded service to the sovereign as honourable. Now that the most important administrative bodies were going to meet almost daily and handle matters that were more numerous and complex, many nobles declined the honour. It is significant that the two colleges in The Hague where the nobles did maintain their presence, the Forestry Office and the Court of Fiefs, probably were not affected by this development.

The nobles could afford to withdraw from office-holding only if they had sufficient alternative income. Precisely in the 1530s, land-leases, the primary source of noble incomes, began to increase sharply.[147] In the first thirty years of the century average lease prices rose 11, 12, and 14 per cent per decade, respectively; but between 1530 and 1540 the average lease price of land rose by 59 per cent. Between 1540 and 1570 the increase slowed to 37, 29, and 23 per cent per decade, but that was still more than the rises in the first thirty years of the century.[148] The purchasing power of lease prices also increased after 1530. Between 1500 and 1530 the real lease price, expressed in wheat, declined steadily, but after 1530 a rise began, lasting until 1560 or 1570. Around 1550 real lease prices had risen to the level of 1500; in 1560 they were 2.5 times as high as in 1530. Based on these figures, the increased prosperity of the nobles after 1530 seems likely.

The simultaneity of these three processes – the decreasing number of nobles in administrative offices, the acceleration of the process of state-formation, and the rise in lease prices – suggests a plausible reconstruction of events. Changes in Brussels led to a far-reaching bureaucratization and professionalization of

---

[143] According to new orders of the Court on 20 Aug. 1531, all councillors had to be present in the chamber from 7 to 10 a.m. and 3 to 5 p.m. in the summer, and from 8 to 11 a.m. and 3 to 5 p.m. in the wintertime. *Groot-placaet-boeck*, II, p. 708; cf. De Schepper, 'Vorstelijke ambtenarij', pp. 358–77.

[144] See above, p. 162.

[145] Van Gelder, 'Hollandse adel', p. 134.

[146] Fruin, *Staatsinstellingen*, p. 72.

[147] See above, pp. 102–3.

[148] Kuys and Schoenmakers, *Landpachten*, p. 58.

the administrative apparatus, in the provinces as well as in Brussels itself. Nobles were not excluded, but office-holding became less appealing to them. The nobles gradually withdrew from those offices that were most influenced by the changes: the Court, bailiffs and sheriffs. This was possible because of a substantial improvement in the incomes nobles received from their lands. Nobles were still allowed to hold offices, but they no longer wanted or needed them.

THE NOBLES IN THE RIDDERSCHAP

As the 'College of the Ridderschap and Nobles of the States of Holland and West-Friesland', its official name, the nobility of Holland had a vote in the meetings of the States. As owners of most of the manors, the nobles were considered to represent the countryside, in contrast to the six voting cities.[149]

The influence of the Ridderschap was greater than the voting relationship of one to six might lead us to suppose. They were the first to cast their vote; if the Ridderschap and Dordrecht, the first of the cities, were in agreement, the rest generally followed suit. The Ridderschap's influence was further increased because it presided over the States, and because the provincial advocate was ex-officio pensionary of the Ridderschap.[150] The Ridderschap also represented the smaller cities.[151] Sometimes, however, these sent their own representatives when discussions concerned them directly.[152] Yet in general people were not in favour of this idea. In 1543 the regent refused to hear the representatives of the small cities during negotiations over the subsidy, and in 1564, when the Court had summoned all the small cities of Holland after they had objected to the policy of the States, the States decided that this was improper and 'tended to the defamation of the States'.[153]

The Ridderschap thus occupied a weighty position in the States. It acted

---

[149] The countryside then known as Zuid-Holland, i.e. the region south of the River Maas, was represented by Dordrecht.

[150] Fruin, *Staatsinstellingen*, pp. 80–2.

[151] In 1522 the nobles were summoned to the States 'on account of the countryside, and the smaller cities' (Van Leeuwen, *Batavia*, p. 762). Although the nobles had not been called when the States had to decide on granting a *gratuiteyt* of 5,000 gulden, the cities demanded that 'the nobles should also be summoned, as representing the small cities and the countryside', whereupon the meeting was postponed until the nobles were present (Van der Goes, *Register*, I, p. 42). Thus P. A. Meilink was mistaken when he stated that the Ridderschap first claimed to represent the small cities in 1528: *Archieven van de Staten van Holland en de hen opvolgende besturen* (The Hague, 1929), I, p. 2.

[152] E.g. in 1540, 1547 and 1559, when the coastal cities of the Noorderkwartier were summoned for discussions of *ankergelden* (anchor-moneys), herring fisheries and a salt-tax (Fruin, *Staatsinstellingen*, p. 80). Other examples can be found in *Hedendaagsche historie*, IV, pp. 106–9; even The Hague, Beverwijk and probably a few Waterlands villages sent representatives to the meeting of the States.

[153] *Res. Holland*, 13 July 1564.

expressly as the representative of rural interests (which coincided with those of the seigneurial lords) in resistance to the urban attempt to destroy industry in the countryside. Thanks in part to noble resistance in the States, the ban of 1531 largely remained a dead letter.[154]

Not all nobles were called to the Ridderschap. In order to be admitted to the college, a candidate had to be a scion of an old noble lineage and hold a high jurisdiction, or at least a manor or a noble ancestral home, directly in fief from the county of Holland.[155] In principle only descendants of old Holland noble families were qualified to appear in the Ridderschap, but nobles from other provinces who held seigneurial possessions in Holland were sometimes also summoned.[156] The list made by the president of the Court of Holland in 1555, discussed at length in chapter 2, distinguished various groups.[157] The largest group consisted of forty-eight persons who met all the criteria. Besides ancient Holland noble families, they included several high nobles who held possessions in Holland (Orange, Horne, Aremberg, Ligne) and a few Utrecht nobles. The second group consisted of a few seigneurs who were not usually enrolled, because they were not noble: the abbots of Egmond and Middelburg, and the burgemeesters of Delft, Amsterdam and Gouda, ex-officio holders of seigneuries belonging to the cities. Then followed the names of thirty-eight lords of the manor who were not regarded as qualified for the Ridderschap for various reasons. The list closed with the names of twenty Holland nobles who possessed no manors. In practice, however, not all nobles who met the criteria attended meetings of the States.

Which nobles attended meetings of the Ridderschap? Beginning in 1525, the nobles in attendance can be traced in the register kept by the provincial advocate Aart van der Goes.[158] Initially the meetings of the States were quite informal affairs. The initiative to call the States lay with the sovereign: in practice that meant his representative, the stadholder or the Court. Thus the secretary could convoke the small cities, while in other instances the defence of their interests was left to the nobles. Likewise, on 8 February 1530, he con-

---

154 Brünner, *Order op de buitennering*, pp. 116–94. Discussion in the States, p. 121.
155 Instruction to Mr Arend Coebel, receiver-general of the States, to remonstrate with the prince of Orange on behalf of the nobles (1565), ARA, Archief van de Staten van Holland, before 1572, inv. no. 2388; ARA, Ridderschap, inv. no. 73; Van Zurck, *Codex*, p. 342; *Hedendaagsche historie*, IV, pp. 91–103.
156 Van der Houve, *Hantvest*, I, p. 235.
157 Appendix 1 of the Dutch edition. Cf. above, pp. 27–9.
158 Van der Goes, *Register*. During his term of office, however, not all meetings were noted, because he was not always present. The notes of Adriaan, his son and successor in office after 1544, are more reliable. After 1555 the registration was even better (Meilink, *Archieven van de Staten van Holland*, p. 4). The lists of nobles appearing in the Ridderschap published by Van der Houve, *Hantvest*, I, pp. 175–83, and Van Leeuwen, *Batavia*, pp. 761–808, are incomplete. Van der Houve goes back only to 1560, and Van Leeuwen lacks most of the meetings between 1560 and 1590, as well as those in 1617 and 1619. Yet they do mention several meetings that are not listed in the published resolutions of the States.

voked the abbots of Egmond and Berne (near Heusden) along with the nobles and cities in order to have them approve a treaty with France, although the clergy was not officially part of the States.[159] The meetings of the States were irregular and infrequent in this period. Between August 1533 and August 1534, for example, the States met only once, and between July 1537 and September 1538 they did not meet at all.[160] This reflects the rather limited significance of the States' meetings in the first half of the sixteenth century. The States had to give their consent to the subsidies and loans, they had to provide their co-operation (often merely decorative) in important acts of government such as rules of succession and peace treaties, but beyond that their participation in government and legislation was largely dependent upon the will of the sovereign. He could consult them when preparing political ordinances, regulations affecting the mints or other important matters, but he could also dispense with them. By contrast, the States themselves, and probably also substantial parts of the population, increasingly regarded the college as a representative body. Since the sovereign needed them in order to collect taxes, they could exercise real influence.[161]

For fifty-five meetings of the States held between 9 February 1525 and 19 February 1530, the names of twenty-two noble attenders are recorded. Six of them attended ten or more times. The other nobles were seldom present: nine nobles appeared only once. Even the nobles who went most frequently attended only a small proportion of the meetings. No one appeared more than twenty-four times. At most meetings half a dozen or fewer nobles were present, and at many meetings the Ridderschap was entirely absent. High nobles very seldom appeared: Jacques de Ligne, who was married to the Wassenaer heiress, came four times; the count of Buren once.

All nobles who came with any frequency to these fifty-five meetings also held important offices in provincial administration. Among them were three councillors of the Court: Jan van Duvenvoirde, lord of Warmond, appeared thirteen times; Gerrit van Assendelft, first ordinary councillor and president from 1528 onward, ten times; Floris Oem van Wyngaerden, lord of IJsselmonde, also ten times. Willem van Alckemade, also known as Willem van Coulster, twenty-four times. With the establishment of the Court of Fiefs in 1520, he had become a judge; earlier he had been a council member, burgemeester, and sheriff of Leiden.[162] Floris van Assendelft, lord of Kijfhoek, younger brother of the

---

[159] Van der Goes, *Register*, I, p. 235.

[160] 'Remonstrantie van het Hof van Holland en de Rekenkamer nopens de administratie van den ontvanger-generaal A. Coebel en de Staten van Holland', ed. P. A. Meilink, *BMHG* 45 (1924): 157–83, at 157.

[161] Ibid., pp. 157–8. Cf. Fruin, *Staatsinstellingen*, pp. 48–9; De Schepper, 'De burgerlijke overheden', pp. 325–6.

[162] Van Son, *De natura et indole curiae Hollandicae*, appendix D; Orlers, *Leyden*, pp. 592, 607, 627; later he became steward of the aristocratic convent of Rijnsburg, 'Actestukken', p. 332.

president of the Court, attended twenty times. He was governor and bailiff of Gouda (1525–55); earlier he had been bailiff and dike-reeve of Schieland and bailiff of The Hague, and in 1534 he became bailiff and sheriff of Oudewater.[163] Those who attended less frequently included several important officeholders such as Adam van der Duyn, bailiff of Putten.[164]

Between 1530 and 1550 this pattern did not change. Those who continued to attend frequently were Floris van Assendelft (d. 1555) and his brother Gerrit (d. 1558), Jan van Duvenvoirde (d. 1544) and Adam van der Duyn (d. 1548). Other frequent attenders were Jasper van Treslong, bailiff of Brill and Voorne (1541–58),[165] and Otto van Egmond, a judge in the Court of Fiefs as well as a member (*registermeester*) of the Chamber of Fiefs and the Delfland polder board.[166] Jacob van der Duyn and Adriaan van Mathenesse belonged to the Schieland polder board, but whether they had other offices is unknown.[167]

The core of the Ridderschap thus consisted of the most important noble office-holders of Holland. The near-permanent attendance of members of the Court is striking. The Court carried out the policies of the sovereign, and in his absence it was charged with calling meetings of the States. Sovereign and representative bodies were thus formally distinguished, but in practice the same persons sat in both. Here the States displayed their origins in the count's council, where the ruler held discussions with noble councillors and delegates from the cities.[168] The States, and in particular the Ridderschap, could only be regarded as a representative body in a very limited sense in this period.

After 1552, however, the political importance of the States increased.[169] As a result of the war with France, taxes rose. Along with the annual ordinary subsidy of 10,000 gulden, which had already been approved in 1548 for the years 1552–4, the States now had to consent to a large number of extraordinary subsidies in rapid succession. The source where the subsidy was ordinarily collected, the *schiltalen* or assessment on wealth, did not flow so freely as to produce all the funds needed. Thus the States were required to find other revenues – a hearth tax, a tax on farms, a tenth-penny on income from real property, rents and tithes, as well as supplemental sales of life annuities. The yearly interest would be paid by an excise tax on wine and beer in the cities and an acreage tax (*morgengeld*) on rural land. Because of their increased responsibilities, the States tried to gain control of the collection and administration of

---

[163] ARA, Grafelijkheidsrekenkamer, registers, inv. no. 492, fos. 159 v., 127 v. and 157 v.; inv. no. 493, fo. 245 v.; Walvis, *Gouda*, p. 75.

[164] Van der Aa, *Biographisch woordenboek*, s.v. Van der Duyn.

[165] He had been sheriff of Haarlem from 1527 to 1536. *Naam-register Haarlem* and ARA, Grafelijkheidsrekenkamer, registers, inv. no. 493, fos. 219 v., 263, 152 v., and 188 v. Bailiff of Den Briel and Voorne, ibid., inv. no. 495, fos. 106, 13, 59, 151 v., 265, 275 v.

[166] Van der Aa, *Biographisch woordenboek*, s.v. Egmond.

[167] Ibid., s.v. Van der Duyn; and *NNBW*, x, p. 592.

[168] On the origins of the States in the count's council: Van Riemsdijk, *Oorsprong*, pp. 384–6.

[169] 'Remonstrantie', pp. 158–9.

funds. Conflicts arose between Arend Coebel, the receiver-general appointed by the States, and Jacob Grammaye, the king's receiver in Holland. The States were able to settle these disputes in favour of their own man.[170]

The States also tried to escape from the guidance of the Court. To meet the increased financial demands of the government, the States had to assemble much more frequently than before. They found it impractical and undesirable to involve the Court, and thus the custom arose that the States themselves decided when they would meet. This led to a conflict between the States and the Court. In 1555 the Court sent a remonstrance to the central administration in Brussels, complaining about the presumption of the States.[171] Simultaneously they protested against the arbitrary action of their own president Assendelft, who did not sign the remonstrance.[172] Since Assendelft often appeared in the Ridderschap during this period and was ex-officio charged with calling the meetings of the States, we can infer that he identified more with the States than with the Court in this matter.

The States now began to distinguish between two kinds of meetings. First, the 'general meetings' in which the sovereign's requests for subsidies were approved: these had to be convoked by the clerk of the Court in the name of the stadholder and the Court. Then there were 'particular meetings' to discuss all other matters that were important to the province. According to the States, the latter meetings could be convoked by the advocate or the receiver of the States, and thus on the initiative of the States themselves.[173] However, the stadholder and the Court did not recognize this claim and insisted that the States could not meet without being called by representatives of princely authority. In 1565 a new conflict on this point arose between the States and the stadholder William of Orange. The States declared 'that it was evident by witnesses, letters and also by a chronicle, that the States could come together by themselves, without needing any consent from the Court, since time immemorial'.[174] Here they expanded the right of convocation, which in the words of their advocate Van den Eynden in 1564 they had limited to extraordinary occasions; now they asserted a general right of convocation and meeting.[175] As representative of the sovereign power, Orange resisted this move. He pointed to his letter of com-

---

[170] Ibid., pp. 159–60.
[171] Pub. ibid., pp. 166–83.
[172] Ibid., p. 162.
[173] ARA, Staten van Holland vóór 1572, inv. no. 2388.
[174] R. C. Bakhuizen van den Brink, 'Eerste vergadering der Staten van Holland, 19 julij 1572', *Studiën en schetsen over vaderlandsche geschiedenis en letteren*, 5 vols. (Amsterdam, 1863–1913), I, pp. 494–550, at 509. Cf. *Res. Holland*, 27 Jan. 1566 (i.e. 1567): Orange declared that the States must no longer meet until the king arrived in the country to re-establish order. The States answered that they had been empowered since time immemorial, not only by privilege but also by usage and custom, to meet at all times that the affairs of the country required.
[175] Bakhuizen van den Brink, 'Eerste vergadering', p. 509.

mission of 1559, which stated that it was his duty to summon the States and prevent their taking action to meet on their own.[176]

Just as the States as a whole tried to gain the right to convoke themselves, so the college of Ridderschap likewise in 1565 pretended that they could decide which nobles would be summoned.[177] The president of the Court, Cornelis Suys, had forbidden the clerk to enrol Johan van Mathenesse, who had tacitly succeeded his father, before the stadholder had given him express orders to do so. Mathenesse had already attended several times. The president's objections to Mathenesse are unknown. His position in the religious question probably did not play a role; in the ensuing conflict, Mathenesse as well as Suys took the king's side. Mathenesse continued to attend the Ridderschap under Alba in 1568, and in 1572 Suys fled with the Court to Utrecht. Suys probably objected in principle to the Ridderschap's pretended right of convocation. The nobles now declared that if one of the members of their college should die, the right to choose a new member belonged to the college itself, without any intervention by the sovereign, his stadholder, the president or the councillors of the Court. To add more weight to their argument, they noted that 'since time immemorial it has always happened thus, as the same is an old, sound and worthy prerogative, right and custom of the said college': all sitting members of the Ridderschap at that moment had allegedly been appointed by co-optation.[178]

It is questionable how accurately the remonstrance of the Ridderschap reflects the situation. Already before 1554 it had been the custom that at meetings of the States when deliberations could not be completed, the six voting cities would specify the date of the next meeting and ask the president to convoke the nobles.[179] It is not clear whether he could convoke whomever he wished. The problem did not arise when Assendelft was president. He is likely to have discussed the choice of newly convoked nobles with the rest of the college; in practice, deceased members were succeeded by their eldest sons. But Suys, the new president of the Court, was not a member of the college, nor were the other Court councillors. Consequently the question of competence to select new members came under discussion. Nevertheless it did not lead to a great conflict, because the troubles that broke out soon afterwards gave an entirely different turn to events.

---

[176] In fact Orange's letter of commission states only that he should summon the States 'quant besoing sera' (as will be needed), not that he should prevent their meeting on their own: *Correspondance de Guillaume le Taciturne*, ed. L. P. Gachard, 6 vols. (Brussels, 1847–57), I, p. 488. Nor do his more extended instructions mention the point, although Fruin thought that could be inferred from the text. The instructions were pub. by Wagenaar, *Amsterdam*, I, p. 371; cf. Fruin, *Staatsinstellingen*, p. 60, and *Correspondentie van Willem den Eersten, Prins van Oranje*, ed. N. Japikse (The Hague, 1934), pp. 310–11.

[177] *Res. Holland*, 27 Sept. 1565.

[178] ARA, Staten van Holland vóór 1572, inv. no. 2388.

[179] 'Remonstrantie', p. 161.

12   Jan Mostaert, 'Abel van der Coulster' (Kon. Mus. voor Schone Kunsten, Brussels). Abel van der Coulster, knight, councillor in the Court of Holland (ca. 1468–1540). He corresponded with Erasmus and found it difficult to implement the harsh decrees against heresy.

The changed character of meetings of the States was reflected in changes in the composition of the Ridderschap. Between 9 April 1560 and 6 April 1563 there were fifty-five meetings of the States.[180] Compared with the meetings held between 1525 and 1530, the frequency increased from an average of eleven per year to eighteen. Consequently membership in the Ridderschap became more time-consuming. The Ridderschap had been transformed, just like administrative office-holding, from an honorary office into a profession. What had been a ceremonial sideline became a busy and demanding occupation. Many nobles must have found the Ridderschap less attractive. The same mechanism that led to a decline in noble office-holding can be observed in the Ridderschap. On 13 July 1560, a meeting had to be postponed 'on account of the absence of the nobles'.[181] There were no more meetings at which the Ridderschap was entirely absent, such as in the 1520s. Later, the poor attendance of the nobles remained a problem. In 1585, when fundamental changes in their constitutional position had occurred, the States passed new regulations. They stipulated that in addition to the member of the Ridderschap who sat in the college of the Deputy Councils, at least three other nobles had to attend all deliberations. If, however, fewer than three nobles were present, these were not allowed to withdraw from the deliberations and decisions that were made. Absent members had to pay a fine, and their absences were carefully recorded, so that a corresponding amount could be deducted from the attendance-moneys.[182]

The second change from 1525–30 is that the number of nobles who took part in the negotiations became much smaller. Only eleven nobles appeared at the fifty-five meetings between 1560 and 1563, half as many known to have attended in the earlier period. But the nobles who were members appeared much more often. Nobles who attended only once practically disappeared.[183] Klaas van Assendelft, son of the late president, was present at forty-six of the fifty-five meetings. Yet the professionalization of the Ridderschap must not be exaggerated: only four members attended more than half of the meetings.

Which nobles did appear in the Ridderschap after 1560? Among the members of the college there were practically no more nobles who occupied government offices, although all who appeared frequently were still members of the polder boards. Klaas van Assendelft and Jacob van der Duyn, lord of Sprange, belonged to the Schieland polder board; Jacob van Duvenvoirde (twenty-four meetings), Willem van Lockhorst (thirty-four meetings), and Gerrit van Poelgeest (twenty-four meetings) were on the Rijnland board; and Otto van

---

180 After the last date, the names of nobles in attendance were no longer recorded in resolutions of the States.
181 *Res. Holland*, 13 July 1560.
182 Ibid., 16 and 17 March 1581.
183 The count of Aremberg, who appeared once (16 Jan. 1562 NS), was an exception.

Egmond van Kenenburg (twenty-four meetings) was on the board of Delf-land.[184] Only Egmond van Kenenburg held other offices: he was a judge in the Court of Fiefs and an officer in the Chamber of Fiefs, but he also belonged to an older generation, having sat in the Ridderschap since 1544. During a meeting of the States on 27 January 1563, when discussion turned to the peat industry, a matter directly related to the polder boards, the provincial advocate noted in the resolution book the presence of Assendelft and Sprange 'from the college of Schieland', and Lockhorst and Poelgeest 'from the college of Rijnland'.[185]

The change in the personnel of the Ridderschap had taken place gradually as a new generation succeeded the former. Floris Oem van Wyngaerden, Court councillor, had died in 1532; his son Jacob, who succeeded to his place in the Ridderschap, held no government offices.[186] Jan van Duvenvoirde, lord of Warmond, another Court councillor, died in 1544; his son Jacob did not hold any office, at least not before the Revolt. In 1548 Adam van der Duyn died; his son Jacob held no office.[187] In 1558 the college lost three members: president Gerrit van Assendelft, whose son Klaas held no offices; Jasper Blois van Treslong, whose son Willem did not appear in the Ridderschap; and the childless Arend van Duvenvoirde, who had been associated with Charles V's court.[188] Only Floris van Assendelft, governor of Gouda, who died in 1555, was succeeded by his son Otto in his governorship as well as Ridderschap; but during the period studied Otto appeared only three times.[189]

The disappearance of office-holders from the Ridderschap was a direct consequence of nobles being less inclined to accept government offices. This development profoundly changed the character of the Ridderschap. Because the office-holders disappeared, the Ridderschap could become more of a representative body. Unintentionally, a distinction arose between institutions of the sovereign and representative bodies of the province. The more representative character of the Ridderschap gave rise to the dispute over the right to select and summon the nobles. It was consistent with an advisory council that the ruler or his delegate would choose his most trusted collaborators as councillors; the principle of co-optation was more suited to a representative body.

Naturally the Ridderschap formed only a minority of the States. But, combined with the increased importance and self-consciousness of the cities, the disappearance of office-holders from the Ridderschap changed the character of the States as a whole. Starting from an organ that had barely any formal powers,

---

[184] *Res. Holland*, 27 Jan. 1563 NS; Van der Steur, 'Johan van Duvenvoirde', p. 246 (Jacob van Duvenvoirde was polder-councillor of Rijnland from 1567 to 1575); Dolk, *Delfland*, p. 711.
[185] *Res. Holland*, 27 Jan. 1563 NS.
[186] *NNBW*, III, pp. 926–7; Van der Aa, *Biographisch woordenboek*, s.v. Oem van Wyngaerden.
[187] Ibid., s.v. Van der Duyn.
[188] *NNBW*, VII, pp. 34–6, VI, p. 121; Obreen, *Wassenaer*, p. 88.
[189] *NNBW*, VII, p. 32; Walvis, *Gouda*, pp. 63 ff.

was dependent on the sovereign and could meet only in order to approve his financial demands, the States became a body that claimed to represent the interests of the province to the sovereign. It was no longer self-evident that the interests of sovereign and people ran parallel to each other. The changed composition of the Ridderschap contributed to the emancipation of the States into a self-conscious body that could take on the leadership of the Revolt in 1572.

Let us once again compare the social position occupied by the Holland nobility at the beginning of the sixteenth century with that on the eve of the Revolt. In the early decades, the foundation of the nobles' social power lay in their dominant position as manorial lords. About 80 per cent of the manors granted to private individuals were in the hands of the nobility. Furthermore, many nobles fulfilled official functions at all levels: in the provincial administration in The Hague, as bailiffs and governors in the rural areas, as sheriffs and magistrates in the cities. Moreover, a fairly large number of nobles did appear, if rather irregularly, in the Ridderschap of the States of Holland, though it had little influence on policy. A small core of nobles who attended more regularly consisted entirely of high office-holders. The nobles thus filled key positions in the administration of the province. No single function was fulfilled only by nobles, nor were all nobles involved in government, but the nobles clearly formed a large part of the provincial political elite.

By 1565 the position of nobles as seigneurial lords had barely changed. They had largely withdrawn from government offices, leaving functions requiring greater judicial expertise and daily activity to professional administrators of bourgeois origin. Moreover, most nobles no longer appeared in the Ridderschap. They abandoned the representation of the countryside and the small cities to a small core of nobles who took part frequently in deliberations of the States. Even these nobles no longer occupied important government offices, except on the polder boards. They were lords, not administrators; and thereby the Ridderschap became more of a representative body.

At the same time another process was taking place, by which the social position of the nobility changed fundamentally. With the rise of mercenary armies consisting primarily of infantry, the nobility lost its significance as a military class. As a consequence, its previous exemption from taxes gradually lapsed. Personal participation in the feudal ban and tax exemption had always been the most important ways in which nobles distinguished themselves from other social groups. Their distinction from the rest of the population therefore became blurred.

175

The result was that the nobles closed themselves off from the rest of society. In the fifteenth century, access to the nobility from below had been open, and it could gradually assimilate the highest levels of the administrative elite. The nobles now raised the psychological barriers against non-nobles. Interest in family history, genealogy, heraldry, and strict endogamy were expressions of this reaction. On the eve of the Revolt, the nobles no longer stood at the centre of power in the province. They can better be described as a class of leisured rural landholders, largely excluded from political power.[190] They were no longer distinguished from the rest of society by political functions and clearly defined privileges, but by such immaterial qualities as birth, rank, style of life and marital choices. They had evolved from a power elite to a status elite.

[190] Van Gelder, 'Hollandse adel', p. 192.

7

Beggars and loyalists

THE COMPROMISE OF THE NOBILITY

The decline of the Holland nobility is often related to that other great event of the sixteenth-century, the Dutch Revolt. Sir William Temple thought that the nobles of Holland were finished off by the war with Spain.[1] According to G. 't Hart, the bourgeoisie assumed the place of the nobility because the latter could not do without the splendour of monarchy.[2] Indeed, with the abolition of the monarchy the opportunity to add new members to the nobility disappeared. Consequently the death warrant of the Holland nobility over the long term was signed and sealed. Such secular demographic considerations probably did not influence the attitude of the Holland nobles during the Revolt. J. L. Price thought that most Holland nobles had more possessions in the South than in the North, and that they therefore chose the king's side.[3] R. Fruin remarked that during the troubles most members of the Ridderschap of Holland were 'Spanish sympathisers'.[4] How did the Holland nobles react to the political problems that arose after the accession of Philip II?

Prior to the 'wonder year' of 1566, Holland had remained relatively quiet.[5] True, the Protestant Reformation had early on found many supporters in the province.[6] In so far as the numbers of persons executed for heresy indicate the popularity of Reform, and not merely the effectiveness of repression, Holland was the most heretically infected province of all the Netherlands.[7] But a great deal of this repression must be attributed to the popularity of the Anabaptist movement between 1530 and 1544. After the middle of the sixteenth century

[1] Temple, *Observations*, p. 85.
[2] 't Hart, *Heenvliet*, p. 204.
[3] Price, *Culture and Society*, p. 59.
[4] Fruin, *Staatsinstellingen*, p. 231.
[5] A. C. Duke and D. H. A. Kolff, 'The time of troubles in the county of Holland', *TvG* 82 (1969): 316–37, at 316.
[6] A. C. Duke, 'Building heaven in hell's despite: the early history of the Reformation in the towns of the Low Countries', in *Britain and the Netherlands*, VII, ed. A. C. Duke and C. A. Tamse (The Hague, 1981), pp. 45–75, at 51–3.
[7] Ibid., p. 45, n. 1. In Holland at least 402 persons were executed on religious grounds before the iconoclasm of 1566, compared with 264 in Flanders, 228 in Brabant, 102 in Friesland, 31 in Utrecht and 23 in Zeeland. In all the provinces combined, more than 1,300 persons were executed for heresy; of those, about 30 per cent were from Holland.

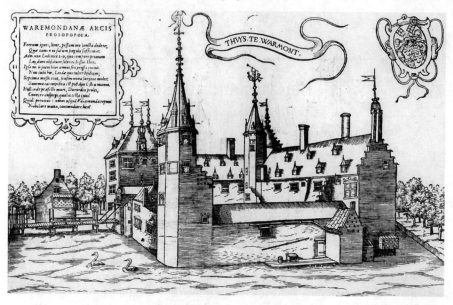

13   Anon. print in Paulus Merula, *Placaten ende ordonnanciën opt stuck van de wildernissen* (1605), Warmond House, the residence of the lords of Warmond from the Duvenvoirde (later Wassenaer) family.

the centre of the Protestant movement shifted to Flanders.[8] The Calvinist variant of the Reformation had barely gained a foothold in Holland before the summer of 1566. During these years the Erasmian moderation and tolerance of the Holland magistrates are striking. The harsh proclamations against heretics issued by the government in Brussels were nowhere received with enthusiasm. Local and provincial administrations followed a policy of passive resistance. The central administration in Brussels had long accused the Court of Holland of being soft on heresy. In 1534 councillors Jan van Duvenvoirde (the lord of Warmond) and Arend Sandelyn, court commissioners for heresy, asked to be relieved of their unpleasant task. They wrote to the stadholder that many people hated them for carrying out their duty, and they could no longer stand 'the sorrow of the poor people in being examined and tortured'. One member sent to Brussels in 1534 to deny the accusation of excessive laxity said that the regent would not have done otherwise, 'seeing the poverty and misery of the prisoners'.[9] In 1539 president Gerrit van Assendelft and councillor Abel van den Coulster were accused of contact with priests who were contaminated with heretical ideas. Van den Coulster was also charged with having spoken scorn-

[8] Ibid., p. 64.
[9] J. S. Theissen, *De regeering van Karel V in de noordelijke Nederlanden* (Amsterdam, 1912), p. 274.

fully about purgatory, and having encouraged the priest Herman Pietersz. to defend Erasmus against his opponents.[10] After the issuance of extremely harsh proclamations against heresy in 1550, the aversion to persecution increased further. In Amsterdam, between 1553 and the coming of the duke of Alba, no one was executed for the faith; in Holland as a whole persecution came to a halt around 1560.[11]

The nobles of Holland were confronted with governmental religious policy in their capacity as seigneurial lords. Some nobles had earlier winked at heresy. In 1536 Joost van Cruijningen protected Anabaptists in his manor of Hazerswoude.[12] When the Anabaptists were nevertheless arrested, the Great Council of Mechelen had to issue an order before the lord of Hazerswoude would allow the bailiff to seize the prisoners' property.[13] The same nobleman had called the heretical priest Angelus Merula to Heenvliet in 1532. Directly after his investiture, Merula began his attack on abuses in the church, reportedly 'to please my Lord of Cruijningen'.[14]

Thus a sympathetic climate was created for the goals of the Confederation or Compromise of the Nobility, which did not seek to introduce Protestantism officially (the goal of its radical Protestant wing), but only to abolish the Inquisition and the proclamations against heretics.

During the summer of 1565, secret discussions between a few Protestant nobles and representatives of the illegal consistories had taken place at the resort of Spa.[15] Their goal was to establish a confederacy of nobles to exercise pressure on the central government. Philip II's refusal to moderate his religious policy, contained in the letters from Segovia, arrived in Brussels in November and strengthened their determination. In early December about twenty young nobles met at the house of the count of Culemborg in Brussels for a Protestant religious service. They then formed a union to fight the Inquisition and the proclamations against heresy; this agreement was called a compromise because the participants were joined by a common oath. Shortly before Christmas, 1565, an act of foundation was signed at a second meeting. According to this text, for the prosperity of the land and the service of the king, the nobles bound themselves to oppose the Inquisition.[16] The terms were kept as general as possible to gain the support of moderate Catholics. The founders made several copies that were circulated throughout the Netherlands, so that as many nobles

---

[10] Ibid., p. 257.
[11] J. J. Woltjer, 'De Vredemakers', *TvG* 89 (1976): 299–321, at 300–1; Duke, 'Building heaven', p. 64.
[12] 't Hart, *Heenvliet*, p. 85.
[13] Theissen, *Regeering Karel V*, p. 281, and 't Hart, *Heenvliet*, p. 85.
[14] 't Hart, *Heenvliet*, p. 85.
[15] M. Dierickx, 'De eerste jaren van Philips II (1555–1567)', *AGN*, IV, p. 337; Rachfahl, *Wilhelm von Oranien*, II, pp. 560–8.
[16] Text in *Archives*, II, pp. 2–7.

14   F. Hogenberg, 'Presentation of the nobles' petition to the Regent Margaret of Parma, 5 April 1566' (Rijksprentenkabinet, Amsterdam).

as possible could show their support by signing them. On 5 April 1566, about two hundred noblemen under the leadership of Hendrik van Brederode presented a petition to the regent, Margaret of Parma.[17] The nobles sought the annulment of the decrees against heresy, and hoped to find a solution in negotiations with the States General. This document was also phrased in such a manner that Catholic nobles could agree with it.[18] Shocked by this dangerous turn of events, the regent told the nobles that, while awaiting a definitive decision, the persecution of heretics would be suspended. After presenting the petition, the leaders left Brussels for the provinces to make propaganda for the Union. During the spring and summer of 1566, many other nobles signed the Compromise and Petition. In total more than four hundred persons (a few of them non-nobles, however) testified in writing to their support for the goals of the Union.[19]

[17] Text of the petition, ibid., II, p. 80.
[18] A comparison of the texts of the Compromise and the petition appears in A. C. J. de Vrankrijker, *De motiveering van onzen Opstand. De theorieën van het verzet der Nederlandsche opstandelingen tegen Spanje in de jaren 1565–1581* (Nijmegen and Utrecht, 1933; reprint, Utrecht, 1979), pp. 8–12.
[19] Dierckx, 'Eerste jaren', p. 337. According to Rachfahl, *Wilhelm von Oranien*, II, p. 567, there were more than 500. For a detailed discussion of sources for the identity of the confederated nobles, and in particular also the Holland members, see ibid., n. 1. The incomplete 'Cathalogue des gentilzhommes confederez', ARA Brussels, Aud., inv. no. 477/5, lists 387 names.

Seventy-eight of the signatories were reportedly of Holland origin. On closer inspection, however, it appears that 24 were either not noble, or nobles from other provinces.[20] Of the remaining 54 nobles, 42 came from old Holland lineages;[21] 12 were originally from other provinces but lived in Holland and owned property there. These 54 nobles bore 27 different family names, of which 20 were from Holland. If about two hundred nobles were living in Holland in this period, these 54 open adherents of the Union formed a significant minority.[22]

It is striking how thick the network of family relations was among the 54 Holland members of the Union. Twenty-two of them (41 per cent) had signed with one or more brothers. In this regard the Holland nobles differed little from those of other provinces. Seventy-eight of the 186 members of the Union who were summoned by the Council of Troubles, an equally high percentage (42 per cent), were condemned along with a father or brother.[23] Josua and Samuel van Alveringen were brothers; they were brothers-in-law of Dirk van der Does, Brederode's steward at his castle Huis te Kleef near Haarlem.[24] Robert and

---

[20] The signers of one copy are listed in Bor, *Nederlantsche oorlogen*; of another, in Van Gouthoeven, *Chronyke*, p. 625, and Van Leeuwen, *Batavia*, pp. 767–8. Te Water (*Verbond*, I, pp. 236–58) has published many names drawn from four lists, known as A, B, C, and D (ibid., IV, pp. 17–43). Nearly all names of Holland signers come from lists A and/or D. After the troubles, the central government made lists of those who were involved in the Confederacy. The 'Cathalogue des gentilzhommes confederez de l'année 1565' lists 387 persons in alphabetical order by their first names and identifies the province from which they came, but it is incomplete. Another list made by the central government contains only Holland nobles, divided into three categories: nobles who signed the act of Union and refused to take a new loyalty oath; nobles who did not sign; and nobles who signed but later recanted (pub. in *Nav* 84 (1935): 158–61; by Rachfahl, *Wilhelm von Oranien*, II, p. 567, n. 1, and identified as ARA Brussels, Aud., inv. no. 531). The sentences issued by the Council of Troubles often report whether the condemned person was a member of the Compromise (*Sententiën*; accords with ARA, Grafelijkheidsrekenkamer, inv. no. 681 *ter*). The register kept for the new loyalty oath to the king in 1567 also gives information about participation in the Confederacy. Apparently, however, not all nobles and vassals of Holland were summoned to swear oaths. The register has been published with annotations by D'Yvoy van Mijdrecht (*Verbond*, pp. 51–85). Cf. ARA, Grafelijkheidsrekenkamer, rekeningen, inv. nos. 4856–60. None of these sources is entirely complete or entirely reliable. Used in combination, however, they give a reasonable picture of the supporters of the Compromise. For some nobles it remains unclear whether they participated. Cf. the list for Friesland in J. J. Woltjer, *Friesland in hervormingstijd* (Leiden, 1962), pp. 318–24, and the list of 186 primarily northern Netherlands members given by Sherrin Marshall Wyntjes, 'Family allegiance and religious persuasion: the lesser nobility and the Revolt of the Netherlands', *The Sixteenth Century Journal* 12 (1981): 43–60. G. Bonnevie-Noël, 'Liste critique des signataires du Compromis des Nobles', *Vereniging voor de geschiedenis van het Belgisch Protestantisme*, 5th series, 3 (1968): 80–110.

[21] Among the signers were three bastards of Brederode (a high noble), who were reckoned among the low nobility, and one bastard of Van den Boetzelaer, who strictly speaking should not be counted among the nobility. This distinction was also apparent from their marital choices: the Brederode bastards married within the Holland nobility, while the Van den Boetzelaer bastard married a non-noble wife.

[22] Van Gelder, 'Hollandse adel', p. 113.

[23] Wyntjes, 'Family allegiance', p. 48.

[24] Te Water, *Verbond*, II, pp. 148–52; Polvliet, *Genealogie van der Does*, pp. 65–6.

Maximiliaan van Blois, known as De Cocq van Neereynen, were also brothers. They were distant relations of the brothers Willem and Jan Blois van Treslong, nephews of Nicolaas van Sandijck.[25] Willem van Treslong was married to Adriana van Egmond, the daughter of Otto van Egmond van Kenenburg. Otto was the brother-in-law of Hendrik Croesingh and a distant relation of the brothers Albrecht and Frederik van Egmond van Meresteyn. The first of these was married to Sara van Brederode, a half-sister of the rebel leader Hendrik van Brederode.[26] By his marriage to Henrica van Egmond van Meresteyn, Jacob van Duvenvoirde, lord of Warmond, was an uncle of Albrecht and Frederik van Egmond. He was likewise an uncle of Gijsbrecht van Duvenvoirde, lord of Obdam, and of his cousin Arend van Duvenvoirde. The fourth Van Duvenvoirde among the nobles of the Union was Dirk, a distant relation of Arend.[27] Gijsbrecht van Duvenvoirde van Obdam was the first cousin of Gijsbrecht van Mathenesse, who was in turn a cousin of Johan van Mathenesse van Wibisma. Van Wibisma's stepfather was Nicolaas van Bronckhorst, who was uncle to the three brothers Gerrit, Jasper and Otto van Poelgeest. The grandmother of Johan and Gijsbrecht van Mathenesse was Maria van Assendelft, a second cousin of president Gerrit van Assendelft; through her they were thus related to the president's son Klaas van Assendelft, his cousin Pauwels van Assendelft and Cornelis van Assendelft, son of a cousin of Klaas and Pauwels. Pauwels van Assendelft was by his marriage to Alferarda van den Boetzelaer (the daughter of the lord of Aldenghoor, from the Cleves branch of the family) distantly related to the Van den Boetzelaers of Asperen. Wessel van den Boetzelaer, who signed the Union along with his one bastard and six legitimate sons, produced the greatest contingent of Union members from one family. By his mother Bertha van Arckel van Heukelom he was also a cousin of Otto van Arckel, lord of Heukelom. Wessel had been married to Françoise van Praet van Moerkercken (who died in 1562); her sister Petronella was married to Herman van Bronckhorst, banneret of Guelderland, lord of Batenburg, whose three sons also joined the Union. Both the Praet and Bronckhorst families were fervent supporters of Protestantism.[28] Wessel's son Rutger was married to Agnes van Bailleul, who came from a Flanders family equally renowned for their heterodox ideas; his son Wessel junior was married to Elizabeth van Bronckhorst en Batenburg. The family ties among the supporters of the Union thus extended over the entire Netherlands.

---

[25] Troost and Woltjer, 'Brielle', pp. 315–16; Te Water, *Verbond*, III, pp. 402–11.
[26] Dek, 'Genealogie Brederode', p. 21.
[27] Obreen, *Wassenaer*. By his marriage to Maria van Hoxwier in 1572, Gijsbrecht van Duvenvoirde became a brother-in-law of Frederik van Egmond: p. 128. She was the daughter of the president of the Court of Utrecht, Hector van Hoxwier and Doed Holdinga; on her mother's side she was related to the Frisian nobility. In 1566 she had married the confederate noble Albert van Huchtenbroek.
[28] Van Gelder, 'Bailleul, Bronkhorst, Brederode', pp. 63–4; Wyntjes, 'Family allegiance', p. 47.

What was the significance of this thick network of family relations? In view of the high rate of endogamy among the Holland nobles, it would have been surprising if there had *not* been so many ties. Nevertheless, family relationships undoubtedly did play a role in the spread of the Compromise. According to the Council of Troubles, Willem van Treslong convinced his brother Jan to sign the petition and attend its presentation.[29] It is unlikely that these were mechanical actions. Although a remarkable number of brothers signed the petition, the number of brothers who did *not* sign was greater. For example, Gijsbrecht van Mathenesse and his cousin Johan van Mathenesse van Wibisma belonged to the Union. But Gijsbrecht's oldest brother Johan, who was a member of the Ridderschap and continued to attend during Alba's time, did not sign; nor did his younger brother Adriaan.

Some family names of Holland nobles do not appear at all in this group. Thus it might be possible to identify a second group of families who were intermarried to the same degree as the members of the Union, but remained outside it.[30] Yet such a correlation between family ties and political choice among nobles outside the Compromise cannot be proved. For example, no member of the Beijeren van Schagen family joined the Union. Johan, lord of Schagen (1544–1618) not only held himself aloof, but also fought under Philip II's stadholder Bossu against the rebels in 1573.[31] In 1568, however, he married Anna van Assendelft, a sister of the Union member Pauwels van Assendelft and a second cousin of Cornelis van Assendelft; Johan's sister Wilhelmina van Schagen married Nicolaas van Bronckhorst, likewise one of the Union nobles.[32] Another example of connections between the Union nobles and others is provided by Splinter van Hargen, lord of Oosterwijk.[33] He remained outside the Union;[34] through his mother Catharina Suys he was related to Cornelis Suys, president of the Court of Holland, who remained loyal to Alba's government and migrated to Utrecht in 1572. In 1571 Splinter van Hargen was enrolled in the Ridderschap under Alba, and he was dike-reeve of Schieland until 1573, when it was reported that he fled owing to the 'troubles'. However, by his marriage to Mechteld Oem van Wyngaerden he was the brother-in-law of Jacob Oem van Wyngaerden, one of the Union nobles, who was condemned by the Council of Troubles because he had been involved in the organization of Protestantism at Leiden.[35] The family of Oem van Wyngaerden presents other examples of differing political choices. At this time in Holland there were two

---

[29] *Sententiën*, p. 155.
[30] Perhaps that was indeed the case in Utrecht and Guelderland. Cf. Wyntjes, 'Family allegiance', p. 45, n. 3.
[31] Dek, *Genealogie graven van Holland*, p. 65.
[32] Te Water, *Verbond*, II, pp. 306–7; according to the 'Cathalogue', Lodewijk van Bronckhorst.
[33] HRA, Collectie Snouckaert, inv. no. 1899.
[34] *Nav* 84 (1935): 159.
[35] *Sententiën*, pp. 48–9.

half-brothers, both named Cornelis Oem van Wyngaerden. One signed the Union and helped to organize the new religion at The Hague. The other did not sign, took the new oath of loyalty to the king in January 1567, became a councillor of the Court of Holland in 1570, and fled to Utrecht in 1572 after the rebels captured Brill.[36]

The accusations made by Granvelle and others that poverty motivated the rebels have been discussed earlier.[37] Pontus Payen maintained that 'most wanted to restore their households, and (as the proverb says) fish in troubled water in order to refill their empty purses'.[38] But it does not appear that the Holland nobles were motivated by financial difficulties. The Holland members of the Compromise formed a good sample of the Holland nobility as a whole. Alongside the extremely wealthy Brederode we find a fair number of nobles who held one or more manors in fief, as well as younger sons who did not hold manors; there were also nobles who were devoid of manors and earned their keep in the service of higher nobles. Administrative office-holders, however, were scarce among the Union nobles of Holland. This is not surprising, since very few nobles held offices at this time. Lodewijk van den Binckhorst, who was active in the spread of the new religion at The Hague, was a *meesterknaap* in the Forestry.[39] Otto van Egmond was an officer of the Chamber of Fiefs.[40] But these office-holders had no responsibility for religious problems. Those who carried out Philip's religious policies, such as councillors of the Court, bailiffs, sheriffs, members of the Chamber of Accounts and treasurers, do not appear on the lists of the Union of Nobles.[41]

Members of the Ridderschap reacted variously to the events. Of the eleven nobles who regularly attended between 1560 and 1563,[42] six signed the Union (Hendrik Croesingh, Arend lord of Duvenvoirde, Gijsbrecht van Duvenvoirde

---

[36] *Sententiën*, pp. 51–3; *Nav* 84 (1935): 161; Smit, 'Omzetting', p. 191; *Memorialen Rosa*, I, p. xlviii. According to D'Yvoy (*Verbond*, no. 22), it was precisely the signer of the Compromise who took the new oath and became a councillor in the Court, while his half-brother had worked for the introduction of the Reformed religion at The Hague, was condemned by the Council of Troubles and fled the country – even though he had not signed the Compromise. This seems highly improbable to me. The same Cornelis van Wyngaerden who was active in The Hague was charged with having received letters from Louis of Nassau with orders to recruit members for the Compromise: would he himself not have signed it? Moreover cf. the 'Cathalogue des gentilzhommes confederez', which reports that the signer was banished.

[37] See above, pp. 94, 114.

[38] Payen, *Mémoires*, I, p. 132.

[39] *Sententiën*, pp. 51–3; Te Water, *Verbond*, II, pp. 212–14; Merula, *Placaten Wildernissen*, p. 25.

[40] His signature is not certain, however: he does appear on the list in Van Leeuwen and Van Gouthoeven, and on Te Water's list D; but he is not in the 'Cathalogue' nor in *Nav* 84 (1935): 158–61.

[41] Nicolaas van Sandijck had been bailiff of Den Briel and Voorne until 1564. Cf. Troost and Woltjer, 'Brielle', pp. 316–18, and Te Water, *Verbond*, III, pp. 402–11. Members of typical office-holding families that were regarded by some as lower nobility, such as Suys and Sasbout, are also lacking among signers of the Compromise.

[42] *Res. Holland*, 1560–3.

lord of Obdam, Otto van Egmond lord of Kenenburg, Gerrit van Poelgeest and Jacob van Wyngaerden). It is not certain whether two others signed (Jacob van Duvenvoirde lord of Warmond and Klaas van Assendelft).[43] Three members of the Ridderschap definitely did not sign (Jacob van der Duyn, Vincent van Lockhorst and Johan lord of Mathenesse). The result was that when the Council of Troubles began its investigation, suspecting everyone who was connected with the Union, six of the eleven sitting members of the Ridderschap had to take flight.

According to the 'Cathalogue des Gentilzhommes confederez' drawn up by the government, support for the Union varied considerably among the provinces of the Netherlands:[44]

Distribution of signers of the Compromise, by provinces

Friesland	87	Walloon Flanders	11
Holland	59	Artois	10
Brabant	46	Luxembourg	10
Namur	30	Guelderland	9
Flanders	21	Mechelen	4
Hainault	19	Foreign	8
Utrecht	17	Unknown	28

The provinces of Zeeland, Groningen, Limburg and Tournai furnished no signers at all. Friesland stands out with a great number of signers, but this figure rests on a misunderstanding on the part of the government. There were no Frisian nobles involved in the drafting of the Compromise and presentation of the Petition. Only in September did about twenty Frisians sign the Compromise. A greater number of Frisians did indeed sign their own Frisian version of the text, known as the Small Compromise. In total about seventy-five Frisians signed one document or the other, testifying to their support for the goals of the Union; but not all of them belonged to the nobility.[45] It is thus no exaggeration to say that Holland produced the greatest number of signers of the Compromise and the Petition. One out of every four male adult nobles signed. The remarkable popularity of this movement in Holland requires further explanation.

---

[43] Jacob van Duvenvoirde signed, according to Van Leeuwen and Van Gouthoeven, and Te Water's list D; but according to *Nav* he was one of the nobles who stayed outside the Compromise. D'Yvoy, *Verbond*, no. 19, says he was not a member of the Confederacy and did not take a new oath. He continued to attend the Ridderschap under Alba's rule, but also after 1572. Klaas van Assendelft, son of the president of the Court who died in 1558, did sign according to Van Leeuwen and Van Gouthoeven, Bor and Te Water D; yet afterwards he denied having been a member (D'Yvoy, *Verbond*, no. 54), and was not, according to the list in *Nav*. He too continued to appear in the Ridderschap under Alba; he died in 1570.

[44] ARA Brussels, Aud., inv. no. 1177/5.

[45] Woltjer, *Friesland*, pp. 148–50, 174–7 and 318–24.

It has been suggested that support for the Compromise was strongest in the distant provinces, where central government was weakest, such as Friesland. Provinces governed by a dissident high nobleman were also supposedly inclined to support the Union.[46] However, while Friesland had many supporters, there were none in Groningen and the Ommelanden, Drente and Overijssel, provinces that were no less particularistic than Friesland and had only shortly before been brought under Habsburg rule. Holland and Zeeland had the same stadholder, and similar experience with central administration. Yet in Holland many nobles supported the Compromise, but in Zeeland none at all. Provincial particularism or the activities of Orange as stadholder cannot explain the popularity of the Union in Holland.

Much more important was the influence of Hendrik van Brederode. While Brederode belonged to the high nobility, he was not endowed with the functions that he might have claimed in accordance with his birth. Perhaps this was owing to the difficulties encountered by his father Reinoud, who had assumed the unbroken arms of Holland and clashed with Charles V; the cause may also lie in Hendrik's impetuous character.[47] Yet Hendrik commanded a band of ordinance and could rely on the services of a number of nobles personally pledged to himself. He was probably the richest nobleman in the province, after Orange and Egmond – and he was one of the greatest fief-holders. The centre of his power lay along the Lek, where he held the sovereignty of Vianen and several surrounding villages. Furthermore, he had extensive possessions near Haarlem and Alkmaar.[48]

By their birth, wealth, and position the Brederodes were the natural leaders of the Holland nobility. Several years later, in 1574, when the nobles brought a complaint to William of Orange about the decline of their position relative to that of the cities, they thought they should apologize, because 'owing to the deaths of lords Brederode, Wassenaer and Egmond' they could turn to no one other than Orange.[49] Brederode enjoyed immense popularity in 1566. The Brederodes pretended (unjustly) to be descended from the counts of Holland.[50] This genealogical misconception, which was not out of line with the fantastic genealogies that the Holland nobles invented for themselves, took on a dangerous political dimension in that turbulent year. Brederode, exercising his sovereign right, had the mint in Vianen strike coins not with the arms of his family (the rampant lion with bar, indicating a cadet branch), but with the unbroken arms of Holland. His portrait was circulated abroad with the legend

[46] Parker, *Dutch Revolt*, p. 69.
[47] Duke and Kolff, 'Time of troubles', p. 317.
[48] Van Gelder, 'Bailleul, Bronkhorst, Brederode', pp. 68–9; De la Fontaine Verwey, 'Le rôle'; Duke and Kolff, 'Time of troubles', pp. 316–18. A modern biography of Brederode is much needed.
[49] Bor, *Nederlantscher oorlogen*, pp. 571–2.
[50] Dek, 'Genealogie Brederode', p. 1.

CO:HO: (*Comes Hollandiae*, count of Holland).[51] During the iconoclasm at the Dominican house in The Hague, one of the rioters cried out, 'We honour no king except for the count of Holland, which is my lord of Brederode; he shall become count of Holland, to whom this monastery belongs, and which his ancestors founded; and if we are no longer allowed to stay here, we shall go to him, where we shall be free!'[52] Five hundred men who embarked at Oosterweel in March 1567 in order to join Brederode's troops declared that 'he was the rightful Lord of Holland, although his ancestors had been appeased with Vianen, and [that he] now with the help of the Calvinists hoped to get it'.[53] In Amsterdam, where Brederode was then staying, there was also a rumour in the spring of 1567 that he would soon become count of Holland.[54]

Thanks to his contacts with high as well as low nobility Brederode was outstandingly qualified to serve as leader of the Compromise.[55] On 5 April 1566 he had taken the lead in presenting the petition to the regent. Thereafter he returned to Holland, where he worked tirelessly to gain supporters for the Union. On 18 May he arrived in the neighbourhood of Haarlem, where he owned a castle, Huis te Cleef. 'Everyone here is Beggar [*gueux*] and double Beggar', he wrote with satisfaction to Louis of Nassau.[56] The city secretary of Haarlem, Dirk Volkertsz Coornhert, did however persuade him to stop his propaganda in Haarlem.[57] A month later Brederode went to Amsterdam on a similar mission. He met with prominent citizens to discuss the Reformation, and while sitting in a carriage he was hailed with enthusiastic shouts of 'vive les gueux'.[58] From Amsterdam he travelled north, where he investigated the status of a polder project he had undertaken; but he also took the opportunity to gain more support for the Union.[59] 'The Beggars here are strewn like sand along the sea', he wrote to Nassau from Bergen.[60] In early July he went to Antwerp, but at the end of August and beginning of September at the time of the iconoclast riots he was back in the north, accompanied by a train of some forty nobles,

---

[51] *NNBW*, x, pp. 121–5.

[52] Smit, *Den Haag*, p. 78. The Frisian nobleman Sjoert Beyma, who was close to Brederode in the summer of 1566, likewise appears to have supported his claim for the count's title (Woltjer, *Friesland*, p. 149).

[53] Godevaert van Haecht, *Kroniek over de troebelen van 1565 tot 1574 te Antwerpen en elders*, ed. R. van Roosbroeck, 2 vols. (Antwerp, 1929–50), I, p. 185.

[54] *Correspondance Guillaume le Taciturne*, II, p. 452. In the fifteenth century the Hooks had also raised the battle-cry: 'Brederode! Brederode! Vrai hoir de Hollande!' (True heir of Holland!): A. G. Jonkees, *Staat en kerk in Holland en Zeeland onder de Bourgondische hertogen 1425–1477* (Groningen and Batavia, 1942), pp. 135–6.

[55] Rachfal, *Wilhelm von Oranien*, I, p. 276.

[56] *Archives*, II, pp. 126–7.

[57] Duke and Kolff, 'Time of troubles', p. 319.

[58] H. F. K. van Nierop, *Beeldenstorm en burgerlijk verzet in Amsterdam 1566–1567* (Nijmegen, 1978), pp. 25–6.

[59] Duke and Kolff, 'Time of troubles', p. 319.

[60] *Archives*, II, p. 130.

'about one hundred horses of this area'.[61] He gave orders to place in safekeeping all valuables from the churches in his manors, and tried to protect the Abbey of Egmond from iconoclasm. After a stay in Egmond, Hoorn and Alkmaar he went via Haarlem and Leiden to Vianen.

Brederode thus travelled a great deal through Holland in the summer of 1566, with the express purpose of gaining support for the Union. He was assisted by a small group of dedicated collaborators. He sent Josua van Alveringen to The Hague to whip up support for the Union.[62] Albert van Huchtenbroeck, Frederik van Egmond and Herbert van Raephorst were sent to Friesland: the first two were married to Frisian noblewomen.[63] Although they had little success initially, the charge was later made against Huchtenbroeck that, without his intervention, Friesland would have stayed outside the troubles.[64] In view of Brederode's position among the nobility of Holland, his activities may well have been the reason that so many Holland nobles joined the Union.

In his propaganda Brederode could exploit existing family links and patronage. Among the members of the Union were his relations by blood and marriage, such as Lancelot and Artus van Brederode, bastards of his father Reinoud. His cousin Arnoud van Brederode, lord of Reynesteyn, was the son of a bastard of his grandfather. Albrecht van Egmond van Meresteyn, by his marriage to Sara van Brederode, bastard daughter of Reinoud, was Hendrik van Brederode's brother-in-law. Lucretia, another illegitimate daughter of Reinoud, was married to Jan van Haeften, thus providing Hendrik a family tie to the Gueldrian signers Jan, Dirk and Frans van Haeften. Lancelot van Brederode, Hendrik's half-brother, was married to Adriana van Treslong, whose father Albert was a second cousin of the Holland signers Jan and Willem van Treslong.[65]

Others were Brederode's clients. Many nobles had gone into his service, either in his band of ordinance, in his household, or as stewards or bailiffs of his manors. From Bergen, Brederode sent Louis of Nassau a petition destined for the regent, which had been signed by many nobles at his request. 'The signers of this letter', he wrote, 'are all persons and gentlemen who are well prepared to do military service *as they are obligated to me*.'[66] ('Ces soubscryps à ce lettre sont

---

[61] Duke and Kolff, 'Time of troubles', p. 133; *Archives*, II, p. 253. Apparently each nobleman had two or three horses.

[62] *Sententiën*, pp. 53–4.   [63] Woltjer, *Friesland*, pp. 148–50.

[64] *Sententiën*, pp. 128–30. Later it appears that Frederik van Egmond, accompanied by Brederode's secretary, Jacob van Ilpendam, made a second trip to Friesland to gain support for the Confederacy. Woltjer, *Friesland*, p. 150.

[65] Dek, 'Genealogie Brederode', p. 21.

[66] *Archives*, II, p. 130 (emphasis mine). The meaning of *ruiterdienst* is rather puzzling. Cf. ibid., pp. 184–5, Hoogstraten to Brederode, 29 July 1566, who ends with the words, 'Monsieur, vous baise les mains cent mille fois, vous offrant mon service et ung *ruiterdienst*' (Sir, I kiss your hands one hundred thousand times, offering you my service and a *ruiterdienst*).

tous gens et jantylhommes quy ont fort byen le moyen de fayre ung reutredeynst *comme il ce me sont oblygé*.') This patronage could take on a very personal character. When Brederode went to Amsterdam in the spring of 1567, the Frisians and other nobles who joined him were described by a contemporary as his 'family'.[67] Jan Blois van Treslong had been in Brederode's service until after the death of his mother, when he inherited landed property and could support himself.[68] His brother Willem van Treslong, who was in Brederode's service in 1566, convinced Jan to sign the Union also.[69] Maximiliaan van Blois, known as De Cocq van Neereynen, had been in Egmond's service, but had resigned to serve Brederode.[70] He became lieutenant of the same company in which his brother Robert served.[71] Dirk van der Does, Brederode's steward at Huis te Cleef, was married to a sister of Samuel and Josua van Alveringen, who likewise entered Brederode's service in 1566.

Brederode's personal influence certainly enhanced the popularity of the Union. Yet it does not explain why an individual nobleman decided to grant or withhold support. Religious conviction was an important motive for many nobles: some were convinced adherents of the new religion. In Leiden, Jacob Oem van Wyngaerden and Arend van Duvenvoirde were among the pathbreakers for the Reformation.[72] Wyngaerden allowed evangelical preachers to enter the city and attended sermons armed with pistols to defend those present against any attacks. He forced the abbess of the convent of Rijnsburg to open the doors of her convent to the Calvinists, and he hindered the sextons of several churches from sounding the bells for Catholic services.[73] Duvenvoirde took advantage of troubled times to go with Herbert van Raephorst and a great number of servants, horses and dogs to the monasteries of Egmond and Heiloo, staying there for a long time at their expense and insulting the abbot of Egmond by making disrespectful remarks about the Catholic mass.[74] Dirk Sonoy, Lodewijk van den Binkchorst and Cornelis van Wyngaerden organized the Protestant movement at The Hague.[75] They brought a preacher there and offered him room and board. The three of them rented a house and a meadow where the sermons could take place. Wyngaerden was also charged with having

---

[67] MS Historische beschrijving van het gepasseerde in Amsterdam omtrent de Reformatie (Historical description of what happened in Amsterdam relating to the Reformation), GA Amsterdam, Archief handschriften, inv. no. 59, fo. 43.

[68] *Correspondance Granvelle*, II, p. 673.

[69] *Sententiën*, p. 65.

[70] *Correspondance Granvelle*, II, p. 648.

[71] Smit, *Den Haag*, pp. 59–60.

[72] D. H. A. Kolff, 'Libertatis ergo. De beroerten binnen Leiden in de jaren 1566 en 1567', *LJ* 58 (1966): 118–48, at 119–20, 133–4.

[73] *Sententiën*, pp. 48–9.

[74] Ibid., pp. 48–50. The abbot of Egmond was the new bishop of Haarlem, Nicolaas van Nieuwland, known as 'dronken Klaesgen' (drunken Nick).

[75] Ibid., pp. 51–3; Smit, *Den Haag*, pp. 31–3.

assured the nuns of Loosduinen that their convent would quickly be remod-
elled as a dovecote. In Voorburg the brothers Ghilein and Johan Zegers van
Wassenhoven and their friend Willem van Treslong had dinner with the local
priest. At table Ghilein slandered the Catholic religion, demanded the priest
hand over the keys to the church, forced his way into the church and broke the
statue of a saint.[76] Johan van Wassenhoven was present at a celebration of the
Lord's Supper in Delft, where the Reformation had also been organized by
several nobles.[77] In Wassenaar Herbert van Raephorst personally participated
in iconoclasm, striking the parish priest, throwing him on the ground and
kicking him. In vandalizing the church he limited himself to the two burial
chapels belonging to his family. He did steal a chalice and, in mockery of the
mass, used it to slake his thirst.[78] Together with Frederik van Egmond and
Cornelis van Assendelft, Raephorst placed a rope around the neck of a cleric in
The Hague and threatened to strangle him because he had preached against
the ministers of the new religion. Assendelft had tried to convert the priest of
Hoogmade to Calvinism by promising him 300 gulden per year. At the same
time he had one of his own children baptized by a Protestant.[79] Wessel van den
Boetzelaer, the lord of Asperen, joined the Union along with his six legitimate
sons and one bastard. The Van den Boetzelaers had been energetic supporters
of the Reform for some time.[80] Their women appear to have played an important role. Wessel's wife Françoise van Praet van Moerkercken came from a
heretical family of Flanders, but she had died in 1562. The Council of
Troubles declared that Wessel had been converted to the new faith by his
'Concubine ou Femme Putaine', Judith van Helmond.[81] His son Rutger came
to the sectaries by his wife Agnes van Bailleul, who was also descended from a
Flemish family known for its heretical ideas.[82] Another son, Otto, was lured
from the orthodox path by his wife Catherijne Ghiselin, first to the Anabaptists,
then to the Calvinists. Wessel himself displayed a lively interest in new ideas. At
the church of Langerak he organized a public disputation between a Mennonite
and a Calvinist preacher.[83] His son Floris was charged with inviting preachers
of both sects to come to his manor of Langerak.[84] In the summer of 1566, the
old lord of Asperen forbade the Catholic mass in his town, and several months
later allowed Protestant preachers to come from Friesland and elsewhere. The

[76] Smit, *Den Haag*, pp. 59–60.
[77] *Sententiën*, pp. 38–40.
[78] Ibid., pp. 39–40; Smit, *Den Haag*, pp. 59–60; Beelaerts van Blokland, 'Wassenaar'.
[79] *Sententiën*, pp. 173–6.
[80] Duke, 'Asperen', p. 207; *Sententiën*, pp. 107, 130–41.
[81] *Sententiën*, p. 130. He had supposedly been a supporter of the new doctrines for four or five
years. According to A. C. Duke, the lord of Asperen had already lapsed in the 1550s, 'Asperen',
p. 208.
[82] Van Gelder, 'Bailleul, Bronkhorst, Brederode', p. 58.
[83] Van Lommel, 'Kerkelijke toestand', p. 441.
[84] *Sententiën*, p. 107.

entire family participated in iconoclasm at Asperen. Lord Wessel opened the gate behind his castle to give entry to the iconoclasts who had come from Culemborg under the leadership of Willem van Zuylen van Nyevelt, lord of Aartsbergen. While Wessel served a meal to his noble guest in the castle, he strictly prohibited the inhabitants of the little town from interfering with the vandalism of their churches. He and his sons supervised this work. Rutger, Daniël, Otto, Floris and the bastard son Wessel (who was sheriff of Asperen) conducted the image breakers from church to church, and they did not regard it as beneath their dignity to take part personally in the destruction. Rutger smashed a stone altar and several days later had the rubble placed in the masonry of the gate of his house. In another monastery the brothers tore up altar-cloths, books and missals; they poured holy oil over the floor and trampled on the sacrament. They also expelled the priest of the St Anne convent from the city.

The aggression of these nobles against the outward symbols of the Catholic mass and their energetic spreading of the new faith show that they supported the Union because they were adherents of the Reform. Yet it would be incorrect to suppose that all the Holland signers were convinced Protestants. Since most Union nobles remained calm in the summer of 1566, less is known about their motives, although many wanted to remain within the Catholic church. The texts of the Union and the petition were deliberately formulated so that as many nobles as possible would join. The Union sought to abolish the harsh decrees against heresy and the Inquisition, not the old church in its entirety. Thus the Union attracted not only Protestants but also moderates who hoped that there would be room in the Netherlands for more than one religion, or those who had as their ideal a broad state church, modelled after the Church of England. Only convinced supporters of Philip's religious policy could not accept the two documents.[85]

The iconoclasm, which began on 10 August in Flanders and broke out in Holland on 23 August, caused the Union to fall apart. At first the events of August 1566 appeared to lead to a victory for the moderates.[86] In the agreement that Margaret of Parma made with the nobles on 23–25 August, she declared that Protestant sermons would be allowed in places where they had already been held. The new religion was now officially tolerated. Although this was only a provisional settlement, no one doubted that the king's final decision would be along the same moderate lines. In exchange, the nobles promised to dissolve the Compromise. Margaret, however, had absolutely no intention of observing this agreement. Public opinion, which previously had sympathized with the perse-

---

[85] On the spectrum of political and religious ideas in this period, see Woltjer, *Friesland*, pp. 93–104, and his 'Het beeld vergruisd?', *Vaderlands Verleden in Veelvoud. Opstellen . . .* (2nd edn, The Hague, 1980), pp. 89–98.

[86] Woltjer, 'Vredemakers', pp. 304–7.

cuted heretics, now began to turn against them. The senseless destruction in the churches, the molesting of clergy, the circumstance that in all places where Protestantism had been introduced the Catholic mass had been made impossible, the perennial fear of radical action by the lower orders – all these factors led moderates to shun the movement. Thus a separation of minds occurred.[87]

At the end of November the central government regained its power and self-confidence, and began using force to wrest back the concessions it had granted to the Protestants. The radical Protestant wing of the Union now grouped themselves around Brederode, in order to fight force with force. Troops were raised; Brederode strengthened the defences of his city of Vianen and tried to make himself master of 's-Hertogenbosch, Utrecht and Amsterdam. His attempts at unleashing an armed revolt ultimately came to naught. The small rebel army was slaughtered at Oosterweel in March 1567; after the capture of Valenciennes, 's-Hertogenbosch and Vianen were also lost. Utrecht opened its gates to government forces under the count of Megen, while Amsterdam admitted the rebel leader but not his troops. Brederode and his disorganized troops had to flee post-haste to Emden. The nobles who did not manage to escape were arrested and executed.

Most nobles meekly watched this drama unfold and accepted the apparently inevitable course of events. When the government demanded a new loyalty oath from all fief-holders and administrative officials in January 1567, most Holland nobles, even those who had signed one of the circulating lists, acquiesced. Only a dozen nobles regarded the new oath as conflicting with their earlier promise to the Union and refused to swear again.[88]

After the collapse of this movement a number of leading nobles fled abroad. More followed after the arrival of the duke of Alba, when the Council of Troubles began its investigation. In all about twenty-five Holland nobles were condemned *in absentia* to exile and confiscation of their property.[89] Others fled without being sentenced. In the Sea-Beggars' fleet or with William of Orange's army, they awaited better times.

THE CIVIL WAR IN HOLLAND

In 1566 iconoclasm had frightened many moderates and driven them into the arms of the government. It would have been prudent for the government to cultivate the loyalty of these groups carefully. Yet Alba did precisely the opposite: by his harsh actions he again alienated the moderates. Thus when a new revolt broke out in Holland after the Sea-Beggars' capture of Brill on 1 April 1572, many people were inclined to choose the lesser of two evils and opened the gates for the rebels.[90]

---

[87] Woltjer, *Friesland*, p. 144. [88] *Nav* 84 (1935): 158–9.
[89] *Sententiën*. [90] Woltjer, 'Vredemakers', pp. 308–9.

The exiles and other refugees from Alba's reign of terror now returned home. But the Holland nobles were divided. Some went over to the rebel forces or defended the cities of Holland besieged by the Spaniards. Jan van Duvenvoirde (1520–73), a younger brother of the lord of Warmond, was a member of the magistracy of Haarlem and a colonel in the city militia during the siege; he died in prison after the city had surrendered.[91] Lancelot van Brederode, Hendrik's bastard half-brother, was also active in Haarlem and executed by the Spaniards.[92] Jan van der Does played an important role when Leiden was besieged.[93] Yet others went into the service of the king, such as Maximiliaan van Cruyningen and Johan van Schagen, who both fought in 1573 at the battle of the Zuiderzee and were taken prisoner by the rebels.[94] Family connections sometimes played a role in the choice of sides: the loyalist stadholder Bossu was an uncle of the lord of Cruyningen.

In the Ridderschap the events of 1572 led to a radical change of membership. The banished members of the Compromise returned and reoccupied their places.[95] On the other hand, those who had served under Alba now had to depart.[96] Only one nobleman, Jacob van Duvenvoirde, lord of Warmond, appeared before the troubles, under Alba, and under the new leadership of the college. The places of the loyalists were taken over by nobles who had not been members of the Ridderschap before, but had actively supported the Revolt, such as Rutger van den Boetzelaer, the son of the old lord of Asperen, Jan van der Does, the defender of Leiden, Adriaan van Swieten, Willem van Zuylen van Nyevelt (the iconoclast, a descendant of an Utrecht family, but lord of Aartsbergen in Holland) and Jan van Woerden van Vliet. Apart from Van Vliet, all these nobles had been members of the Union. The Ridderschap thus consisted almost exclusively of persons who had been active in 1566; most were supporters of the Reformation.

The revolution of 1572 also led to changes in the important administrative offices. The Court of Holland and the Chamber of Accounts, which had compromised themselves under Alba with persecutions and confiscations, fled before the advancing rebels to the relative safety of Utrecht; they had to be replaced.[97] Many bailiffs, sheriffs and stewards had likewise been involved in

---

[91] Van der Steur, 'Johan van Duvenvoirde', p. 247.

[92] Te Water, *Verbond*, II, p. 299.

[93] *NNBW*, VI, p. 426.

[94] A. W. E. Dek, 'Genealogie der heren van Cruijningen', *JbCBG* 11 (1957): 79–120, at 104, and Holleman, *Dirk van Assendelft*, p. 333.

[95] The names of the nobles reappear only in the printed resolutions of Holland in 1575. Those returning were Arend van Duvenvoirde; Gijsbrecht van Duvenvoirde, lord of Obdam; Otto van Egmond van Kenenburg; Gerrit van Poelgeest and Jacob van Wyngaerden. Hendrik Croesinck was the only signer of the Compromise who did not return.

[96] Jacob van der Duyn, Vincent van Lockhorst, and Johan van Mathenesse. Klaas van Assendelft and Arend de Jode, who had attended in Alba's time, had both died in 1570.

[97] Smit, 'Omzetting'.

the persecutions and could not be kept in office either. This change of person-nel led to the return of the nobles in many administrative offices. Perhaps the appointment of nobles rested on a deliberate policy of William of Orange. Prior to the revolutionary meeting of the States in Dordrecht in 1572, Orange had instructed his delegate Marnix to negotiate with the States about 'the rulers and governors of the cities in Holland, desiring their counsel and advice therein, that they would themselves name *Noblemen, who would be qualified thereunto* and [Marnix] would present unto them those who would be available to His Grace'.[98] Indeed, more nobles were available at this time. Before the Revolt the prosperity of many nobles had made it possible for them to withdraw from offices. In 1572 and subsequent years, however, financial considerations may have motivated them to seek such appointments. Under Alba's rule, many nobles had to flee their country, leaving their property behind. All these nobles had a clear material interest in the success of the Revolt. A merchant could continue his trade in exile because he maintained his business contacts and could keep his capital out of Alba's hands with relative ease. A craftsman took his specialized knowledge with him into exile and could probably find work abroad. But a nobleman, whose capital consisted primarily of farms and seigneurial rights, had little to live on in exile. Trade or manual labour would cause him to lose his noble status.[99] Most nobles took service in the Sea-Beggars' fleet or in Orange's army. An exception was Willem van Zuylen van Nyevelt, who earned his living at Wesel as a bookbinder.[100] It was important for these nobles to regain their properties, which had fallen into the hands of the enemy. Jan van der Does of Leiden complained that after the relief of the siege he was 'destitute of all means of maintaining himself and his wife and his small children, since all of his and his wife's property lying in enemy territory has been frustrated (noting that the same has been confiscated); and furthermore nearly all of his household goods and possessions for the maintenance of himself and his family have been pledged as collateral or sold'.[101]

Thus Holland nobles returned to the service of their country. In the new Court of Holland in 1572 and 1573 eleven councillors were appointed: five of them belonged to the nobility.[102] The Chamber of Accounts, which had never

---

[98] Cited by Bakhuizen van den Brink, 'Eerste vergadering der Staten', p. 530 (emphasis mine). Apparently sheriffs, bailiffs and governors are meant here.

[99] Cf. J. C. A. de Meij, *De watergeuzen en de Nederlanden 1568–1572* (Amsterdam and London, 1972), pp. 154–5. [100] Te Water, *Verbond*, III, p. 85.

[101] 'Over de belegering van Leiden en het kapiteinschap van Johan van der Does', *Kron HG* 2 (1846): 150–61, at 158–60.

[102] Jacob van Duvenvoirde, the old lord of Warmond, who was summoned to the Ridderschap before the troubles, in Alba's time, and after 1572; Gerard Oem van Wyngaerden; Cornelis van den Bouchorst; Dirk van Bronckhorst and Artus van Brederode (*Memorialen Rosa*, II, p. xlviii–il). Dirk van Egmond van de Nyenburg probably did not belong to the noble family of Egmond: see J. Belonje, 'De afkomst van het geslacht van Egmond van de Nijenburg', *JbCBG* 9 (1955): 39–75.

been a noble domain, did not now become noble. Only Lodewijk van de Binckhorst, a former member of the Compromise, was appointed a master of accounts in 1572.[103] But several nobles were appointed bailiffs: Gerard van Berckenrode in Kennemerland, Willem van Dorp in Delfland, Pieter van Rhoon in Putten, Willem van Zuylen van Nyevelt in South Holland.[104] The bailiwicks that were tied to governorships were already for the most part in the hands of nobles, but here too some had to be replaced. Many nobles were appointed: Adriaan van Swieten in Gouda, Daniël van den Boetzelaer in Loevestein, Willem van Zuylen van Nyevelt at Muiden in 1580.[105] In the large cities of Holland, however, nobles did not return to the office of sheriff.

THE PACIFICATION

The division of the Holland nobility was ended by the Pacification of Ghent, the peace agreement made by the States General and the rebellious provinces in November 1576. According to its terms, the confiscation of goods of the disputing parties was reversed: the former rebels recovered those of their possessions that lay in areas controlled by the States General, and supporters of the king got back their possessions in Holland and Zeeland. Prisoners were released. A general reconciliation of the Holland nobles was now possible.

Those who had hoped for a lasting solution to the difficulties were cheated. In the south the enmities were resumed shortly afterwards, but among the Holland nobles the old divisions did not return. In the long years of war that followed, most of them remained willy-nilly on the side of the rebellious States. Thus Johan van Schagen had remained Catholic and kept aloof from the Union. In 1571 he appeared in the Ridderschap under Alba,[106] and in 1573 he fought on the Spanish side. He was captured, and for a time Sonoy seized his possessions in the name of Orange. Yet several years after the Pacification, Schagen resumed his place in the Ridderschap; in 1579 he was a deputy for Holland in the States General, in 1582 he was its president, in 1595 he became a member of the Council of State, in 1605 again delegate to the States General, and in 1615 member of the Deputy Councils for South Holland.[107] Maximiliaan van Cruijningen, who had also fought for the king, became general of artillery in the States army (though he had to give up the post again under Leicester) and member of the Council of State.[108] Both men remained Catholics.

[103] Van Gouthoeven, *Chronyke*, pp. 110–12.
[104] ARA, Grafelijkheidsrekenkamer, registers, inv. no. 496, fo. 11; inv. no. 498, fo. 121 v. and 147 v.; Dolk, *Delfland*, p. 707; M. Balen Jansz., *Beschrijvinge der stad Dordrecht* (Dordrecht, 1677), p. 7.
[105] ARA, Grafelijkheidsrekenkamer, registers, inv. no. 498, fo. 45; Walvis, *Gouda*, p. 80.
[106] Van Epen, 'Ridderschap', p. 8.
[107] Holleman, *Dirk van Assendelft*, p. 333; Dek, *Genealogie graven van Holland*, p. 65.
[108] Dek, 'Genealogie Cruijningen', p. 55.

Material considerations may have played a significant role in the choice of Holland nobles for the States' side. On 28 October 1579 the States confiscated all goods, incomes and rents in Holland of residents who had chosen the side of the enemy or the Malcontents.[109] This regulation largely served to bind the nobles to the States' side. Without their goods they could not 'live nobly'. Only three high nobles who owned extensive possessions in Hainault, Flanders and Brabant could allow themselves to remain loyal to the king of Spain. These were Philips van Egmond (son of Lamoraal, who was executed in 1568), the count of Ligne, who was in possession of the Wassenaer inheritance, and the countess of Aremberg, the successor to the estates of the Naaldwijk family. In 1579 the States ordered the seizure of their goods.[110]

Most indigenous nobles, however, continued to live in Holland and had few possessions outside the province. Some tried to remain friendly to both sides: Anthonie van Woerden van Vliet, who had lived with his family in Mechelen until 1579 but owned goods in Holland, asked for a 'lettre de reconciliation' from the king; at the same time he requested permission to continue living in Haarlem. This was granted, but he could not simultaneously enjoy the income from his possessions in areas under royal control.[111] Another example is Philippe de la Torre, who had settled in The Hague with Parma's permission. He had inherited possessions in Holland from his uncle François de Cocq van Opijnen, and he sought Parma's protection although he declared that he wanted to continue living in Holland.[112]

The year 1572 signified a caesura for the Ridderschap. Royal sympathizers had to flee, and those banished under Alba returned. The Ridderschap was purged and filled with supporters of Orange, mostly Protestants. After 1576, however, the divisions became less sharp, and over the longer term continuity was restored. The Catholic lord of Schagen received a seat in the college, and his heirs continued to appear even though they remained Catholic. Johan van Mathenesse (1533–1602) likewise changed his affiliation later. He had shunned the Confederacy, and had attended the sessions under Alba. In 1572 he stayed abroad, but after the Pacification he again became a member of the Ridderschap, the Council of State, and the Deputy Councils. This friend of Oldenbarnevelt remained Catholic, but his heirs, who were also recorded among the nobility, did not keep the faith of their ancestors.[113]

Religion was not a criterion for admission to the Ridderschap, but loyalty to the young Republic was. In the first years of the Republic, until about 1600,

[109] *Res. Holland*, 28 Oct. 1579.
[110] Ibid., 20 Aug., 28 Oct. 1579; cf. Wilson, *Queen Elizabeth*, pp. 48–50.
[111] ARA Brussels, Aud., inv. no. 1472/1.
[112] Ibid.
[113] J. J. de Geer, 'Proeve eener geschiedenis van het geslacht en de goederen der Heeren van Mathenesse', *Berigten van het Historisch Genootschap* 3, 1st part (1850): 44–129; Van der Zee, *Matenesse*, p. 75; Den Tex, *Oldenbarnevelt*, II, p. 251.

four of the twelve or thirteen nobles who attended regularly were Catholic: Warmond (Duvenvoirde), Mathenesse, Poelgeest and Schagen. Even in 1656, when the apostolic vicar Jacobus de la Torre drew up a list of Catholic office-holders in Holland, two of the thirteen regular attenders, Warmond and Schagen, were still Catholic.[114]

The relative moderation of the Dutch Revolt is evident from the fact that of the ten families who attended frequently before 1563, only two disappeared from the Ridderschap: the lords Van der Duyn and Van Lockhorst. Although he remained Catholic, Nicolaas van der Duyn, the lord of 's-Gravenmoer (d. 1649), did become dike-reeve of Delfland and an officer of the Forestry. His son Adam (1639–93) became a general in the States' army, master of the hunt and master of the stables to William III, and dike-reeve of Delfland; his son Adriaan (1683–1753) was again enrolled in the Ridderschap in 1724, from which his family had been absent for a century and a half.[115]

CONCLUSION

Between 1565 and the early years of the Republic much changed in the short term, but little over the longer term. In Holland there was much sympathy for the Compromise of the Nobles, but only a few of its supporters were militant Calvinists. The iconoclasm of 1566 led to division. Under Alba, the radical wing of the Union had to leave the country. In 1572 the situation was reversed: the radicals returned and the supporters of the king had to take flight. Yet the Pacification of Ghent created the possibility of reconciliation. Nobles who had appeared in the Ridderschap under Alba could now return. The Ridderschap displayed the same pattern as most city councils of Holland, where continuity also reigned over the long term.[116]

The question of the partisan choices of the Holland nobles thus has no simple answer. During the confused years of the troubles and civil war, some chose one side, some the other; most probably tried to remain neutral. After 1579, when hopes for an early agreement between the parties had vanished, the choice of the nobles became easier. They primarily chose the side where their

[114] W. J. F. Nuijens, *Geschiedenis der Nederlandsche beroerten in de 16e eeuw*, 8 vols. (Amsterdam, 1865–70), I, pp. 282–90. On Catholics in the Holland Ridderschap, see W. J. J. C. Bijleveld, 'De Roomsch-Catholieken in de oude Hollandsche Ridderschap', *NL* 45 (1927): 306–9, and the subsequent polemic, pp. 336–41. More fundamental is J. C. Naber, 'Dissenters op 't kussen. Eene bijdrage tot de staatkundige geschiedenis der Vereenigde Nederlanden', *De Tijdspiegel* (1884), issue 2, pp. 45–57, who shows that in Holland Catholics were never officially excluded from office-holding.

[115] *NNBW*, IX, pp. 541–2; Van der Aa, *Biographisch woordenboek*, s.v. Van der Duyn. Lockhorst was a loyalist in 1572 but later went over to the Ridderschap of Utrecht: Van Epen, 'Ridderschap', p. 4.

[116] J. C. Boogman, 'De overgang van Gouda, Dordrecht, Leiden en Delft in de zomer van het jaar 1572', *TvG* 57 (1942): 81–112.

possessions lay. In Holland that meant that the States seized the properties of Egmond, Aremberg and Ligne, but the majority of the old Holland nobles retained their possessions.

Let us close this chapter with an exception that probably proves the rule, but shows how complicated the relationships were: the De Jeude or De Jode family, who lost their possessions in Holland as a result of the Revolt. Arend de Jode (1510–70) was Lord of Hardinxveld and had been governor of the fortress of Loevestein since 1545.[117] He remained outside the Compromise, and, although he did not swear a new oath of loyalty to the king, he remained faithful to the government.[118] He appeared in the Ridderschap under Alba and also kept his governorship of Loevestein. In the latter capacity he was killed in 1570, during the attack by Orange's troops. It was not exceptional that De Jode had chosen the king's side, but it certainly was unusual that his widow Maria van Boisot abandoned the ancestral manor of Hardinxveld and took her children to settle in Brussels. A closer look at the circumstances makes this decision understandable. Maria van Boisot was much younger than her husband: when he died in 1570 at the age of about sixty, she was thirty-five. She was burdened with four small children and a stepdaughter from Arend's previous marriage. Moreover, as a result of the All Saints' Day flood of 1570, the village of Hardinxveld was under water. The young widow therefore decided to 'stick the spade in the dike' and returned to her family in Brussels. The De Jode family continued to live in the south, where the daughters were married, and the last son and heir, Jan de Jode, died in 1641.

---

[117] On Arend de Jode, *NNBW*, VI, p. 864; Van der Aa, *Biographisch woordenboek*, s.v. De Jode; on the family: *Nav* 42 (1892): 226–76, and HRA, Collectie Snouckaert, inv. no. 2338.
[118] D'Yvoy van Mijdrecht, *Verbond*, no. 131.

8

Integration and apartheid

THE NOBLES AS SEIGNEURS

In the Dutch Republic the manors still served as the foundation of the nobles' political power. On the basis of their possession of manors the Holland nobles were represented in the States, and thereby they had access to high offices. Until 1650 the nobles remained the most important holders of manors, though their relative position declined.[1] While nobles had held about 80 per cent of the manors in 1585, by 1650 their share fell to about 60 per cent. Holland nobles, nobles from other provinces and non-nobles now each held about 30 per cent of the manors in fief. Between 1585 and 1650 the number of non-noble seigneurs doubled, from 26 to 52. Moreover, the number of manors held by cities increased from 3 to 14.[2]

A survey of the lords and manors located in the bailiwick of Rijnland in 1667 illustrates the continuing aristocratic character of manorial holdings (table 8.1).[3] In Rijnland the nobles had retained an overwhelming share of the manors. The seigneurie of Rijnsburg, a fief formerly held by the abbess of the aristocratic convent there, was now managed by the Ridderschap of Holland, so that its revenues benefited the nobility. The most important noble seigneurs were the lords of Wassenaer, as the members of the Duvenvoirde family now called themselves. Five members of this family together held nine manors. The nobles in Rijnland were above all holders of manors with high justice. Of the twenty-four manors with low justice, they held only five; but they had seventeen of the twenty-six manors with high justice.[4]

Ten manors were in the hands of nine non-noble lords. They could hardly be described as 'bourgeois'. Most possessed foreign titles of knighthood or nobility and thus belonged to what Schoockius called *nobiles recentiores*. 'Lord

---

[1] See appendices 5 and 6 of the Dutch edition.
[2] See Van Nierop, 'Quaede regiment'.
[3] Van Leeuwen, *Costumen Rijnland*, pp. 16–22.
[4] The nine Holland nobles who held manors in Rijnland in 1667 were: Johan baron van Wassenaer, lord of Warmond (4 manors); Lord Gerrit van Poelgeest (2); the dowager lady of Brederode, widow of Reinoud van Brederode (2); Gerard van Wassenaer (1); Diederik van Wassenaer (1); *jonkheer* Karel Oem van Wyngaerden (3); *jonkheer* Arend van Wassenaer, lord of Duvenvoirde (2); Lord Jacob van Wassenaer, knight, lord of Obdam (1); Lord Wigbold van der Does (3).

Table 8.1 *Manors in Rijnland, 1667*

Holders of manors	Number of total manors	Percentage of manors granted	Percentage held in fief
Holland nobles	20	40	49
Other nobles	2	4	5
Non-nobles	10	20	24
Cities	6	12	15
No indication	3	6	7
Manors not granted in fief	9	18	0
Totals	50	100	100

Cornelis de Vlamingh van Oudshoorn, knight', lord of Oudshoorn and Gnephoek, came from an Amsterdam family of merchants and regents that pretended to trace its ancestry back to the noble family of Oudshoorn. Yet only after the purchase of the manor in 1627 did they dare to assume the double surname of De Vlamingh van Oudshoorn.[5] Johan Nooms, 'knight and baron of the Holy Roman Empire', lord of Aarlanderveen, was related to De Vlamingh van Oudshoorn. Their fathers had been partners in a trading business.[6] The widow of *jonkheer* Dirk van der Laen, *jonkheer* Pieter van Kuyk van Mierop, George de Hertoghe and Maria van Reigersberg, and the widow of Willem van Liere, lord of Oosterwijk, had no less aristocratic allure.[7] Yet they did not belong to the old nobility: rather, they illustrate a phenomenon that has been called 'the aristocratization of the regents in the Republic'.[8] In 1667 the city of Leiden held five manors in Rijnland, while Delft had one. The cities placed great importance on the possession of manors as a means to economic and political domination of the countryside. The opportunity to repress cheap industrial competition in the surrounding areas was a significant incentive for cities to buy manors.[9]

Although the nobles still had a very prominent place as lords of the manor in

[5] Elias, *Vroedschap*, I, p. 505. Cf. his pp. 279 and 233, note *e*, and A. de Roever Nzn., 'De Vlaming van Oudshoorn', *Amsterdamsch Jaarboekje* (1891): 105–22.

[6] Elias, *Vroedschap*, I, p. 431.

[7] Dirk van der Laen probably was descended from the noble family of that name, which was not enrolled in the Ridderschap of Holland, however. On Pieter van Kuyk van Mierop, cf. Van der Aa, *Biographisch woordenboek*, s.v. Cornelis van Cuyk van Myerop. On George de Hertoghe: *NNBW*, I, p. 1090. Maria van Reigersberg came from the patriciate of Zeeland; her husband Willem van Liere was descended from a noble family: Van der Aa, *Biographisch woordenboek*, s.v. Willem van Liere.

[8] D. J. Roorda, *Partij en factie. De oproeren van 1672 in de steden van Holland en Zeeland* (Groningen, 1978), pp. 37–58, and his 'De regentenstand in Holland', *Vaderlands Verleden in Veelvoud*, 2nd edn (The Hague, 1980), pp. 221–40.

[9] Jansma, 'Laat-middeleeuwse stad'.

the mid-seventeenth century, their relative position had declined in comparison with a century earlier. In general new owners, whether cities or aristocratic burghers, could only have bought their manors from nobles. Yet this does not indicate that the nobles as a whole were impoverished.[10] Often other nobles came forward as purchasers of these manors. But because nobles did not buy all the manors offered for sale, urban burghers did eventually gain a foothold.

To what extent was the Revolt a cause of the transfer of manors to non-noble holders? The general revolt that broke out in 1576 did not last long. After the duke of Parma had managed to separate the so-called Malcontents from the rebel camp, Egmond, Ligne and Aremberg, who had many possessions in Holland, chose the king's side, and the States of Holland seized their property.[11] Yet, after Philips van Egmond died in 1590, his brother and heir Lamoraal returned to Holland. Lamoraal's attempts to recover his fiefs failed, partly because the States wanted to reserve for themselves the high justice on his manors, and partly because they did not trust Lamoraal's politics or morals. Since he was known as a libertine and was suspected of having been involved in the assassination of the prince of Orange, they wanted to keep him out of the States assembly. Lamoraal and his two sisters, who also lived in Holland, did receive great sums of money from the States, more than the income from his properties. But, as a result of his extravagant lifestyle, Lamoraal was in the end declared bankrupt and his confiscated properties were sold.[12]

In accord with the Twelve Years' Truce concluded in 1609, the States lifted the seizures of properties belonging to persons who resided in enemy territory. Ligne and Aremberg decided to take no risks and sought to liquidate their possessions in Holland, although Ligne was not able to find buyers for some of his possessions until after the Peace of Westphalia in 1648. Forty manors held by Egmond, Aremberg, and Ligne thus came on the market. Twenty nobles, of whom sixteen came from Holland families, bought these manors, as did thirteen burghers and three cities. Four manors were not granted in fief and remained with the States of Holland (table 8.2). When these high nobles chose the Spanish side, they made it possible for others to obtain manors, but the nobility did not disappear as a result.

Yet the number of manors held by the nobility is only one aspect of power relations in the countryside. Within the manors, the authority of the lord increased as a consequence of the Revolt. Just as the Revolt strengthened city administrations, so it strengthened lords of the manors.[13] The titles on which the lord based his authority were the same, but the circumstances and concepts

---

[10] See above, pp. 133–4.
[11] *Res. Holland*, 20 Aug., 28 Oct. 1579.
[12] Wijs, *Leenstelsel*, pp. 45–102.
[13] S. J. Fockema Andreae, MS inventory of the *huisarchief* of the lords of Warmond, GA Leiden, pp. 6–7. J. L. Van der Gouw, *Het ambacht Voorschoten* (Voorburg, 1956), p. 34.

Table 8.2 *Sales of manors by Egmond, Aremberg and Ligne*

Manors sold to:	Holland nobles	Other nobles	Burghers	Cities	States	Total
Egmond	2	1	7	0	4	14
Aremberg	6	2	1	0	0	9
Ligne: during truce (1609–21)	4	1	2	3	0	10
Ligne: after 1648	4	0	3	0	0	7
Totals	16	4	13	3	4	40

of administrative law held by the new rulers had changed. Calvin had recognized lesser authorities under the sovereign – estates or orders to which the people owed absolute obedience. Since nobles held by far the greatest number of manors at the end of the sixteenth century, they were the order who most clearly represented authority in this sense. Furthermore, the theorists made no distinction between urban and rural administration. Village government rested not with the institutions developed by villagers themselves, but rather with the noble seigneur. Initially the bailiff of Rijnland tried to act as a higher 'magistrate' in relation to the seigneurs exercising low justice within his jurisdiction. These attempts, begun in 1573, had apparently failed by 1588.[14] The high jurisdictions, however, did not fall under the bailiff's authority. As the bailiff of Rijnland tried to assume attributes of urban administration, so did the lords in their high jurisdictions. As long as local interests did not oppose him, the lord could rule unchallenged, because contemporary political thought supported him. Questions of authority were regarded as questions of property, and property rights were protected by judges even when that property involved governing authority. Thus before the Revolt the lord of Warmond had never occupied himself with local by-laws, but after 1585 he repeatedly did so.[15] The lord's appointment of members to many administrative bodies is another power in Warmond that was only exercised after the Revolt. The administrative powers of the lord, such as granting permission for trades and businesses, also date from this period. In granting permission to notaries and in managing religious properties, the lord was specifically placed in the same position as city administrators by the States.[16]

Under the governments of Charles V and Philip II, the powers of the seigneurs were limited, primarily by the increasing activities of the Court of

[14] S. J. Fockema Andreae, 'Aantekeningen over het baljuwschap Rijnland', *TvR* 14 (1931): 236–64.
[15] Van der Steur, 'Johan van Duvenvoirde', pp. 221–4.
[16] Fockema Andreae, MS Huisarchief Warmond, p. 7.

Holland.[17] In the Republic the private lords again felt the wind in their sails. They successfully opposed the granting of manors to polder boards. Not only the cities acquired manors, but in the early years of the Republic a *sterfman* (an individual, as opposed to an institution of mortmain) representing the 'common inhabitants' of a polder was sometimes invested with a manor. In 1592 Herman Oem was invested with half of the manor of Puttershoek, 'for the benefit of the common inhabitants of Mijnsheerenland van Moerkerken', and in 1605 and 1608 Matthijs van Asperen was invested with the seigneurie of Hardinxveld and the high justice of Papendrecht, 'for the benefit of the common inhabitants of the Alblasserwaard'.[18] But around 1630 these experiments ended, and in 1642 the investiture of manors for the benefit of collective groups was regarded as undesirable 'as unprecedented in this country'.[19]

THE MEETING OF THE STATES: NOBLES AND CITIES

During the Republic the nobles also had to deal with the increasing importance of the cities and their regents in the States of Holland. In numbers alone, the Ridderschap had to share the meeting hall with eighteen cities instead of six.[20] In 1581 the burdens of war made it desirable to involve more cities in the decision-making of the States. Thus it was decided to invite a number of smaller cities for the duration of the war.[21] This marked a definitive end to the right of the Ridderschap to represent the small cities. In 1627 the nobles stated that they had 'formerly in the time of the sovereigns', represented the small cities: apparently they regarded the loss of this right as a *fait accompli.*[22]

They had a different view of their right to represent the countryside. When the cities questioned this right, the nobles defended themselves vigorously and successfully. As representatives of the countryside the nobles had sometimes had differences with the cities, such as in 1531 regarding rural industries, but their right of representation itself was not disputed. There were signs of difficulties when the nobles complained to Orange in 1574, 'as champions and protectors of the countryside, seeing and noticing the great injustice and evil done by the cities of Holland, which do nothing else than depriving [the nobles]

[17] Van Gelder, 'Hollandse adel', pp. 138–40.
[18] Repertoria op de leenregisters, ARA, Leenkamer, inv. no. 231, fo. 690 v.–691; inv. no. 230, fos. 92 v. and 386.
[19] Rijpperda Wierdsma, *Politie en justitie*, pp. 210–11.
[20] Fruin, *Staatsinstellingen*, p. 234.
[21] *Res. Holland*, 16 March 1581. The final version of the regulation of the States of Holland (*Groot placaet-boeck*, III, p. 87) mentions only 'de Edelen ende Steden, die men gewoonlijck is te beschrijven, ende tot noch toe beschreven zijn geweest' (the nobles and cities, which are customarily enrolled, and have been enrolled up to now). The phrase 'geduyrende den Oorlogh' (during the war) has disappeared.
[22] Pieces concerning the right of the Ridderschap to represent the rural areas, ARA, Ridderschap, inv. no. 63.

of their liberties and privileges against all law and fairness, and deprive the rural areas of their old liberties, customs and trades'. As 'champions of the countryside', the nobles asked the stadholder to maintain rural privileges and to allow no changes without hearing the Ridderschap.[23] The exact cause of this complaint is unknown, but in 1579 the right of the Ridderschap to represent the rural areas was again specifically confirmed after a request by the countryside of Voorne to send their own representative to the States. Voorne and Brill claimed that they did not belong to Holland because the former lords of Voorne had not been vassals of the counts of Holland. The States did admit the city of Brill, but refused entry to the rural area of Voorne on the grounds that all rural areas were already represented by the Ridderschap.[24]

Nevertheless the cities did look enviously upon the monopoly position of the nobles, and in 1627 a conflict broke out in the States about the representation of the countryside. It began when a commission was established to review assessments for the poundage, the ground-tax in the cities and villages of Holland. The nobles were to select one member, but they insisted on choosing two, 'for the sake of the countryside'. More fundamental, however, was their opposition to the proposal that three commissioners appointed by the cities would have authority over manors that had not been granted in fief, but remained directly under the control of the provincial government, or 'in the count's bosom'.[25] The nobles could not allow this to happen. They prepared a note in which they once again stated clearly that they represented the entire countryside, and not only the manors held by private lords.[26] After the matter had been postponed several times, it ended with a partial victory for the nobles. The Ridderschap itself would appoint an extra commissioner who would supervise the entire countryside, without making any distinction between manors that had been granted in fief and manors 'in the count's bosom'. This did not resolve the conflict in principle, because the cities had said that they 'could not permit the lord nobles to represent the countryside', and they did not want to retract this statement.[27]

Ten years later difficulties surfaced again. The Ridderschap informed the States in February 1637, that they had invited stadholder Frederick Henry to participate in future deliberations of their college. The cities could not object, because the Ridderschap had the right of co-option; but they did protest against a passage in the act stating that the nobles represented the countryside. Several delegates declared that they would have to discuss this point with their constituencies. When the resolutions had to be confirmed at the next meeting,

---

[23] Bor, *Nederlantscher oorlogen*, pp. 571–2.
[24] *Res. Holland*, 12 Feb. 1579.
[25] Ibid., 13 Jan. 1627.
[26] ARA, Ridderschap, inv. no. 63. A copy of the remonstrance of the nobles is found in GA Amsterdam, Archief Burgemeesters, Lands- en gewestelijk bestuur, inv. no. 136 R 10–7.
[27] *Res. Holland*, 28 July 1627.

Haarlem and Leiden stated that they could not support this formulation, but this had no practical consequences.[28]

The matter came up again in 1685, when according to a report by the French ambassador, the count d'Avaux, the Amsterdam delegate to the States declared 'that the countryside is no more dependent on the nobles than on the magistrates of the cities, and that in Amsterdam there are people more noble, and who contribute more to the state, both in money and in counsel, than the seven nobles who are present . . . If the nobles want to make something of it, Messieurs of Amsterdam have the arms and hands to make themselves felt'.[29]

Attacks on the right of the Ridderschap to represent the countryside were a consequence of the increasing importance and self-consciousness of the cities. The aggressive words of the Amsterdam delegate would have been unthinkable in the sixteenth century. But the nobles defended their position well, and the matter was never decided in favour of the cities.[30] The cities regarded this as an anomaly, but they accepted it. They never contested the right of the nobility to attend the States. Even in the eighteenth century, when there were few Holland noble families left and their significance as lords of the manors had declined further, the cities did not contest this privilege. The reason lay in the conservative respect for the constitution of the Republic, with its emphasis on ancient rights and privileges, which gave the cities their own special position.

The influence of the Ridderschap in the States was greater than their numerical vote, now one-nineteenth of the total.[31] Most matters were settled by majority vote, but unanimity was required to decide on war and peace, or changes of government. If agreement could not be reached, the matter had to be referred to a neutral commission.[32] In practice this regulation was unwieldy: since decisions still had to be made, matters sometimes were not allowed to come to a vote. The members took turns 'advising', and finally the grand pensionary 'concluded'. The Ridderschap could exercise considerable influence on the final 'conclusion' because the grand pensionary was also the pensionary of the Ridderschap, and normally stated the views of that college. Also, the nobles were the only ones who represented the rural areas, and they could state their advice first, 'as being the oldest, most prominent and most lordly'.[33] This did not mean, however, that the nobles could follow an independent course.[34]

[28] Ibid., 5 Feb., 19 March 1637.
[29] Jean Antoine d'Avaux, *Négociations en Hollande depuis 1679 jusqu'en 1684*, ed. E. Mallet, 6 vols. (Paris, 1752–3), IV, pp. 324–5.
[30] Fruin, *Staatsinstellingen*, p. 232.
[31] See above, p. 166.
[32] *Res. Holland*, 17 March 1581; *Groot placaet-boeck*, III, p. 88. On the order of meeting of the States, cf. Fruin, *Staatsinstellingen*, pp. 235–6; on the influence of the Ridderschap, Fockema Andreae, *Nederlandse staat*, pp. 43–4.
[33] Van der Houve, *Hantvest*, I, p. 11.
[34] Aalbers, 'Factieuze tegenstellingen', p. 412.

Many important matters were not handled by the States as a whole, but by smaller commissions. Here the influence of the nobles was even greater. It was the custom to appoint one or more members of the Ridderschap to all commissions and important administrative colleges; often these nobles acted as presiding officers.[35] The Ridderschap had the right to a fixed number of members in the administrative colleges of Holland and the United Provinces. At the higher level, the Ridderschap named one delegate to the States General, one to the Council of State, one each to the Admiralties of Rotterdam and Amsterdam. In provincial administration the Ridderschap selected several members of the Forestry Office and the polder councils, the chairman of the Deputy Councils of South Holland and two councillors of the Court of Holland. All members of the Court had to be jurists, except those appointed by the Ridderschap.[36] Outside the actual government, the nobles selected one member of the college of curators of the University of Leiden and two directors of the East India Company. Finally, many *ad hoc* commissions of the States were selected jointly by the cities and the nobles.[37] For some functions the nobles appointed their delegates directly, while for others they made nominations. By virtue of his quality, the oldest member of the Ridderschap was entitled to occupy the chairmanship of the Deputy Councils of South Holland. The lieutenant-forester was generally a member of the Ridderschap. The nobles made a list of three candidates, from which the States as a whole chose one. The noble curator of the University of Leiden was appointed directly until 1679; afterwards a list of three names was prepared for the stadholder's choice.[38]

The connection between membership in the Ridderschap and high-office-

---

[35] ARA, Ridderschap, inv. no. 73; *Hedendaagsche historie*, IV, pp. 99–100, 131–2, 243; *Res. Holland*, 7 March 1706; *Groot placaet-boeck*, II, p. 779.

[36] Kluit, *Hollandsche staatsregeering*, III, pp. 445–6, and *Hedendaagsche historie*, IV, p. 243. Yet cf. the MS 'Namen van ruwaard, stadhouders, presidenten, enz.', ARA, Hof, no inv. number, but available in the reading room, fo. 143 v., which states that the councillors nominated by the nobles could use the title *Jonker* in place of *Meester* (master, or graduate in law): 'sijnde evenwel de Jonkers altijd gepromoveerde ad gradum doctoratus vel licentiatus in iure' (although the *jonkers* likewise always hold the degree of doctor or master of law).

[37] In 1649 the Ridderschap had obstructed all appointments for some time, because they demanded membership in the Generaliteitsrekenkamer (Generality Chamber of Accounts) and three seats on the Court (J. E. Elias, *Geschiedenis van het Amsterdamsche regentenpatriciaat* (The Hague, 1923), p. 125). Cf. *Res. Holland*, 5 May 1654 and 28 April 1665: the nobles requested a permanent place in the Generaliteitsrekenkamer 'gelijck in alle andere collegiën' (as in all other colleges). Apparently the nobles were successful, because both a document referring to appointments, dating from the end of the seventeenth century (ARA, Ridderschap, inv. no. 73), and *Hedendaagsche historie*, IV, pp. 99–100, report that in this college one seat was reserved for a representative of the nobles.

[38] ARA, Ridderschap, inv. no. 73. Two members of the Court were chosen by the stadholder from three persons nominated by the Ridderschap (MS 'Namen van ruwaard', fo. 143). In the eighteenth century the *besognes* of the States-General consisted of eight members and one clerk. Each province sent one member, but Holland sent two, as a rule the *raadpensionaris* and a member of the Ridderschap. By this means the nobles had a fairly great influence on the national government.

holding, which had existed in the beginning of the reign of Charles V, was re-established during the Republic. Yet the relation was now reversed: previously, the high-office-holders were the ones who attended the Ridderschap; now, membership in the Ridderschap gave access to high offices. The character of these offices had indeed changed greatly. Nobles could now be found in genuine regent-offices.[39] A civil service in the modern sense was unknown in the Dutch Republic. Administrative tasks had to be fulfilled by those who were 'qualified' by their wealth and social standing. The members of the Ridderschap, a small group with the leisure for rule, could make their contribution to the typical regent-government of the Republic. Along with the urban regents, noble regents took part in all important administrative bodies. The influence of the nobles in the colleges of the Republic could sometimes be greater than that of the cities because a nobleman was appointed for life, while the ten Holland cities that sent delegates to the States General and the Council of State had to take turns, occupying offices for three years at a time, at six-year intervals. Members drawn from the Ridderschap thus generally had more continuity, seniority and experience – which, if they were skilful, they could convert into greater political influence.[40]

Finally, the significance of the Ridderschap increased as a result of the Revolt when, together with the cities, it evolved from a representative body to the bearer of sovereignty in the province. Naturally the power of the nobles did not grow as much as that of the cities. But in an absolute sense their power did increase. Sir William Temple was impressed by the political significance of the nobility in Holland:[41]

Though they have all together but one voice equal to the smallest town; yet they are very considerable in Government, by possessing many of the best Charges both Civil and Military, by having the direction of all the Ecclesiastical Revenue that was seized by the State upon the Change of Religion;[42] and by sending their deputies to all the Councils both of the Generalty and the Province, and by the nomination of one Counsellor in the two great Courts of Justice.[43] They give their Voice first in the Assembly of the states, and thereby [lend] a great weight to the business in consultation.

---

[39] On regent offices: A. T. van Deursen, 'Staatsinstellingen in de Noordelijke Nederlanden 1579–1780', *NAGN*, V, pp. 350–87, at 376–80.
[40] ARA, Ridderschap, inv. no. 73; *Hedendaagsche historie*, IV, pp. 99–100; Gabriëls, *De Edel Mogende Heeren*, p. 553.
[41] Temple, *Observations*, pp. 58–9.
[42] This is incorrect; nobles administered only the property of the formerly aristocratic convents of Rijnsburg and Leeuwenhorst.
[43] This should probably read: two councillors in the Court.

THE MEETING OF THE STATES: THE COMPOSITION OF THE
RIDDERSCHAP

During the Republic, as in the earlier period, not all nobles were enrolled in the Ridderschap. The tendency to restrict access to the college, already manifest in the reign of Philip II, was even more pronounced. In 1565 the Ridderschap came into collision with William of Orange when it asserted the right of co-option. Because the troubles soon distracted everyone's attention, this encounter had no consequences.[44] Under Alba, co-option was naturally out of the question. The provincial advocate Jacob van den Eynden was arrested in 1568 and charged with having summoned nobles to the Ridderschap on his own initiative, denying access to qualified Catholics.[45] In 1572 the 'revolutionary' States usurped the right to summon themselves. Although the political situation was too confused to speak of formal rights, the prince of Orange, the man acting behind the façade of the first 'free' meeting of the States, now recognized the right of the States to call themselves.[46] As a result of the Revolt, the States became sovereign. Under those circumstances, no other body or person could be expected to summon the members, because this would undermine their sovereignty. The new independence of the States naturally implied the independence of its constituent parts, and in 1581 the States officially established the right of the Ridderschap to enrol new members.[47]

Which nobles appeared in the Ridderschap? When the college was purged in 1572, only nobles who actively supported the Revolt were summoned. Most had belonged to the Compromise of the Nobility and sympathized with the new religion. Several years later, however, some nobles who had appeared under Alba returned to the college. After 1585 the Ridderschap consisted of a fixed group of ten to twelve nobles who attended nearly all sessions. Most of the families who had risen to prominence during the Revolt retained their place in the college during the Republic. Only when the seigneurial possessions that established eligibility for membership were inherited by another family, or when a lineage died out, did a family disappear from the Ridderschap. Thus the lords of Assendelft disappeared in 1617, and the lords of Egmond van Kenenburg followed suit in 1618.[48] The Van Zuylen van Nyevelt family did not return to the college after the death of Willem van Zuylen in 1609, perhaps because the family was actually from Utrecht. A small number of noble families

---

[44] See above, p. 170.
[45] Whether this charge, which the pensionary denied, was true is impossible to determine from the printed resolutions of Holland because the names of the nobles attending do not appear after 1564. P. A. Meilink, 'De verdediging van Mr Jacob van den Eijnden voor den Raad van Beroerten', *BMHG* 45 (1924): 184–205, at 192, 202.
[46] Bakhuizen van den Brink, 'Eerste vergadering der Staten', pp. 506–9.
[47] *Res. Holland*, 17 March 1581; *Groot placaet-boeck*, III, p. 87.
[48] Holleman, *Dirk van Assendelft*, pp. 377–82; Dek, *Genealogie van Egmond*, p. 87.

now distributed the spoils. They divided among themselves the most important administrative posts and the substantial incomes attached. In 1590 the attendance-money for the Ridderschap as a whole was fixed at 4,500 gulden.[49] The revenues from the former aristocratic convents of Rijnsburg and Leeuwenhorst, which went to sitting members of the college, were also significant. The nobles thus had an interest in keeping the number of enrolled members small and their incomes high. In practice the right of co-option was limited to ensuring that deceased members were succeeded by their oldest son, and that no new families joined them. During the first stadholderless period (1650–72) the spirit of nepotism reached its peak when the Ridderschap officially specified what had long been established custom. The nobles declared in 1666 that the oldest son of a deceased member would automatically be admitted to the Ridderschap when he had reached the age of twenty-five. Other members could be admitted only by a majority vote; those from outside Holland required a unanimous vote. When a deceased member had no son or grandson, his eldest brother or his brother's male descendant would succeed him.[50] Co-option, nepotism, the distribution of lucrative offices among a small circle: the political culture of the nobles was identical to that of their urban regent counterparts in the seventeenth-century Dutch Republic.

Nevertheless, the Ridderschap was not entirely immune to outside influences. Tension between the two poles of power, the States and the stadholder, was a constant factor. Just like the autonomous urban councils, the Ridderschap sometimes had to bow to the will of the stadholder. In 1618 and 1672 the stadholder was able to make the States do his bidding. By purging the city councils, he secured the appointment of magistrates who supported his party. Through their delegates to meetings of the States, he influenced the policy of the States of Holland. The stadholders also attempted to gain influence over the first member of the States, the Ridderschap.

In the political struggles of the Twelve Years' Truce (1609–21), the majority of the Ridderschap took Oldenbarnevelt's side.[51] After Oldenbarnevelt's arrest, Maurice sought to purge the Ridderschap as he had purged the provincial advocate's supporters from the city councils in September and October of 1618. Naturally he did not have the right to appoint or dismiss the nobles, but he could put pressure on them. At the suggestion of the only supporter of the contra-Remonstrants in the Ridderschap, the recently converted Johan van

---

[49] *Res. Holland*, 20 Jan. 1590. Previously the attendance-money came to 3,000 gulden; it was now increased by 50 per cent, 'mits in alle vergaderingen in competenten getale komende' (provided that a sufficient number come to all meetings). Cf. Fruin, *Staatsinstellingen*, p. 233; also *Res. Holland*, 9–29 Sept. 1632, 8–23 Dec. 1632, and 12–29 Jan. 1633, when it was proposed to increase the attendance-money of the nobles. Apparently nothing came of it.

[50] Aitzema, *Saken*, v, p. 857; cf. Fruin, *Staatsinstellingen*, p. 234. The Ridderschap of Utrecht imposed a similar rule in 1667: ARA, Ridderschap, inv. no. 73.

[51] Den Tex, *Oldenbarnevelt*, III, p. 645.

Duvenvoirde, the college was requested to enrol the lords of Brederode, Van Swieten, Van den Bouchorst (the lord of Wimmenum), Van Raephorst and Van Lijnden van Kronenburg, who were presumably thought more sympathetic to Maurice's policy.[52] Shortly afterwards one of them, Adriaan van Swieten, became the investigative judge at the trial of Oldenbarnevelt. The newly named members belonged to old Holland noble lineages, so that no constitutional objections could be made to their appointment.[53] Van Lijnden actually belonged to the Gueldrian nobility, but as lord of Kronenburg he was the successor to his mother, who came from the Amstel van Mijnden family. As such he could assert a positive right to membership.

The situation was different when Maurice expressed the wish that henceforth his supporters François van Aerssen, lord of Sommelsdijk, and Daniël van Hertaing, lord of Marquette, should also be admitted. Both of them held manorial possessions in Holland, but they did not belong to the Holland nobility. Hertaing belonged to a noble family from Hainault, while Van Aerssen came from Brussels and was not even noble. It should not be surprising that there was great resistance in the Ridderschap. Of the fourteen members present, eight voted against Van Aerssen and seven against Hertaing. Among the opponents, it is noteworthy that, besides Oldenbarnevelt's supporters Mathenesse, Obdam, Schagen and Warmond, there were also three newly named nobles – Van Swieten, Van Raephorst and Van Lijnden van Kronenburg. Apparently they thought the criterion that only nobles of Holland origin should be seated in the college was more important than the power politics of the moment. Maurice pressured the Ridderschap. If they did not want to enrol his clients, they would have to expel his opponents. This threat was enough to persuade Schagen, Swieten and Kronenburg. On the condition that it would not set a precedent, the college decided on 19 January 1619 to admit Sommelsdijk and Marquette.[54]

The admission of both of his supporters was not enough to satisfy Prince Maurice. On 29 October 1619 the Ridderschap discussed a proposal by the Deputy Councils to strike from their membership both sons-in-law of Oldenbarnevelt, Cornelis van der Myle and Reinoud van Brederode, lord of Veenhuizen.[55] This purge did not take place without resistance. The lords of Wyngaerden, Schagen and Mathenesse took up the cause of the threatened nobles, and Mathenesse voted against their exclusion from the Ridderschap. Some were amazed that Mathenesse himself was not excluded: he was known as a champion of the Remonstrants and an active supporter of Oldenbarnevelt.

---

[52] Ibid., and *Res. Holland*, 19 Sept., 10 and 22 Oct. 1618.
[53] On Swieten, see Den Tex, *Oldenbarnevelt*, III, p. 647.
[54] ARA, Ridderschap, inv. no. 73; S. Barendrecht, *François van Aerssen, diplomaat aan het Franse hof (1598–1613)* (Leiden, 1965), p. 1.
[55] Not to be confused with Walraven van Brederode, who was enrolled in the Ridderschap as a supporter of Maurice.

The services he had performed for his country and the fact that he would be outvoted anyway were probably the reasons. In any case the proposal to exclude Van der Myle and Veenhuizen was approved. In a gesture singularly lacking in subtlety, the newly appointed member Marquette was charged with informing both lords of their exclusion.[56]

Later the stadholders again attempted to influence the States by means of the Ridderschap. *Jonker* Louis of Nassau, a bastard son of Maurice and thus a nephew of Frederick Henry, was enrolled in 1636. In the following year Frederick Henry himself was admitted to the Ridderschap with the imposing title of 'First Noble', which previously had been held by the Brederodes. Immediately after he became stadholder in 1672, William III likewise wanted to strengthen his position in the States. He had himself enrolled as First Noble and took steps to enroll three of his partisans in the Ridderschap. Yet the sitting members had agreed in January to admit no new members for four years, except of course the eldest sons of deceased members, in conformity with the regulations of 1666. In 1674, however, the stadholder successfully forced the appointment of his candidates.[57]

Although the Ridderschap's right of co-option was never contested, in practice it was subject to limitations. In times of crisis the stadholder was able to exercise great influence on the composition of the college – as indeed Oldenbarnevelt had done in the appointment of his sons-in-law and protégés Veenhuizen and Van der Myle.[58] Yet over a longer period that influence appears rather limited. Of the five noble members favoured by Maurice in 1618, Swieten attended the Ridderschap only until 1622, and Kronenburg until 1626. Their descendants were not enrolled in the college. Brederode, Bouchorst and Raephorst remained, but, since members of the Brederode family had appeared earlier, Raephorst and Bouchorst were the only newcomers who acquired lasting places. Marquette died in 1625; his son did not succeed him in the Ridderschap.[59] After François van Aerssen's death in 1641, his son Cornelis was immediately enrolled. Yet his support of William II's *coup d'état* in 1650 made his position untenable: the States refused to grant him amnesty. They agreed only after Cornelis had promised not to appear in the Ridderschap again, and the family vanished from the Ridderschap forever.[60] Oldenbarnevelt's sons-in-law Veenhuizen and Van der Myle, who had first

---

[56] *Res. Holland*, 29 Oct. 1619; G. Brandt, *Historie der Reformatie en andere kerkelijke geschiedenissen in en omtrent de Nederlanden*, 4 vols. (Amsterdam, 1671–1704), IV, p. 77; H. A. W. van der Vecht, *Cornelis van der Myle 1579–1642* (Sappemeer, 1907), pp. 114–15; Den Tex, *Oldenbarnevelt*, III, p. 645.

[57] Fruin, *Staatsinstellingen*, p. 234.

[58] On Oldenbarnevelt's influence in the Ridderschap, see Den Tex, *Oldenbarnevelt*, II, p. 250.

[59] Van der Aa, *Biographisch woordenboek*, s.v. Hartaing.

[60] *NNBW*, III, pp. 8–12. Cornelis van Aerssen's defence (15 July 1651) is found in Aitzema, *Saken*, III, p. 588.

been struck from the list and then banished, returned to the college in 1632 with only the representative of Leiden showing any sign of displeasure. In general, the upheavals of 1618 and 1619 were regarded as bygones. Outsiders, even those as powerful as Maurice in 1618, had limited power to influence the composition of the college.

AN ARISTOCRATIC REPUBLIC

Much has been written about the 'aristocratization' of regents in the Republic, also known as 'the betrayal of the bourgeoisie'.[61] This phenomenon saw the urban regents giving up their activities in trade and industry in order to adopt an aristocratic style of life. They tried to get knighthoods and patents of nobility from foreign monarchs, drew up fanciful family trees to show their noble origins, acquired manors or noble properties, and adorned themselves with noble names, titles and coats of arms. Most writers situate this phenomenon in the second half of the seventeenth century,[62] but there were already signs of it in the sixteenth century. Around 1570 Hadrianus Iunius noted that 'many foreigners, artisans, ropemakers, ribbon-makers and merchants' children are creeping into that order' (i.e. the nobility of Holland).[63] That was certainly an exaggeration, but in 1566 Johan van Oldenbarnevelt registered himself as a student at Louvain as 'Johannes Reynerii ab Oldenbarnevelt, *nobilis*'. Apparently the registrar did not believe him, because he added the words *sub specie nobilis*, 'passing himself off as a nobleman'.[64] Through marriage and purchase, Oldenbarnevelt did acquire various manorial possessions, calling himself 'lord of De Tempel' (after one of his manors). He married off his daughters to noblemen and apparently preferred the company of nobles to that of patricians.[65]

Members of the Egmond van de Nyenburg family also pretended on insufficient grounds to belong to the nobility. In the first half of the sixteenth century they were known only by their patronymic, a clear sign of plebeian origins. Yet they were governors of the castle of Nyenburg for the count of Egmond;

---

[61] See esp. D. J. Roorda, 'The ruling classes in Holland in the seventeenth century', in J. S. Bromley and E. H. Kossman (eds.), *Britain and the Netherlands* (Groningen, 1964), II, pp. 119–31; and J. A. Faber, 'De oligarchisering van Friesland in de tweede helft van de zeventiende eeuw', *AAGB* 15 (1970): 39–64.

[62] T. S. Jansma, 'De economische en sociale ontwikkeling van het Noorden', *AGN*, VI, pp. 89–146, at 138. Roorda, 'Ruling classes', pp. 229–38, gives the phases of the process of aristocratization, which had already begun before 1650. Roorda, *Partij en factie*, p. 39. Faber, 'Oligarchisering', pp. 43–61.

[63] Cited from the Dutch translation of Iunius' *Batavia: Een seer cort doch clare beschrijvinge vande voornaemste ghemuerde ende ongemuerde steden ende vlecken van Holland ende West-Vriesland* (Delft, 1609), p. 32.

[64] Den Tex, *Oldenbarnevelt*, I, pp. 50–1.

[65] Ibid., pp. 88–103.

moreover they held possessions from the Egmond Chamber of Fiefs. After 1550 they began to use the name Egmond van de Nyenburg and declared they were descended from a bastard branch of the noble family. In 1580 Dirk van Egmond van de Nyenburg, councillor in the Court and later president of the High Council of Holland and Zeeland, bore the unbroken arms of the counts of Egmond.[66]

In the seventeenth century this phenomenon became more prevalent. A pamphleteer wrote scornfully in 1608 about 'the great pantaloons that had to suffer only a few years ago, but now are great lords, build houses like churches, and hold state as if they were of the best nobility, yea, even far exceed them in splendour'.[67] In Amsterdam Dirk de Vlamingh, after his purchase of the seigneurie of Oudshoorn, became Dirk de Vlamingh van Oudshoorn; his cousin and business partner Willem Nooms bought Aarlanderveen.[68] Long before the middle of the century, Johan Huydecoper had become lord of Maarsseveen, Jacob de Graeff lord of Zuid-Polsbroek, and Gerard Schaep lord of Kortenhoef.[69] It was perhaps unjustly said that Frans Banningh Cocq's father had been a beggar, but in any case he had begun his career as an apothecary's assistant. Frans, the central figure in Rembrandt's *Nightwatch*, became knight, lord of Purmerland and Ilpendam, president of the polder board and lieutenant-forester of the recently drained Purmer and Wormer polders.[70] The Zeeland patrician family Manmaker (possibly from *mandmaker* = basketmaker) provides a colourful example of aristocratization. In 1601 Jacob Manmaker had himself invested with the seigneurie of Hofwegen. In 1637 his nephew *lord* Adriaan *van* Manmaker was likewise invested, and in 1643 it was the turn of Adriaan's son *jonkheer* Charles van Manmaker. Their lifestyle had little to do with the non-noble making of baskets, but much with the making of men.[71]

Adriaan Pauw (1585–1653) was the grandson of an Amsterdam grain merchant who had entered the city council after the *Alteratie* of 1578. He studied in Leiden, began as a merchant in Amsterdam, became pensionary of that city, councillor and master of accounts in the Chamber of Accounts, pensionary of Holland, director of the East India Company, curator of the University of Leiden and a member of several diplomatic missions. In 1613 he received a knighthood from James I, and in 1624 Louis XIII made him a knight in the order of St Michael. He received from the French king the right to add the

[66] Belonje, 'Egmond van de Nyenburg', p. 55.
[67] *Schuyt-praetgens*, fo. A 1 v.
[68] Elias, *Vroedschap*, I, pp. 233, 279, 431; see above, p. 200.
[69] J. C. van Dillen, *Van rijkdom en regenten. Handboek tot de economische en sociale geschiedenis van Nederland tijdens de Republiek* (The Hague, 1970), p. 288.
[70] Elias, *Vroedschap*, I, p. 406.
[71] Repertoria op de leenregisters, ARA Leenkamer, inv. no. 230, fo. 353 v. Cf. Van der Aa, *Biographisch woordenboek*, s.v. Adriaan van Manmaker.

French lily to his arms, and from the English king the English rose – and he did so. In 1620 he was invested with the castle and seigneurie of Heemstede, which he had bought for 36,000 gulden; henceforth he styled himself 'lord of Heemstede'. Later he bought additional manors. In 1630 his son Nicolaas married Anna van Lockhorst, who was related to a noble family that had previously held Heemstede. But Pauw used the castle of Heemstede only as a country house and continued to live in the city.[72]

Not only the regents of Holland, but also persons of humble origins found a noble name attractive. Thus in 1609 a certain Pieter Harmansz. van Percijn (a Holland noble name) was named magistrate (*schepen*) in the city of Alkmaar: 'he wants to be known by this name, because five years ago he called and wrote himself Clock and always signed thus, being not in the least of that [noble] origin. His father was a miller from Het Gooi and ran a mill here called de Rootoren, by the watergate . . . and afterwards became a beer-merchant. He did not have a good name.'[73] The Antwerp artist Joost van Egmond (1601–74), a pupil of Rubens and court-painter to Louis XIII and Louis XIV, was the son of a Leiden carpenter. Perhaps he could ascribe his origin to the village of Egmond, but certainly not to the family of counts. Nevertheless he painted 'a great painting showing the Genealogy of the House of the Counts of Egmond', on which he had reserved a place for himself as well as his legitimate and bastard children. Yet he failed in an attempt to obtain a declaration from the Antwerp city government that he was 'Justus verus d'egmont, dict de Meresteyn'.[74]

Such pretensions were a thorn in the side of the genuine old nobility. In a pamphlet written at the time of the negotiations for the Peace of Westphalia, an Utrecht nobleman mocked the fact that Adriaan Pauw was not noble and had adorned himself with a foreign title of knighthood. Pauw was an 'homme de néant' (man of nothing), his father a 'cruel and enterprising man'; he 'raised himself up from the base people only to serve as judge, jury and executioner of Oldenbarnevelt'. The author censured 'the money-grubbing scoundrels, my lords Bicker and Pauw', who had brought along a knighthood from hated France 'in order to be called "Your Honour"'. The argument was of course purely political, but its author apparently expected that such abuse would add weight to his views.[75] Martinus Schoockius as well as Simon van Leeuwen complained about newly rich burghers who acted like nobles.[76] Van Leeuwen confirmed that 'among the old nobles this has always been unbearable and is

---

[72] J. C. Tjessinga, *Schets van het leven van Adriaan Pauw* (Heemstede, 1948), pp. 7–18; Repertoria op de leenregisters, ARA, Leenkamer, inv. no. 246, fo. 151.

[73] W. A. Fasel, *Alkmaar en zijne geschiedenissen. Kroniek van 1600–1813* (Alkmaar, n.d.), pp. 26–7.

[74] M. G. Wildeman, 'Het voorgeslacht van Joost van Egmondt', *Wap* 16/17 (1913): 316–18.

[75] Cited by Tjessinga, *Adriaan Pauw*, p. 37.

[76] Schoockius, *Belgium*, pp. 128–30, 132; Van Leeuwen, *Redeningh*, p. 33.

taken badly'.[77] Arend van Buchell wrote contemptuously about the *Sturmius* (Storm?) family, who garnered more derision than honour by vaunting their fancied nobility at the house of the lord of Brederode.[78] According to the same source, Rutger van den Boetzelaer, lord of Asperen, gave a box on the ears to Wouter van Oudshoorn, lord of Craijenstein, 'a man of absolutely no nobility, though rich', who had prided himself on buying the manor of Wulven from an impoverished relation of Van den Boetzelaer.[79]

The snobbery of these new men did not pose a serious threat to the position of the nobility. But the situation did frighten its lower ranks, those who claimed noble descent, but had ceased to live nobly and gradually had been assimilated into the urban patriciate. They were exposed to pressure from both sides: on the one hand, the aristocratic aspirations of the regents threatening to over-shadow them, and on the other hand the increasing exclusiveness of the Ridderschap families. Their response was a combination of aristocratization and revalorization of noble identity, which could be called a 're-aristocratization' of the lower nobility.

Alckemade was an old Holland noble lineage.[80] In the early sixteenth century members of the family worked in administrative offices in The Hague and in the city administrations of Haarlem and Leiden.[81] A branch of the Alckemades settled in Amsterdam: through office-holding and marriage they were assimilated to the Amsterdam patriciate. Floris Maartensz van Alckemade (d. 1572) was magistrate (1544), councillor (1546) and burgemeester (1568) of Amsterdam.[82] After the *Alteratie*, however, the family remained Catholic and took no part in city administration. In 1614 Floris' grandson Sybrand van Alckemade took advantage of the lifting of the seizure of properties belonging to persons living in enemy territory to buy the old ancestral homestead, Oud-Alckemade. The castle had fallen into ruin, in part because of the siege of Leiden, and was heavily burdened with debt. In 1622 Sybrand began the reconstruction of the house, where he and his descendants henceforth lived as true nobles.[83] It is indicative of the value placed on aristocratic origins that by

---

[77] Van Leeuwen, *Redeningh*, p. 16.
[78] Van Buchell, *Diarium*, p. 254.
[79] Ibid., pp. 258–9; Destombe, *Van den Boetzelaer*, pp. 186–8.
[80] In 1305 Hendrik van Alckemade was invested with Oud-Alckemade. Fockema Andreae, Renaud and Pellinck, *Kastelen*, p. 67.
[81] Jan van Alckemade was bailiff of Kennemerland (1513–17) and sheriff of Haarlem (1524), ARA, Grafelijkheidsrekenkamer, registers, inv. no. 492, fos. 121 v., 189. Floris van Alckemade was on the Leiden Council in 1481, as was Hendrik van Alckemade in 1510. Willem van Alckemade was likewise a Leiden councillor, burgemeester (1504), and sheriff (1509–15), but later attended the Ridderschap regularly as lord van den Coulster. He became polder-councillor of Rijnland, councillor in the Court of Fiefs in 1520 and steward of the aristocratic convent of Rijnsburg: Orlers, *Leyden*, pp. 592, 607, 617; 'Actestukken', p. 332.
[82] Allard, 'De Alkemaden'.
[83] Van Lommel, 'Genealogie der Alckemades', pp. 312–13; 'Een jachtruzie', pp. 124–31. Cf. Fockema Andreae, Renaud and Pellinck, *Kastelen*, illustrations 6, 7, 8.

1604 Sybrand had an official act drawn up to show that not only had the Alckemades been fief-holders in the fourteenth century, but that they had also been relations of the lords of Egmond.[84]

Another example is provided by the Alkmaar regent family of Teylingen, which probably descended from the noble lineage of that name. Augustein van Teylingen (b. ca. 1475) and his son used the broken arms of Teylingen as their seal; one generation later the bar was removed, and after 1625 the descendants generally used the title *jonker*.[85]

Just as Sybrand van Alckemade bought Oud-Alckemade, so Pieter van der Does, a bailiff and dike-reeve of Rijnland, bought the Huis Ter Does at Leiderdorp. The house had not belonged to the family for a long time, and for the previous fifty years had been in the hands of Amsterdam merchants.[86] By living in an old castle or on a homestead bearing the family name, families could raise their status. But sometimes members of *déclassé* noble families bought a manor that had never been held by their family. This was primarily a social and political investment, because the possession of a manor could open the road to the Ridderschap, with all the concomitant status, prestige, power and income.

Around the beginning of the sixteenth century, the Van den Bouchorst family held offices in the magistracy of Leiden. Their ancestral castle of Hoge Boekhorst at Noordwijkerhout had been inherited through the female line by the Van Woerden van Vliet family.[87] Adriaan van den Bouchorst was burgemeester in 1478 and was recorded as a member of the Council in 1481; Gijsbert was on the Council in 1510, Dirk between 1519 and 1574.[88] Cornelis was a member of the rebel Court of Holland between 1572 and 1574.[89] In 1612 Nicolaas van den Bouchorst made use of the suspension of property seizures during the Truce to buy the manor of Wimmenum from the prince of Ligne.[90] In 1618, as a supporter of Maurice, he took a seat in the Ridderschap, and in 1624 he became bailiff and dike-reeve of Rijnland. In 1636, his son Amelis followed him into office and, on Nicholaas's death in 1640, into the Ridderschap.[91] Thus the lords of Bouchorst transformed themselves from urban nobles of Leiden, barely distinguishable from the patriciate, into landed nobility, members of the Ridderschap, and holders of the highest offices of the Republic.

---

[84] Declaration regarding investitures of land in the Alckemade family etc. (1604), ARA, HA Oud-Alkemade, inv. no. 142.

[85] Wüstenhoff, 'Geslachten van Teijlingen', p. 448. On the devaluation of the title *jonkheer*, see above, p. 37.

[86] P. N. van Doorninck, *Inventaris van eene verzameling charters betrekking hebbende op de geslachten van der Does, Duivenvoorde en Mathenesse* (Haarlem, 1895), pp. 21–6; Fockema Andreae, Renaud and Pellinck, *Kastelen*, illustrations 25–9.

[87] Fockema Andreae, Renaud and Pellinck, *Kastelen*, p. 70.

[88] Orlers, *Leyden*, pp. 591–7.

[89] *Memorialen Rosa*, I, p. il.

[90] Repertoria op de leenregisters, ARA, Leenkamer, inv. no. 247, fo. 430.

[91] W. A. Beelaerts van Blokland, 'Groot-Haesebroek', *LJ* 27 (1934): 1–21, at 6–7.

For these urbanized lower nobles the path to nobility was shorter than for the bourgeois regents, who had 'taken their family trees out of the air or wrought them from Amadis of Gaul', as one snob put it.[92] They dusted off their old coats of arms and associated themselves with an older tradition. They had no need for foreign titles. Not a single Holland nobleman appears on the list of Netherlanders knighted by foreign monarchs in the seventeenth century.[93] In a century that valued noble titles so highly, their prestige rose on its own. To the extent that the gradual extinction of noble lineages reduced the number of nobles, their social prestige increased.[94] The Holland nobles carefully guarded their exclusivity by defending their privileges, by emphasizing their social distance from other groups, and most of all by endogamy.

It was precisely this exclusivity that Sir William Temple regarded as the most striking characteristic of the Holland nobility:

These are in their Customs, and manner, and way of living, a good deal different from the rest of the people; and having been bred much abroad, rather affect the Garb of their Neighbour-Courts, than the popular air of their own Countrey. They value themselves more upon their Nobility, than men do in other Countreys, where 'tis more common; and would think themselves utterly dishonoured by the marriage of one that were not of their rank, though it were to make up the broken Fortune of a Noble Family, by the Wealth of a Plebean. They strive to imitate the French in their Meen, their Clothes, their way of Talk, of Eating, of Gallantry, or Debauchery; And are, in my mind, something worse than they would be, by affecting to be better than they need; making sometimes but ill Copies, whereas they might be good Originals, by refining or Improving the Customs and Virtues proper to their own Countrey and Climate. They are otherwise an Honest, Well-nature'd, Friendly, and Gentlemanly sort of men, and acquit themselves generally with Honour and Merit, where their Countrey employs them.[95]

CONCLUSION

In the time of the Republic the Holland nobility was confronted with the increasing significance, power, wealth, and pretensions of the cities, the urban burghers and other non-nobles. As lords of the manor they lost ground to persons of bourgeois origin. They had to share their place in the States with eighteen instead of six voting cities. In social life newcomers increasingly tried to emulate their lifestyle. How did the nobility respond to the 'rise of the bourgeoisie'?

First, the Holland nobility never had a monopoly on the exercise of political power. At the beginning of the sixteenth century the nobles had to share their

---

[92] Cited in Tjessinga, *Adriaan Pauw*, p. 13.
[93] *Nav* 14 (1864): 259.
[94] Cf. Van Dillen, *Rijkdom en regenten*, p. 285; Schöffer, 'De Republiek', pp. 179–80.
[95] Temple, *Observations*, pp. 85–6.

prominent position with non-noble persons in practically all areas. During the reign of Charles V, a few non-noble persons and cities already held manors. The nobles did not have a monopoly of important administrative offices either: on the contrary, their share actually declined after 1530. The nobles never had a majority or even parity with the cities in the States. Genteel patrician families with semi-noble appearances who were attracted to the nobility also existed before the Revolt. In this regard nothing really new happened after 1585. Indeed, it is difficult to find a period in European history when the bourgeoisie was *not* rising. Yet these processes increased in speed, extent and significance during the early years of the Republic, and the nobility had to respond.

It is remarkable how well the Holland nobility adjusted to the new circumstances. Nobles of Holland and their relatives from other provinces still held a majority of the seigneuries. Their authority within their jurisdictions increased. In the meetings of the States, the nobles had an influential position as representatives of the countryside: their views carried more weight than the simple vote would suggest. In administrative colleges of the province and the generality they often exercised more influence than other members.

The Dutch Republic was an aristocratic regent-republic. Power lay with the regents, persons who came from a small number of patrician families and divided the most important offices among themselves. The regents were qualified to rule by their wealth, origins and connections. The regents of Holland were primarily urban; by their origins, social circles and marital connections they were clearly distinguished from the nobility. Yet the Holland nobility did not find itself on the periphery of power. They reacted to the changed circumstances by transforming themselves into rural counterparts of the urban regents. Like the urban councillors, they distributed the lucrative offices among themselves. They too formed a group that had the leisure to rule, qualified by origin, tradition, education, wealth and connections. The agreement made by the Ridderschap in 1666, which practically blocked newcomers from access to their college, echoes the tendencies to exclusivity found in urban councils about the same time. Like the urban councils, the Ridderschap was divided by factional strife.[96] Their ambivalent relationship with the stadholder, by which the latter sometimes gained his way but could not maintain his influence over a longer period, mirrors the difficult relationship between the urban regents and the House of Orange.

Together with the urban regents, the Holland nobility constituted the administrative elite of the Republic.[97] In meetings of the States, the administra-

---

[96] Aalbers, 'Factieuze tegenstellingen', pp. 417–45.

[97] Here I limit my considerations to the period up to ca. 1650, but the statement also applies to the early eighteenth century, when the number of noble families was sharply reduced. The image of a single power elite in the Republic, formulated hypothetically, appears also in Schilling, 'Aufstand der Niederlande', p. 231.

tive colleges, the admiralties, the board of curators of Leiden University and the polder boards we find both nobles and urban regents, more often working together than in opposition. In social life, however, the nobles adhered to a strict apartheid. If a social group consists of those persons who intermarry,[98] then the nobility and the regent-aristocracy formed two distinct groups. The nobles did not allow themselves to be pushed aside by the regents. With remarkable success the nobles adapted to the new power relationships in the Dutch Republic.

[98] Mousnier, 'Problèmes de méthode', p. 20.

9

Conclusion: knights and regents

This book began with a contrast between the splendid funeral procession of Jan van Wassenaer in 1524 and the laconic remark of Fynes Moryson at the end of the sixteenth century, that the nobility of Holland had been rooted out and that the remaining nobles lived as burghers and enjoyed no prestige whatsoever. The contrast accords with the images Johan Huizinga evoked in his two master-works, *The Waning of the Middle Ages* and *Dutch Civilisation in the Seventeenth Century*. How did the nobility of Holland contribute to and participate in the transition from the middle ages to the modern era?

Both poles of this rough opposition need shading. Around 1500 Holland was not a society dominated by the nobility, let alone a 'feudal' society. Everything that would give the seventeenth century its modern appearance was already present in embryonic form. Half of the population lived in the cities, and the cities dominated the States. The nobility constituted less than one-half per cent of the population, a minute proportion in absolute terms as well as relative to those in other countries. Nevertheless, the other half of the population lived in the countryside and was subject to the lordship and jurisdiction of that handful of noble families. Nearly all commanders of fortified places, and half or more of the members of important administrative bodies in The Hague were nobles. One out of every two bailiffs in charge of governing the countryside was noble, and half of the larger cities had noble sheriffs. Nor were the cities themselves as bourgeois as one might suppose. Descendants of noble lineages sat in the councils of Dordrecht, Haarlem, Delft and Leiden. The nobles as a group owned but a small share of the land, owing to their small number; yet many individual nobles were large landowners. In exchange for the duty of noble fief-holders to serve the count as heavily armed knights in the feudal ban, they received fiscal exemptions. The other privileges of the nobility were limited, but the bearers of noble blazons enjoyed universal respect. To summarize: at the beginning of the sixteenth century, the nobility formed a small part of the total population, but an influential and significant part of the political elite.

As for the seventeenth century, was it really so 'bourgeois' as Huizinga maintained? True, more people lived in cities, cities had extended their influence over the countryside as well as in the States, and urban regents dominated provincial administration. The nobility's share of the population had become even smaller. As holders of the manors the nobles had to accept the presence of non-noble newcomers. In city governments, few nobles were to be found. But the Holland nobility had not disappeared. They still held about 60 per cent of the seigneuries. Their voice still carried special weight in the States. In higher administrative colleges of the generality and the province, delegates of the Ridderschap played a part far out of proportion to their numbers. In its emulation of the old knightly nobility, the bourgeoisie of the Republic did not succeed in assimilating to the nobility. The nobility had lost most of its privileges, but these had never been very important. Its social prestige had not declined. In short: the nobility in the seventeenth century still constituted a prominent part of the provincial elite.

Yet this conclusion does not imply that nothing had changed between 1500 and 1650. Economic change, the rise of the state, the Reformation and the Revolt presented challenges to the nobles. Their response to these challenges testifies to their great vitality. There was no 'crisis' of the Holland nobility. The history of the nobility in the age of the Dutch Revolt is a success story. Its success was based on three assets: wealth; the ability to adapt to changing political circumstances; and the will to survive as a separate social group.

Defective sources do not allow us to make an exact balance sheet of noble revenues and expenditures. But there are enough indications to confirm H. A. Enno van Gelder's judgment that the Holland nobles were prosperous on the eve of the Revolt, and to extend his conclusion to the entire period studied. Many nobles expanded their holdings of land and manors. Their prosperity was founded on the ownership of farms, which they leased out at steadily rising rents. Seigneurial rights constituted a much smaller portion of their capital. Some rights also brought in increasing revenues, such as tithes and fishing rights. Other rights yielded fixed sums that lost their significance over time owing to inflation. Revenues of the latter type formed only a small part of the total incomes of the nobles, and did not undermine their prosperity. Nevertheless the close connection of noble revenues and agricultural conjuncture made them vulnerable. After the middle of the seventeenth century, the increasing economic problems of the nobility can probably be related to the falling trend of agricultural prices.

Not all nobles shared in the fruits of rural prosperity. Some went bankrupt or were forced to give up part of their holdings. But it is a sign of the economic resilience of the nobility as a whole that many properties that came on the market were bought by other nobles. Their substantial revenues were often counterbalanced by high expenses, for maintaining their social position required great sums of money. Presumably some nobles were brought to bankruptcy by conspicuous consumption, and not by some structural economic cause such as the tendency of fixed incomes to lag rising prices. Moreover, these noble expenditures should not be seen simply as extravagance, but more as an investment, the 'cost of acquisition' or 'intangible goodwill' in modern corporate balance sheets. One was only a true noble if one lived as a noble – and that was expensive.

It is unclear to what extent office-holding contributed to noble incomes. But there is no reason to doubt a contemporary statement that those who wished could live well from their offices. This was no less true for the noble regents during the Republic.

The position of the nobility was also affected by political change. The most significant transformation had already occurred between 1530 and 1550, well before the Revolt. While the nobles retained their dominant position as manorial lords, their position as office-holders declined. Nobles continued to hold military offices and certain functions that had an aristocratic appeal, but they withdrew from the more demanding posts, which were changing from honorary to professional positions. Fewer nobles presented themselves for the offices of Court councillor, bailiff, sheriff and urban magistrate.

Much is unclear about these developments. Yet it is plausible that the nobles withdrew voluntarily. The concentration of authority in Brussels and the increasing bureaucratization made office-holding less attractive. Simultaneously, their rising revenues from land allowed them to live as leisured gentlemen on their manors.

During the early sixteenth century, high-office-holders were also the most prominent members of the Ridderschap. Since the nobles held fewer offices, the personal link between administration and justice disappeared. This development aided in the evolution of the provincial States into a more truly representative institution after 1550 – one that was eventually able to shoulder responsibility for the Revolt.

Finally, another development of the early sixteenth century was the ending of assimilation of high-office-holders into the nobility. As nobles withdrew from political life, they closed themselves off socially and did not allow new blood in their ranks. The result of these developments was the separation of nobility and political elite. At the beginning of the century, the nobility and the administrative elite formed two largely overlapping groups. Many nobles were provincial office-holders; simultaneously many attended the States of Holland, albeit infrequently. After mid-century the nobles stood on the periphery of administration, except for their role as seigneurial lords. On the eve of the Revolt, the nobles were still an elite in terms of wealth and status, but no longer a power elite.

To what extent did the loss of political power motivate the nobles to unite in the Compromise of the Nobility? H. A. Enno van Gelder long ago discredited the economic explanation of the Revolt of the nobility. Instead, he sought the cause of their discontent primarily in the administrative reforms of Charles V and Philip II. The freedom and independence of noble seigneurs were restricted in many ways, most of all by the increasing importance of the Court of Holland. The Court consisted of professional jurists, arrogated to itself all kinds of powers from lesser judicial bodies, made decisions with reference to Roman and canon law, and took insufficient account of noble interests in its appointments to bailiff's courts.[1] 'And behind this Court stood the central government, ruled by a female regent of foreign origin, in the name of a foreign sovereign, supported by a council of learned lawyers, only some of whom were noble, and even these were from other provinces.'[2] Van Gelder concluded that 'against all this, only joining together could protect them: dozens of nobles signed at the first call for the Compromise, dozens more joined ranks behind the Prince of Orange when he raised the standard of revolution against this hated authority'.[3] According to Van Gelder, for the nobles the Revolt was a reaction against the loss of administrative independence and privileges. This position, however, finds little support in the sources. Neither the Compromise and Petition, nor other documents indicate that the nobles wanted to restore their threatened position as manorial lords, nor that they sought readmission to administrative offices.

What was the impact of the Revolt on the fortunes of the nobility? The Compromise of the Nobility was very popular in Holland. Brederode, its leader, was one of the most influential nobles in Holland: he was able to mobilize many lesser nobles for his cause. Some members of the Compromise were dedicated to religious reform, while others merely opposed the religious policy of the king. The iconoclast riots in the summer of 1566 caused the Union to split into a radical wing under Brederode that wanted to fight on for the new religion, and a moderate wing that was willing to accept the restoration of the government's authority. After the arrival of the duke of Alba, the radicals were forced into exile. In 1572, however, the balance shifted to the other side, when the 'Beggars' returned and those who had carried out royal policies had to flee. This led to the appointment of many nobles to vacant administrative posts. Most had been members of the Compromise, and many had joined the reformed church, in exile if not earlier. The years of division were ended by the Pacification of Ghent in 1576: those who had appeared in the Ridderschap in Alba's time could then return. After 1579, when the Revolt changed into a lengthy war, most Holland nobles continued to live in the province – and thus voted with their feet for the rebels. This had little to do with their political or religious convictions – indeed, most of them probably stayed Catholic – but only with the fact that their possessions were situated in Holland. Since the greatest part of their wealth consisted of landed property, they could live nobly only in Holland. A few high nobles such as Ligne, Aremberg and Egmond, whose properties

[1] Van Gelder, 'Hollandse adel', pp. 138–40 and 134.
[2] Ibid., p. 140.
[3] Ibid., p. 141.

15   G. van Honthorst, 'Jacob van Wassenaer-Obdam' (Private collection). Jacob van Wassenaer (1610–65), lord of Wassenaer, Obdam, etc., lieutenant-admiral of Holland.

were primarily located in Walloon areas of the south, chose the king's side, probably for the same reasons.

Consequently, continuity prevailed over the long term. This is not to suggest that the Revolt changed nothing. The Revolt of the Netherlands was deeply conservative in character. Sixteenth-century state-building was based on a strengthening of monarchical authority, centralization of justice, administration, legislation and patronage; the undermining of traditional corporate privileges; and the employment of a professional bureaucracy dependent on the monarch alone. In the United Netherlands these developments were averted by the Revolt. Conservatism has undoubtedly been a factor in history, but it has never achieved its goal, the maintenance of the status quo. Nor did it accomplish this in the Dutch Republic. The tendency toward centralization was destroyed in the rebellious provinces, and an extreme particularism gained the upper hand. Sovereignty lay not in the States-General of the United Provinces but with the provincial States; and in the last analysis, with its constituent members, the voting cities, whose delegates could not make decisions without an express mandate. Therefore, the main beneficiaries of the Revolt were the urban regents, who in part supported the Revolt and in part tried to curb it where it became too radical.

The conservative, particularistic character of the Revolt was the reason for the success of the Holland nobility in adapting to the new circumstances in the Republic. In the first place, it now shared in the sovereignty that had fallen to the States. The nobles formed a minority, but as first member of the States and the only representative of the countryside, they were certainly not a negligible one. Second, nobles continued to hold the greatest share of the manors. No one thought of abolishing this archaic form of government. On the contrary, the conservative revolution strengthened the position of manorial lords, just as it had strengthened urban governments. Finally, in the administrative colleges of the province and the generality the nobles played a disproportionately large role. The personal link between the Ridderschap and the administrative colleges, which had been lost during the reign of Charles V, returned during the Republic. If the cities and urban governments profited from the Revolt, the nobles did so as well.

Naturally not all Holland nobles took part in provincial administration. But in nearly all regent-colleges a member of the nobility was present. They were well-suited for their role as rural regents. Regents are usually defined as those qualified to rule by their wealth and social origin. The nobles were certainly richly endowed, and, if birth was a criterion, they could easily overshadow the most genteel urban regents. The Republic's form of government was aristocratic, a government of 'the best' citizens, and the Holland nobles must certainly be reckoned among that group. The political elite consisted of delegates from both the patriciate and the nobility. Thanks to the collapse of the monarchy, both groups were able to develop to the fullest.

It is all the more remarkable that the political integration of the nobility and patriciate was not coupled with social rapprochement between the two groups. By their marital choices, their 'customs, manners and way of living', they remained clearly distinct. We might summarize the history of the Holland

16   Cornelis Anthonisz., 'Genealogical series of the lords of Brederode', ca. 1550–1 (detail, Rijksprentenkabinet, Amsterdam). The series begins with Zuphriidus, a younger son of the count of Holland. Thus the Brederodes also bore the lion rampant of Holland on their coat of arms, but above it was a bar indicating that they were a cadet branch.

nobility as economic prosperity, political integration and social apartheid. But the story would not be complete without noting a disadvantageous consequence of the Dutch Revolt. Through the collapse of the monarchy, the means of raising new persons to the nobility disappeared. Consequently, the Holland nobility was doomed to extinction. As the number of nobles declined, they became ever more aristocratic, and their social status was ever more exclusive. But they had to pay a high price for it.

16 *(cont.)*

16 (cont.)

16 (*cont.*)

Bibliography

Note: The alphabetical order here used follows Dutch practice, 'ij', for example, being treated as 'y'.

UNPUBLISHED SOURCES

Algemeen Rijksarchief, The Hague
Huis Duivenvoorde, inv. no. 36.
Financie van Holland, inv. no. 440.
Grafelijksheidsrekenkamer, registers, inv. nos. 492–6, 498; rekeningen, inv. nos. 681 *ter.* 4454, 4455, 4862–6.
Graven van Holland, inv. no. 885.
Heerlijkheid Hardinxveld, inv. no. 1.
Heerlijkheid 's-Heeraartsberg, Bergambacht en Ammerstol, inv. nos. 258, 259, 260, 262, 262-a, 264.
Familie Heereman van Zuijtwijck, provisional inv. no. 34.
Hof van Holland, inv. nos. 29, 5653, 5654.
Landsadvocaat Johan van Oldenbarnevelt, prov. inv. no. 1015.
Leen- en registerkamer van Holland, inv. nos. 226–53.
Heerlijkheid Lisse, inv. nos. 4, 6, 17.
Heerlijkheid Mijnsheerenland van Moerkerken, inv. no. 40.
Nassause Domeinraad na 1581, inv. nos. 8171–211.
Huis Oud-Alkemade, inv. no. 142.
Ridderschap en Edelen van Holland en West-Friesland, prov. inv. nos. 63, 73.
Staten van Holland, before 1572, inv. no. 2388.
Staten van Holland 1572–1795, inv. no. 1788.
Familie Wassenaer van Rozande, inv. no. XVI-z.
Collectie handschriften VII, Coll. W. G. van Oyen, inv. no. 11.

Algemeen Rijksarchief, Brussels
Audiëntie, inv. nos. 477/5, 1177/5, 1184, 1472/1, 1475/5, 1704/1.

Rijksarchief Noord-Holland
Heerlijkheid Oosthuizen, inv. nos. 32, 38, 39, 43, 47.

Gemeentearchief Amsterdam
Archief Burgemeesters, Lands- en gewestelijk bestuur, inv. no. 136 R 10–7.
Archief Burgemeesters, stadsrekeningen van de jaren 1531, 1560, 1590, 1619.

Bibliography

Familiearchief Bicker, inv. nos. 674, 718.
Familiearchief De Graeff, inv. no. 433.
Handschriften, inv. no. 59.

Gemeentearchief Leiden
Huisarchief van de heren van Warmond, inv. nos. 66, 67, 71, 76.
Secretarie-archief 1575–1851, inv. no. 7542.

Archief van het hoogheemraadschap Rijnland
Morgenboek van Aalsmeer, Aarlanderveen, Alkemade, Alphen, Esselikerwoude, Hille-
gom, Katwijk en Valkenburg, Koudekerk, Lisse, Noordwijk en Noordwijkerhout,
Warmond.

Archief van het hoogheemraadschap van de Alblasserwaard
Inv. no. 649.

Archief van de Hoge Raad van Adel, The Hague
Collectie Snouckaert.

Koninklijke Bibliotheek, The Hague
Naam en wapenen der Hoog Edele Heeren welke in de Ridderschap van de Provincie
van Holland en West Vriesland zijn beschreven geweest (MS 135 A 27).

Centraal Bureau voor de Genealogie, The Hague
D. G. van Epen. 'De Ridderschap van Holland en West-Friesland. Namen, stamdelen
en kinderen der beschreven edelen' (MS).

PRINTED SOURCES AND WORKS

Aa, A. J. van der, K. J. K. van Harderwijk and G. D. J. Schotel, *Biographisch woordenboek
der Nederlanden*, 21 vols., Haarlem, 1852–78.
Aalbers, J., 'Factieuze tegenstellingen binnen het college van de ridderschap van Hol-
land na de Vrede van Utrecht', *BMGN* 93 (1978): 412–45.
'Actestukken betreffende de verkiezing van vrouwe Elburch van Langerak tot abdis van
Rijnsburg in 1553 en eene Informatie, tegelijkertijd gehouden', *BGBH* 23 (1898):
321–71.
Aitzema, Lieuwe van, *Saken van Staet en oorlogh in, ende omtrent de Vereenigde Nederlanden
beginnende met het jaar 1621*. 6 vols., 2nd edn, The Hague, 1669–72.
Allard, H. J., 'Nadere aantekeningen over de Alkemaden', *BGBH* 1 (1873): 374–80.
Anonymus Belga, *De adel*, Alkmaar, 1786; Kn 21299; by P. de Wacker van Zon.
Archives ou correspondance inédite de la Maison d'Orange-Nassau, ed. G. Groen van Prin-
sterer, 1st series, 8 vols. and supp., Leiden, 1835–47; 2nd series, 5 vols., Utrecht,
1857–61.
Armstrong, C. A. J., 'Had the Burgundian government a policy for the nobility?', in
Britain and the Netherlands, II, ed. J. S. Bromley and E. H. Kossmann, Groningen,
1964, pp. 9–32.
Avaux, Jean Antoine d', *Négociations en Hollande depuis 1679 jusqu'en 1684*, ed. E. Mallet,
6 vols., Paris, 1752–3.
Baars, C., *De geschiedenis van de landbouw in de Beijerlanden*, Wageningen, 1973.

Bibliography

Baelde, M., *De collaterale raden onder Karel V en Filips II, 1531–1578*, Brussels, 1965.
'Edellieden en juristen in het centrale bestuur der zestiende-eeuwse Nederlanden
(1531–1578)', *TvG* 80 (1967): 39–51.
'De Nederlanden van Spaanse erfopvolging tot beeldenstorm, 1506–1566', in *De Lage
Landen van 1500 tot 1780*, ed. I. Schöffer, H. van der Wee and J. A. Bornewasser,
Amsterdam and Brussels, 1978, pp. 38–101.

Bakhuizen van den Brink, R. C., 'De adel', *Cartons voor de geschiedenis van den Nederlandschen vrijheidsoorlog*, 3rd edn, The Hague, 1891, pp. 1–78.
'Eerste vergadering der Staten van Holland, 19 julij 1572', *Studiën en schetsen over
vaderlandsche geschiedenis en letteren uit vroegere opstellen bijeen verzameld en
vermeerderd*, 5 vols., Amsterdam, 1863–1913, I, pp. 494–550.

Balen Jansz., Matthijs, *Beschrijvinge der stad Dordrecht*, Dordrecht, 1677.

Barendrecht, S., *François van Aerssen, diplomaat aan het Franse hof (1598–1613)*, Leiden,
1965.

Beeck Calkoen, J. F. van, *Onderzoek naar den rechtstoestand der geestelijke goederen in
Holland na de Reformatie*, Amsterdam, 1910.

Beekman, A. A., *Het dijk- en waterschapsrecht in Nederland vóór 1795*, 2 vols., The Hague,
1904–7.
Geschiedkundige atlas van Nederland, 19 vols., The Hague, 1912–39.

Beelaerts van Blokland, W. A., 'Het geslacht van Mathenesse', *NL* 39 (1921): 34–9, and
375–6.
'Groot-Haesebroek', *LJ* 27 (1934): 1–21.
'Wassenaar in den geuzentijd', *LJ* 23 (1930–1): 67–97.

Belonje, J., 'De afkomst van het geslacht van Egmond van de Nijenburg', *JbCBG* 9
(1955): 39–75.
Ter Coulster, Wormerveer, 1946.

Beverwijck, Johan van, *'t Begin van Hollant in Dordrecht. Mitsgaders der eerster Stede
beschryvinge, regeringe, ende regeerders*, Dordrecht, 1640.

Billacoix, F., 'La crise de la noblesse Européenne, 1550–1650. Une mise au point',
RHMC 23 (1976): 258–77.

Bindoff, S. T., *Tudor England*, Harmondsworth, 1967.

Bitton, Davis, *The French Nobility in Crisis 1560–1640*, Stanford, 1969.

Blécourt, A. S. de, *Ambacht en gemeente. De regeering van een Hollandsch dorp gedurende de
17e, 18e en 19e eeuw*, Zutphen, 1912.
'Heerlijkheden en Heerlijke rechten', *TvR* 1 (1918–19): 45–107, 175–90 and
489–519.

Blockmans, W. P., and J. van Herwaarden, 'De Nederlanden van 1493 tot 1555:
binnenlandse en buitenlandse politiek', *NAGN*, V, pp. 443–91.

Blockmans, W. P. et al. 'Tussen crisis en welvaart: sociale veranderingen 1300–1500',
NAGN, IV, pp. 42–86.

Blok, P. J., 'De financiën van het graafschap Holland', *BVGO* 3rd series, 3 (1886):
36–130.

Boitet, Reinier, *Beschrijving der stadt Delft*, Delft, 1729.

Bonnevie-Noël, G., 'Liste critique des signataires du Compromis des Nobles', *Vereniging voor de geschiedenis van het Belgisch Protestantisme*, 5th series, 3 (1968): 80–110.

Bontemantel, Hans, *De regeeringe van Amsterdam, soo in 't civiele als crimineel en militaire (1653–1672)*, ed. G. W. Kernkamp, 2 vols., The Hague, 1897.

Boogman, J. C., 'De overgang van Gouda, Dordrecht, Leiden en Delft in de zomer van het jaar 1572', *TvG* 57 (1942): 81–112.

Bor, Pieter, *Oorsprongk, begin ende vervolgh der Nederlantscher oorlogen*, 4 vols., Amsterdam, 1679–84.

Bort, Pieter, 'Hollants leenrecht', *Alle de wercken*, 3rd edn, Leiden, 1731, pp. 1–370.

Boxhorn, Marcus Zuerius, *Toneel ofte beschryvinge der steden van Hollant*, Amsterdam, 1634.

Brandt, G., *Historie der Reformatie en andere kerkelijke geschiedenissen in en omtrent de Nederlanden*, 4 vols., Amsterdam, 1671–1704.

Brokken, H. M., 'De creatie van baanderheren door de graven Willem IV en Willem V', *Holland. Regionaal-historisch tijdschrift* 11 (1979): 60–4.

Het ontstaan van de Hoekse en Kabeljauwse twisten, Zutphen, 1982.

Bruch, H., 'Hoe kwamen de Geuzen aan hun naam?', *Spiegel Historiael* 2:12 (1976): 655–60.

Brünner, E. C. G., *De order op de buitennering van 1531. Bijdrage tot de kennis van de economische geschiedenis van het graafschap Holland in de tijd van Karel V*, Utrecht, 1918.

Bruinvis, C. W., *De Alkmaarse Vroedschap tot 1795*, n.p., 1904.

Buchell, Arend van, *Diarium*, ed. G. Brom and L. A. van Langeraad, Amsterdam, 1907.

Burema, L., *De voeding in Nederland van de middeleeuwen tot de twintigste eeuw*, Assen, 1959.

Bijleveld, W. J. J. C., 'De Roomsch-Catholieken in de oude Hollandsche Ridderschap', *NL* 45 (1927): 306–9 and 336–41.

Bijleveld, W. J. J. C., and W. Nolet, 'Het klooster van St Ursula of der Elfduizend Maagden in Warmond', *BGBH* 43 (1925): 40–58, and 45 (1927): 54–76.

Cobban, Alfred, *The Social Interpretation of the French Revolution*, Cambridge, 1964.

Cornelissen, J. D. M., *Waarom zij geuzen werden genoemd*, Tilburg, 1936.

Correspondance de Guillaume le Taciturne, ed. L. P. Gachard, 6 vols., Brussels, 1847–57.

Correspondance de Philippe II sur les affaires des Pays-Bas, ed. L. P. Gachard, 6 vols., Brussels, 1848–1936.

Correspondance du Cardinal Granvelle, ed. E. Poullet and Ch. Piot, 12 vols., Brussels, 1877–96.

Correspondentie van Willem den Eerste, Prins van Oranje, ed. N. Japikse, The Hague, 1934.

Craandijk, J., 'De geschiedenis van Nicolaas van Assendelft', *BVGO* 4th series, 10 (1912): 1–38.

Cuminius, Wilhelmus, *Disputatio politica de nobilitate*, Groningen, 1641.

Dek, A. W. E., *Genealogie van de graven van Holland*, The Hague, 1954.

'Genealogie der heren van Cruijningen', *JbCBG* 11 (1957): 79–120.

Genealogie der heren en graven van Egmond, The Hague, 1958.

'Genealogie der heren van Brederode', *JbCBG* 13 (1959): 105–46.

Destombe, J. W., *Het geslacht van den Boetzelaer. De historische ontwikkeling van de rechtspositie en de staatkundige invloed van een belangrijk riddermatig geslacht*, ed. C. W. L. van Boetzelaer, Assen, 1969.

Bibliography

Deursen, A. T. van, *Het kopergeld van de gouden eeuw*, 4 vols., Assen, 1978–80; Eng. edn: *Plain Lives in a Golden Age: Popular Culture, Religion and Society in Seventeenth-Century Holland*, tr. Maarten Ultee, Cambridge, 1991.

'Staatsinstellingen in de Noordelijke Nederlanden 1579–1780', *NAGN*, v, pp. 350–87.

Devyver, André, *Le sang épuré. Les préjugés de race chez les gentilshommes français de l'Ancien Régime (1560–1720)*, Brussels, 1973.

Dierickx, M., 'De eerste jaren van Philips II (1555–1567)', *AGN*, iv, pp. 305–49.

Dijk, H. van, and D. J. Roorda, 'Het patriciaat van Zierikzee tijdens de Republiek', *Archief. Mededelingen van het koninklijk Zeeuwsch genootschap der wetenschappen* (1979): 1–126.

Dillen, J. G. van, *Het oudste aandeelhoudersregister van de Kamer Amsterdam der Oost-Indische Compagnie*, The Hague, 1958.

Van rijkdom en regenten. Handboek tot de economische en sociale geschiedenis van Nederland tijdens de Republiek, The Hague, 1970.

Dissel, E. F. van. 'Grond in eigendom en huur in de ambachten van Rijnland omstreeks 1545', *Handelingen en mededelingen van de Maatschappij der Nederlandsche Letterkunde* (1896–7): 152–4.

Dolk, T. F. J. A., *Geschiedenis van het hoogheemraadschap Delfland*, The Hague, 1939.

Doorninck, P. N. van, *Inventaris van eene verzameling charters betrekking hebbende op de geslachten van der Does, Duivenvoorde en Mathenesse*, Haarlem, 1895.

Dorp, Arend van, *Brieven en onuitgegeven stukken*, ed. J. B. J. N. de van der Schueren, 2 vols., Utrecht, 1887–8.

Duke, A. C., 'Building heaven in hell's despite: the early history of the Reformation in the towns of the Low Countries', in *Britain and the Netherlands VII: Church and State since the Reformation*, ed. A. C. Duke and C. A. Tamse, The Hague, 1981, pp. 45–75. Reprinted in *Reformation and Revolt in the Low Countries*, London and Ronceverte, 1990, pp. 71–100.

'An inquiry into the troubles in Asperen, 1566–1567', *BMHG* 82 (1968): 207–27.

Duke, A. C., and D. H. A. Kolff, 'The time of troubles in the county of Holland', *TvG* 82 (1969): 316–37. Reprinted in *Reformation and Revolt in the Low Countries*, London and Ronceverte, 1990, 125–51.

Durand, Yves, ed., *Hommage à Roland Mousnier. Clientèles et fidélités en Europe à l'époque moderne*, Paris, 1981.

Elias, Johan E., *Geschiedenis van het Amsterdamsche regentenpatriciaat*, The Hague, 1923.

De Vroedschap van Amsterdam, 2 vols., Haarlem, 1903–5.

Elton, G. R., *Reformation Europe, 1517–1559*, New York, 1963.

Enklaar, D. T., *De ministerialiteit in het graafschap Holland*, Assen, 1943.

Eppens tho Eqart, Abel, *Kroniek*, ed. J. A. Feith and H. Brugmans, 2 vols., Amsterdam, 1911.

Faber, J. A., 'Drie eeuwen Friesland. Economische en sociale ontwikkelingen van 1500 tot 1800', *AAGB* 17 (1972).

'De Noordelijke Nederlanden van 1480 tot 1780. Structuren in beweging', *NAGN*, v, pp. 196–250.

'De oligarchisering van Friesland in de tweede helft van de zeventiende eeuw', *AAGB* 15 (1970): 39–64.

Bibliography

Fasel, W. A., *Alkmaar en zijne geschiedenissen. Kroniek van 1600–1813*, Alkmaar, n.d.

Feenstra, Hidde, *De bloeitijd en het verval van de Ommelander adel (1600–1800)*, Groningen, 1981.

Flandrin, Jean-Louis, *Familles, parenté, maison, sexualité dans l'ancienne société*, Paris, 1976.

Fockema Andreae, S. J., 'Aantekeningen over het baljuwschap Rijnland', *TvR* 14 (1931): 236–64.

Het hoogheemraadschap van Rijnland; zijn recht en zijn bestuur van den vroegsten tijd tot 1857, Leiden, 1934.

De Nederlandse staat onder de Republiek, 7th edn, Amsterdam, 1975.

'De Rijnlandse kastelen en landhuizen in hun maatschappelijk verband', in S. J. Fockema Andreae, J. G. N. Renaud and E. Pellinck, *Kastelen, ridderhofsteden en buitenplaatsen in Rijnland*, Arnhem, 1974, 1–20.

Fontaine Verwey, H. de la, 'Le rôle d'Henri de Brederode et la situation juridique de Vianen pendant l'insurrection des Pays-Bas', *Revue du Nord* 40 (1958): 297–302.

Foreest, H. A. van, *Het oude geslacht van Foreest 1250–1570*, Assen, 1950.

Fox, J., 'Baljuwen en schouten in Holland. Hoe bij de Derde Afdeling van het Algemeen Rijksarchief naar hun benoeming te zoeken', *Holland. Regionaal-historisch tijdschrift* 12 (1980): 35–7.

Fruin, R., *Geschiedenis der staatsinstellingen in Nederland tot den val der Republiek*, ed. H. T. Colenbrander, 2nd edn, The Hague, 1922.

Verspreide geschriften (*VG*), 10 vols., The Hague, 1900–5.

Gabriëls, A. J. C. M., 'De Edel Mogende Heeren Gecommitteerde Raaden van de Staaten van Holland en Westvriesland, 1747–1795. Aspecten van een buitencommissie op gewestelijk niveau', *TvG* 94 (1981): 527–64.

Geer, J. J. de, 'Proeve eener geschiedenis van het geslacht en de goederen der Heeren van Mathenesse', *Berigten van het Historisch Genootschap* 3, 1st part (1850): 44–129.

Gegevens betreffende roerend en onroerend bezit in de Nederlanden in de 16e eeuw, ed. H. A. Enno van Gelder, 2 vols., The Hague, 1972.

Gelder, H. A. Enno van, 'Bailleul, Bronkhorst, Brederode', *Van beeldenstorm tot pacificatie. Acht opstellen over de Nederlandse revolutie der zestiende eeuw*, Amsterdam and Brussels, 1964, pp. 40–79.

'Friesche en Groningsche edelen in den tijd van den Opstand tegen Spanje', *Historische opstellen opgedragen aan prof. dr. H. Brugmans . . .*, Amsterdam, 1929, pp. 78–94.

'De Hollandse adel in de tijd van de Opstand', *TvG* 45 (1930): 113–50.

Nederlandse dorpen in de 16e eeuw, Amsterdam, 1953.

'1548: De eenheid voltooid', *Van beeldenstorm tot pacificatie. Acht opstellen over de Nederlandse revolutie der zestiende eeuw*, Amsterdam and Brussels, 1964, pp. 9–39.

Genicot, L., *L'économie rurale Namuroise au bas moyen âge*, 2 vols., Louvain, 1960.

Geurts, P. A. M., *De Nederlandse Opstand in pamfletten*, Nijmegen, 1956; reprint Utrecht, 1978.

Geyl, P., *Geschiedenis van de Nederlandse stam*, 6 vols., (paperback edn) Amsterdam and Antwerp, 1961–2.

Gillissen, J., 'Les phases de la codification et l'homologation des coutumes dans les XVII provinces des Pays-Bas', *TvR* 18 (1950): 36–67 and 239–90.

Goes, Aert van der, and Adriaen van der Goes, *Register van alle die dagvaerden bij deselve*

Bibliography

Staten gehouden mitsgaders die resolutiën, propositiën ende andere gebesongneerde in de voirsz dagvaerden gedaen, 6 vols., The Hague, n.d. (ca. 1750).

Gosses, I. H., *Welgeborenen en huislieden. Onderzoekingen over standen en staat in het graafschap Holland*, Groningen, 1926.

Goubert, Pierre, *L'Ancien Régime. I: La société*, Paris, 1969; Eng. edn, *The Ancien Régime, 1600–1750*, tr. Steve Cox, London, 1973.

Gouthoeven, Wouter van, *D'oude chronyke ende historiën van Holland, Zeeland ende Utrecht*, 2nd edn, The Hague, 1636.

Gouw, J. W. van der, *Het ambacht Voorschoten*, Voorburg, 1956.

'Schieland als koloniaal gebied van Rotterdam', *Rotterdams Jaarboekje* (1977): 235–55.

Grapperhuis, F. H. M., *Alva en de tiende penning*, Zutphen, 1982.

Groenendijk, L. F., 'Piëtisten en borstvoeding', *Pedagogisch tijdschrift/Forum voor opvoedkunde* 1 (1976): 583–90.

Groenhuis, G., *De predikanten. De sociale positie van de gereformeerde predikanten in de Republiek der Verenigde Nederlanden voor ± 1700*, Groningen, 1977.

Groot, Hugo de, *Inleidinge tot de Hollandsche rechtsgeleerdheid*, ed. F. Dovring, H. F. W. D. Fischer and E. M. Meyers, 2nd edn, Leiden, 1965.

Nederlantsche jaerboeken en historiën. Sedert het jaar MDLV tot het jaar MDCIX, Amsterdam, 1681.

Groot placaatboek vervattende alle placaten . . . der Staten 'slands van Utrecht . . . tot het jaar 1728 ingesloten, ed. J. van de Water, 3 vols., Utrecht, 1729.

Groot placaet-boeck vervattende de placaten . . . van de . . . Staten Generaal der Vereenigde Nederlanden ende van de . . . Staten van Hollandt en West-Vrieslandt mitsgaders van de . . . Staten van Zeelandt, ed. C. Cau, 9 vols., The Hague, 1658–1796.

Guillaume, H. L. G., *Histoire des Bandes d'Ordonnance des Pays-Bas*, Brussels, 1873.

Haecht, Godevaert van, *Kroniek over de troebelen van 1565 tot 1574 te Antwerpen en elders*, ed. R. van Roosbroeck, 2 vols., Antwerp, 1929–50.

Haks, Donald, *Huwelijk en gezin in Holland in de 17de en de 18de eeuw*, Assen, 1982.

Handvesten, privilegiën, vrijheden, voorregten, octroyen en costumen: mitsgaders sententiën . . . der stadt Dordrecht, ed. Pieter Henrik van de Wall, Dordrecht, 1790.

Hart, G. 't, *Historische beschrijving der vrije en hoge heerlijkheid van Heenvliet. Met inventaris en regestenlijst van het huisarchief der Vrijheren van Heenvliet*, n.p., 1949.

Harten, J. D. H. 'Het sociaal-economische leven, geografie en demografie 1500–1800', *NAGN*, v, pp. 37–77.

Hedendaagsche historie of tegenwoordige staat der Vereenigde Nederlanden, 23 vols., Amsterdam, 1739–1803.

Henry, L., *Anciennes familles Génévoises. Etude démographique XVIe–XXe siècle*, Paris, 1956.

'Démographie de la noblesse Brittanique', *Population* 20 (1965): 692–704.

Hexter, J. H., 'The myth of the middle class in Tudor England', *Reappraisals in History*, London, 1961, pp. 71–116.

Holleman, F. A., *Dirk van Assendelft, schout van Breda en de zijnen*, Zutphen, 1953.

Hooft, P. C., *Nederlandsche historiën*, 2 vols., 4th edn, Amsterdam, 1703.

Horden Jz., P., *Een kleine geschiedenis van het land van Vianen*, n.p., 1953.

Hortensius, Lambertus, *Over de opkomst en den ondergang van Naarden*, ed. P. H. Peerlkamp and A. Perk, Utrecht, 1866.

Bibliography

Houve, Matthijs van der, *Hantvest of Charte Chronyk vande landen van Oud-Batavien, Oud-Vriesland, Oud-Francenland*, 2nd edn, Leiden, 1646.

Hüffer, M., *De adellijke vrouwenabdij van Rijnsburg, 1133–1574*, Nijmegen and Utrecht, 1923.

Huizinga, J., *Verzamelde Werken*, 9 vols., Haarlem, 1948–53.

Hulkenberg, A. M., *Het huis Dever te Lisse*, Zaltbommel, 1966.

'Het kasboek van Jan van Mathenesse, heer van Dever, 1587', *LJ* 54 (1962): 50–66.

'Het huwelijkscontract en het testament van Janus Dousa (van der Does)', ed. J. A. Feith, *Algemeen Nederlandsch Familieblad* 5 (1888): 157–63.

Immink, P. W. A., 'De Hollandsche "welgeborenen"', *Verslagen en mededeelingen van de Vereeniging tot uitgave der bronnen van het oude vaderlandsche recht* 10 (1948): 253–89.

Informacie up den staet, faculteit ende gelegentheyt van de steden ende dorpen van Hollant ende Vrieslant, ed. R. Fruin, Leiden, 1866.

Iunius, Hadrianus, *Batavia, in qua praeter gentis et insulae antiquitatem, originem, decora, mores, aliaque ad eam historiam pertinentia, declaratur quae fuerit vetus Batavia etc.*, Leiden, 1588; Dutch edn, *Een seer cort doch clare beschrijvinge vande voornaemste ghemuerde ende ongemuerde steden ende vlecken van Holland ende West-Vriesland*, Delft, 1609.

'Een Jachtruzie van voor 200 jaar', *LJ* 13 (1916): 124–31, published anonymously.

Jacobs, J. F., and M. Thierry de Bye Dólleman, 'Het familiekroniekje van Ysbrant van Spaernwoude', *JbCBG* 18 (1964): 81–116.

James, Mervyn, *Family, Lineage and Civil Society in the Durham Region 1500–1640*, Oxford, 1974.

Jansen, H. P. H., *Hoekse en Kabeljauwse twisten*, Bussum, 1966.

Hollands voorsprong, inaugural lecture, Leiden, 1976.

Jansen, P. C., 'Verraad in Holland', *Tijdschrift voor Sociale Geschiedenis* 9 (1977): 295–8.

Jansma, T. S., 'Het economisch overwicht van de laat-middeleeuwse stad t.a.v. haar agrarisch ommeland, in het bijzonder toegelicht met de verhouding tussen Leiden en Rijnland', *Tekst en uitleg. Historische opstellen aangeboden aan de schrijver bij zijn aftreden als hoogleraar aan de Universiteit van Amsterdam*, The Hague, 1974, pp. 35–53.

'De economische en sociale ontwikkeling van het Noorden', *AGN*, vi, pp. 89–146.

Raad en Rekenkamer in Holland en Zeeland tijdens hertog Philips van Bourgondië, Utrecht, 1932.

Janssens, P., 'De Zuidnederlandse adel tijdens het Ancien Régime (17e–18e eeuw)', *TvG* 93 (1980): 445–65.

Jonkees, A. G., *Staat en kerk in Holland en Zeeland onder de Bourgondische hertogen 1425–1477* (Groningen and Batavia, 1942).

Kaper, Ronnie, 'De Hollandse adel, 1500–1660: huwelijk en gezin', *Skript. Tijdschrift voor geschiedenisstudenten* 2:3 (1980): 48–61.

Kerckhoffs-de Heij, A. J. M., *De Grote Raad van Mechelen en zijn functionarissen 1477–1531*, 2 vols., Amsterdam, 1980.

Kieft, C. van de, 'De feodale maatschappij der middeleeuwen', *BMGN* 89 (1974): 193–211.

Kloos, J., *Noordwijk in de loop der eeuwen*, Noordwijk, 1928.

Bibliography

Klooster, L. J. van der, 'De juwelen en kleding van Maria van Voorst van Doorwerth', *Nederlands Kunsthistorisch Jaarboek* 31 (1980): 50–64.

Kluit, A., *Historie der Hollandsche staatregeering tot aan het jaar 1795*, 5 vols., Amsterdam, 1802–5.

Koenigsberger, H. G., 'Patronage and bribery during the reign of Charles V', *Estates and Revolutions. Essays in Early Modern European History*, Ithaca and London, 1971, pp. 166–75.

'Property and the price revolution (Hainault, 1474–1573)', ibid., pp. 144–65.

Kolff, D. H. A., 'Libertatis ergo. De beroerten binnen Leiden in de jaren 1566 en 1567', *LJ* 58 (1966): 118–48.

Koning, Jacobus, *Geschiedenis van het slot te Muiden en Hoofts leven op hetzelve*, Amsterdam, 1827.

Kosters, J., *Eenige mededeelingen over Oud-Nederlandsch jachtrecht*, Arnhem, 1910.

Kramer, C., 'De datering van Hendrik Laurensz. Spieghels zinspel Numa ofte Amptsweygheringe', *Jaarboek Amstelodamum* 66 (1974): 80–95.

Kronenberg, H., 'Verhouding tussen adel en patriciaat in Deventer', *Bijdragen en Mededelingen van de Vereeniging tot Beoefening van Overijselsch Regt en Geschiedenis* 65 (1960).

Kuttner, Erich, *Het hongerjaar 1566*, 3rd edn, Amsterdam, 1974.

Kuys, J., and J. T. Schoenmakers, *Landpachten in Holland, 1500–1650*, Amsterdam, 1981.

Labatut, Jean-Pierre, *Les noblesses européennes de la fin du XVe siècle à la fin du XVIIIe siècle*, Paris, 1978.

Leeuwen, Simon van, *Batavia illustrata ofte oud-Batavien, vervattende de verhandelinge van den adel en regeringe van Hollandt enz.*, The Hague, 1685.

Costumen, keuren ende ordonnantiën van het baljuwschap ende lande van Rijnland, Leiden, 1667.

Redeningh over den oorspronck, reght, ende onderscheyt der edelen, ende wel-geborenen in Hollandt; mitsgaders der selver voor-rechten, soo die nu zijn, ofte van aloude tijden zijn geweest, Leiden, 1659.

Loens, Pieter, *Kort begrip van den staet, en 't onderscheyd der persoonen mitsgaders 't recht daar uyt voortkomende*, Leiden, 1726.

Lommel, A. van, SJ, 'De kerkelijke toestand der gemeente Langerak in den Alblasserwaard, A° 1567, 27 jan.', *BGBH* 10 (1882).

'Fragment eener genealogie der van Alckemades', *Nav* 23 (1873): 312–14.

Maanen, R. C. J. van, 'De vermogensopbouw van de Leidse bevolking in het laatste kwart van de zestiende eeuw', *BMHG* 93 (1978): 1–42.

Macfarlane, K. B., 'Bastard feudalism', *Bulletin of the Institute of Historical Research* 20 (1943–5): 161–80.

Matthaeus, A., *De nobilitate, de principibus, de ducibus etc. libri IV*, Amsterdam, 1686.

Meerkamp van Embden, A., 'De Prins en de staat van eersten edele in Zeeland', *Prins Willem van Oranje 1533–1933*, Haarlem, 1933, pp. 101–24.

Mees, W. C., *Lamoraal van Egmond*, Assen, 1963.

Meij, J. C. A. de, *De watergeuzen en de Nederlanden 1568–1572*, Amsterdam and London 1972.

Bibliography

Meilink, P. A., *Archieven van de Staten van Holland en de hen opvolgende besturen*, 1: *Archief van de Staten van Holland vóór 1572*, The Hague, 1929.

'De verdediging van Mr Jacob van den Eijnden voor den Raad van Beroerten', *BMHG* 45 (1924): 184–205.

Mellink, A. F., *De wederdopers in de Noordelijke Nederlanden 1531–1544*, Groningen, 1953; reprint Leeuwarden, 1981.

Memorialen van het Hof (den Raad) van Holland, Zeeland en West-Friesland van den secretaris Jan Rosa, ed. A. S. de Blécourt and E. M. Meijers, 3 vols., Haarlem, 1929.

Merula, Paulus, *Placaten ende ordonnanciën op 't stuck van de Wildernissen*, Dordrecht, 1605.

Montesquieu, C. L. de Secondat de la Brède et de, *De l'esprit des lois*, ed. Gonzague Truc, 2 vols., Paris, 1956.

Moryson, Fynes, 'Moryson's reis door en zijn karakteristiek van de Nederlanden', ed. J. N. Jacobsen Jensen, *BMHG* 39 (1918): 214–305.

Mousnier, Roland, 'The Fronde', in *Preconditions of Revolution in Early Modern Europe*, ed. R. Forster and J. P. Greene, Baltimore and London, 1970, pp. 131–59.

Les hiérarchies sociales de 1450 à nos jours, Paris, 1969.

'Problèmes de méthode dans l'étude des structures sociales des XVIIe et XVIIIe siècles', *La plume, la faucille et le marteau. Institutions et société en France du Moyen Age à la Révolution*, Paris, 1970.

ed., *Problèmes de la stratification sociale. Deux cahiers de la noblesse, 1649–1651*, Paris, 1965.

Muchembled, R., 'Famille, amour et mariage: mentalités et comportements des nobles artésiens à l'époque de Philippe II', *RHMC* 22 (1975): 233–61.

Murris, R., *La Hollande et les Hollandais aux XVIIe et XVIIIe siècles vus par les Français*, Paris, 1925.

Naam-register van de Heeren van de Regeering der Stad Haarlem, van de ministers van dien; en van derzelven commissien; alsmeede van eenige ampten en employen binnen dezelve, Haarlem, 1733.

Naber, J. C., 'Dissenters op 't kussen. Eene bijdrage tot de staatkundige geschiedenis der Vereenigde Nederlanden', *De Tijdspiegel*, issue 2 (1884), pp. 45–57.

Een terugblik. Statistische verwerking van de resultaten van de informacie van 1514, 1885–90; reprint Haarlem, 1970.

Nepveu, J. I. D., 'Gerrit van Bevervoorde, wegens schaking van Anna Magdalena van Reede te Brussel ter dood gebracht', *BMHG* 8 (1885): 29–44.

Nierop, H. F. K. van, *Beeldenstorm en burgerlijk verzet in Amsterdam 1566–1567*, Nijmegen, 1978.

'"Het quaede regiment". De Hollandse edelen als ambachtsheren, 1490–1650', *TvG* 93 (1980): 433–44.

Nieuw Nederlands Biografisch Woordenboek, ed. P. C. Molhuysen and P. J. Blok, 10 vols., Leiden, 1911–37.

Niphuis-Nell, M., 'Veranderingen in de duur van de gezinsfasen', in *Gezin en samenleving*, ed. C. J. M. Corver et al., Assen, 1977, pp. 82–90.

Noordegraaf, L., *Daglonen in Alkmaar 1500–1850*, n.p., 1980.

Nuijens, W. J. F., *Geschiedenis der Nederlandsche beroerten in de 16e eeuw*, 8 vols., Amsterdam, 1865–70.

Bibliography

Obreen, H. G. A., *Geschiedenis van het geslacht van Wassenaer*, Leiden, 1903.

Een onderscheyt boeckje ofte tractaetje vande fouten en dwalingen der politie in ons vaderlant, Amsterdam, 1662; Kn 8670.

Ontdeckinge van de valsche Spaensche Jesuijtische Practijcke, The Hague, 1618; Kn 2632, by Cornelis van der Myle.

Ontstaan der grondwet. Bronnenverzameling. Eerste deel 1814, ed. H. T. Colenbrander, The Hague, 1908.

Orlers, J. J., *Beschryvinge der stadt Leyden*, 2nd edn, Leiden, 1641.

'Over de belegering van Leiden en het kapiteinschap van Johan van der Does', *Kron HG* 2 (1846): 150–61.

Parival, Jean de, *Les délices de la Hollande. Oeuvre panégirique*, Leiden, 1661.

Parker, Geoffrey, *The Dutch Revolt*, London, 1977.

Europe in Crisis 1598–1648, Glasgow, 1979.

Payen, Pontus, *Mémoires*, ed. A. Henne, 2 vols., Brussels and The Hague, 1861.

Perroy, E., 'Social mobility among the French *noblesse* in the later middle ages', *PP* 21 (1962): 25–38.

Petit, Jean-François Le, *Nederlandtsche Republycke, bestaende in de Staten so generale als particuliere van 't Hertochdom Gelder, Graefschap van Hollant, etc.*, Arnhem, 1615.

Polvliet, C. J., *Genealogie van het oud adellijk geslacht van der Does*, The Hague, 1893.

Post, R. R., *Kerkelijke verhoudingen in Nederland vóór de Reformatie van ± 1500 tot ± 1580*, Utrecht and Antwerp, 1954.

De roeping tot het kloosterleven in de 16e eeuw, Amsterdam, 1950.

Practijcke van den Spaenschen Raedt, n.p., 1618; Kn 2618.

Press, Volker, *Calvinismus und Territorialstaat. Regierung und Zentralbehörden der Kurpfalz 1559–1619*, Stuttgart, 1970.

Presser, J., *De Tachtigjarige Oorlog*, 5th edn, Amsterdam, 1975.

Price, J. L., *Culture and Society in the Dutch Republic during the 17th Century*, London, 1974.

Rachfahl, Felix, *Wilhelm von Oranien und der niederländische Aufstand*, 3 vols., The Hague, 1906–24.

Regt, W. M. C., 'De burcht Groot-Poelgeest', *LJ* 4 (1907): 93–112.

'Remonstrantie van het Hof van Holland en de Rekenkamer nopens de administratie van den ontvanger-generaal A. Coebel en de Staten van Holland', ed. P. A. Meilink, *BMHG* 45 (1924): 157–83.

Renaud, J. G. N., *Het huis en de heren van Heemstede*, Heemstede, 1952.

'De Rijnlandse kastelen in hun krijgsbouwkundige betekenis', in S. J. Fockema Andreae, J. G. N. Renaud and E. Pellinck, *Kastelen, ridderhofsteden en buitenplaatsen in Rijnland*, Arnhem, 1974, pp. 21–52.

Rendorp, Joachim, *Verhandeling over het recht van de jagt*, Amsterdam, 1777.

Rendorp, Petrus, *De origine ac potestate ordinum sub comitibus Hollandiae*, Leiden, 1782.

Renier, G. J., *The Dutch Nation, an Historical Study*, London, 1944.

Resolutiën van de Heeren Staaten van Holland en Westvriesland, 276 vols., The Hague, n.d. (ca. 1750–98).

Ridder-Symoens, H. de, 'Adel en Universiteiten in de zestiende eeuw. Humanistisch ideaal of bittere noodzaak?', *TvG* 93 (1980): 410–32.

Bibliography

Riemsdijk, T. van, 'De oorsprong van het Hof van Holland', *Geschiedkundige opstellen aangeboden aan Robert Fruin*, The Hague, 1894, pp. 183–208.

Roever Nzn., A. de, 'De Vlaming van Oudshoorn', *Amsterdamsch Jaarboekje* (1891): 105–22.

Rogier, L. J., *Eenheid en scheiding, Geschiedenis der Nederlanden 1477–1813*, 3rd edn, Utrecht and Antwerp, 1973.

Geschiedenis van het katholicisme in Noord-Nederland in de 16de en 17de eeuw, 3 vols., Amsterdam, 1946–8.

Romein, J., 'De functie van een historische fictie. De vermeende afstamming der Germanen uit Troje in verband met het begrip translatio imperii', *Historische lijnen en patronen. Een keuze uit de essais*, Amsterdam, 1971, pp. 13–22.

Geschiedenis van de Noord-Nederlandsche geschiedschrijving in de middeleeuwen, Haarlem, 1932.

Romein, J., and A. Romein, *De lage landen bij de zee. Geïllustreerde geschiedenis van het Nederlandse volk*, 3rd edn, Utrecht, 1949.

Roorda, D. J., *Partij en factie. De oproeren van 1672 in de steden van Holland en Zeeland*, Groningen, 1978.

'De regentenstand in Holland', *Vaderlands Verleden in Veelvoud. Opstellen over de Nederlandse geschiedenis na 1500. I: 16e–18e eeuw*, 2nd edn, The Hague, 1980, pp. 221–40.

'The ruling classes in Holland in the seventeenth century', in J. S. Bromley and E. H. Kossman (eds.), *Britain and the Netherlands*, Groningen, 1964, II, pp. 109–32.

Rosenfeld, Paul, 'The provincial governors from the minority of Charles V to the Revolt', *Standen en Landen* 17 (1959): 1–63.

Rowen, H. H., ed., *The Low Countries in Early Modern Times*, New York, 1972.

Rijpperda Wiersdma, J. V., *Politie en justitie. Een studie over Hollandschen staatsbouw tijdens de Republiek*, Zwolle, 1937.

Salverda de Grave, J. J., 'Twee inventarissen van het huis van Brederode', *BMHG* 39 (1918): 1–72.

Schepper, H. de, 'De burgerlijke overheden en hun permanente kaders 1480–1579', *NAGN*, V, pp. 312–49.

Rechter en administratie in de Nederlanden tijdens de zestiende eeuw, inaugural lecture, Alphen aan den Rijn, 1981.

'Vorstelijke ambtenarij en bureaukratisering in regering en gewesten van 's Konings Nederlanden, 16e–17e eeuw', *TvG* 90 (1977): 358–77.

Schepper, H. de, and P. Janssens, 'De Raad van State in de landsheerlijke Nederlanden en zijn voortgang op gescheiden wegen, 1531–1588/1948', *450 jaar Raad van State*, The Hague, 1981, pp. 1–35.

Scherft, P., *Het sterfhuis van Willem van Oranje*, Leiden, 1966.

Schilling, Heinz, 'Der Aufstand der Niederlande: bürgerliche Revolution oder Elitenkonflikt?', in *Zweihundert Jahre amerikanische Revolution und moderne Revolutionsforschung*, ed. Hans Ulrich Wehler, Göttingen, 1976, pp. 177–231.

Schöffer, I., 'Did Holland's golden age coincide with a period of crisis?', in *The General Crisis of the Seventeenth Century*, ed. Geoffrey Parker and Lesley M. Smith, London, Henley and Boston, 1978, pp. 83–109.

Bibliography

'De Republiek der Verenigde Nederlanden, 1609–1702', in *De Lage Landen van 1500 tot 1780*, ed. I. Schöffer, H. van der Wee and J. A. Bornewasser, Amsterdam and Brussels, 1978, pp. 167–267.

'La stratification sociale de la République des Provinces-Unies au XVIIe siècle', in *Problèmes de stratification sociale: Actes du colloque international (1966)*, ed. Roland Mousnier, Paris, 1968, pp. 121–32.

Schoockius, M., *Belgium Federatum, sive distincta descriptio Reipublicae Federati Belgii*, Amsterdam, 1652.

Schotel, G. D. J., *De abdij van Rijnsburg*, 's-Hertogenbosch, 1851.

Schueren, J. B. J. N. de van der, 'Eenige mededeelingen omtrent het regulieren-convent en andere geestelijke goederen onder Leijderdorp', *BGBH* 10 (1882): 210–39.

Schuyt-praetgens, op de vaert naer Amsterdam, tusschen een lantman, een hovelinck, een borger, ende schipper, n.p., n.d. [after Easter 1608]; Kn 1450.

Sententie gegeven op het interinement van Brieven van pardon, noopende d'ontschakinge van seecker Jonge-Dochter gedaan by Gerrit van Raephorst (ged. 15 juli 1515), n.p., n.d.; Kn 9; reprint 1664; Kn 8960.

Sententiën en indagingen van den Hertog van Alba, ed. J. Marcus, Amsterdam, 1735.

Slicher van Bath, B. H., *Geschiedenis: theorie en praktijk*, Utrecht and Antwerp, 1978.

Sloet, L. A. J. W., 'Gerrit van Bevervoorde schaakt iure militari juffer Anna Magdalena van Rheden in het jaar 1589', *BVGO*, 2nd series, 10 (1880): 259–92.

Smit, J., *Den Haag in geuzentijd*, The Hague, 1922.

'De omzetting van het Hof van Holland', *BVGO*, 6th series, 2 (1925): 179–223.

Smit, J. W., 'The present position of studies regarding the revolt of the Netherlands', in *Britain and the Netherlands*, 1, ed. J. S. Bromley and E. H. Kossmann, London, 1960, pp. 11–28.

Smith, E., 'Koop of spel. Eenige aanteekeningen uit de geschiedenis van den aankoop door Amsterdam der ambachtsheerlijkheden van Amstelveen, Sloten, Sloterdijk en Osdorp van Reinoud van Brederode in 1529', *Jaarboek Amstelodamum* 36 (1939): 39–86.

Son, Henricus Stephanus van, *De natura et indole curiae Hollandicae (vulgo het Hof van Holland) sub comitibus*, Leiden, 1783.

Spieghel, Hendrick Laurensz., 'Zinspel Numa ofte Ambtsweigeringe', in *Noordnederlandse rederijkersspelen*, ed. N. van der Laan, Amsterdam, 1941, pp. 295–320.

'Staat van onkosten van den heer van den Boetzelaer van Langerak gemaakt als afgezant in Frankrijk 1619–1622', ed. F. H. C. Drieling, *Kron HG* 5 (1849): 15–18.

Steur, A. G. van der, 'Johan van Duvenvoirde en Woude, 1547–1610, heer van Warmond, admiraal van Holland', *Hollandse Studiën* 8 (1975): 179–273.

Stone, Lawrence, *The Crisis of the Aristocracy, 1558–1641*, Oxford, 1965.

The Family, Sex and Marriage in England 1500–1800, London, 1977.

Temple, William, *Observations upon the United Provinces of the Netherlands*, ed. George Clark, Oxford, 1972.

Terdenge, H., 'Zur Geschichte der holländischen Steuern im 15. und 16. Jahrhundert', *Vierteljahrschrift für Sozial- und Wirtschaftsgeschichte* 18 (1925): 95–167.

Tex, Jan den, *Oldenbarnevelt*, 5 vols., Haarlem and Groningen, 1960–72; abridged Eng. ed, 2 vols., Cambridge, 1973.

Theissen, J. S., *De regeering van Karel V in de noordelijke Nederlanden*, Amsterdam, 1912.

Bibliography

Thierry de Bye Dólleman, M., 'Genealogie Van Ruyven', *JbCBG* 20 (1966): 140–73. 'Het geslacht Berckenrode', *JbCBG* 12 (1958): 81–132.

Tjessinga, J. C., *Schets van het leven van Adriaan Pauw*, Heemstede, 1948.

Den Triumph vanden oorloch ende de mis-prijsinghe vanden peys seer genoechlijck ende corts-wijlich om te lesen [Leiden], 1608; Kn 1978.

Troeyer, P. B. de, *Lamoraal van Egmont. Een critische studie over zijn rol in de jaren 1559–1564 in verband met het schuldvraagstuk*, Brussels, 1961.

Troost, W., and J. J. Woltjer, 'Brielle in hervormingstijd', *BMGN* 87 (1972): 307–53.

Uytven, R. van, 'Sociaal-economische evoluties in de Nederlanden vóór de Revoluties (veertiende-zestiende eeuw)', *BMGN* 87 (1972): 60–93.

Vandenbroeke, Chr., F. van Poppel, and A. M. van der Woude, 'De zuigelingen- en kindersterfte in België en Nederland in seculair perspectief, *TvG* 94 (1981): 461–91.

Vecht, H. A. W. van der, *Cornelis van der Myle, 1579–1642*, Sappemeer, 1907.

Vermaseren, B. A., 'Het ontstaan van Hadrianus Junius' "Batavia"', *Huldeboek Pater Dr Bonaventura Kruitwagen*, The Hague, 1949, 407–26.

Vigliana. Bronnen, brieven en rekeningen betreffende Viglius van Aytta, ed. E. H. Waterbolk and Th. S. H. Bos, Groningen, 1975.

Vrankrijker, A. C. J. de, *De motiveering van onzen Opstand. De theorieën van het verzet der Nederlandschen opstandelingen tegen Spanje in de jaren 1565–1581*, Nijmegen and Utrecht, 1933; reprint Utrecht, 1979.

Vries, Jan de, *The Dutch Rural Economy in the Golden Age*, New Haven and London, 1974.

Vries, O., 'Geschapen tot ieders nut. Een verkennend onderzoek naar de Noord-Nederlandse ambtenaar in de tijd van het Ancien Regime', *TvG* 90 (1977): 328–49.

Vrugt, M. van de, *De criminele ordonnantiën van 1570. Enkele beschouwingen over de eerste strafrechtcodificatie in de Nederlanden*, Zutphen, 1978.

Wagenaar, Jan, *Amsterdam in zyne opkomst, aanwas, geschiedenissen*, 3 vols., Amsterdam, 1760–7.

Walvis, J., *Beschrijving der stad Gouda*, Gouda and Leiden, 1713.

Water, J. W. te, *Historie van het verbond en de smeekschriften der Nederlandsche edelen*, 4 vols., Middelburg, 1776–96.

Wildeman, M. G., 'Het voorgeslacht van Joost van Egmondt', *Wap* 16/17 (1913): 316–18.

Wilson, Charles, *Queen Elizabeth and the Revolt of the Netherlands*, London and Basing-stoke, 1970.

The Transformation of Europe 1558–1648, London, 1976.

Win, P. de, 'De adel in het hertogdom Brabant van de vijftiende eeuw. Een ter-reinverkenning', *TvG* 93 (1980): 391–409.

Winter, J. M. van, 'De middeleeuwse ridderschap als "classe sociale"', *TvG* 84 (1971): 262–75.

Ministerialiteit en ridderschap in Gelre en Zutphen, Groningen, 1962.

Ridderschap. Ideaal en werkelijkheid, Bussum, 1965.

Wittert van Hoogland, E. B. F. F., *De Nederlandsche adel, omvattende alle Nederlandsche adellijke geslachten in de Noordelijke en Zuidelijke Nederlanden*, The Hague, 1913.

Woltjer, J. J., 'De "alderrijcste" te Leiden in 1584', in *Leidse facetten*, ed. D. E. H. de Boer, Zwolle, 1982, pp. 23–34.

243

Bibliography

'Het beeld vergruisd?' *Vaderlands Verleden in Veelvoud. Opstellen over de Nederlandse geschiedenis na 1500. I: 16e–18e eeuw*, 2nd edn, The Hague, 1980, pp. 89–98.

Friesland in hervormingstijd, Leiden, 1962.

'De Vredemakers', *TvG* 89 (1976): 299–321.

Wood, James B., *The Nobility of the Election of Bayeux*, Princeton, 1980.

Woude, A. M. van der, 'Demografische ontwikkeling van de Noordelijke Nederlanden 1500–1800', *NAGN*, v, pp. 102–68.

'Het Noorderkwartier', *AAGB* 16 (1972).

Wrigley, E. A., *Bevolkingsvraagstukken in verleden en heden*, n.p., 1969; Eng. edn, *Population in History*, New York, 1969.

Wüstenhoff, D. J. M., 'De geslachten van Teylingen', *Wap* 8 (1904): 265–80, 289–304, 401–16, 433–48.

Wyntjes, Sherrin Marshall, 'Family allegiance and religious persuasion: the lesser nobility and the Revolt of the Netherlands', *The Sixteenth Century Journal* 12 (1981): 43–60.

'Survivors and status: widowhood and family in the early modern Netherlands', *Journal of Family History* 7 (1982): 396–405.

Wijs, J. A., *Bijdrage tot de kennis van het leenstelsel in de Republiek Holland*, The Hague, 1939.

Yvoy van Mijdrecht, M. L. d', *Verbond en smeekschriften der Nederlandsche edelen. Vermeerderd met eenige aantekeningen en verrijkt met bijna alle de facsimilés door G. J. Beeldsnijder*, n.p., n.d. [Utrecht, 1833].

Zee, C. A. van der, *Matenesse en het Huis te Riviere*, Schiedam, 1939.

Zurck, Eduard van, *Codex Batavus, waer in het algemeen kerck en burgerlijck recht van Hollant, Zeelant, en het ressort der admiraliteit kortelijck is begrepen*, Delft, 1711.

Index

Aa, Philips van der, 137
Adrichem family, 44, 159
Adrichem, Wilhelmina Adriaansdr van, 84–5
Adrichem van Dorp family, 74
Aerssen, François van, 210, 211
Aerssen van Sommelsdijck, Cornelis van, 121, 211
Aertsz, Pieter, 28
Alba, duke of, 25, 117, 171, 179, 192, 193, 194, 196, 197, 198, 208, 223
Alblas, van, family, 158
Alblas, Cornelia Jan Willem Jan Reyersdr, 31
Alckemade family, 17, 45n, 74, 78, 159, 215–16
Alckemade, Floris Maartensz van (d.1572), 215
Alckemade, Jacob van, 111n
Alckemade, Sybrand van, 17, 135, 215–16
Alckemade, Willem van, 153, 160n
Alckemade, Willem van (also known as Coulster), 168
Aldegonde, Lady van St, 137
Alkemade, Jan van, 158n
Almonde family, 159
Almonde, Dirk van, 158n
Alveringen, Josua van, 39, 181, 188, 189
Alveringen, Samuel van, 181, 189
Alveringen, Zeger van, 152
Alys, Mathurin, 79–80
Amstel en Mijnden, van, family, 210
Amstel en Mynden, Anthonie van, 93
Arckel, van, family, 77
Arckel van Heukelom, Bertha van, 182
Arckel van Heukelom, Otto, 182
Aremberg, countess of, 196
Aremberg, counts of, 38, 96, 146, 147, 167, 198, 201, 223
Asperen, Matthijs van, 203
Assendelft family, 42, 130, 132, 146
Assendelft, Adriana van, 89, 90
Assendelft, Anna van, 78, 183
Assendelft, Bartoud van, 27, 137
Assendelft, Beatrix van, 141
Assendelft, Catharina van, 121

Assendelft, Cornelis van, son of Otto, 130, 182, 183, 190
Assendelft, Dirk van, 83, 97, 141, 144
Assendelft, Floris van (brother of Gerrit), 81, 86, 108, 141, 146, 160n, 168, 169, 174
Assendelft, Gerrit van (ca. 1487–1558), 6n, 24, 70, 78–82, 121, 141, 146, 149, 150, 153, 160n, 168, 169, 170, 171, 174, 178
Assendelft, Hugo van, 6n, 149
Assendelft, Jan van (brother of Gerrit), 141
Assendelft, Jan van (cousin of Otto), 130
Assendelft, Jan van (uncle of Gerrit, d.1480), 83
Assendelft, Klaas van (father of Gerrit, d.1501), 82, 83, 121, 140
Assendelft, Klaas van (nobleman not summoned to Ridderschap), 28
Assendelft, Klaas van (1517–70, son of Gerrit), 79–81, 130, 134, 173, 174, 182, 185
Assendelft, Margaretha van, 89, 90
Assendelft, Maria van, 182
Assendelft, Nicolaas van (nephew of Gerrit), 146
Assendelft, Otto van (nephew of Gerrit), 81, 86, 130, 133, 134, 146, 174
Assendelft, Pauwels van, 137, 182, 183
Assonleville, Christoffel d', 114
Aubigny, 74
Avaux, count d', 205

Bailleul, Agnes van, 182, 190
Banning Cocq, Frans, 213
Bekesteyn family, 44, 158
Berckenrode family see Berckenroede
Berckenrode, Dirk van, 28
Berckenrode, Gerard van, 195
Berckenrode, Gerrit van, 158n
Berckenroede family, 44, 72, 74, 75, 158
Bergen, marquis of, 39, 146
Bernemicourt, Anna van, 129
Beveren, lord of, 13, 161
Bevervoirde, Gerrit van, 88, 90, 91
Beijeren, Sabina van, 112

Index

Beijeren van Schagen family, 42, 161, 183, 158, 210
Beijeren van Schagen, Adriana van, 145
Beijeren van Schagen, Diederik van, 60n
Beijeren van Schagen, Floris Karel van, count of Warfusé, 131
Beijeren van Schagen, Jan van (ante 1450–post 1518), 161
Beijeren van Schagen, Jan van (ante 1517–1542), 161
Beijeren van Schagen, Johan van (1544–1618), 78, 113, 130, 134, 145, 161, 183, 193, 195, 196, 197
Beijeren van Schagen, Josina, 161
Beijeren van Schagen, Wilhelmina van, 183
Beijeren van Schagen, Willem van, 131, 196
Beyma, Sjoert, 187n
Bicker, 214
Binckhorst, Lodewijk van den, 150n, 184, 189, 195
Blois, Robert, 182
Blois, Maximiliaan van (known as De Cocq van Neereynen), 182, 189
Blois van Treslong, see Treslong
Boechorst family, 159
Boetzelaer, van den, family, 49n, 130, 132, 182, 190–1
Boetzelaer, Alferarda van den, 182
Boetzelaer, Daniël van den, 191, 195
Boetzelaer, Elburg van den (ca. 1505–68), 123
Boetzelaer, Floris van den, 130, 133, 191
Boetzelaer, Frederik Hendrik van den, 89
Boetzelaer, Gideon van den, 110, 130–1
Boetzelaer, Otto van den, 190–1
Boetzelaer, Philip Jacob van den, 60n
Boetzelaer, Rutger van den, 182, 191, 193, 215
Boetzelaer, Rutger Wessel van den, 131, 133
Boetzelaer, Sophia (dowager) van den, 75
Boetzelaer, Walraven van den, 85
Boetzelaer, Wessel van den (1529–75), 115, 123, 182, 190–1
Boetzelaer, Wessel van den (bastard son), 191
Boetzelaer, Wessel, jr (son of Rutger), 182
Boisot, Maria van, 198
Bol, Josina, 84
Bont, Gerrit de, 137n
Boot, Aart, 152
Borsselen family, 26, 73
Borsselen, Anna van, 13
Borsselen, Frank van, 153
Borsselen, Margaretha van, 84
Borsselen, Wolfert van, 153n
Bosschuyzen family, 44, 159
Bosschuyzen, Coen van, 157n

Bosschuyzen, Gomme van, 156n
Bosschuyzen, Jacob van, 158n
Bosschuyzen, Willem van, 156n, 160n
Bossu, Maximiliaan de Hennin, count of, 14, 153n, 183
Bouchorst, van den, family, 100, 216
Bouchorst, Adriaan van den (1478), 216
Bouchorst, Adriaan van den (1542), 100
Bouchorst, Amelis van den (d.1603), 101
Bouchorst, Amelis van den (1613–69), 137, 216
Bouchorst, Cornelis van den, 194n, 216
Bouchorst, Dirk van den (1519–74), 216
Bouchorst, Gijsbert van den (1510), 216
Bouchorst, Nicolaas van den, 101, 210, 211, 216
Boxhorn, Marcus Zuerius, 10, 11, 29, 45n, 49
Boxtel, baron of, 91
Brecht, lord of, 43
Brederode family, 34, 38, 39, 41, 66, 77, 131, 186–9, 211, 215
Brederode, Arnoud van, 188
Brederode, Artus van, 188, 194n
Brederode dowager lady of, 199n
Brederode, Hendrik van (1531–68), 39, 112, 130, 160, 161, 180–2, 186–9, 192, 223
Brederode, Johan Wolfert van (1599–1655), 60n, 65, 77, 210
Brederode, Lancelot van, 188, 193
Brederode, Lucretia van, 188
Brederode, Reinoud van, lord of Veenhuizen, 60n, 71, 210–11
Brederode, Reinoud III van (1492–1556), 39, 41, 96, 128, 133, 142–4, 146, 153n, 186
Brederode, Reinoud IV van, 91
Brederode, Sara van, 182, 188
Brederode, Walraven van (1462–1531), 84
Brederode, Walraven van (1547–1614), 26
Brederode, Walraven van (1597–1620), 91
Brederode, Wolfert van (d.1679), 65
Bronchorst family, 77, 158
Bronchorst, Andries van, 137
Bronchorst, Willem van, 137
Bronckhorst family, see Bronchorst
Bronckhorst, Andries van, 149
Bronckhorst, Anthonis van, 153
Bronckhorst, Dirk van, 194n
Bronckhorst, Herman van, 182
Bronckhorst, Joost van, 151, 152, 158n
Bronckhorst, Nicolaas van, 182, 183
Bronckhorst en Batenburg, Elizabeth, 182
Buchell, Arend van, 26, 34, 88, 91–2, 133, 215
Bueckelaer family, 158
Buren, count of, 161, 168

246

Index

Burgundy, Charlotte of, 13
Burgundy, Jacqueline of, 13
Burgundy, Maximilian of, 13, 14, 116, 128
Bye, Joris de, 130

Camons, Willem van, 31n
Carnisse, lord of, 163
Carondelet, Jan, 1
Cats, George van, 134
Cats, Klaas Lievensz van, 149
Cats, Maria van, 73
Charles the Bold, 153
Charles V, Emperor, 8, 13, 24n, 31, 32, 33, 35, 41, 50, 122, 126, 133, 142, 147, 152, 153, 159, 164, 186, 202, 207, 222, 225
Chasseur, Catharina le, 79–81
Cocq van Opijnen, François de, 196
Coebel, Arend, 170
Conincx, Frederik, 89, 90
Coornhert, Dirk Volkertsz, 187
Coppier, Jacob, 152
Cornelis, Brother, 114, 125
Coulster, van den, family, 44, 158, 159
Coulster, Abel van den, 6n, 149, 150, 172, 178
Coulster, Florens and Ysbrand van den, 157n
Cralingen family, 77
Cralingen, Daniël van, 85
Cralingen, jonkvrouw van, 89
Croesingh, Cornelis, 134, 153n
Croesingh, Hendrik, 182, 184
Cruyningen, Johan van (d.1559), 128, 133
Cruyningen, Joost van (d.1543), 13, 83, 144, 179
Cruyningen, Joost van (d.1547), 13, 160
Cruyningen, lords of, 12–15, 17, 43, 117, 132, 146
Cruyningen, Maximilian van, 13–15, 128, 133, 193, 195
Culemborg, count of, 43, 179
Culemborg, countess van, 85

Damman, Theophilus, 70–1
Does, van der, family, 17, 42, 48, 52n, 73, 101, 159
Does, Adrian van der, 155
Does, Anna van der, 101
Does, Dirk van der, Mr, 137
Does, Dirk van der, Brederode's steward, Member of Compromise, 181, 189
Does, Dirk van der, lord of Noordwijk, 155, 156n
Does, Dirk van der, son of Jan, 48
Does, Hendrik van der, 72, 158n
Does, Jacob van der, 72

Does, Jan van der (Janus Dousa), 17, 39, 48, 60n, 83, 137, 193, 194
Does, Josina van der, 75
Does, Pieter van der, 134, 216
Does, Reinier van der, 152
Does, Steven van der, 60n, 101
Does, Wigbold van der, 60n, 71, 199n
Domburch, Jacob van, 126
Dorp, van, family, 44, 71, 132, 149, 158, 159
Dorp, Adriaan van, 2, 129, 134
Dorp, Arend van (ca. 1530–1600), 116–18, 125, 129, 132
Dorp, Arend van (1599–1652), 141
Dorp, Cornelis van, 129, 134
Dorp, Frederik van, 60n
Dorp, Jeroen van, 1
Dorp, Josina van, 85
Dorp, Magadalena van, 85
Dorp, Willem van, 195
Dousa, Janus, see Does, Jan van der
Drenckwaert, van, family, 158
Driebergen, Cornelie van, 134
Dussen, van der, family, 44, 159
Duveland, Pieter van, 137
Duvenvoirde family, 15–17, 39, 41, 42, 43, 45n, 51n, 116, 139, 158, 199
Duvenvoirde, Arend van (d.1483), 15, 16, 155
Duvenvoirde, Arend van (d.1558), 174
Duvenvoirde, Arend van (1528–ca. 1599), 25, 182, 184, 189
Duvenvoirde, Arnoldina van, 16
Duvenvoirde, Dirk van, 160n, 182
Duvenvoirde, Gijsbrecht van, lord of Den Bossche (d.1510), 16, 155
Duvenvoirde, Gijsbrecht van, lord of Obdam (1540–80), 16, 182, 184
Duvenvoirde, Jacob van, baron of Wassenaer, lord of Obdam (1610–65), 16, 60n, 141, 244
Duvenvoirde, Jacob van, baron of Wassenaer, lord of Obdam (1635–1713), 199n
Duvenvoirde, Jacob van, lord of Obdam (1574–1623), 137
Duvenvoirde, Jacob van, lord of Warmond (1509–77), 16, 54, 141, 145, 173, 174, 182, 193, 197
Duvenvoirde, Jan van (m. 1504), 60n
Duvenvoirde, Jan van, burgemeester of Haarlem, younger brother of the lord of Warmond (1520–73), 73, 193
Duvenvoirde, Jan van, lord of Duvenvoirde (d.1544), 16, 54
Duvenvoirde, Jan van, lord of Warmond, judge, 6n, 16, 24, 149, 150, 153, 160n, 168, 169, 174, 178

Index

Duvenvoirde, Johan van, later van Wassenaer, lord of Voorschoten, (1578–1647), 18, 118, 136, 209–10

Duvenvoirde, Johan van, lord of Warmond, admiral of Holland (1547–1610), 16, 25, 77, 100, 113, 116, 134, 135, 141, 142, 144, 193

Duvenvoirde, Johan van Wassenaer, lord of Warmond (1622–87), 199n

Duvenvoirde, lord of, 1

Duvenvoirde, Maria van, 16

Duvenvoirde, Maria van, 55

Duvenvoirde, Willemina van, 15

Duvenvoirde-Starrenburgh, Pieter van, 60n

Duvenvoirde-Wassenaer, Arend van, 60n

Duyn, van der, family, 25, 49n, 52n

Duyn, Adam van der (bailiff of Putten before 1540), 169, 174

Duyn, Adam van der (cited 1599, 1620), 25, 137

Duyn, Adam van der (1639–93), 197

Duyn, Adriaan van der (1683–1753), 197

Duyn, Jacob van der, lord of Sprange, 169, 173, 174, 185

Duyn, Nicolas van der (d.1649), 197

Duyn, Philipotte van der, 75

Duyn, Willem van der (1537–1607), 75

Egmond family, 51n, 132

Egmond, Adriana van, 182

Egmond, Batholomeus van, 2

Egmond, counts of, 36, 38, 39, 112, 129, 134, 141, 146, 198, 201, 223

Egmond, Frederik van, 182n, 188

Egmond, Frits van, 190

Egmond, Jan van (1438–1516), 39, 153n, 154

Egmond, Jan II van, 39, 147

Egmond, Johan van, 137

Egmond, Joost van (1601–74), 214

Egmond, count Karel van, 155

Egmond, Karel van (son of Lamoraal), 127, 133

Egmond, Lamoraal van (1522–68), 39, 74, 111, 127, 133, 153n, 154–5, 160

Egmond, Lamoraal van, jr, 133, 201

Egmond, Otto van, judge, 169, 184

Egmond, Philips van (d.1590), 196, 201

Egmond van de Nyenburg family, 212–13

Egmond van de Nyenburg, Dirk van, 194n, 213

Egmond van Kenenburg family, 41

Egmond van Kenenburg, Otto van, 173–4, 182, 185

Egmond van Meresteyn family, 41, 73

Egmond van Meresteyn, Albrecht van, 182, 188

Egmond van Meresteyn, Frits van, 182

Egmond van Meresteyn, Henrica van, 182

Enklaar, D. T., 44

Eussum, Caspar van, 101

Everaerts, Nicolaas, 6n, 149

Eynden, Jacob van den, advocate, 170, 208

Faget, Simon du, 89

Foreest family, 44, 49n, 73, 74, 158

Foreest, Andries van, 84

Foreest, Cornelis van, 73

Foreest, Dirk Jacobsz van, 111n

Foreest, Herpert van, 73

Foreest, Jan van (d.1501), 73

Foreest, Jan van (1498–1557), 73

Foreest, Koen van, 33–4, 37

Foreest, Magdalena van, 73

Foreest, Pieter van, 62

Foreest, Willem van, 34

Frederick Henry, stadholder, 15, 52n, 204, 211

Fruin, Robert, 94, 177

Gattinara, Mercurino, 164

Gavere, lord of, 161

Gelder, H. A. Enno van, 12, 95–6, 113, 126, 138, 140, 142, 221–3

Genicot, L., 45

Ghiselin, Catherijne, 190

Goes, Aart van der, 167

Gouthoeven, Wouter van, 10, 20, 29, 33, 45n, 46, 49, 50, 95, 129

Graeff, Jacob de, 213

Grammaye, Jacob, 170

Grand, Guillaume le, 152

Granvelle, Cardinal, 12, 94, 184

Grebber, Catharina de, 86–8, 90

Grotius, Hugo, 12, 37, 94

Gijsbrechtsz, Jacob, 126

Haeften, Dirk van, 188

Haeften, Frans van, 188

Haeften, Jan van, 188

Haer, jonkvrouw van der, 86, 88, 90

Halewyn, Lodewijk van, 2

Hardenbroeck, Johan van, 131

Hardinxveld, lord of, 105, 107

Hargen, Splinter van, 183

Hargen, van, family, 52n

Hart, G. 't, 11, 177

Heemstede, Jan van, 158n

Heemstede, lords of, 17, 134

Heerartsberg, lord of 's-, 126

Heerman family, 159

Helmond, Catharina van, 79

Helmond, Judith van, 190

Index

Henry VIII, king of England, 114
Hertaing, Daniël van, lord of Marquette, 210, 211
Hertoghe, George de, 200
Heuckesloot, Maria van, 73
Heukelom, Henrika van Arckel van, 86
Hey, Johannes, 75
Hogelande, Jasper Lievensz van, 6n
Hohelohe, 52n
Holdinga, Doed, 182n
Hooft, Pieter Cornelisz, 12, 94
Hoogstraten, countess of, 146
Hoogstraten, Frans van, 158n
Horne, count of, 36, 38, 39, 74, 146, 155, 167
Houve, Matthijs van der, 95
Hoxwier, Hector van, 182n
Hoxwier, Maria van, 182n
Huchtenbroek, Albert van, 182, 188
Huguette, 80
Huizinga, Johan, 10, 220
Huydecoper, Johan, 213

Immink, P. W. A., 45
Isselt, Jan van, and daughter, 88, 90
Ivrea, *jonkvrouw* d', 89

James I, king of England, 213
Jansz, Jacob, 28
Jasper, Otto, 182
Jode, de, family, 52n, 152, 158, 198
Jode, Arend de (1510–70), 198
Jode, Jan de (d.1641), 198
Jonge, Cornelis de, 152
Jonge, Engelram de, 126
Jonge, Jacob de, 28, 152
Jonge, Joos de, 152
Junius, Hadrianus, 30, 46, 49, 212

Kenenburg, lord of, 163
Knollys, Sir Francis, 88
Knollys, Thomas, 88, 91
Koningsveld, Sibilla van, 126
Kuyk van Myerop, Pieter van, 89
Kyffhoeck, Alijd van, 79, 83

Laen, van der, family, 44, 45n, 159
Laen, Dirk van der, 200
Laen, Gerard van der, 113
Laen, Hendrik van der, 137
Laen, Nicolaas van der, 150
Lalaing, 74
Lebesteijn, Vincent van, 152
Leeuwen, van, family, 45n
Leeuwen, Simon van, 10, 11, 30, 33, 37, 49, 69, 95, 214

Lefebvre, Roeland, 129, 132
Leicester, Robert Dudley, earl of, 6, 52n, 195
Lier, Johanna van, 137
Liere, Willem van, 200
Ligne, counts of, 16, 38, 39, 118, 147, 167, 196, 198, 201, 223
Ligne, Jacques de, 168
Ligne, prince of, 146, 216
Lockhorst family, 43, 159
Lockhorst, Anna van, 214
Lockhorst, Cornelis van, 34
Lockhorst, Gerrit van, 156n, 158n, 160n
Lockhorst, Vincent van, 185
Lockhorst, Willem van, 173, 174
Loo, van, family, 44, 158, 159
Loo, Aechte Potter van der, 73
Loo, Albrecht van, 6n, 152, 153
Loo, *jonkvrouwe* van, 137
Loo, Margaretha van, 71
Louis XIII, king of France, 213, 214
Louis XIV, king of France, 214
Luxemburg, Françoise van, 39, 161
Lijnden van Kronenburg, Anthonis van, 210, 211

Malsen family, 132
Manmaker family, 213
Manmaker, Adriaan van, 213
Manmaker, Charles van, 213
Manmaker, Jacob, 213
Mansfeld family, 74
Margaret of Austria, 161, 164
Margaret of Parma, 50, 180, 191
Marnix van St Aldegonde, Philips van, 194
Mary of Hungary, 164
Mathenesse family, 42, 66
Mathenesse, Adriaan van (d.1557), 6n, 169
Mathenesse, Adriaan van (d.1574), 183
Mathenesse, Florentina van, 131
Mathenesse, Gijsbrecht van (ca. 1645–70), 64, 131, 133
Mathenesse, Gijsbrecht van (d.1598), 182, 183
Mathenesse, Jan van, 6n
Mathenesse, Johan van (1488–1522), 100
Mathenesse, Johan van (1538–1602), 77, 103, 163, 171, 196, 197
Mathenesse, Johan van (ca. 1595–1653), 64, 68, 182, 183, 185, 210
Mathenesse, Johan van, lord of Lisse (1547–1624), 97, 101, 135, 137, 144
Mathenesse, Maria van, 16
Mathenesse, Nicolaas van (post 1508–64), 100, 128
Mathenesse, Nicolaas van (fl. 1599), 137
Mathenesse, Willem van (d.1653), 64

Mathenesse, Willem van (d. ca. 1671), 65
Mathenesse van Wibisma, Johan van, 182, 183
Maurice of Nassau, 52n, 85, 129, 209–12, 216
Maximilian, Emperor, 24n, 159n
Meresteyn, *see* Egmond van Meresteyn
Merode, Jan van, and daughters, 88, 90
Merode, lord of, 146
Merula, Angelus, 13, 179
Merula, Paulus, 152
Merwede, van der, family, 77
Mierop, van, family, 152
Mierop, Cornelis Vincentsz, 26
Mierop, Jacob Vincentsz, 26
Mierop, Pieter van Kuyk van, 200
Mierop, Vincent Corneliszoon van, 26
Montesquieu, 7
Montfoort, burgrave of, 146
Montigny, 39
Morgan, Sir Thomas, 88, 91
Moryson, Fynes, 5, 6, 7, 11, 46, 49, 69, 220
Myerop, *see* Mierop
Myle, Adriaan van der (d.1590), 60n, 111n
Myle, Adryaen van der, shareholder of East-India Company, 111n
Myle, Arend Cornelisz van der, 28, 31–2, 111n
Myle, Cornelia van der, 137
Myle, Cornelis van der, 32, 71, 137, 210–11
Myle, Johan van der, 137

Naeltwijck family, 74
Nassau, Adriana van, 83, 144
Nassau, Emilia of, 125
Nassau, Hendrik van, 154, 161
Nassau, Louis van, 112, 128, 187, 188
Nassau, Louis van (bastard, 1636), 211
Nassau-Siegen, Anna Johanna, countess of, 65
Nath, van der, Mr, 89
Nooms, Johan, 200
Nooms, Willem, 213
Noordwijk, Anna van, 16
Nuyssenberg, Willem van, 31n
Nyenrode, Jan van, 157

Obdam, Jacob van (admiral, 1603), 16, 210
Obdam, Jacob van (admiral, 1653), 16
Occo, Pompejus, 24n
Oem, Herman, 203
Oem Jacobsz, Jacob, 157n
Oem van Wyngaerden family, 42, 45n, 183–4
Oem van Wyngaerden, lord of, 1, 2, 210
Oem van Wyngaerden, Cornelis, judge, 149, 150, 184

Oem van Wyngaerden, Cornelis, member of Compromise, 184, 189
Oem van Wyngaerden, Dirck, 157n
Oem van Wyngaerden, Mr Floris, 6n, 16, 149, 153, 160n, 168, 174
Oem van Wyngaerden, Gerard, 194n
Oem van Wyngaerden, Jacob (1525–1604), 16, 157n, 160n, 174, 183, 185, 189
Oem van Wyngaerden, Joost van, 86
Oem van Wyngaerden, Karel, 199n
Oem van Wyngaerden, Martina, 86
Oem van Wyngaerden, Mechteld, 183
Oldenbarnevelt, 28, 32, 71, 129, 137, 209–12, 214
Orange, *see* William I, Maurice, Frederick Henry, etc.
Ouderamstel, Heyman Jacobsz van, 157n
Oudheusden, 149
Oudshoorn, jonker Willem van, 113
Oudshoorn, Wouter van, 215

Parival, 49
Parma, duke of, 196, 200
Pauw, Adriaan (1585–1653), 213–14
Pauw, Nicolaas, 214
Pauwels, Adriaan, 162
Payen, Pontus, 12, 94, 184
Percijn, Pieter Harmansz van, 214
Persijn, 74
Philip II, king of Spain, 14, 31, 32, 33, 36, 50, 127, 177, 179, 184, 202, 208, 222
Philip the Fair, 2, 32
Pieck, Geertruid, 135
Pieck, Judith Wilhelmina, 64–5, 68
Piennes, lord of, 1
Pietersz, Herman, 179
Poelgeest family, 42, 45n, 159
Poelgeest, Gerrit VIII van (ca. 1490–1549), 100, 122
Poelgeest, Gerrit IX van (ca. 1520–64), 173, 174
Poelgeest, Gerrit X van (ca. 1545–1614), 100, 134, 182, 185, 197
Poelgeest, Gerrit XII van (ca. 1625–78), 100, 131, 199n
Poelgeest, Gerrit XIII van (d.1713), 132
Poelgeest, lords of, 17, 100, 101, 131
Polyander van den Kerckhoven, Johan, 15, 71, 128, 145
Praet van Moerkercken, Françoise van, 182, 190
Praet van Moerkercken, Petronella van, 182
Praet van Moerkercken, Willem van, 78
Presser, Jacques, 11
Price, J. L., 11, 177

Raephorst family, 73, 159
Raephorst, lord of, 1
Raephorst, Gerrit van, 86–8, 89–90
Raephorst, Herbert van, member of the
Compromise, 90, 188, 189, 190
Raephorst, Herbert van, member of
Ridderschap (1618), 210, 211
Rataller Doubleth, George, 85, 89, 90
Rataller, Philips, 71
Reede, Anna Magdalena van, 88, 90, 91
Reigersberg, Maria van, 200
Renesse, Frederick van, 149
Renesse, Gerrit van, 155
Renier, G. J., 140
Renoy, Gerrit van, 24n, 28, 152
Reyd, Everhard van, 111
Rhoon family, 159
Rhoon, Boudewijn van, 137
Rhoon, Frederick van, 86
Rhoon, Jan van, 137
Rhoon, Pieter van, 137, 195
Rochus, 144
Romein, Jan and Annie, 10, 94
Ruychrock van de Werve family, 27n
Ruyven family, 44, 72
Ruyven, Jan van, 73
Rijnsburg, abbesses of, 122–5

Sandelyn, Arend, 178
Sandijck, Nicolaas van, 182
Sasbout family, 184n
Sasbout, Arend, 24n, 28
Sasbout, Joost, 6n, 149, 153
Schaep, Gerard, 213
Schagen family, *see* Beijeren van Schagen
Schagen, lord of, 1, 134
Schenck van Tautenburgh, Maria, 122
Schoockius, Martinus, 21, 24, 34, 37, 69, 199
Schoten family, 158
Schumpeter, Joseph, 20
Solms-Braunfels, Louise Christina, 65
Sonoy, Diederik (Dirk), 150n, 189, 195
Spaernwoude family, 44, 72
Spaernwoude, Gerrit van, 84
Spanghen, 1
Spieghel, Hendrik Laurensz, 162–3
Stalpert, family, 152
Stalpert, Jacob, 153
Stone, Lawrence, 7, 47
Sturmius (Storm?) family, 215
Suys, Cornelis, 150, 171, 184n
Suys, Pieter, 137
Swaef, Johannes de, 61
Swieten, van, family, 132, 159
Swieten, Adriaan van (1532–84), 129, 193,
195

Swieten, Adriaan van (d.1629), 129
Swieten, Adriaan van (1593–after 1630), 130
Swieten, Adriaan van (1618), 210, 211
Swieten, Cornelis van (d.1544), 129
Swieten, Geertruid van, 71
Swieten, Jan van, 158n
Swieten, Maria van, 71
Sijl, van, 74
Sypesteijn, Johan van, 113

Taffin, Jean, 61
Temple, Sir William, 11, 46, 49, 70, 140,
177, 207, 217
Tetroede family, 44, 159
Tex, Jan den, 140
Teylingen family, 78, 216
Teylingen, Augustein van, 216
Teylingen, Maria van, 82
Teyng, Frans, 162
Thienen, Andries van, 113
Tilburg, lord of, 137
Toll, van, family, 34
Torre, Jacobus de la, 197
Torre, Philippe de la, 196
Treslong family, 158
Treslong, Adriana van, 188
Treslong, Albert van, 188
Treslong, Jan Blois van, 182, 183, 188, 189
Treslong, Jasper van, 158n, 169, 174
Treslong, Willem van, 174, 182, 183, 188,
189, 190

Valckesteyn, Gillis van, 158n
Vierlingh, Andries, 112
Viglius, 42
Vlaminck, de, family, 142, 213
Vlaminck van Oudshoorn, Dirck de, 142, 213
Vlamingh van Oudshoorn, Cornelis, 200
Vliet, *see* Woerden van Vliet
Voerst, Maria van, 136
Vries, Jan de, 98

Waelwijck, lord of, 43
Warmond, Johan van (admiral), 16
Warmond, lady of, 105, 106
Warmond, lords of, 62, 96, 99–100, 103–4,
115, 163, 202, 210; *see also* Duvenvoirde
Wassenaer family, 38, 41, 49n, 77, 141
Wassenaer, Andries (bastard), 31n
Wassenaer, Arend van, lord of Duvenvoirde,
199n
Wassenaer, Catharina, 13
Wassenaer, Diederik van, 199n
Wassenaer, Gerard van, 199n
Wassenaer, Jan van, 1–5, 7, 39, 153n, 160,
220

Wassenaer, lords of, 16–17, 135, 145, 199; *see also* Duvenvoirde
Wassenaer, Maria van, 147
Wassenaer, Willem van, 25
Werff, Pieter Adriaansz van der, 163
Werve, Hendrik van der, 137
Werve, Lodewijk van der, 126
William I, king of the Netherlands, 49
William I, prince of Orange (William the Silent), 14, 36, 38, 39, 40, 52n, 61, 73, 103, 112, 117, 120, 126, 146, 153n, 167, 170, 171, 186, 192, 194, 195, 201, 203, 208
William II, prince of Orange, stadholder, 8, 211
William III, prince of Orange, stadholder, 211
Woerden van Vliet, Anthonie, 162, 196

Woerden van Vliet, Jan, member of the Ridderschap, 193
Woerden van Vliet, Johan van, commander of Oudewater, 108
Woude, Jacoba van, 16
Wyngaerden family, *see* Oem van Wyngaerden

Zegers, Guillam, 149
Zegers van Wassenhoven, Ghilein, 190
Zegers van Wassenhoven, Johan, 190
Zoudenbalch family, 43
Zoutelande, Gielis van, 126
Zuid-Polsbroek, lord of, 102
Zuylen family, 43
Zuylen van de Haer, Elizabeth, 83
Zuylen van Nyevelt family, 43, 208
Zuylen van Nyevelt, Willem van, 191, 193, 194, 195, 208

CAMBRIDGE STUDIES IN EARLY MODERN HISTORY

Edited by Professor J. H. Elliott, University of Oxford, Professor Olwen Hufton, Harvard University, and Professor H. G. Koenigsberger

The Old World and the New, 1492–1650* *J. H. Elliott*

The Army of Flanders and the Spanish Road, 1567–1659: The Logistics of Spanish Victory and Defeat in the Low Countries Wars* *Geoffrey Parker*

Calvinist Preaching and Iconoclasm in the Netherlands, 1544–1569 *Phyllis Mack Crew*

Neostoicism and the Early Modern State *Gerhard Oestreich*

Prussian Society and the German Order: An Aristocratic Corporation in Crisis *c.* 1410–1466 *Michael Burleigh*

Richelieu and Olivares* *J. H. Elliott*

Society and Religious Toleration in Hamburg 1529–1819 *Joachim Whaley*

Absolutism and Society in Seventeenth-Century France: State Power and Provincial Aristocracy in Languedoc* *William Beik*

Turning Swiss: Cities and Empire 1450–1550 *Thomas A. Brady Jr*

The Duke of Anjou and the Politique Struggle during the Wars of Religion *Mack P. Holt*

Neighbourhood and Community in Paris, 1740–1790 *David Garrioch*

Renaissance and Revolt: Essays in the Intellectual and Social History of Modern France *J. H. M. Salmon*

Louis XIV and the Origins of the Dutch War *Paul Sonnino*

The Princes of Orange: The Stadholders in the Dutch Republic *Herbert H. Rowen*

The Changing Face of Empire: Charles V, Philip II and Habsburg Authority, 1551–1559 *M. J. Rodriguez-Salgado*

Frontiers of Heresy: The Spanish Inquisition from the Basque Lands to Sicily *William Monter*

Rome in the Age of Enlightenment: The Post-Tridentine Syndrome and the *Ancien Régime* *Hanns Gross*

The Cost of Empire: The Finances of the Kingdom of Naples in the Time of Spanish Rule *Antonio Calabria*

Lille and the Dutch Revolt: Urban Stability in an Era of Revolution *Robert S. Duplessis*

The Armada of Flanders: Spanish Maritime Policy and European War, 1568–1668 *R. A. Stradling*

The Continuity of Feudal Power: The Caracciolo di Brienza in Spanish Naples *Tommaso Astarita*

*Titles available in paperback are marked with an asterisk**

DATE DUE